Congratulations
To: a Good Shooter
from: R. Roland Brinkmeyer
Club Shot 1978

The Pennsylvania - Kentucky Rifle

THE PENNSYLVANIA-KENTUCKY RIFLE

by HENRY J. KAUFFMAN

BONANZA BOOKS • NEW YORK

This edition published by Bonanza Books
a division of Crown Publishers, Inc.,
by arrangement with The Stackpole Company.
D E F G H

Printed and Bound in the United States of America

Preface

THE HISTORY OF FIREARMS is dotted with examples of inventions and evolutions of different arms. The range and usefulness of these vary from small incidental improvements to the creation of entirely new weapons. Among the great and interesting evolutions one finds a rifle that was made in America by gunsmiths who migrated from their homes in central Europe in the first half of the eighteenth century. These men brought rifles with them which had short, octagonal barrels with a large bore. The stocks were made of walnut wood and a cavity was cut into the butt of the gun to carry patches, and was covered with a sliding cover of wood. For reasons of utility or patriotism, or both, this European arm was slowly discarded and a better rifle was made to take its place. This new rifle had a long octagonal barrel with a smaller bore than found on its European ancestor. It had a full stock made of maple wood and in the butt end a cavity to carry patches was covered with a brass plate, which was fastened to the butt with a hinge. This rifle was the best arm in the world for killing game or men at great distances.

The rifle was originally an invention of craftsmen who lived in central Europe; and because many of them settled in Pennsylvania, Pennsylvania became famous for its rifles and riflemakers. The great demand for rifles in the new world created a need for these Pennsylvania products in other areas of America; and there is no doubt that Pennsylvania riflemakers emigrated to Maryland, Virginia, North Carolina, Kentucky, Ohio, New York, and the New England states where they continued to work in the traditions of the craft which they learned in Pennsylvania. Near the borders of Pennsylvania there was little departure from the style of Pennsylvania rifles, but at more distant points it is known that new styles were created.

No contemporary record of the eighteenth century is known to indicate the names attached to the rifles made in any of these regions in America; however, in the decade after the Battle of New Orleans a ballad was written about the battle and Andrew Jackson and his riflemen from Kentucky.

This romantic description seems to have started the practice of calling muzzle-loading rifles "Kentucky Rifles," regardless of the place where they were made. In 1848 a riflemaker in Pittsburgh stated that he was a manufacturer of the "celebrated Kentucky Rifle." The use of the term was popularized and made permanent by Dillin when he wrote his famous book and called it *The Kentucky Rifle.* In this book he recognized that rifles were made in many areas in America, but he used it as a generic term and made no attempt to segregate them according to their regional styles and peculiarities.

Since 1924, when Dillin published *The Kentucky Rifle*, a great deal of research has been done on the subject of muzzleloading rifles made in America. The increased knowledge on the subject has led to a recognition of the fact that rifles made in New England frequently have stocks made of walnut wood, that New York gunsmiths carved different designs than Pennsylvania craftsmen, and that rifles made in Ohio are frequently more profusely inlaid with silver than rifles made in Pennsylvania. It is also recognized that rifles made in St. Louis show some Pennsylvania qualities, but were made specifically for use in the opening of the west.

This intensive study of the rifle in America has resulted in a number of studies relating to rifles made in specific areas. This one, with a short excursion into nearby Maryland, is confined to rifles made in Pennsylvania and is therefore called the *Pennsylvania-Kentucky Rifle*. The *Ohio-Kentucky Rifle* and the *Plains Rifle* will be published as well as other studies about this fascinating subject.

HENRY J. KAUFFMAN
Lancaster, Pennsylvania

Acknowledgments

For their generous cooperation, the author is grateful to:

Mr. Joseph Aiken, Alexandria, Virginia.

The Berks County Historical Society, Reading, Pa.

Mr. Donald Berkbile, Washington, D. C.

Mr. Howard Blackmore, London, England.

Mr. E. H. Blettner, Hanover, Pa.

Mr. Ray Burkhardt, Jr., Shippensburg, Pa.

Mr. T. J. Cooper, Port Royal, Pa.

Mr. John Cummings, Doylestown, Pa.

Mr. Samuel S. Dyke, Lancaster, Pa., who was especially helpful in locating data about gunsmiths who worked in Lancaster County, Pennsylvania.

Mr. Herman Dean, Huntington, West Virginia.

Mr. R. A. Farber, Bedford, Pa. rendered a valuable service by supplying data about gunsmiths who worked in Bedford County, Pennsylvania.

Mr. Reaves Geohring, Lancaster, Pa.

Mr. Joseph Haney, Pottsville, Pa.

Mrs. Olive S. D'Arcy Hart, London, England.

Mr. Earl S. Heffner, Bethlehem, Pa. Mr. Heffner supplied important biographical data about the Moll family of gunsmiths.

Mr. Luther Heisey, Lancaster, Pa.

Dr. Jamest T. Herron, Cannonsburg, Pa. whose manuscript material about gunsmithing in Western Pennsylvania has been of much value in writing this survey.

Mr. Calvin Herring, Allentown, Pa.

Mr. Frank Horton, Winston-Salem, North Carolina.

Dr. Eric Hulmer, Harmony, Pa.

Mr. Charles Kauffman, York, Pa.

Mr. Joe Kindig, Jr., York, Pa. The author and the collecting fraternity are indebted to Mr. Kindig for the contributions he has made to this book. His extensive collection of firearms was always available for study, and photographs of some of his fine guns can be found among the illustrations. Mr. Kindig's wide knowledge of firearms was frequently drawn upon by the author and the response was always informative and graciously given.

The Lancaster County Historical Society, Lancaster, Pa.

Mr. Jerry Lestz, Lancaster, Pa.

Mrs. B. W. Luttenberger, Lancaster, Pa.

Mr. Robert McAfee, Jr., Pittsburgh, Pa. Mr. McAfee has made an outstanding contribution to the book by researching most of the tax assessment lists of counties in western Pennsylvania. The accuracy and scholarly nature of his contribution is particularly appreciated by the author.

Mrs. Frank Mish, Jr., Falling Waters, West Virginia.

The New York Historical Society, New York, N. Y.

Mrs. Paul Niemeyer, Doylestown, Pa.

Mr. Lloyd Norris, Breckenridge, Pa.

Dr. Burl N. Osburn, Willow Street, Pa.

The Historical Society of Pennsylvania, Philadelphia, Pa.
Mr. Harold Peterson, Washington, D. C.
Mr. Carl Pippert, Washington, D. C.
Dr. Carl P. Russel, Orinda, California.
Mrs. Leroy Saunders, Reading, Pa.
Dr. Alfred Shoemaker, Kutztown, Pa.
Mrs. Arthur B. Shelton, Chevy Chase, Maryland.
Mr. Stanley Skonieczki, Millersville, Pa.
Mr. Ray Smith, New Berlin, Pa.
Mr. James Swartz, Doylestown, Pa.
Mr. Albert Toth, Belfast, Pa.
Mr. G. F. Thompson, Wednesbury, England.
Mrs. Ellen Watt, Latrobe, Pa.
Mr. V. H. Woods, Birmingham, England.
Mr. Sam Woodside, Chicago, Illinois.
Mrs. Harlan Wilson, Zelienople, Pa.
The Historical Society of York County, York, Pa.

Finally, I am grateful to my wife, Zoe T. Kauffman, who made most of the line drawings found throughout the book; and to my sister, Florence Kauffman, who spent many hours looking for gunsmiths in the United States Census of 1850.

Contents

Chapter 1

The Rifle In Europe

THE MAJOR FUNCTION of this book is to inform the reader about the development and use of the rifle in Pennsylvania. It is obvious for reasons of time, space, and interest, that this preliminary survey of the rifle in Europe cannot encompass all of the details concerning this famous arm; however, some information about its origin and development will be given in this chapter for those who have an interest in the subject.

That the invention of rifling cannot be positively attributed to one man is understandable, for five hundred years ago the invention was not considered as important as it is today, and there was little likelihood of its being recorded at the time that it occurred. That the rifle was invented in Germany, or adjoining territory, is a reasonable conclusion, for central Europe was the workshop of the world at the time of the Renaissance. Despite the fact that there is uncertainty regarding the origin of the rifle, there is some agreement among authorities on the subject that gun barrels with grooves were first made by Gaspard Kollner, of Vienna, in the late fifteenth century, or Augustus Kotter in Nuremberg in 1520. An excerpt from Deane's *Manual of the History and Science of Fire-arms*, London, 1853, presents the situation as it is generally accepted today.

> Yet it is to the Artizans of Germany, that the Rifle owed its origin at the close of the 15th century. In 1498, grooved barrels (with straight grooves) were the arms of the citizens of Leipsic at target practice, and towards the middle of the next century in 1520, Augustus Kotter, or Koster, of Nurenberg, became celebrated for the perfection of his so-called rose or star-grooved barrels, having a spiral form.

The reader should be aware that the form and function of rifled barrels changed from the time of their invention until their use in Pennsylvania. Slow-burning powder formed a residue in early smoothbore guns of the fifteenth century that not only reduced the efficiency of the gun, but also necessitated frequent cleaning of the barrel. It is claimed by some authorities that the original object in grooving a barrel was to provide a space for the fouled gunpowder to accumulate and have less ill effect on the performance of the gun. The same authorities advance the idea that the earliest grooves were straight and therefore had little function, except to reduce the friction between the ball and the barrel and to provide a place for the fouled gunpowder to accumulate. It has been suggested that some grooves made at a later time by an indifferent gunsmith were so irregular that a spiraled effect was suggested

1

to him. Further experimentation with the spiraled grooves proved that they were better than the straight ones, and thereafter the practice of making straight grooves in gun barrels was discontinued.

It is the opinion of other experts that grooves were made in a spiral form from the start, because the craftsmen were aware of the spinning motion of the arrow and they tried to give a similar action to the round bullet. They knew that a bullet, spinning on its axis, would maintain a straight line as nearly as gravity and air resistance would permit, and if the bullet had any irregularities of form or density the unsymmetrical balance in form or weight would be canceled by its whirling motion. An examination of some of the earliest rifled barrels reveals that they have from six to twelve grooves; and, as there is no uniformity in the twist of the grooves, the conclusion naturally drawn from this survey is that grooves were always twisted and that there was considerable experimentation to determine the best combination of grooves and twist.

It is also interesting to note that the windage (loss of pressure around a bullet) of the early smoothbore was reduced in the rifled barrel. A bullet which was slightly oversize for the bore of the rifle before it was rifled was beat into the barrel with a mallet and a ramrod. If this bullet did not fill the grooves by the time it was rammed to the breech, the expanding pressure of the powder is thought to have fully forced it into the grooves. This loading procedure not only reduced or almost eliminated windage, but also greatly improved the accuracy of the ball, which wobbled out of the barrel of a smoothbore gun.

The early use of straight grooves versus spiraled grooves will probably never be settled to the satisfaction of all interested parties; however, there is no doubt that the accuracy of guns was greatly improved with a grooved barrel. A quotation from the *Citizen and His Shooting Festivals* by Gustav Freytag tells that, "quarrels must have arisen sometimes concerning this at Public shooting matches, for in 1563, Elector August of Saxony decided that rifled barrels should be only allowed, if all the shooters agreed to it." It should be noted that improvement of performance was gradually obtained by the constant experimentation of the gunsmiths with grooves and spiraling. There were half twists, three-fourth twists, and full twists in a 3-4 foot barrel; when better gunpowder became available, the experiments had to be repeated, for the more powerful powder was stripping the ridges from the ball and causing the rifle to perform like a smoothbore.

Although the wobbling of the bullet was eliminated by giving a spiral motion to the ball, the matter of eliminating fouled gunpowder remained a constant problem. It is obvious that a small residue of foul powder was left in the barrel after each shot and the accumulating powder made recharging and shooting increasingly difficult. The problem was solved by the use of a greased patch; first mentioned by Alonzo Martinez de Espinar, who explained, in 1644, that without the greased patch only two shots could be made with a rifle; but a dozen shots could be made without cleaning the barrel, if a greased patch were used. This improved method of loading and shooting a rifle is attributed by many writers to Pennsylvania gunsmiths, but its description by Espinar at a much earlier time clearly indicates that the improvement was first used in Europe.

Although rifles were first used in Germany in the first half of the sixteenth century, the student of American firearms should be aware that the rifle of that period had few of the characteristics found in a Pennsylvania product of the eighteenth century. The German gun did have a rifled barrel, but the exterior shape of the barrel was round in the tradition of earlier smoothbore guns. It had a very simple lock mechanism, called a matchlock, which was only a slight improvement over the earlier method of igniting the barrel by hand. A description of the stock of such a gun from the catalogue of the Wallace Collection in London focuses attention on the fact that, although this early gun was related to the Pennsylvania rifle, the relationship was a very distant one:

> Stock of pear-wood, inlaid with engraved stag's horn with an intricate ornament of foliage and strapwork involving amorini, fauns, birds, and grotesque figures of men and animals. On either side of the breech strap are figures of Venus and Mercury; on the fore-end Jupiter, Chronos, Apollo, and Mars; on the heel of the butt, Diana. On a small panel of mother-of-pearl on the underside is engraved the date 1598, while above the lockplate is stamped the letter N. There is no trigger guard, but to take its place the butt is stepped underneath on the right side to accommodate the fingers. The over-all length of the gun is 48 4/5.

The next step in the evolution of the style of the German rifle is called the wheel-lock stage. There was little in the design and function of early rifles with wheel locks that resembled the Pennsylvania rifle of the eighteenth century. It was a nearer relative than the matchlock gun, for, in addition to its having a rifled bore, the exterior shape of the barrel was octagonal, and in the rear of the stock a butt-trap box with a sliding cover was located.

Although this butt trap is called a patch box by Americans, there is considerable doubt that it was the equivalent of the patch box on a Pennsylvania rifle. In the first place, it is called a butt trap by informed men who are familiar with the form and function of German rifles. If it had served as a storage place for greased patches, it is likely that they would have known about it and expounded on such an inter-

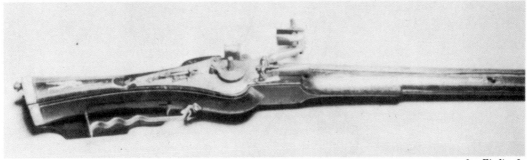

Joe Kindig, Jr.

PLATE 1

European rifle with wheel lock. c. 1600. These rifles often have octagonal barrels which are etched, engraved, or chiseled with designs of foliage, animals, or human figures. They have back and foresights, the latter frequently are made of brass. The number of grooves varies, however, many of them have eight.

The stocks are usually made of fruit wood or walnut and are frequently overlaid with a myriad of designs made of horn. The simple lines and lack of profuse ornamentation in this rifle makes it attractive to connoisseurs of Pennsylvania rifles.

esting function of this cavity. In the second place there is no residue of grease found in these cavities to indicate that greased patches were carried in them. This situation does not completely eliminate their being used for greased patches, but is does suggest that they were used to store some object or material that was reasonably clean.

The lock of the wheel-lock gun was the most complicated mechanism ever used to ignite a gun and needs no further explanation here, as it had little influence on Pennsylvania guns.

The following description of the barrel on a seventeenth century wheel-lock gun does suggest that it was slowly assuming the shape that finally appeared on the Pennsylvania rifle.

> Long slender octagonal barrel, slightly engraved with scroll-work at the breech and muzzle, brass fore and back sights. A sighting groove runs along the top facet from the breech strap to a point one-and-a-half inches in front of the back sight. At the end of this groove a maker's stamp is inlaid in brass, and beyond is engraved the date 1645. Exceptionally small bore with multiple grooved rifling. The barrel is 43½ long.

In the late seventeenth century the true ancestor of the Pennsylvania rifle was created by German gunsmiths. In this period some major changes in design and mechanism occurred which might have been precipitated by the invention of the flintlock in 1630. Although the earliest flintlock guns were highly decorated, there was a definite trend toward a simplification of the entire gun. The flintlock was smaller, easier and cheaper to make, and did not have to be wound with a key like its predecessor, the wheel-lock. The simplification of the lock mechanism continued until the lock on a German rifle was very similar to the simple, hand-made locks of the early Pennsylvania rifle.

The barrel continued to be octagonal on the flintlock rifles and there was a range of barrel lengths. The chiseled decoration of some of the fine wheel-lock guns was continued on the guns with flintlocks. Also, the slow transition in the shape of the stock should be noted from the early wheel-lock to the flintlock.

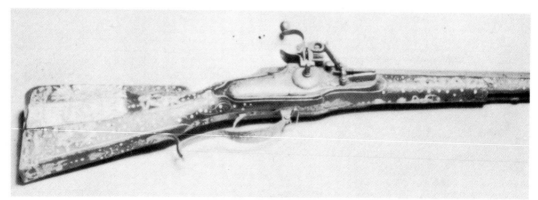

Joe Kindig, Jr.

PLATE 2

German rifle with wheel lock. c. 1640. Although this gun is profusely decorated, the embryo form of the Pennsylvania rifle can be seen in this early German arm. The contour of the stock, the shape of the trigger guard, and the position of the patch box, suggest the later "Jaeger rifle" and the early Pennsylvania rifle.

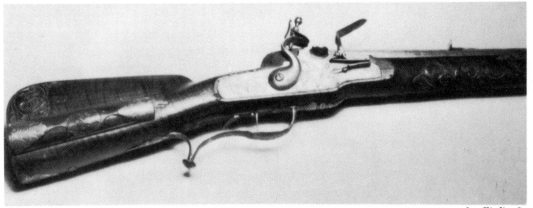

PLATE 3

German rifle with flintlock. c. 1650-1670. Although the shape of the flintlock on this rifle is identical to that of the wheel lock, which preceded it, the form and function of the rifle shows evidences of the change from the early European rifle to the early Pennsylvania rifle.

The straight stock of the early wheel-lock gun, which was not rested against the shoulder, was changed to a stock with a drop that could be comfortably rested against the shoulder, while taking aim and shooting. This new procedure permitted a better aim to be taken, and the recoil was absorbed by the body rather than by the arms as in the use of the wheel-lock gun. There was also a marked departure from the guns profusely inlaid with horn to a more sparsely inlaid gun stock using sheet silver, brass, and silver wire. The butt trap was moved from the bottom of the stock to the middle and the sliding lid was made of wood instead of bone, as on the earlier guns.

The gun which the Pennsylvania gunsmiths copied was called the Jaeger, which was the favorite hunting rifle of many men in central Europe at the end of the seventeenth and the beginning of the eighteenth centuries. This gun was called a

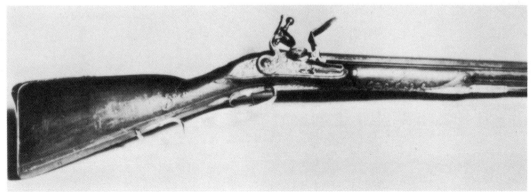

PLATE 4

Rifle with flint lock, full stock of walnut, brass mountings, and octagonal-to-round barrel 54 inches long with Weliceslaus Sporer engraved on the top facet of the barrel.

The lock and trigger guard of this rifle show the European ancestry of parts used on early rifles made in Pennsylvania. The screw on the rear extension of the trigger guard is a detail which was used by several early gunsmiths in Lancaster County.

"Jaeger" because it was the weapon of the men who hunted big game in central Europe. It had a relatively short (30 to 36 inch, a few 40 inches) rifled, octagonal barrel with a caliber of .60 to .75. It was heavy in the breech end with a pleasing taper toward the muzzle where the cross dimension increases a bit. This flare on the barrel at the muzzle makes it a much more attractive gun part, but has nothing to do with the performance of the gun. Some makers engraved their names on the top facet of the barrel; others stamped on barrel designs that are often meaningless to today's collectors.

The stocks are of walnut or fruit woods, and invariably reach to the muzzle of the barrel. Some of the earliest guns of this type were profusely carved from end to end, while the later models are carved on the cheek side of the butt with only a few scrolls on each end of the cheek rest. The lock and lock-bolt plate are seated in a panel, which is raised from the stock and terminates in a tear drop pattern at the rear of the lock. A rib is carved along the fore stock next to the barrel and a combination of flutes and ribs is found sometimes along the ramrod. They were also frequently carved at the point where the ramrod tail pipe is fastened to the stock. The stock was quite thick at the butt plate, some reaching a thickness of two and one-half inches.

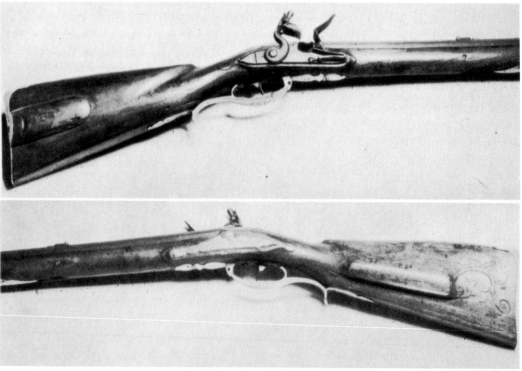

Joe Kindig, Jr.

PLATE 5

Rifle with flint lock, full stock of walnut, brass mountings, and octagonal barrel. This rifle is a "border-line example" and could have been made in Europe or Pennsylvania. The carving on the cheek side of the stock, the patch box cover of wood, and the contour of the stock make the place of its production uncertain. Its unmarked octagonal barrel suggests production in Pennsylvania in the first half of the eighteenth century.

The early eighteenth century lock had a flint mechanism and somewhat highly ornamented lock plates. There were chiseled designs of hunting scenes, which usually included men, dogs, and animals. The lock plates were five to six inches long and about one and one-fourth inches wide. The bottom edge of the lock plate was usually concave to fit the contour of the gun. The bottom side of the pan was usually angular, instead of round, and there was no bridle to the frizzen.

The mountings of these rifles are usually brass, and one is known to have inlays of silver on the cheek side. Simple designs are engraved on the tail of the butt plate, the lock-bolt plate and the trigger guard, which are obviously influenced by the ornate designs of earlier guns.

The previous discussion obviously focuses attention on the fact that many of these rifles were highly ornamented in comparison with early Pennsylvania guns, but a few were made so simply that it is very difficult to determine where they were made. A local wood expert, who was born in Europe, contends that German walnut was lighter in color than American walnut; and, after the finish is removed, an almost positive identification can be made. This statement has been confirmed in the writer's few experiences with the problem of identification. Some of the rifles have locks which closely resemble the hand-made locks found on early Pennsylvania rifles; this not only increases the difficulty of identification, but also adds support to the theory that the early hand-made lock used on the Pennsylvania rifle was made in Germany. The barrels on these guns are invariably octagonal; and some are not signed, which increases the suspicion that they were made in America, for most European gunsmiths placed some means of identification on the barrels.

It should not be presumed that the rifle was used only in central Europe before its introduction into Pennsylvania. It was used in other areas but the design and mechanism of the Pennsylvania rifle can be traced directly to the German rifle and, for that reason, others will not be discussed here. Additional information on the European ancestry of the Pennsylvania rifle will be given in the next chapter.

Chapter 2

The Rifle In Pennsylvania

THE EUROPEAN ANCESTRY of the Pennsylvania Rifle has been established beyond any doubt. It has been pointed out that for two hundred years, 1500-1700, the rifle underwent a series of changes culminating in the simple rifle which the early settlers doubtless brought with them to America. The designing of arms has never been a static matter; and, when the scene of rifle production was shifted from Central Europe to Pennsylvania, the process that was started abroad continued here. During the next hundred and fifty years, through experimentation and adaptation, a new rifle was developed in Pennsylvania to meet the needs of a nation which was truly perched on the frontier. Although it had its limitations in design and ornamentation, it was extremely accurate and very satisfactory for killing men or game at great distances. The Pennsylvania rifle subsequently influenced the design of arms throughout western Europe and had an influence as far-reaching there as the earlier European arms had previously had on America.

The development of the rifle in Pennsylvania can be divided into three distinct phases, the first being the period of transition.

The period of transition in Pennsylvania might be described as the time when the style of European arms was slowly changing to one that was Pennsylvania in character. The period cannot be accurately dated, for no one knows when it started, and we are equally ignorant as to when it ended; however, for reasons of convenience, it might be thought of as the fifty-year span from 1725 to 1775. It is probable that guns were made in Pennsylvania before that time, and it is very probable that transition-style guns were made in the backwoods of Pennsylvania after 1775; but by and large, this was the period of time·when the new Pennsylvania rifle evolved.

The uncertainties of this early period of rifle production in Pennsylvania are in unhappy contrast to the precise dating of advances in European arms. It is said that the flintlock was invented about 1630, but there is no way to form an estimate as to when the first hinged patch box was placed on a rifle in Pennsylvania. This unfortunate situation exists because Pennsylvania was very primitive in the first half of the eighteenth century. And, although there might have been some early production of rifles elsewhere in Pennsylvania, the bulk of the early work occurred in a frontier province, called Lancaster County after 1729.

In order to completely understand the difficulties involved in determining the time of the earliest production of rifles in Pennsylvania, the reader should be aware of the inadequate resources for research on the subject. One of the most informative

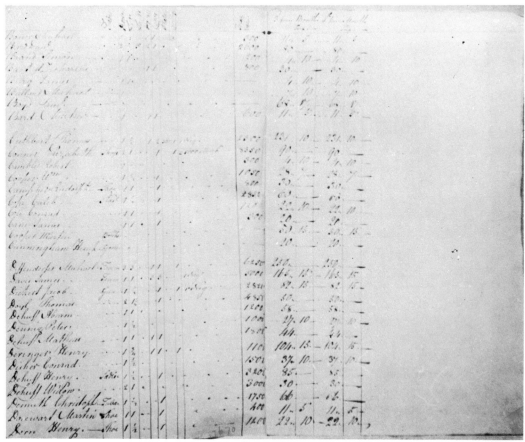

PLATE 6

A page from the tax assessment list for the borough of Lancaster for the year 1780. Jacob Dickert is obviously listed as a gunsmith in this one.

and accurate sources of information are the tax assessment lists, which are under the jurisdiction of the Commissioners of the various counties. The indifferent care which these precious documents receive in most cases indicates that they are of little use in the operation of civil law today. The earliest ones are invariably missing; in Lancaster County *all* of them previous to 1750 are missing, and the early ones that have survived are usually in poor condition because of neglect and inadequate storage accommodations. It is not unusual to find that their location is unknown to courthouse employees, and some employees will contend that they never existed. If a sizable quantity of lists is found, the researcher is often faced with failure because the assessors neglected to record the occupation of the men who were taxed. It is interesting to note that the gunsmith was a respected man in a community; and if any occupations are listed, the gunsmith is invariably included.

The second best source of information about early gunsmiths is the deeds and wills of these men. Fortunately, these records are usually complete and well cared for in most courthouses; and their contents, alphabetically indexed, are readily available. This procedure has its limitations, for the name of a man must be known

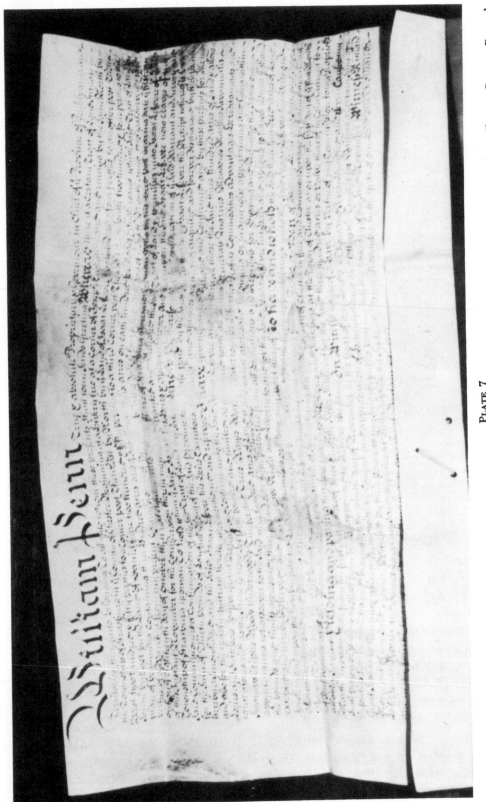

PLATE 7

This deed is a record of the transfer of a property from the proprietor, William Penn, to a resident of Strasburg Township, Chester County, Pennsylvania. After 1729 Strasburg Township was a part of Lancaster County, Pennsylvania. The new owner of the land was named Lefevre; however, there is no evidence that he was a gunsmith.

to find data about him; the tax lists are of great value in discovering names of gunsmiths that are not known. The data in deeds varies, although the occupation of the purchaser, or vendor, of the real estate is usually mentioned, and in some rare cases his former residence. Such a disclosure was found in a deed recorded for Henry Lechler, who moved to Carlisle from Lancaster in 1798. Sometimes because the deed is involved in the settlement of an estate, family relationships are mentioned, as in the case of a Matthius Roessor property in Lancaster, the deed to which mentions the name of his son, Peter. Wills can be equally valuable in recording the occupation of the deceased, and they of course furnish an approximate date of the death of the person being investigated.

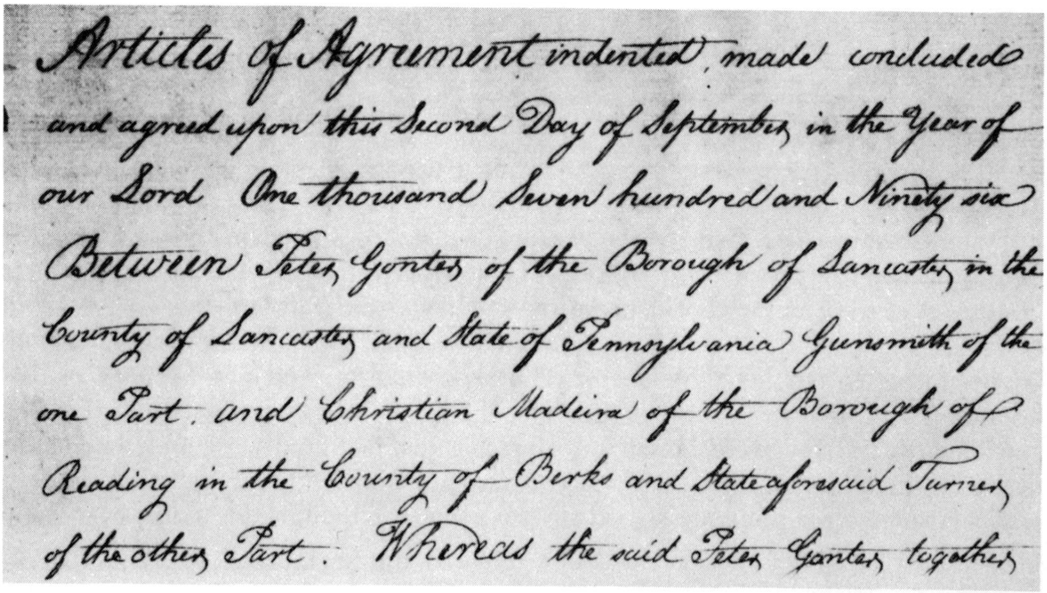

Articles of Agreement indented, made concluded
and agreed upon this Second Day of September in the Year of
our Lord One thousand Seven hundred and Ninety six
Between Peter Gonter of the Borough of Lancaster in the
County of Lancaster and State of Pennsylvania Gunsmith of the
one Part, and Christian Madeira of the Borough of
Reading in the County of Berks and State aforesaid Turner
of the other Part. Whereas the said Peter Gonter together

Joe Kindig, Jr.

PLATE 8

In the eighteenth century the occupation of parties involved in the transferring of a property was often mentioned in the deed for the property.

The records of the Moravian Church in Pennsylvania are very informative because a Moravian community was a communal corporation and all of its activities are a matter of church record. Unfortunately, some of the most valuable ones remain to be translated from German to English, although some are now available in English. A few scattered sources such as bills, day books, and military records, add some details to the total picture; but before the Revolution such records were rare and are difficult to find. There are no business directories for the transition period known to exist in Pennsylvania.

The early production of rifles in Pennsylvania is further obscured by the fact that the earliest gunsmiths failed to sign their products. This neglect is particularly mysterious because the German guns of the early eighteenth century examined by the writer are signed, as are a great many of the German guns illustrated in the catalogue of the Wallace Collection, in London, and quite a few are dated.

Although the identification of early Pennsylvania rifles is a baffling and hazardous procedure, in each gun there is some evidence to suggest the time and place where it was made. It has been pointed out that some guns are virtually impossible to identify as European or American. Such an uncommon, but not impossible, situation could arise if a European gun were brought to America and the stock was broken so that the gun was no longer usable. The metal parts would then be placed in the hands of a gunsmith, who would restock the gun in a native wood, such as walnut or cherry. To identify such a gun would defy the ingenuity of the most discriminating authority, and the fact is obvious that it is not wholly a European gun or an American one. It is likely that such incidents occurred, for the inventory of a man named John Henry, who died in 1747, lists "a set of tools for stocking guns" but there are no tools such as anvils, tongs, etc., for doing any metal work. This man must have been engaged in the business of restocking guns or stocking guns for another who produced only the metal parts.

Some guns are more easily identified than the one suggested in the previous example. These guns have stocks that are made of maple wood. The use of maple was not an exclusive Pennsylvania procedure, but it was much more common here than in any other part of the world. These stocks have thick butt plates, a patch box with a sliding cover of wood, without the overlay of metal on the cover that is frequently found on their European counterparts. The stock is rarely carved, but a few have vestiges of carving on the cheek side of the stock near the butt end. They have about 40 inch octagonal barrels, which were originally rifled; but now are usually smooth bored of about 50 caliber. The lack of rifling is ordinarily explained by the fact that because the barrels were made of soft iron, the ridges were worn out from shooting and loading, or they were bored out after big game disappeared and the hunter needed a smoothbore rather than a rifle. There are front and rear sights on the barrels, and some were probably signed by the makers, although the writer cannot recall seeing a very early rifle with a signature.

The mountings on these early guns are usually made of brass, and the parts are sparsely engraved. The butt plate, like the trigger guard and the lock-bolt plate, were usually cast and show a rough texture on the inside, where they have not been finished. The ramrod pipes were made of heavy sheet brass, and are usually simple cylinders with a ring or a band filed near the ends. The trigger guards are long and shallow and show definite relationship to the trigger guards of the Jaeger rifle.

The lock plates are usually plain, except for a few slashes filed across the tail, behind the hammer; and the bottom edge is either straight or convex to fit the contour of the gun at the point where the lock is placed. The lock-bolt plate on the left side of the rifles is a thick piece of brass with beveled edges. Most of these details are illustrated in the early maplestocked gun from the M. T. Stewart Collection.

It is important to note that the sliding cover of wood on rifle patch boxes is not a guarantee of early production, for this arrangement was used by Pennsylvania gunsmiths over a long span of years. A flintlock rifle with such a patch box cover is in the author's collection; it was made in the Allentown area early in the nineteenth century. The late use of this early feature on a rifle can be explained by the fact that gunsmiths in that area seemed to cling to old traditions longer than those in other

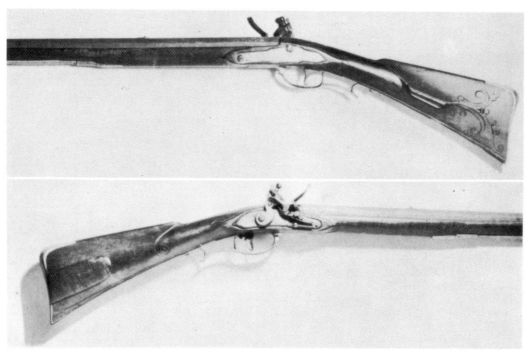

M. *T. Stewart*

PLATE 9

Rifle with flint lock, stock of maple, brass mountings, patch box cover of wood, octagonal barrel 43½ inches long.

parts of Pennsylvania. It should also be pointed out that a cover of wood was much less costly than one of brass. The elimination of a ferrule on the forestock and a ramrod tailpipe are other evidences of economy in this particular rifle.

A rifle in the Kindig collection can be regarded as another gun of the transition period because it has some of the features of the Pennsylvania rifle and some of the Jaeger rifle. It has a heavy, thick stock, which is carved on the cheek side of the butt and on the forestock along the ramrod. The lock plate and hammer have convex surfaces in the tradition of early lock making. The mountings are made of cast brass. The butt plate is almost flat, and the trigger guard is quite shallow and long. The unsigned octagonal barrel has a front and rear sight.

Despite the fact that this rifle has a number of characteristics usually associated with the Jaeger rifle of central Europe, it has one feature that indicates its having been produced in Pennsylvania: the substitution of a brass patch box cover for the earlier cover of wood. This change can be easily understood, for the cover of wood was not attached to the stock of the rifle; in addition to being cumbersome to use, there was always the possibility that it might be lost. The high mortality of wooden covers from old rifles is evidence that a great many of these covers were lost. It must be admitted that the wooden cover was compatible with the contour and general design of the gun, but the ingenious gunsmiths of Pennsylvania obviously created a new and better cover.

The new cover of brass had essentially the same size and shape as its predecessor, for the function of the patch box was not changed. The major improvement in

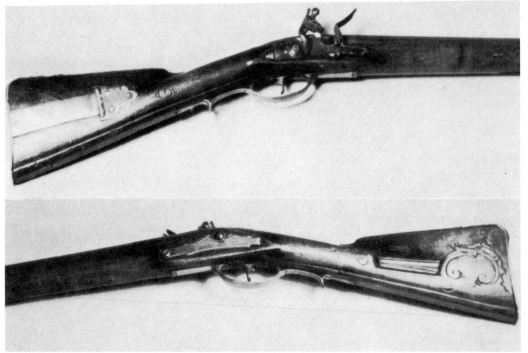

Joe Kindig, Jr.

PLATE 10

Rifle with flint lock, full stock of maple, brass mountings, and octagonal barrel. The flat butt plate, the thickness of the butt, the early lock with its convex lock plate, the simple incised carving on the cheek side of the butt, and the two piece brass patch box all point to the fact that this is one of the earliest rifles made in Pennsylvania. Its style and period suggest that it was made in Lancaster County, Pennsylvania. Rifles of this type are extremely rare.

the cover was the use of a hinge to attach it to the stock. The contents of the patch box were easily available in this new arrangement, and the possibility of loss was completely eliminated. In addition, the introduction of a bright piece of metal on the right side of the butt gave the gun a distinctive feature and identified it as the product of a Pennsylvania gunsmith.

The decorative possibilities of this new idea seem to have been immediately obvious to the gunsmiths, for though the lid was straight and plain, it was attached to a brass finial with a hinge having a leaf motif in its outline. The three screws holding this plate to the stock were arranged in the form of a triangle, which tied in with the shape of the plate and conformed with the general shape of the stock as well. A few lines were usually engraved on the lid and finial to relieve the severe plainess of the two pieces. Just where and when this new patch box cover was created will never be known, but it was doubtless the most drastic alteration in the transition from the European rifle to the Pennsylvania rifle.

A rifle in the Clegg collection indicates an effort on the part of the gunsmith to relieve the plain and uninteresting side edge of the lid. The use of wire inlay was an old European custom, and the gunsmith merely adapted it to a new concept in the decorating of rifles in Pennsylvania. The use of brass wire along the edges of the patch box in this gun is a pleasing feature, but other gunsmiths had other ideas on the subject.

One of the most interesting variations from the straight edge of the patch box was to use a scallop design around its entire outer edge, except where it overlapped the butt plate, where it conformed to the contour of the butt plate.

A floral motif was used in the finial of the patch box, and the early use of a pierced pattern is also found in this interesting example. The use of three screws to fasten the finial to the stock was continued, and the simple engraved line of the Clegg gun was expanded to a profuse pattern on the patch box, although the engraved pattern is not as important as the substitution of the scalloped edges for the earlier straight edges of the lid.

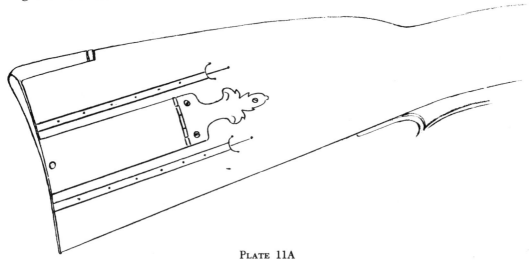

PLATE 11A

A two-piece patch box with wire inlay and a suggestion of a "Roman nose" is found on the stocks of rifles made in Berks County in the transition era.

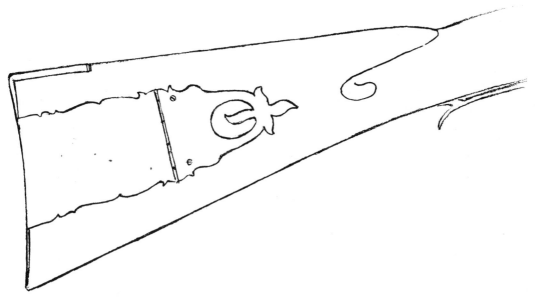

PLATE 11B

Unique patch box cover made of brass. It is obviously a transition pattern from the early, simple two–piece cover to the later, more elaborate, four-piece pattern. Its engraved pattern is so badly worn that no attempt was made to reproduce it.

Joe Kindig, Jr.

PLATE 12

Rifle with flint lock, full stock of maple, brass mountings, octagonal barrel 45 inches long with
J. Graeff engraved on the top facet of the barrel.

This rifle is unquestionably one of the first ones made in Lancaster County with a four-piece brass
patch box. Some of the first patch boxes were plain, but this one has a few lines engraved on it
suggesting the standard Lancaster pattern which appears on rifles made at the end of the eighteenth
century.

The final step in the evolution of the patch box came when a gunsmith separated the scalloped edge, which certainly must have ripped some coats or shirt
sleeves, and fastened these edges permanently to the gun. The lid again became a
long rectangular strip of brass, hinged to a finial, which was fastened to the stock
with the three screws. This general pattern of a patch box was used until the small
round or elliptical one replaced it in the middle of the nineteenth century. Although
a chronological development is implied in this discussion, it must be understood
that all of these patterns probably did not develop as precisely as suggested.

The guns of the transition period are interesting and important to collectors
and historians, but few collections are known to the author having more than a
few examples of these early guns. This situation arises from the fact that the guns
are often difficult to identify as Pennsylvania products, and they lack the glamor
of later guns. Some advanced collectors have a few transition guns to compare
with their guns made in the second period of production, which Joe Kindig, Jr.,
prefers to call the "Golden Era of Gun Making in Pennsylvania." Although attractive
and accurate guns were made before and after this period, the author concurs
with Mr. Kindig in his belief that between 1775 and 1830 the gunsmiths of Pennsylvania reached the apex of their craft. This was the period when long slender guns
were made with beautiful maple stocks, carved with the skill of the finest wood-
carvers, and ornamented with brass mountings engraved in the finest traditions of
the engraver's art in Pennsylvania. The reader's attention, however, should be focused on the fact that this superior product did not come into full bloom precisely
in 1775 nor did it completely fade when the first gun of the percussion era was
made.

It is an easily recognized fact that the urgencies of war create a strong demand
for arms, and the impact of the American Revolution on production in Pennsylvania
probably followed a typical pattern. All the gunsmiths were engaged in producing
arms for the soldiers, which suggests the output of arms increased, but the quality
of arms deteriorated. The acquiring of thousands of muskets from France probably
reduced the demand for local products, but the necessity for repair work and replacement certainly continued. The demands on Pennsylvania gunsmiths must

have been particularly acute while the army was encamped at Valley Forge. When hostilities ceased in 1780, the resources for arms production were greater than the demand and some readjustment in personnel and facilities was doubtless necessary.

Some gunsmiths, particularly the ones who had been recruited from the allied trade of blacksmithing, probably returned to their former occupations because there was a more urgent need for ploughshares than guns in the new nation. Some aggressive men like Jacob Ferree, Henry Albright, and Peter Resor, migrated to the frontier at different points from Chambersburg to Pittsburgh and set up shops to participate in the new economic developments west of the mountains. The less imaginative men stayed in the East and worked for leaders in the field like Jacob Dickert, George Eyster, Jacob Sell, Peter Gonter, and others who played an important role in the creation of the true Pennsylvania rifle.

This discussion of the evolution of firearms in early Pennsylvania focuses attention on the fact that the completely new rifle was not created by one man at one time and place. It might be presumed that one craftsman developed a profusely engraved patch box about the time of the Revolution and that another envisioned a longer, slender barrel at the same time. In a distant town another craftsman made a lighter gun while his neighbor was experimenting with the most effective number of grooves to cut in a barrel. Although all this experimentation was occurring in a reasonably small portion of Pennsylvania, considerable time would obviously be required to bring all these details to the attention of most of the gunsmiths. Ultimately most of the fine makers incorporated all of these features in their guns, but when and by what means the evolution occurred will doubtless never be fully known. It has been determined with some degree of certainty that the finest Pennsylvania rifles were created sometime between the Revolution and the end of the eighteenth century.

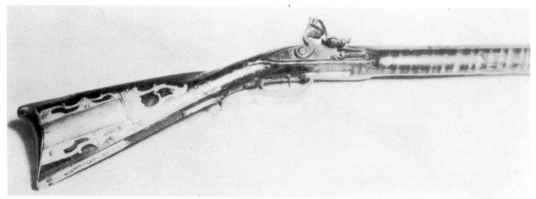

Joe Kindig, Jr.

PLATE 13

Rifle with flint lock, full stock of curly maple, brass mountings, and octagonal barrel with G. Eyster engraved in script letters on the top facet of the barrel.

This gun is really a lavish display of the gun maker's craft. The lace-like quality of the patch box decoration, the extensive use of C scrolls on the bas-relief carving, and the profusely engraved patterns on the brass work are evidences of Eyster's skill. He made unusual use of the cross-hatching technique in his carving and his engraving. He also used a great many screws to hold the brass mountings to the stocks. There are twelve screws in the patch box.

Few of his products are signed, but his style can be recognized by anyone who has seen a number of his guns. He is known to have made both rifles and fowling pieces.

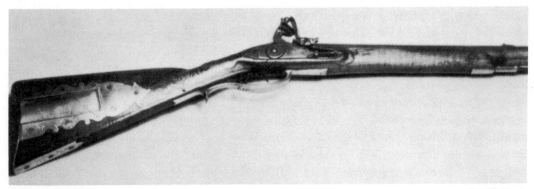

Joe Kindig, Jr.

PLATE 14

Rifle with flint lock, full stock of curly maple, brass mountings, and octagonal barrel 45 inches long with J. P. Beck engraved on the top facet of the barrel.

Some collectors attribute Beck's rifles with wooden patch box covers to the early part of his career, and the style of this gun places it among the earliest that he made. It is obvious that he made both styles of patch boxes throughout most of his career. It is possible that he liked wooden covers and they reduced the price of a rifle from one with a brass patch box.

The rich, but simple, details of many of his products establish him as one of Pennsylvania's outstanding craftsmen. He made rifles, pistols, and fowling pieces. His superior ability as a craftsman is evident in all of his products.

It is difficult to describe exactly the rifle made in Pennsylvania late in the eighteenth and early nineteenth centuries, for, although there was a constant style, each maker introduced variations in his products that in modern terminology might be called "trade marks." Not all of these variations can be discussed, however, some typical examples are the bird finial that Beyer used on his patch boxes, carving of George Eyster, and the engraving of Isaac Hains.

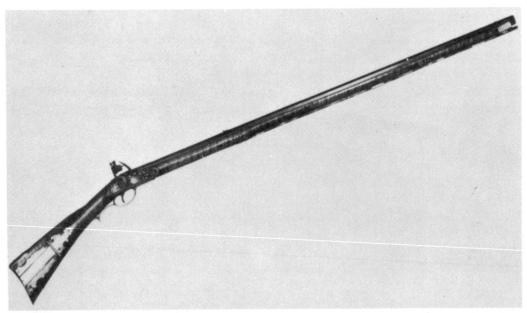

Wilson Collection

PLATE 15

Typical proportions of a rifle made in Lancaster in the late eighteenth century. This one is signed C. Gumpf.

Because a gun was built around the barrel, it seems reasonable to describe first the barrels of the Pennsylvania flintlock rifles of the Golden age. The barrel was usually octagonal throughout, although some makers used the older pattern of octagon-to-round. The octagonal pattern was heavy at the breech and tapered slowly toward the muzzle, where it sometimes flared a bit to make the pattern more attractive than a uniform tapering pattern would have been. Many makers engraved their names in script letters on the top facet of the barrel, and research has proved that their engraved signatures on the barrel often closely resemble their written signatures. A few men like J. Haeffer of Lancaster engraved their names in block letters. A few makers like Jacob Sell signed their full names; many, like P. Gonter, used one initial and their last name; and in very rare cases, for example, used their first two initials and their last name like J. P. Beck. The appearance of two names, like Dickert and Gill, is rarely found. On the top facet of some barrels is stamped an Indian head or crossed tomahawks, which are thought to be proof marks. On the side facets of some barrels the barrel maker stamped his name or initials, leaving the top facet on which the gunsmith could place his name. The barrels range in length from forty to forty-eight inches, although any longer than forty-four must be considered rare. The front and rear sights were attached by slipping them into a slot shaped like a dovetail on the top facet of the barrel.

The lugs on the bottom of the barrel have either round holes or rectangular slots through which pins or strips of metal pass to hold the barrel to the stock. It is doubtful if any barrels of the flintlock period were originally equipped with patent breeches, but they were often added to flint gun barrels when the guns were changed to percussion ignition. The width over the flats of the barrels is about 1 to 1⅛ inches at the breech and ⅞ to 1 inch at the muzzle, although larger and smaller exceptions can doubtless be found. Only a few guns of the flintlock period retain their original bores, which are rarely less than 35 or over 60 caliber. The number of grooves varies with each maker; but six to eight are most common, with one twist in forty inches. The barrels were finished by several applications of a liquid that accelerates rusting, which was arrested by a final application of oil.

As has been pointed out, some of the earliest Pennsylvania rifles were stocked in walnut wood, others have stocks of plain maple, and a few were stocked in curly maple. By the end of the eighteenth century the gunsmiths were using curly maple for most of their fine guns. The contrasting values of the light and dark veins in the wood added interest to the stock, and after years of use the deep red-brown color

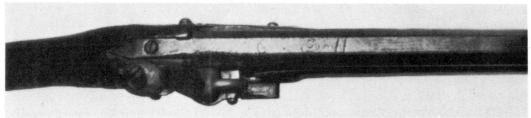

Wilson Collection

PLATE 16

The engraved signature of C. Gumpf on the top facet of a rifle barrel shows the style used late in the eighteenth and early nineteenth centuries. Some of them can be easily read while others cannot be read even with the assistance of a magnifying glass. This one is in about average condition.

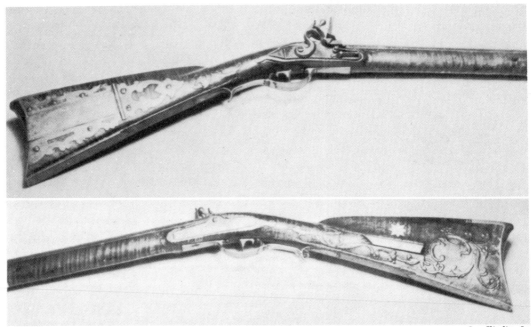

Joe Kindig, Jr.

PLATE 17

Rifle with flint lock, full stock of curly maple, brass mountings, and octagonal barrel marked C. Welshantz on the top facet.

This rifle establishes C. Welshantz as one of the fine craftsmen of York, Pennsylvania, in the last quarter of the eighteenth century. The design of his patch box, the delicacy of his carved patterns on the cheek side, and his clever use of the graver establish him as a master craftsman. The similarity of his work to Martin Frey's, another gunsmith of York, Pennsylvania, is evident in the patterns carved in bas-relief on the stocks of their rifles.

which the maple acquired was an excellent "back drop" for the mountings of polished brass. The massive size of the earlier rifles was noticeably reduced to make the gun long, slender, and graceful. The butt became thinner, the wrist was smaller, and the forestock became a fragile shell of wood that was frequently split or broken away entirely by an indifferent user. The most distinguishing feature of the late eighteenth and early nineteenth century stock was the pattern, carved in bas-relief on the cheek side of the butt, around the breech tang and at the rear of the bottom ramrod pipe.

Although Pennsylvania gunsmiths decorated their rifles in a number of ways, the rifle with a carved stock is considered the *piece de resistance* in most collections. The importance of this feature can be attributed to the difficulty of carving curly maple and the resulting decorative quality which the carving gave to the gun. Most of the designs were original with the gunsmith who used them, although the master's influence on the apprentice can be detected on some guns. Interlacing scrolls were the most popular motif, and a few craftsmen were partial to carved deer or lions. Some gunsmiths used geometric patterns, and others used a combination of many basic ideas.

Although the decorative addition which these carved patterns made to fine guns is important, the reader's attention should be focused on the fact that they are particularly useful in identifying the makers of many unsigned guns. It appears that after a gunsmith selected a pattern, or motif, to carve on his guns, he often continued using this pattern, with minor variations, over a long span of years. It is also known that many fine craftsmen did not sign all of their guns, and without some comparative means of identification the makers of these unsigned guns would never be identified. It is obvious, therefore, that when an expert can compare unsigned guns with signed specimens, he can make attributions with considerable skill and certainty, particularly when makers with a consistent style, like Frederick Sell and George Eyster, are involved. The carved gun will probably always be considered the apex of the art of the gunsmith, for those proficient in this skill are usually superior in all phases of the art of gun making. The brass mountings of the rifles made in the late eighteenth and early nineteenth centuries resembled those used on the rifles of the late portion of the transition era. Their simple functional form was continued; however, they obviously became a medium in which the gunsmith could display his skill and imagination as an engraver. Occasionally a two-piece patch box of the earlier period appears on a gun made late in the century, but it was then engraved in the tradition of the period rather than left plain as it would have been thirty years earlier. Such a gun is illustrated which was made by Stoeffel Smith and is dated 1794. The typical patch box of the late eighteenth century was made of four separate pieces: the lid, the finial, and two side plates. The outline of the finial seems to have followed the same patterns in certain geographical areas; for example, the daisy finial on the patch box was favored by many craftsmen in Lancaster County. Berks County craftsmen developed a spear pattern, while craftsmen in York County favored a drooping feather pattern.

It has been previously pointed out that the surface of the earliest brass patch boxes was very plain or engraved with only a few scrolls. The tempo of decoration increased until virtually the whole patch box was covered with a profusion of designs. Different ways for releasing the lid were improvised by various makers, and the patch box became almost a separate work of mechanical and decorative ingenu-

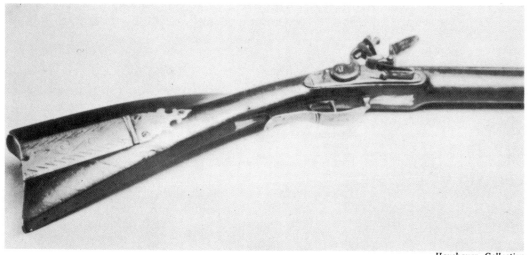

PLATE 18

Haushauer Collection

Rifle with flint lock, stock of plain maple, brass mountings, and octagonal barrel with Stoeffel Smith, 1794, inlaid with silver on the top facet of the barrel.

Herman Dean

PLATE 19

Rifle with flint lock, brass mountings, silver inlays, full stock of curly maple, and octagonal barrel with Jno. Shriver engraved on the top facet of the barrel.

The design and workmanship of the patch box of this gun is typical of the superb work done in the golden era of gun making in Pennsylvania The carving on the cheek side is also the work of a master craftsman.

ity. Later the side plates and finial were pierced to add interest to the contour and the engraving; and the unit became a mass of ornamentation that has few, if any, counterparts in American craftsmanship.

To this elaborately decorated patch box were added a few silver inlays. Many craftsmen used an eight-pointed star in the cheek piece with interesting variations in design and surface enrichment. On the wrist a circle or an ellipse was also inlaid, on which the owner's initials were sometimes to engraved.

A few of the better craftsmen used the wire inlay technique to ornament their guns, but it was never used as widely here as in Europe. Both silver and brass wire were used, although silver wire seems to have been used on the finer guns. Two guns made by J. P. Beck, which have inlays of silver wire, are known to the writer.

In the nineteenth century an unattractive change was made in the patch box design by exposing a strip of the stock between the lid and the side plates. Some of the earlier patch box finials were used in this new arrangement, but they seem ill-suited to their new environment. The surface continued to be profusely engraved, but the

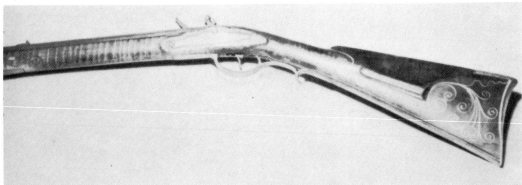

John Fonderwhite

PLATE 20

Rifle with flint lock made by J. Sees. The technique of decorating with wire inlay was not used by many rifle makers in Pennsylvania. The design in the inlay was obviously inspired by the traditional C scrolls which were carved in bas-relief by many makers.

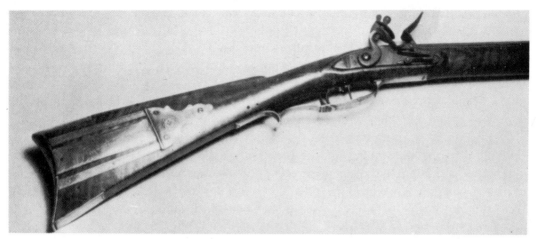

PLATE 21

The second style of four-piece patch box used by gunsmiths in Lancaster County, Pennsylvania. This rifle was made by C. Gumpf between 1810 and 1820.

designs indicate that the originality of the early makers was rapidly disappearing. The work of old masters like Dickert and Gonter, in this period is difficult to identify if the signature is missing from the top facet of the barrel.

Some of the makers of flintlock guns in the nineteenth century followed the traditions of craftsmanship set by the earlier craftsmen. Men like John Armstrong and Melchoir Fordney excelled in certain phases of the work, and made rifles of fine quality. Armstrong included strips of silver inlay in some of his carved patterns, and thereby suggested a wider use of this technique than had previously been employed. Later, barrel pin escutcheons of silver were quite common, and a half-moon and eagle replaced the eight-pointed star of craftsmen. The widest use of this technique occurred in the percussion era which followed. A description of the locks used in this era can be found in the chapter on locks.

There might be some question by cynics and collectors of more modern arms about the desirability of calling the late eighteenth and early nineteenth centuries the "Golden Age of Gun Making in Pennsylvania"; however, the fact that the rifle of this period was an attractive and effective arm is difficult to dispute. It must be admitted that by earlier European standards, the Pennsylvania flintlock rifle was not an outstanding achievement in arms decoration. European museums are full of wheel-lock rifles, which were made in Central Europe, and the surrounding area, some of which were brought to America about ten years ago with the treasures from the Vienna Museum. These guns are superb examples of craftsmanship in carving, inlaying, and chiseling. It should be noted, however, that these European guns are representative products of a highly developed system of hand crafts which made comparable products in areas like textiles, ceramics and metal smithing. The Pennsylvania rifle is a representative product of a primitive system of hand crafts which also produced comparable products in textiles, ceramics, and metal smithing. Within the framework of this primitive system of hand crafts the Pennsylvania gunsmiths produced a gun that was unique. They introduced a patch box cover that was not only original but also functional and attractive. They popularized a type of wood for gun stocks that aided materially in making the Pennsylvania rifle a unique arm. They reduced the bore and increased the length of the barrel until it was the most efficient rifle in the world. The resulting increased speed of the bullet with lower trajectory brought it to the attention of all arms experts in the western world. The statement of General George Hanger, a British officer in the American Revolution, might briefly summarize the achievement of the period. He said, "I never in my life saw better rifles (or men who shot better) than those made in America."

It might be surmised by the reader that rifles made in Pennsylvania after the "Golden Age of Gun Making" showed evidence of less creativity on the part of the gunsmiths, although the rifles were certainly not less effective as weapons in the era of percussion ignition. The outstanding exception to this trend of uniformity were the gunsmiths of Bedford County, who reached the apex of their craft in the middle of the nineteenth century.

It is important to notice at the outset of the last period of rifle production in Pennsylvania that the major influence of the period came from Europe, although this time it came from England instead of central Europe. In the spring of 1806 a clergyman, named Forsyth appeared in London and announced that he had solved a problem that had been plaguing English gunsmiths for a long time. The unreliability of the flintlock had set many minds to thinking and some advance had been made in the substitution of fulminates for the earlier gun powder; but, until the appearance of Forsyth, no practical way to use them had been discovered. Forsyth had invented a chamber which held a small amount of detonating powder; when its

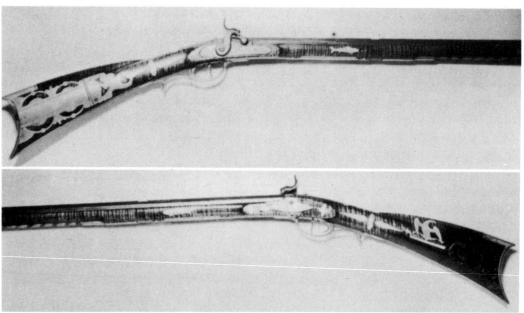

T. J. Cooper

PLATE 22

Rifle with percussion lock, full stock of curly maple, brass mountings, silver inlays, octagonal barrel 36 inches long signed on the top facet J. Long.

The lace effect in the side plates of the patch box and the eagle finial make this a very attractive product of Long. The fine curl of the wood and the silver inlays, including a fish and an eagle, suggest that this is one of his masterpieces.

firing pin was struck by the hammer, sparks were forced into the barrel and the gun quickly discharged. After some skirmishes with the British Ordnance Office, Forsyth turned to manufacturing guns. He hired James Purdy to make the guns while he supervised, and from the time of his patent in 1807 until 1819, Forsyth refined and improved his system of ignition. It was an "uphill" fight, for many die-hards stuck to their flintlock guns. The invention of the copper cap and its subsequent standardization sealed the fate of the flintlock; and by the 1830's, Pennsylvania gunsmiths were busy converting guns to percussion ignition and making new ones equipped with this useful mechanism.

The Forsyth invention had an extremely important influence on arms performance and design, but it was only one of the factors which changed the appearance and improved the performance of rifles after the 1830's in Pennsylvania. The invention of faster burning gunpowder at about the same time also had a tremendous influence. The long barrels of the earlier guns were not only attractive but were needed for the slow burning powder to spend its force before the bullet left the muzzle. When faster burning powder became available, the barrels became shorter; and, although no efficiency was sacrificed, the shorter barrels are less attractive to most collectors than the longer ones.

Finally, the adoption of mass production methods for producing guns and gun parts had a two-fold effect on rifle production in Pennsylvania. It thinned the ranks of individual gunsmiths, for establishments like the Henry factory at Boulton, and the Leman Rifle Works in Lancaster might easily have forced twenty-five to fifty gunsmiths out of business or into the factories to become employees of manufacturers like Henry and Leman. These two factories were joined later by the Enterprise Gun Works at Pittsburgh; so that, after the Civil War, only a sprinkling of gunsmiths were engaged at the trade.

The second effect of mass production was the uniformity in the quality of the rifles made at the time. Although Henry Leman did make a few presentation pieces, as did some of the other men like Fordney and Drepperd, the bulk of the factory output lacked the originality of the earlier individual makers. Finally, the produc-

Vincent Nolt

PLATE 23

Rifle with percussion lock, half stock of maple, brass mountings, and octagonal barrel marked H. Leman, Lancaster, Pa.

This is an early half-stock made by Leman in his factory at Lancaster, Pennsylvania. This rifle is identical to earlier rifles with a full stock, except for the shortened stock and the rib under the barrel.

tion of thousands of "half stocks" with round or elliptical brass patch boxes brought the craft of gun making to its lowest aesthetic level, and unfortunately to its demise.

The barrel of the percussion rifle continued to be octagonal in shape, but the flare at the muzzle seems to have been completely dropped. The elimination of the flare can be easily understood, for any departure from a uniformly tapering barrel would have created extra work with no corresponding improvement in the function of the gun. This statement is not meant to imply that rifles were no longer attractive but that they no longer had the little flourishes in design that earlier smiths seemed so eager to provide in their products. A few octagon-to-round barrels were used in the percussion era, but they are very rare. The outside dimension of the barrel at the muzzle was ¾ of an inch to 1 inch, with some exceptions like the massive barrels of Huntington County guns, which were as big as 1⅛ inch at the muzzle. Barrel lengths were generally decreased until they got to thirty six inches, although the late Pittsburgh makers charged extra only for lengths beyond forty-two inches. The barrels had front and rear sights, which were fitted into a dovetail-shaped cut in the top facet of the barrel. James Bown and Sons supplied at their regular price a rear elevating sight for distances up to three hundred yards. For longer distances they recommended globe and peep sights. The bore of the Pennsylvania rifles was slowly reduced in diameter, for big game was rapidly disappearing and squirrel hunting seemed to be taking its place. Some barrels had a caliber as small as 25 with a uniform or gain twist. Although some of the older gunsmiths continued to engrave their names on the top facet of the barrels, the new fashion was to stamp them in block letters, and often the name of the city in which the gunsmith worked was stamped under or following the maker's name. Some gunsmiths engraved their barrels profusely with geometric designs at the breech and the muzzle and some added designs in front of and behind the rear sight.

The development of the patent breech in the percussion era was necessitated by the fact that the weakest part of the barrel in the flintlock era was at the breech, for there the only separate part of the barrel was joined to it by threads. The procedure of joining another part in the same area would obviously further reduce the ability of the barrel to withstand the great pressure of the charge when

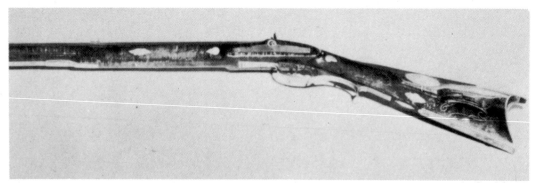

A. Orr Johnston

PLATE 24

Rifle with percussion lock, full stock of maple, brass mountings, silver inlays, and octagonal barrel marked J. H. Johnston on the top facet of the barrel.
The incised carving on this rifle is typical of the work found on fine rifles of the percussion era.

it exploded. The patent breech was really a separate end of the barrel about two or three inches long, the breech tang and the nipple being integral parts of the metal casting. This casting was filed and fitted into the barrel in a way that provided more strength than had previously been supplied by the thread of the breech plug. This procedure not only increased the strength of the barrel where it was most needed, but also permitted easy removal and replacement of the entire end after it had been badly eaten away by the fulminates of the percussion cap. J. Bown & Sons made these points about their patent breech. "Patent Breech, with vent screw, so it can be taken out in case of burnt powder accumulating in the chamber, or should you put a bullet in your barrel without powder, you can put sufficient powder into the chamber to blow out the ball."

A description of a barrel for a percussion gun, found in a Brown and Hirth catalogue of 1883, gives specific details concerning the material of which a barrel was made at that time.

> "Our Standard Steel Barrels are made from the same material as the best Cast Steel, the only difference is that it is not so highly carbonized; many call it decarbonized steel, which is perhaps the proper name. Every barrel is drilled from a solid bar, and we warrant them equal in material and finish to any Rifle Barrel in the country. We except none."

The brown finish on the barrels of earlier guns was used by makers as long as muzzle-loading guns were made.

Curly maple continued to be the favored wood for stocking rifles throughout the percussion era, although many late gunsmiths seem to have lacked the discrimination of earlier craftsmen in selecting fine wood. Some craftsmen on the frontier continued to use wood with fine grain, especially those in Bedford County. Leman and a few other makers found it more convenient to mark an artificial curl on their plain maple stocks than to hunt choice wood for the thousands of guns they were producing. The late Pittsburgh makers offered guns stocked in plain maple, curly maple or walnut.

A few of the old-timers who were making flintlock guns in the percussion era carved some of their stocks in the early tradition of craftsmanship, but it is very uncommon to find a carved rifle by Melchoir Fordney, Fredrick Sell, or Andrew Kopp that always had a percussion lock. A great many craftsmen did some incised carving on the cheek side of the butt, as J. H. Johnston did on the gun illustrated here. The cheek piece always had to be carved; and in the late period the Pittsburgh makers carved a round one, instead of one with a straight bottom.

The over-all length of the stock was naturally shorter to conform to the shorter barrels, the butt end became thinner, and the wrist often became heavier, with a resulting lack of grace in its contour. It should be noted that the Bedford County gunsmiths produced a very graceful rifle, while the style of many other makers was slowly deteriorating.

The old-timers of the percussion period continued to use mountings similar to those used on guns with flintlocks. The form of the mountings was particularly slow to change. for there was little, if any, change in their function. Most of them were made of cast brass, although a few eastern Pennsylvania makers and a number of makers in Pittsburgh often used mountings of German silver on their fine guns. The four-piece patch box, with a strip of the stock exposed between the lid and the side plates, was continued by most makers, although there were definite trends toward uniformity in size and pattern. Many of the patch box finials in 1840-1850 followed a keyhole or bee hive pattern. John Shuler of Liverpool used them, as did also the Gumpfs and the Gibbs in Lancaster. The round patch box was introduced in the decade before the Civil War, and was popular as long as muzzle loading rifles were made. The thinner stock required a narrower butt plate and trigger guard. The curve on the butt plate became so sharp that it appears to be unsuited to the portion of the body which supported it. Only one screw was needed to hold the new lock in place so the long lock-bolt plate was discarded in favor of a simple washer which at times was engraved or had a fancy outline. A rib was fitted to the bottom of the barrel in half-stocked guns and a pewter ferrule was cast on the forestock, where the ramrod entered the stock. Escutcheon plates were provided for the barrel pins and various inlays were used in other portions of the stock.

Although the inlays on the cheek-pieces and the wrists of rifles had only a decorative function, the wide use of barrel pin escutcheons in the early part of the percussion era suggests that inlays came to have a dual function. An extensive examination of rifles will reveal that many of the stocks are broken and chipped in the area of the barrel pins from frequent removal and replacement of the pins. It is obvious that, if a small piece of metal with a hole in its center for the movement of the barrel pin were inlaid at such spots, the wood would be protected from such damage. The practice of using escutcheons at barrel pins was followed by gunsmiths throughout Pennsylvania in the era of percussion ignition.

In the early part of the period they were made of sterling, brass, and occasionally German silver. The patterns were shapes such as ellipses, fish, or half moons, and many of them were cleverly engraved. Most of the later inlays were made of German silver and they were less frequently engraved than in early times.

It is obvious that the second function of inlays was to decorate and when motives of function and decoration were combined, there could be little quarrel with the fact that their use enhanced the physical appearance of the rifle. A time did come, how-

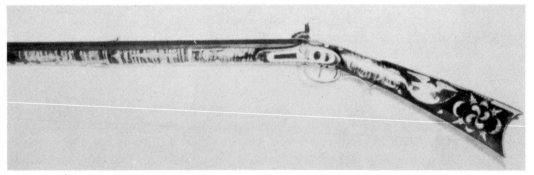

T. J. Cooper

PLATE 25

Rifle with percussion lock, full stock of curly maple, brass mountings, silver inlays, set triggers, octagonal barrel 38 inches long with B. J. Koughe on the top facet.

The "Take Down" feature of the stock and its numerous inlays are unusual features of this rifle. The workmanship on the entire rifle is of unusually high quality.

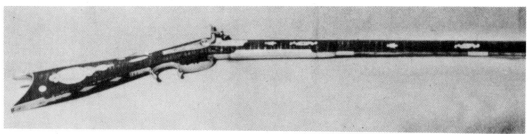

Hiram Ball

PLATE 26

Rifle with percussion lock, full stock of curly maple, silver mountings, silver inlays, set triggers, octagonal barrel 38 inches long with C. Flowers on the top facet of the barrel.

The silver plate protects the stock from the flash of the percussion cap, the "wear plate" on the stock between the trigger guard and the bottom ramrod pipe, and the delicate design of the inlays are evidences of Flower's superiority as a gunsmith in western Pennsylvania. The interesting design of the finial on the toe-plate should also be noted.

ever, when gunsmiths seemed to throw discretion to the winds and inlaid pieces of metal indiscriminately over most of the stock. Hearts, and diamonds, and tear drops were popular motifs of the late period and some makers continued to use fish as long as decorative inlays were used. A fine gun in the Hiram Ball Collection by Charles Flowers shows how inlays could be used by combining good taste with function. The three gun catalogues of late Pittsburgh makers examined by the author show no guns that have more than barrel pins escutcheons, nor is there a suggestion that such guns could have been orderd from them.

There were other important features on guns of the percussion era such as double-set triggers, hickory ramrods with a screw attachment, bar locks, and double hook trigger guards. The following quotation is a complete description of a gun sold by J. Bown & Sons in Pittsburgh in 1883.

Half Stock Kentucky Muzzle-Loading Rifle

No. 5 Half stock Rifle, fine enterprise iron barrels, which finishes equal to steel; not a flaw or seam of any kind. With full length rib, solid steel patent breech, full scroll percussion vent screw in the breech, best steel double hair triggers, with set screw to regulate the pull of the trigger in making fine shooting. Full Westley bar locks, steel inside, beautifully shaped hammer, steel nipples, German silver mountings, with double hook guard, toe pieces and patch box escutcheons and bolt loop to hold stock on the barrel; full-sized ramrod, with ball screw and ferrule on top end to use in loading conical ball as well as round ball; fine curly maple stock, with round cheek piece, so as to rest the cheek on the stock when shooting. We rifle all No. 5. Rifles up to 36 inches, both in our increased or gain twist, over 36 inches. This Rifle has sporting rear elevating sight graduated up to 300 yards; over 300 yards no open sight can be used with accuracy. Over that distance globe and peep sights should be used. This is one of the finest gotten up Muzzle Loading Rifles in this country for the money. It is finished in superior style, and every care taken to insure accuracy in shooting. Bullet mould fitted for round balls. We furnish each rifle with a muslin cover. Price $20.00.

No. 6. Same style as No. 5, with fine curly maple stock, standard steel barrels, German silver mountings, with muzzle turned down for starter, made in superior style, long and round balls, raised sights, fine set triggers $25.00

GENEALOGICAL

COMPILED AND F

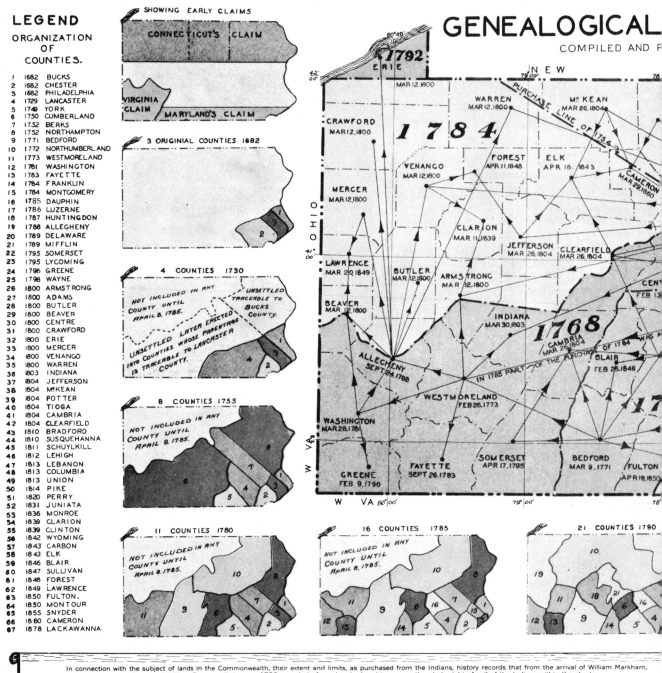

SHOWING EARLY CLAIMS

LEGEND

ORGANIZATION OF COUNTIES.

1	1682	BUCKS
2	1682	CHESTER
3	1682	PHILADELPHIA
4	1729	LANCASTER
5	1749	YORK
6	1750	CUMBERLAND
7	1752	BERKS
8	1752	NORTHAMPTON
9	1771	BEDFORD
10	1772	NORTHUMBERLAND
11	1773	WESTMORELAND
12	1781	WASHINGTON
13	1783	FAYETTE
14	1784	FRANKLIN
15	1784	MONTGOMERY
16	1785	DAUPHIN
17	1786	LUZERNE
18	1787	HUNTINGDON
19	1788	ALLEGHENY
20	1789	DELAWARE
21	1789	MIFFLIN
22	1795	SOMERSET
23	1795	LYCOMING
24	1796	GREENE
25	1798	WAYNE
26	1800	ARMSTRONG
27	1800	ADAMS
28	1800	BUTLER
29	1800	BEAVER
30	1800	CENTRE
31	1800	CRAWFORD
32	1800	ERIE
33	1800	MERCER
34	1800	VENANGO
35	1800	WARREN
36	1803	INDIANA
37	1804	JEFFERSON
38	1804	McKEAN
39	1804	POTTER
40	1804	TIOGA
41	1804	CAMBRIA
42	1804	CLEARFIELD
43	1810	BRADFORD
44	1810	SUSQUEHANNA
45	1811	SCHUYLKILL
46	1812	LEHIGH
47	1813	LEBANON
48	1813	COLUMBIA
49	1813	UNION
50	1814	PIKE
51	1820	PERRY
52	1831	JUNIATA
53	1836	MONROE
54	1839	CLARION
55	1839	CLINTON
56	1842	WYOMING
57	1843	CARBON
58	1843	ELK
59	1846	BLAIR
60	1847	SULLIVAN
61	1848	FOREST
62	1849	LAWRENCE
63	1850	FULTON.
64	1850	MONTOUR
65	1855	SNYDER
66	1860	CAMERON
67	1878	LACKAWANNA

CONNECTICUT'S CLAIM

VIRGINIA CLAIM

MARYLAND'S CLAIM

3 ORIGINIAL COUNTIES 1682

4 COUNTIES 1730

NOT INCLUDED IN ANY COUNTY UNTIL APRIL 8, 1785.

UNSETTLED TRACEABLE TO BUCKS COUNTY.

UNSETTLED LATER ERECTED INTO COUNTIES WHOSE PARENTAGE IS TRACEABLE TO LANCASTER COUNTY.

8 COUNTIES 1755

NOT INCLUDED IN ANY COUNTY UNTIL APRIL 8, 1785.

11 COUNTIES 1780

NOT INCLUDED IN ANY COUNTY UNTIL APRIL 8, 1785.

16 COUNTIES 1785

NOT INCLUDED IN ANY COUNTY UNTIL APRIL 8, 1785.

21 COUNTIES 1790

In connection with the subject of lands in the Commonwealth, their extent and limits, as purchased from the Indians, history records that from the arrival of William Markham, Deputy of William Penn, until the year 1792, a period of one hundred and ten years, the whole right of soil of the Indians within the charter bounds of Pennsylvania, was extinguished by the following thirty-three treaties and purchases:

1. 1682, JULY 15. Deed for lands between the Falls of Delaware and Neshammonys Creek, confirmed by William Penn, October 24, 1682.
2. 1683, JUNE 23. Deed for "lands lying betwixt Pemmapecka and Neshemineh Creek *** and backward of the same, and to run two days journey with an horse, up into the as the said River doth go."
3. 1683, JUNE 25. Wingebone's release for lands "lying on the west side of the Schuylkill, beginning from the first falls *** and backward of the same as far as my right g
4. 1683, JULY 14. Deed for lands between Schuylkill and Chester Rivers.
5. 1683, JULY 14. Deed for lands between Schuylkill and Pemmapecka Creeks.
6. 1683, SEPTEMBER 10. Keketappan's deed "for his half of all his lands betwixt Susquehanna and Delaware which lieth on the Susquehanna side."
7. 1683, OCTOBER 18. Machaloha's deed "for lands from the Delaware River and Chesapeak Bay, and up to the Falls of the Susquehanna."
8. 1684, JUNE 3. Manghougsin's release "for all his land on Perkioming."
9. 1684, JUNE 7. Richard Mettamicont's release "for lands on both sides Pemmapecka Creek on the Delaware."
10. 1685, JULY 30. Deed for lands "between Pemmapecka and Chester Creeks, and back *** as far as a man can go in two days" from a point on Conshohocken Hill.
11. 1685, OCTOBER 2. Deed for lands between Duck and Chester Creeks, and backward from Delaware, "as far as a man could ride in two days with a horse."
12. 1692, JUNE 15. Acknowledgment of satisfaction for land "lying between Neshamina and Poquessing *** and extending backwards to the utmost bounds of the Province."
13. 1696, JANUARY 13. Col. Thomas Dongan's, formerly Governor of New York, deed to William Penn for lands on both sides of Susquehanna, from the lakes to the "Chesapeak
14. 1697, JULY 5. Taminy's deed for the lands between Pemmopeck and Neshaminy, and "as far back as a horse can travel in two summer days."
15. 1700, SEPTEMBER 13. Deed of the Susquehanna Indians for the lands on "both sides of the Susquehanna and next adjoining the same, and comprising Dongan's Deed." (No.
16. 1701, APRIL 23. Ratification of Dongan's Deed and the Deed of September 13, 1700 (No. 14), "by the Susquehanna, Shawona, Potowmack, and Conestogoe Indians."
17. 1718, SEPTEMBER 17. Deed of release by the Delaware Indians for "the lands between the Delaware and Susquehanna Rivers, from Duck Creek *** to the Lehigh Hills."

PLATE 27

COMPLIMENTS OF
GENEVIEVE BLATT
Secretary
DEPARTMENT OF INTERNAL AFFAIRS

OF THE COUNTIES
BUREAU OF LAND RECORDS - 1933
ION - 1944

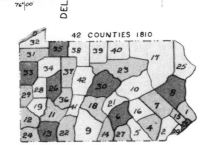

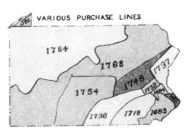

VARIOUS PURCHASE LINES

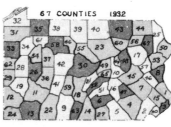

67 COUNTIES 1932

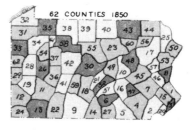

62 COUNTIES 1850

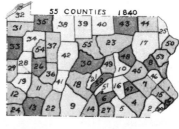

55 COUNTIES 1840

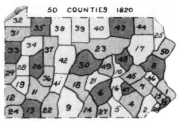

50 COUNTIES 1820

25 COUNTIES 1800

42 COUNTIES 1810

DATES OF THE VARIOUS TREATIES & PURCHASES

FIRST PURCHASE
1 JULY 15 1682

6 DEEDS & RELEASES
2 JUNE 23 1683
3 JUNE 25 1683
4 JULY 14 1683
5 JULY 14 1683
6 SEPT 10 1683
7 OCT 18 1683

9 DEEDS & RELEASES COVERING THIS AND FORMER PURCHASES
8 JUNE 3 1684
9 JUNE 7 1684
10 JULY 30 1685
11 OCT 2 1685
12 JUNE 15 1692
13 JAN 13 1696
14 JULY 5 1697
15 SEPT 13 1700
16 APR 23 1701

SUSQUEHANNA & DELAWARE INDIANS
17 SEPT 17 1718
18 DEC 16 1720
19 MAY 31 1726

SCHUYLKILL INDIANS
20 SEPT 7 1732

FIVE INDIAN NATIONS
21 OCT 11 1736
22 OCT 25 1736

WALKING PURCHASE
23 AUG 25 1737

NINE INDIAN NATIONS
24 AUG 22 1749

TREATY OF ALBANY
25 JULY 6 1754
26 OCT 23 1758

NEW PURCHASE
27 SEPT 5 1768
28 NOV 5 1768

LAST PURCHASE
29 OCT 23 1784
30 DEC 21 1784
31 JAN 21 1785

PRESQUE ISLE
32 JAN 9 1789
33 MAR 3 1792

'20, DECEMBER 16.   Deed settling controversy respecting boundary of the lands arising from dispute concerning distance a man and a horse can each travel in a day.

'26, MAY 31.   Deed for lands on both sides of Brandywine Creek.

'32, SEPTEMBER 7.   Deed for lands between "Lechay Hills and Kekachtanemin Hills," between Schuylkill and its branches, and the branches of Delaware.

'36, OCTOBER 11.   Deed "for all the said River Susquehanna with the lands lying on both sides thereof," eastward to the head of the branches, or springs running into the Susquehanna, and westward "to the setting of the sun," and from its mouth northward "to the hills or mountains called Kekachtanemin."

'36, OCTOBER 25.   The preceding deed declared by the Indians to include the lands on the Delaware, "and all the lands on both sides of the River Susquehanna from the mouth thereof as far northward, * * * to the ridge of Hills called Tyoninhaschta."

'37, AUGUST 25.   Deed comprising the "Walking Purchase," or, "as far as a man can go in one day and an half" from the westerly branch of Neshamony to the Delaware.

'49, AUGUST 22.   Deed for lands from the "Kekactany Hills to Maghonioy Mountain," and between Susquehanna and Delaware on the north side of "Lechawachsein Creek."

'54, JULY 6.   Deed at Albany for the lands on the west side of Susquehanna River, from Kittochtinny Hills to a mile above the mouth of Penn's Creek, "thence northwest and by west, as far as the Province extends to its western lines. * * * thence to the southern boundary, * * * thence by the southern boundary to the * * * Kittochtinny Hills, * * * thence by the south side of the said Hills to the Beginning."

'58, OCTOBER 23.   Deed of surrender of part of the Purchase of 1754, and new boundaries declared and confirmed.

'68, SEPTEMBER 5.   The end of "Nittany Mountain assumed as a station," per deed made, and surveys not usually made north thereof.

'68, NOVEMBER 5.   Deed at Fort Stanwix, commonly called the "New Purchase," extending from northeast to southwest corner of Commonwealth.

'84, OCTOBER 23.   Deed explaining the boundary at the treaty at Fort Stanwix and Pine Creek, declared to have been the boundary designated by the Indians, commonly called the "Last Purchase."

'84, DECEMBER 21.   Deed declaring Lycoming to be the boundary.

'85, JANUARY 21.   Deed at Fort Stanwix and Fort McIntosh for the residue of the lands within the Commonwealth, made October 23, 1784, and January 21, 1785.

'89, JANUARY 9.   Indian cession of lands at Presque Isle including the Triangle.

'92, MARCH 3.   On October 3, 1788, an Act was passed authorizing the Supreme Executive Council to draw on the State Treasurer for a sum of money for defraying the expense of purchasing from the Indians lands on Lake Erie. It is usually called the "Purchase of the Triangle." It contains 202,187 acres.

Chapter 3

County Characteristics

Lancaster County

IT WAS SUGGESTED in an earlier chapter that certain patterns for rifles were developed in different areas in Pennsylvania. There is an implication in this statement that each geographical area in which rifles were made had a unique effect on the patterns that were used there. Although there is evidence of regional styles, it must be clearly understood that these styles are not a direct outcome of geographical conditions.

It seems logical to conclude that designs for rifles in Pennsylvania might be attributed to, or connected with, patterns of European arms. The logical question then arises: why were certain styles used in different parts of Europe? It is doubtful if the answer to this question will ever be known, and it must be pointed out that research for this survey has not even suggested a reasonable answer to that problem.

The development of distinctive styles for rifles in Pennsylvania can be partially explained by noting some contributing factors which assisted in the procedure. The prevalence of distinct patterns in various localities of Pennsylvania can be attributed to the use of certain gun patterns by several gunsmiths in a particular area. These designs were attractive and functional, so they were learned by the apprentices, who in turn taught them to their apprentices. Since these gunsmiths lived in a particular geographical or political subdivision of Pennsylvania, the pattern was named for the area in which it was used. These areas roughly conform to county boundaries, so certain designs have become known by the names of the counties in which they were used. The discussion of each county style is prefaced with a brief history of the county so that the reader may gain some historical perspective in the development of regional patterns or designs.

Every one is aware that Penn's first purchase from the Indians was divided into three counties, Bucks, Philadelphia, and Chester. Subsequent purchases extended his holdings; and, when Lancaster County was formed in 1729, it was a massive triangle with a base on the Maryland line and the present site of Pottsville at its apex. A number of other counties were later formed from it, until it finally assumed the size and location that it has today.

At first Pennsylvania was largely an English colony, but as a result of Penn's visit to the Rhine valley, a number of Germans and Swiss came to live in Penn's "Holy Experiment." The following names, among others, are found in the early group

PLATE 28

View of Lancaster taken from *The History of Lancaster County* by I. Daniel Rupp and published by Gilbert Hills in 1844. The tallest steeple can be easily identified as part of Trinity Lutheran Church on South Duke Street.

which migrated from the continent: Hans Martin, and his sons Martin and John; Hans Herr; John Rudolph Bundley; Martin Kendig; Jacob Miller; Martin Oberholtz; Hans Funk; Michael Oberholtz; and Wendell Bowman. On April 11, 1711, the Surveyor General divided their purchase into as many parts as the group had previously agreed upon. Additional land in Strasburg Township was surveyed in 1712 for Amos Strettle, who divided his 3389 acres into smaller tracts, some of which were bought by Henry Shank, Ulrich Brackbill, Augustine Widower, Alexander Fridley, Martin Miller, George Snavely, Christian Musser, Andrew Shultz, John Fouts, Jacob Stein, John Hackman, John Bowman, Valentine Miller, Jacob Hain, John Herr, Henry Carpenter, Daniel Ferree, Isaac Lefever, Christian Stoner, John Beiers, Hans Lein, Abraham Smith, John Jacob Hoover, Septimus Robinson, Samuel Hess, Samuel Boyer, and John Musgrove. There is no proof that any of these men were gunsmiths; however, the names of later gunsmiths in Lancaster County suggest that they or their ancestors were among the earliest settlers of the county.

It is a well-established fact that when colonists left their homes in Europe for America, they brought a range of craftsmen with them who would be helpful in establishing a balanced economy in the new world. And it was pointed out in an earlier chapter that the rifle was invented in the German and Swiss provinces from which these settlers came. So it must be presumed that a number of gunsmiths came to Pennsylvania and pursued their trade here, as quickly as they could be spared from the urgent labor of building houses and clearing land for agricultural purposes.

It is recorded in Rupp's *History of Lancaster County,* published in Lancaster in 1844 by Gilbert Hills:

> Martin Meylin, son of Hans Meylin, was the first gunsmith within the limits of Lancaster County; as early as 1719, he erected a boring mill, on what is known as Meylin's run, on the farm owned by Martin Meylin, West Lampeter Township. He was esteemed one of the most skillful workmen in iron of his day. He was an active member of the colony, and transacted much of their business abroad.

It must be obvious to all readers that this important statement lacks documentation and therefore must be considered a secondary source of information. A gun with the initials M. M., or perhaps W. W., filed on the top facet of the barrel does not add authenticity to the Rupp statement; and, unfortunately, the records in the Lancaster County Courthouse have nothing positive to offer on the trade of Martin Meylin. The Rupp statement must be accepted with an open mind and with the hope that it will be substantiated someday; but, until then, the researcher must move to the earliest documented data available concerning gunsmithing in Lancaster County, Pennsylvania.

It is a strange coincidence that the records of the two earliest gunsmiths known to have worked in Lancaster County start in 1740. One of these men is the famous Matthias Roesser, who was born in Germany in 1708 and came to America in 1736. At the time of his death in Lancaster in 1771, a document connected with the settling of his estate states that he was a gunsmith and that he had bought a tract in Lancaster from James Hamilton in 1740. The record does not indicate that he was a gunsmith in 1740, but since he was then thirty-two years old, it seems safe to presume that he had already served his apprenticeship in Germany, for that period usually terminated when a youth reached the age of twenty-one.

The second gunsmith living in Lancaster County in 1740 was Henry Mull, who also bought a property at that time from James Hamilton. This information is found in Deed Book C., Page 251, 1775 in the Lancaster County Courthouse. It is entirely possible that Henry Mull was a brother of John Moll, one of the early gunsmiths of Northampton County. Perhaps the second letter in the name of one of these men was indistinctly written on a ship's list or a legal document and it was less confusing to continue with the new spelling than the correct old one. It is also possible that an attempt was made to Anglicize the name by changing the "o" to "u" or vice versa. Henry Mull moved to Huntington Township, York County, Pennsylvania, and is

PLATE 29

These brass mountings are typical of the first rifles made in Lancaster County with a four-piece patch box.

listed as a gunsmith there in the tax assessment list of 1783. One gun is known to the author that is attributed to Henry Mull; however, his and Roesser's products might be described as extremely rare. Other gunsmiths known to have worked in the transition period in Lancaster County are Jacob Dickert, Joshua Baker, Christopher Breidenhardt, John Henry, John Newcomer, John Miller, Issac Hains, Joel Ferree, and Peter Gonter.

There is documentary proof that these gunsmiths made guns in Lancaster County before the Revolution, but virtually no signed specimens of this early period have survived, and the provenance of the early guns must be determined on circumstantial evidence. Such an approach to the important matter of identification might seem hazardous, but it is known that styles in guns changed slowly, and it might be safely presumed that guns made about 1790 in Lancaster County will in some ways resemble guns made in the same county in 1765. It seems obvious that by working backward from signed rifles made after the Revolution to unsigned rifles made before the Revolution, some similarities in the two periods can be detected. Such a procedure can be followed in all the areas in which rifles were made in the transition period; however, attributions must be made with the knowledge that the Pennsylvania style was only emerging at that time and there are apt to be more similarities than differences in guns made in different regions. In other words, guns made in the transition period are apt to be quite European in their general character but have a few embryonic regional qualities of Pennsylvania guns.

A specific example of the survival of a European style in most areas of Pennsylvania was the use of a wooden cover for the patch box. Such guns were made in Lancaster County, although it is thought that the two- and four-piece patch boxes of brass were also used there in the transition period. There seems to be no doubt that the four-piece patch box with a daisy finial was used in Lancaster County in the late transition period. The release for the lid of the patch box was usually placed in the top extension of the butt plate. The trigger guards were long and shallow and the back extension was sometimes attached with a screw instead of a stud and a pin.

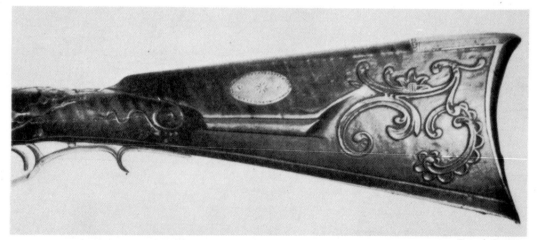

Reaves Goehring

PLATE 30

C Design carved in bas-relief on the butt of a Lancaster rifle by Peter Brong. The traditional two C's in a horizontal position has been extended to include a third C in a vertical position.

This method is a direct copy of German guns of an earlier period. The lock-bolt plate pattern was quite consistent, and generally followed the pattern illustrated.

Although few rifles made in Pennsylvania in the transition period were carved, it should be noted that the patterns on carved rifles made in Lancaster County are very similar. The carving appears on the cheek side of the butt where a few lines emanate from the cheek rest and spread into a form which resembles two capital C's, with a few extra flourishes to make them more decorative. They are usually in a horizontal position and one faces up while the other faces down.

The discussion of Lancaster County guns of the transition era might be terminated with the warning that some Lancaster characteristics will probably be found on guns made in other areas. This situation has occurred, because Pennsylvania rifles were first made in Lancaster County, and therefore many gunsmiths were trained there, then moved to less competitive territory, and carried their patterns with them. The decision that Pennsylvania rifles were first made in Lancaster County, is based on the facts that Lancaster was the first county formed in which rifles were made, the earliest records of rifle production are found in Lancaster County, and a number of rifles have survived that are thought to have been made there.

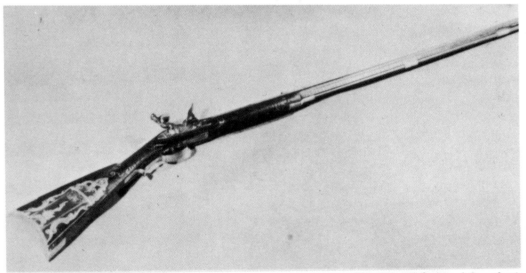

The Historical Society of Pennsylvania

PLATE 31

Rifle with flint lock, brass mountings, full stock of curly maple which is beautifully carved in bas-relief designs on the cheek side of the butt, around the breech tang, and below the bottom ramrod pipe. On the top facet of the octagonal barrel, Isaac Hains is engraved in script letters. This rifle is the product of a master craftsman and is in its original perfect condition. The patch box is in an attractive and rare pattern of the late eighteenth century.

It has been pointed out that an embryo Lancaster pattern can be found in rifles of the late transition era, but in the "Golden Age" the true Lancaster pattern matured. The stock was less massive, it was often longer, and more profusely decorated than in the early period. The typical Lancaster stock can be frequently identified by a butt which is shaped like a triangle. The base of the triangle is the butt plate and the two straight lines of the top and bottom of the stock converge in an apex at the breach end of the barrel. The illustration shows such a form on a Dickert and a Hoak rifle of the late eighteenth century. This form can be observed on guns made by DeHuff, Haeffer, Hoak, Gonter, and others.

The carved double C pattern on the cheek side of the butt was continued by many craftsmen, although sometimes it was raised rather than incised. It should be

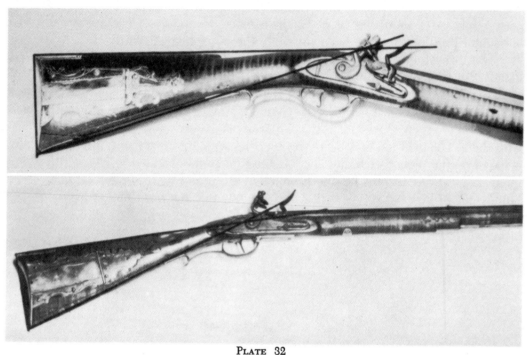

PLATE 32

Two rifles made in Lancaster in the late eighteenth century with butts which are triangular in form. The straight top and bottom edges of the stock are joined by a butt plate that is almost flat. The top one is by Dickert, the other by J. Hoak.

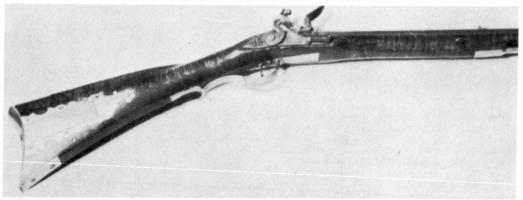

Joe Kindig, Jr.

PLATE 33

Rifle with flint lock, full stock of curly maple, silver and brass mountings, and octagonal barrel 42 inches long.

This rifle has two very unusual features, it has a bona fide date 1796 engraved on the lid of the patch box and all of the patch box (except the lid) is made of silver. It was probably made in Lancaster County but there are no marks on the barrel to suggest the maker's name.

The curve of the butt plate on this rifle shows the pattern that was used by gunsmiths in Lancaster in the 1790's.

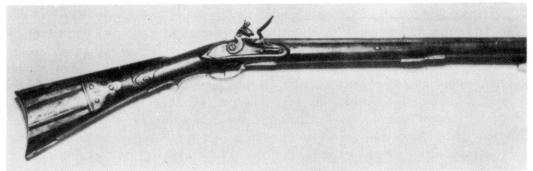

Vincent Nolt

PLATE 34

Rifle with flint lock marked Sweitzer (Lancaster), full stock of curly maple, brass mountings octagonal barrel 43 inches long, marked P. Gonter in block letters on the top facet of the barrel.

This rifle has a patch box similar to the pattern used by Dickert, Brong, Eberman, and other gunsmiths of Lancaster in the first quarter of the nineteenth century.

noted, however, that Lancaster gunsmiths are not famous for the quality of their carved guns.

By the end of the eighteenth century the radius on butt plates became sharper and they were narrower to conform to the more slender stocks of the period. The release for the lid of the patch box was generally placed in the front extension of the butt plate, as it was in earlier rifles. The trigger guard continued to be long and shallow, although the screw found in the back extension of transition guns rarely appears in the guns of the late eighteenth century.

The four-piece patch box was used by all gunsmiths, some of whom engraved extravagant designs on them. The daisy finial was very popular, although a pattern resembling a trillium was used by some craftsmen. In the nineteenth century the solid side plates were dropped for narrow strips, which were separated from the lid by a strip of the stock. Some of the earlier finials were continued with the new arrangement, but were less attractive in their new setting.

A new and less attractive lock-bolt plate was also introduced in the nineteenth century. A few gunsmiths, such as Melchoir Fordney, engraved the lock-bolt plates, but the new pattern shows definite influence of mass production, in contrast to the pleasing individual shapes used on earlier rifles. It might also be noted that the shape of the panel in which the lock-bolt plate was placed was not influenced by the shape of the plate.

PLATE 35

Typical lock-bolt plate of a late flint or early percussion rifle made in Lancaster County. The chequering is also another feature of many rifles made in Lancaster County.

The stocks of the percussion period have the typical triangular shape at the butt. They are a bit shorter to conform to shorter barrels, the wrist is often quite thick, frequently checkered; and plain maple again was very popular for stocks. Butt plates are narrower with more radius and the patch-box release is only on rare occasions retained in the top extension of the butt plate. Henry Gibbs and J. Fordney used a few inlays in their stocks, but never the profusion that was used by men like Douglass, Johnson, and Joe Long. H. Leman used an artificial grain on his stocks. The long patch boxes were used by some men, but were later replaced by simple brass castings, either round or elliptical, a few of which were engraved, but most of which were plain.

By the middle of the nineteenth century Lancaster styles were similar to most of the others in the State and only the work of Henry Leman can really be identified without referring to the signature on the top facet of the barrel. Lancaster production of muzzle-loading guns ceased when the doors of the Leman rifle works were finally closed in 1887.

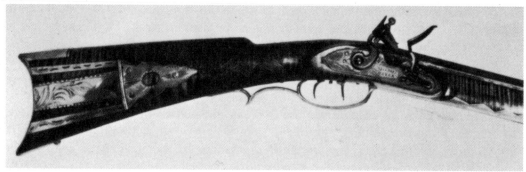

T. J. Cooper

PLATE 36

Rifle with flint lock, full stock of curly maple, brass mountings, set triggers, and octagonal barrel marked H. Gibbs. The radius of the butt plate, the chequered wrist, the set triggers, and the engraved patch box might be found on a rifle made in Lancaster in the late portion of the flintlock period or the early portion of the percussion era.

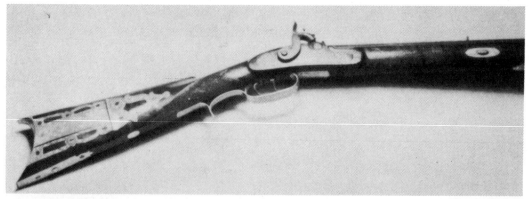

Reaves Goehring

PLATE 37

Rifle with percussion lock, half stock of curly maple, mountings of German silver, set triggers, octagonal barrel marked Eicholtz & Bros.

Very few rifles are known to have been made in Lancaster with mountings of German silver. The tulip finial on the toe-plate is a pleasing feature for a Lancaster rifle.

Berks County

Although Berks County was not erected until 1752, the reader should be aware that its growth paralleled that of Lancaster county more nearly than the date would indicate. The following excerpt from the *History of Berks County*, by Morton L. Montgomery, 1886, supplies some interesting data about its early development:

> Very nearly all (the settlers) landed at Philadelphia, and thence the great majority proceeded towards the interior districts and the head waters of streams. This is particularly the case with the Schuylkill and its tributaries. The settlements between the Schuylkill and the Delaware were numerous before 1700. Every decade thereafter found them farther northward from the Wissahickon to the Perkiomen, from the Perkiomen to the Manatawny, and from the Manatawny to the Maiden Creek. And so they proceeded between the Schuylkill and the Susquehanna Rivers.

During the second quarter of the eighteenth century the area continued to grow; and small centers of population became established in places like Douglass, Exeter, Maiden-Creek, Manatawny, Heidelburg, Crumru, Bethel, Brecknock, and Longswamp. Manufactures were carried on in all parts of the county; and carpenters, masons, shoemakers, gunsmiths, blacksmiths, spinners, weavers, and other craftsmen were helping to create a new county of importance in Pennsylvania. The mining of iron ore and the production of iron by a number of furnaces were of great importance in the growth of this new county. Colebrookdale Furnace was located on one of the branches of the Manatawny, within a mile of the present site of the borough of Boyertown. It was said to have been erected in 1720, or a few years earlier, and was doubtless one of the earliest furnaces in Pennsylvania. Such furnaces were significant contributors to Pennsylvania's prominence in the production of rifles and other arms.

On January 13, 1738, the Honourable George Thomas, Lieutenant-Governor of the province, laid before the Council two petitions requesting that a separate county be formed to be named Berks. One petition was signed by people living in the northern part of Philadelphia County and the other by inhabitants of the northeast portion of Lancaster County. These people pointed out that the great distance between their homes and the established county seats at Philadelphia and Lancaster created a hardship for them in transacting their legal business and in the enforcement of the law. They requested that a new "Seat of Justice" be more conveniently located for their use.

Despite constant prodding of the Council by the Lieutenant-Governor, no action was taken on this matter. On May 19, 1739, a petition was again presented to the Council for their consideration. It was again laid aside without action. The petitioners waited six years before renewing their request for a separate county; this one received the same treatment. On February 4, 1752, York and Cumberland Counties having been formed in the meantime, the Berks County group presented their final petition for the forming of a new county; and on March 11, 1752, the Speaker of the House reported that the bill, having been enacted into law, was signed by the governor. After fourteen years of effort, the county of Berks became a reality.

PLATE 38

Replica of the courthouse, and other buildings, which stood at the intersection of Fifth and Penn Streets in Reading, Pennsylvania, in the eighteenth century. The centers of most Pennsylvania towns which were laid out by the proprietors had the same general plan.

Although the area which became Berks County had a population of 10,000 in 1748, there were no large centers of population located within its boundaries. The prospect of becoming a new county doubtless stimulated interest in selecting a site for a county seat and in the fall of 1748 a town was laid out on the banks of the Schuylkill, to be called Reading, after the county-town of Berkshire, England. In 1749 the sale of lots was announced, and by 1751 seven lots were sold. In 1752 thirty-three lots were sold, and in 1753, eighty-four.

It is fortunate that the names and occupations of the earliest plot owners are known. The earliest gunsmith known to have worked in Berks County was John Schreidt, who bought a lot in Reading in 1758. It is also interesting to note that a tax assessment list has been preserved in the library of the Berks County Historical Society which shows that Wolfgang Hacka was living in Reading in 1758. The occupations of none of the residents are listed in this important document, but this man was undoubtedly the Wolfgang Haga who is listed as a gunsmith in Reading from the mid-1760's until his death in 1796. The spelling of his name in the tax list can be attributed to a German assessor who spelled names as he pronounced them. It might be mentioned that many of the earliest tax assessment lists were written in German. In 1761 William Graeff bought a lot in the town, and his occupation was listed as a "lock and gunsmith."

The reader's attention must be called to the fact that the documented dates for these gunsmiths does not preclude the possibility of their having worked there at an earlier time. For example, if Wolfgang Haga was eighty years old when he died in 1796, he would have been only forty years old in 1756, and could easily have

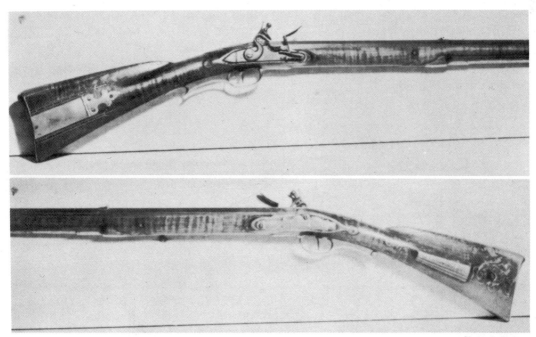

Clegg Collection

PLATE 39
Rifle with flint lock, full stock of curly maple, brass mountings, and octagonal barrel.

been making guns for ten years before that time. Schreidt and Graeff might also have been middle-aged men when they made their purchases and could have been making guns at an earlier time.

It is most unfortunate that very few Berks County gunsmiths of the eighteenth century signed their guns, and, as a result, there is little opportunity to work backward as could be done in Lancaster County. Since no rifle of any period signed by any of these three early men is known, the makers of the few Berks County rifles of the transition period in existence must remain anonymous.

In Berks County there seems to have been the same survival of style from the transition period to the Golden Age as was noted in Lancaster County; however, the problem of identification of early rifles is much more difficult because fewer of the later rifles were signed by their makers. Despite the scarcity of signed rifles and the survival of European styles, some regional qualities can be found in the rifles of Berks County in the transition era.

There were, of course, rifles with wooden patch-box covers, but there is certainly nothing definite about that feature, so they must be by-passed for rifles with other characteristics. Since the brass patch box was an American invention, rifles with these appendages must be given important consideration. It has also been mentioned that two-piece patch boxes made up of a simple brass lid and finial were very early; so rifles with such patch boxes and other qualities of Berks County must be regarded as the work of the transition period.

The rifle illustrated in Plate 11 with a rectangular lid hinged to a finial with three lobes was a pattern used in Berks County for many years. The lobes on this early gun are engraved to suggest a leaf effect, although this feature was generally dropped on later patch boxes. The attractive brass wire inlay was also later replaced by side plates in the four-piece patch box, which was used in the "Golden Age."

The butt plates were thin to conserve metal, and the extension on the top of the butt was small with a number of very shallow facets. The trigger guards were long and wider than usual, and the lock-bolt plate was thick with attractive bevels around the outer edge.

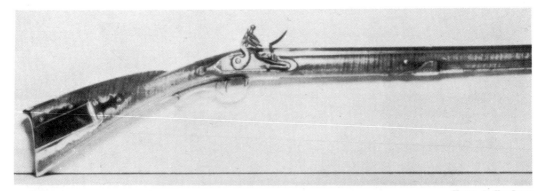

Henry J. Kauffman

PLATE 40

Rifle with flint lock, full stock of curly maple, brass, mountings, and octagonal barrel 43 inches long. This rifle with its unmarked barrel, its plain brass mountings, and its stock with a "Roman nose" comb is a typical product of Berks County craftsmen in the last quarter of the eighteenth century. A few were probably made in the first quarter of the nineteenth century.

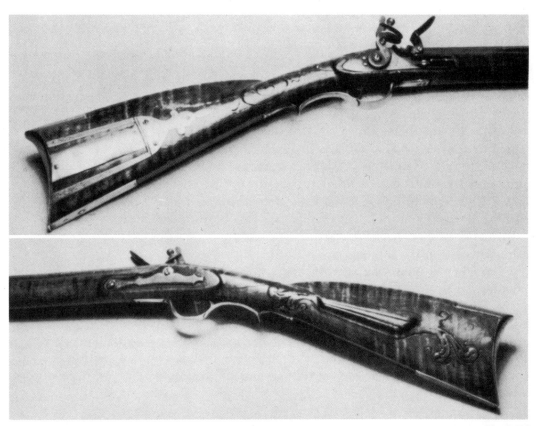

Lloyd Nolt

PLATE 40A

Rifle with flint lock, curly maple stock, brass mountings, octagonal barrel 40 inches long with S. Pannabecker engraved on the top facet in script letters. The lock-bolt plate, the carved patterns, and the contour of the stock suggest production in the eighteenth century, but the style of the patch box is definitely of the early nineteenth century. Barrels signed by the Pannabeckers are not uncommon, but complete guns by any of them are quite rare.

The moulded cheek rest on the early rifles is a rich detail, and a few scrolls on the cheek side of the butt carved in bas-relief are attractive and distinctive of guns made in the area. Many gunsmiths also carved in bas-relief a scroll at the end of the bottom ramrod pipe. Although this treatment is not particularly attractive, it was done in a bold manner that often aids in identifying a gun of the region. The lock and lock-bolt plate are set in carved panels that conform to their shapes and generally terminate in a tear drop at the rear. A few rifles have simple moulded edges along the ramrod, and some stocks have a decorative line carved along the bottom edge of the butt from the trigger guard to the butt plate. This feature was also carried in the pattern of many later gunstocks. There is a slight suggestion of a "Roman nose" on some early stocks, but that feature really matured in the next period.

Although there were departures from the early pattern of rifles in the Golden Age, the later rifles were really only refined examples of the early ones. The patch box became the common four-piece style, with little or no engraving; and the finial was elongated to make it more streamlined. The trigger guard, butt plate, and lock-bolt plate were a bit less bulky; and many rifles had toe-plates with finials that resembled the finials on the patch boxes. The toe-plates were usually fastened with screws.

The ferrule on the end of the forestock was one of the unique features of the period, giving it a convex instead of a square end, like most rifles. This end seems to have been made of one piece of metal and must have been cast, for there is no evidence of hammer work on them, as is found on other brass parts. This feature was carried into the percussion period.

Although the stocks of the "Golden Age" in Berks County were a bit more bulky than in other areas, they were attractive specimens of the gunsmith's art. At this time the "Roman nose," which was a sharply rounded comb in the butt of the rifle, came into wide usage and became the most significant identifying feature of a rifle made in the Berks County area. It was used from Womelsdorf to Allentown and as far north as Berks County craftsmen migrated. In its restrained form it was very attractive and distinctive, although some gunsmiths exaggerated it to the point where it might be regarded as offensive.

The "Roman nose" was used by gunsmiths late in the flint era along with the patch-box finial with three lobes; however, an additional point was frequently found on the top lobe, as in the illustrated rifle made by Samuel Pennabacker. Although this gun was made near the end of the "Golden Age," it obviously has features that became popular in the percussion era, particularly the four-piece patch box with strips of the stock showing between the lid and the side plates. The butt plate radius became sharper, the toe-plate was simplified, and the percussion gun with carving in bas-relief is a rarity.

Northampton County

It has been pointed out that the first major nucleus of English-speaking peoples in Pennsylvania formed at Philadelphia. This site acted as a geographical hub, from which spokes extended to the west and north. Along spokes, which were rivers and land thoroughfares, masses of immigrants moved to find new homes. At first the spokes were short and terminated in the three first counties. Later the spokes became longer; and people moved into the areas which became Lancaster, Berks, and Northampton Counties. The fact that Berks and Northampton Counties were not formed as early and were more distant counties does not imply that they were not thickly populated. The frontier areas were organized into counties sooner because of their greater need for law enforcement agencies.

Because the embryo Northampton County adjoined the Delaware River; it seems safe to presume that it was visited by traders before 1700, and it is likely that a few squatters moved into the area soon after the turn of the century. The records indicate, however, that there was no village of any size long before the county was organized in 1752. The delay in its growth might partially be explained by the fact that the Blue Mountain region was less attractive to the Germans than the rich farm lands of Lancaster and Berks Counties. As has been noted, the great migration from Germany in 1709 and 1710 was largely absorbed by the land between Philadelphia and the

PLATE 41

Gunsmiths lived and worked in log buildings like this one in Bethlehem, Pennsylvania.

Susquehanna. The second great influx of Germans after 1725, however, seems to have been attracted to the north and it is from that time that the area grew rapidly until it was established as a separate county in 1752.

An interesting incident in connection with acquiring part of the land for Northampton County might logically be included here because an important gun is connected with the episode. On August 25, 1737, a meeting was held by representatives of the proprietors and the Indians at Durham, to determine a mutually satisfactory plan for the acquisition of land from the Indians. It was agreed that the purchase of 1686 be extended by having a man start walking from a point at Wrightstown in Bucks County, and continue as far as he could walk in one and one-half days.

Three men were selected, Edward Marshall, Solomon Jennings, and James Yeates. The walk took place on September 19 and 20, 1737. At sunset of the first day Marshall had walked to the northern base of the Blue Mountain. Yeates and Jennings were unable to continue with Marshall, who walked about seventy-four miles in a day and a half.

Although the Indians did not value this land highly, for their best hunting grounds were to the north and in New York State, they protested the walk when the boundary line was drawn. Thereafter, they were belligerent and finally joined in the French and Indian War in 1755-58. Marshall and his family were killed by the Indians while they lived in the area of the present site of Stroudsburg.

In the Bucks County Historical Society Museum there is a maple-stocked rifle with a wooden cover on its patch box, which was carried by Marshall on this walk. This rifle is unquestionably one of the earliest Pennsylvania rifles extant and is an excellent example of craftsmanship in wood and metal. It can be viewed any day the museum is open.

At the time of its erection, Northampton County included all the land now contained in the counties of Northampton, Lehigh, Carbon, Monroe, Pike, Wayne, and Susquehanna. The first petition for the County was read on May 11, 1751. In March, 1752, Governor Hamilton signed the document to create the County. Its name was not the choice of its residents, for Thomas Penn had previously sent a letter to America directing that some land be laid out for a town at the forks of the Delaware, which should be called Easton, and whenever a new county was formed, it was to be called Northampton. It is evident that the proprietors were determined to see that the hordes of German settlers should live in areas with English names.

It is obvious from Penn's instructions that Easton was destined from the first to be the county seat. The procedure for selecting the site of this county seat is important to note, for it was a very poor choice, and one which the residents would doubtless not have made. The town was on a low site, surrounded by hills that discouraged expansion, and ill-suited to raise the produce needed by the residents of the town. There were few roads and these were very poor. The town grew slowly; its only asset was that it was the "county seat." In 1750 only two or three houses were standing there, one of which had been built in 1739 by David Martin, who owned the ferry. His ferry-house was a one-story log building, famous for its frequent use for negotiating Indian treaties. The proprietors sold lots with the condition attached that the purchaser had to build a house not less than twenty feet square with a stone chimney. Some of the earlier chimneys were made of slabs of wood, covered with mud on the inside and outside to minimize the danger of fire. In 1763 there were sixty houses in the town, all of log construction.

It is interesting to note that the tax list for 1763 included the occupations of the men living in Easton in that year. The following trades and properties were represented at that time: 2 weavers, 2 butchers, 3 laborers, 1 grist and saw-mill, 6 taverns, 3 stores, 5 carpenters, 3 masons, 1 hatter, 1 locksmith, 1 smith, 1 gunsmith, 2 tailors, 1 skin dresser, 1 saddler. Our attention naturally focuses on the three men who were smiths of some type. Unfortunately nothing additional is known about the gunsmith, Ephraim Blum. No guns bearing his name are known to the writer, nor is there any information about him in subsequent years. The locksmith, Henry Young, was very likely the progenitor of several gunsmiths. John Young is listed as a gunsmith in the tax assessment list of 1786 and a firm known as Wm. Young and Bros. was engaged in the gun business in Easton in the mid-nineteenth century. The 1763 tax list also

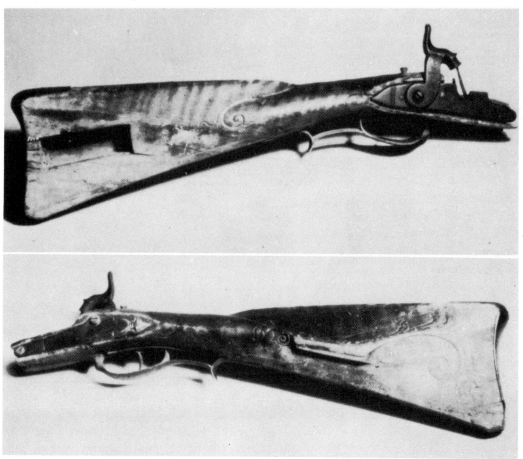

Reaves Goehring

PLATE 42

Butt end of the rifle with a flint lock, brass mountings, and a stock of curly maple, which is carved in the incised technique. The barrel of this rifle is missing so that its maker cannot be identified, but it is clearly a product of a Northampton County craftsman in the transition period.

includes a man named Abraham Berlin and lists him as a smith. An Easton tax list of 1782 lists a man named Abraham Berlin as a barrel-smith; it is very likely that both listings refer to the same man. The fact that Isaac Berlin is known to have been a gunsmith in 1800-1805 in Berwick Township, Adams County, and that he is known to have lived at Easton at an earlier time, suggests that Abraham was the father and Isaac, the son. It might also be pointed out that John Moll, who lived in Northampton County, and died in 1794, was one of the early producers of guns there. A normal work span of forty years would have permitted him to produce guns as early as 1754.

The documented evidence of gunsmiths working in Northampton County before the Revolution substantiates the fact that rifles were made there in the transition era of gunmaking in Pennsylvania. It is also important to note that some rifles have survived that are attributed to the smiths of the County.

The early Northampton gunsmiths seem to have been partial to plain maple for the stocks, with some incised carving on the cheek side of the butt. The most unusual feature of the stock, however, is the fact that the wrist has a longer horizontal axis than a vertical axis. The trigger guards are long and wide, the butt plates are thin with a small extension on top of the butt, and the rear end of the lock-bolt plate often terminates in a pointed tail or in the shape of an arrow head.

PLATE 43

Many of the rifles made in Northampton County had incised carving on the stocks, and the wrist of the stock was thicker horizontally than vertically. The sketch shows the proportions of a butt from a rifle made in the transition period.

It seems reasonable to presume that some of the early gunsmiths who worked in Northampton County also worked in the Golden Age of gun making, and that some of the features found on early guns were used on those made throughout the eighteenth and early nineteenth centuries. A rifle made by J. Rupp after the Revolution proves this hypothesis to be true. In the early portion of the nineteenth century John Moll, Jr., Adam Angstadt, and Jacob George, both of the latter living in Berks County near Northampton County, continued the two-piece patch box, the thick horizontal axis of the wrist, the plain maple, and the incised carving. A few guns were carved in relief, but such a gun from Northampton County is a rarity. Finally, it might be pointed out that nowhere in Pennsylvania did gunsmiths cling to early patterns as long as they did in Northampton County. The late eighteenth and early

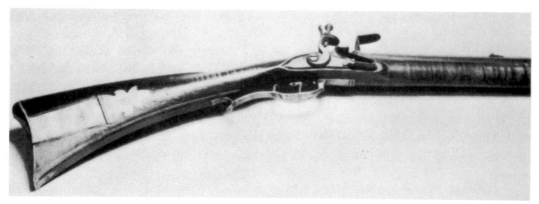

PLATE 44

Rifle with flint lock, full stock of curly maple, brass mountings, and octagonal-to-round barrel 42 inches long, marked J. Rupp in script letters on the top facet of the barrel.

This gun is obviously a product of a Northampton County gunsmith in the late eighteenth century. The incised carving on the cheek side of the butt, the two-piece patch box, and the sweeping curve in the bottom edge of the butt are typical of guns made in Northampton County. An Indian design is carved in the stock in front of the trigger guard. Many rifle stocks of this region were made of plain maple rather than curly maple.

nineteenth century products of these gunsmiths differed from those of the transition era largely in the fact that they were lighter, longer, and more ornamented than the earliest ones.

Although the Henry Gun Factory was started by William Henry II at Nazareth in the 1780's, the writer has never seen a long gun that can be identified as a product of this famous gunsmith. A number of guns are extant that have W. H. on the top facet of the barrel, but they lack qualities that would permit positive attribution to William Henry II. It might be pointed out, however, that many gunsmiths in the Northampton County area used initials rather than their names to mark their products. This practice has led to certain attributions such as suggesting that a gun

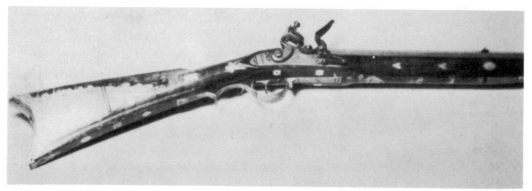

PLATE 45

Rifle with flint lock, full stock of curly maple, brass mountings, inlays of silver, bone, and brass, and octagonal barrel 45 inches long with Peter Moll engraved on brass plates, which are inlaid on the top of the barrel. Other brass inlays on the top facet have Hellertown, Warranted, May 26, 1826 and No. 40 engraved on them.

This unusual product of Peter Moll has over forty inlays in the stock and quite a number of brass inlays in the top facet of the barrel. It is interesting to speculate for whom such a gun was made.

with a D. B. on the barrel was made by Daniel Boone. It is obvious that attributions must be made on the basis of style and period rather than on a convenient matching of initials to names.

The Henry factory was inherited by J. J. Henry, the son of William II, who became a prolific producer of guns in the late 1820's and early 1830's for the American Fur Company. Some ledgers of the American Fur Company, which bought large quantities of rifles from him for trade with the Indians, are preserved in the library of the New York Historical Society. These ledgers record certain business transactions with Henry and include details describing the guns that he made for them. A copy of one page is presented here through the courtesy of the New York Historical Society.

Although the writer has seen a few long guns with J. Henry on the top facet of the barrel, it is not uncommon to find locks on Pennsylvania rifles which bear his name. They closely resemble English locks of the period and seem to be of comparable quality.

In 1812 Lehigh County was formed from part of Northampton County, of which Allentown became the county seat. Some of the Molls worked in Allentown, while others worked in a small town to the south called Hellertown. Their products were typical of the Golden Age and the percussion era which followed.

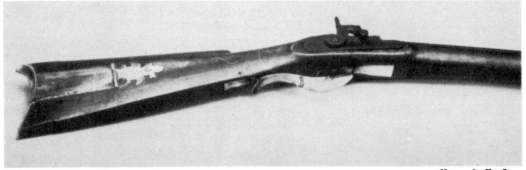

Henry J. Kauffman

PLATE 46

Rifle with percussion lock, full stock of maple painted red, brass mountings, octagonal barrel 41 inches long.
The red paint and the general style of the rifle suggest that it might have been made by a gun-smith in the Northampton County area for the "Indian trade."

There was little change in the rifles of the percussion era from the ones made in the Golden Age. The two-piece patch box continued to be popular with most gun-smiths, some of which were engraved with simple geometric patterns. An unusually large lock-bolt plate is found on some rifles and the bottom ramrod pipe often has a large flange at the bottom, where it overlaps the stock.

The late rifles of Northampton and Lehigh counties might be described as typical of the Golden Age, but with a minimum of ornamentation.

Dauphin County

Events in the gradual shaping of Dauphin County are in sharp contrast to those that preceded the creation of other counties east of the Susquehanna. While streams of settlers were virtually flooding into the counties along the southern border of Pennsylvania, the region to the north was comparatively ignored. This indifference can be explained by a number of reasons.

It is obvious and reasonable that the first centers of population outside of Philadelphia should have been established in the adjoining areas of Bucks and Chester Counties. Their proximity to the Philadelphia markets and the convenience of living in general contributed to their rapid growth. The second periphery of settlement around Philadelphia passed roughly through Easton, Reading, and Lancaster. The third wave of settlement started at York and swung toward the present site of Harrisburg and Pottsville. This movement culminated in the forming of Dauphin County in 1785.

It might also be emphasized that the terrain of the Dauphin County area was less attractive to the German farmers than that of the earlier settlements. The poorness of the soil and the greater distance to markets worked against the development of the more distant areas. The vacuum caused by the German farmers avoiding this area also had repercussions on gun production there. While gunsmiths were busy from Lancaster to Northampton Counties, the Indians of Dauphin County were trading furs with the few Scots and Irish who ventured into the upper regions of the Susquehanna.

The fact that the Dauphin County area was part of Lancaster County before they were separated also helps to explain its late creation. No part of the Dauphin County area was a great distance from Lancaster, when compared with some parts of Cumberland County, which extended from the Susquehanna River to the Ohio line. In addition, the presence of Indian villages in the Blue Mountain area discouraged people from making permanent settlements in the region. In the beginning of the eighteenth century the region was too far from Philadelphia to be inhabited, and by the middle of the century prospective settlers were scared away by unrest and impending war with the Indians. The erection of Fort Hunter and other forts along the Blue Mountains is evidence of the danger involved in living there. Apparently this danger did not subside completely after the French and Indian War, for another thirty years passed before the county was created.

Middletown, a post town in Swatara Township, is the oldest town in the county, having been laid out in 1755 by George Fisher, who lived on a large tract of land which he received from his father, John Fisher, a Philadelphia merchant. The area was later inhabited by other Quakers from Philadelphia, who enjoyed a lucrative business with local settlers and traders moving back and forth on the Juniata and Susquehanna Rivers. The town was incorporated in 1829 and was a center of trade for many years. An extract from the *History of Dauphin County*, Vol III, p. 459, tells of a gunsmith who lived in the town in the nineteenth century.

James Campbell was born November 17, 1805, three miles north of Middletown. He was educated in the common schools, and learned the trade of blacksmith and gunsmith at Harrisburg, and followed these trades throughout his life.

After completing his apprenticeship with his brother-in-law, George Kunkle, he went to Middletown, and established himself as a gunsmith on North Union Street. He died July 21, 1856.

The first settlement of importance at the present site of Harrisburg was made in 1719 by a native of Yorkshire, England, named John Harris. The plan for Harrisburg was not drawn up until 1785 and it immediately became the county seat of Dauphin County. It was first named Harris' Ferry but in 1786, the Executive Council renamed it Louisburg, in honor of Louis XVI of France. The name was later changed to Harrisburg, in honor of John Harris, the original settler of the site. In 1810, Harrisburg was selected as the seat for the Government of Pennsylvania; in 1812, the legislature met there for the first time.

Although rifles were produced in a number of areas in Dauphin County, the place of greatest interest to gun collectors is Lebanon Township, where the famous maker, J. P. Beck, lived. Originally, it was a very large township in the northern part of Lancaster County, but, in 1739, the Court at Lancaster created Bethel Township from the northern end of Lebanon Township. The first settlers in the area were Germans, who lived in log houses with puncheon floors. In 1750 Lebanon Township had only 150 taxable residents.

In 1813 Lebanon County was created from parts of Dauphin and Lancaster Counties and the town of Lebanon became the county seat. The town grew slowly so that by 1821 it had only about three hundred dwellings.

It is doubtful if many rifles were made in the county in the transition period. J. P. Beck, who was born in the early 1750's, made rifles with wooden patch box

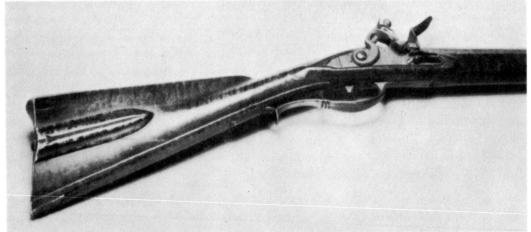

Carl Pippert

PLATE 47

Rifle with flint lock, brass mountings, full stock of curly maple, and octagonal barrel with J. P. Beck engraved on the top facet of the barrel.

The simple and graceful lines of this rifle are evidence that J. P. Beck was one of the finest of the Pennsylvania gunsmiths. The simple molded pattern of the patch box cover adds an interesting decorative note to the simple pattern of the butt. The hand-made lock is also a very compatible feature of the rifle.

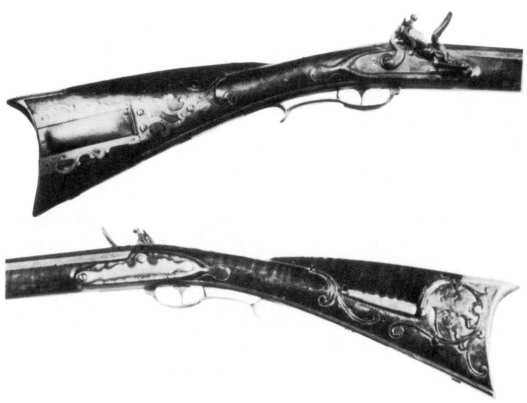

Herman Dean

PLATE 48

Rifle with flint lock, full stock of maple, brass mountings, octagonal barrel with P. Berry engraved on the top facet of the barrel in script letters.

The design of the patch-box finial seems to have been used only by Berry and is one of the factors which assist in identifying his products. The carving on the cheek side of the butt is another of Berry's original designs. Berry is known to have made a few fowling pieces. Any of his guns would be a valuable asset to a collection of Pennsylvania guns.

covers, but they are essentially in the style of rifles made in the Golden Era. None of the other makers are known to have worked before the Revolution.

It is an unfortunate fact to report that the rifles made in the Golden Age do not have strong county characteristics. This deficiency might be attributed to the fact that the area was greatly influenced by craftsmen from Lancaster and Berks Counties. One line of communication and trade was up the Susquehanna River from Lancaster County; the other line came into the county from Berks County. There is no doubt that the gunsmiths of Dauphin County either came from these two areas or were greatly influenced by the styles that had been developed there in earlier times. For example, it is obvious that J. P. Beck was influenced by a Lancaster pattern in shaping his stocks and a "Roman nose" is easily discernible in some of the guns made by N. Beyer, who probably worked in the eastern part of Dauphin County near Berks County.

From the writer's point of view, the J. P. Beck rifles with wooden patch box covers belong in the second era of rifle production in Pennsylvania. The rifles lack the massive stock of the early rifles; they are frequently signed and their ornamentation is compatible with the Golden Age rather than with the transition era. It should be mentioned that Beck developed a style of his own in his later rifles. His four-piece brass patch boxes are extravagant displays of engraving, and his carving in bas-relief covered the cheek side of the butt end of his guns. His carving shows little kinship with either Lancaster or Berks County styles. His use of silver wire inlay was an attractive feature of several of his guns. Although the style and technique of his carving closely resemble that of N. Beyer, and C. Beck, it cannot be said that they established a strong Dauphin County style. Both Beyer and Beck engraved a curious arrangement of letters on the bottom facet of some of their barrels (J. N. K. J.), which is believed to stand for "Jesus Nazareth, King of the Jews."

Peter Berry and Martin Shell also made guns that were extravagantly carved and have similarities that might suggest their working in the same area. The thin butts of Peter Berry's guns are an exception to the general practice of Pennsylvania gunsmiths of the late eighteenth century. Some of Peter Berry's rifles have a comb, which might be regarded as a restrained version of the "Roman nose."

There is much variation in the style of patch boxes in the county and the lock-bolt plates are quite thick, but also vary in style from maker to maker. The shallow trigger guards are typical of the period throughout the other counties.

It is known that very few gunsmiths worked in Dauphin and Lebanon Counties in the percussion era, and the ready availability of gun parts in hardware stores apparently discouraged the creation of a late style. A few makers, such as S. Miller and John Shell, probably made rifles in the 1840's; but there is little regional evidence in their products that they worked in the area. In the 1840's S. Miller was the only gunsmith working in the borough of Lebanon; this suggests that there was little demand for rifles there or that they were imported from Lancaster, where twenty-two gunsmiths were working in the borough and a great many were scattered throughout the county. Some gunsmiths worked in Harrisburg after the Revolution

Park Emery

PLATE 49

Rifle with flint lock, full stock of curly maple, brass mountings, and octagonal barrel marked S. Miller in script letters on the top facet of the barrel.
The lock on this rifle indicates that it was made by S. Miller in the late flintlock period. One might reasonably expect to find such a patch box on a rifle with a percussion lock. Miller is known to have worked in the percussion era.

and into the percussion era, but their products are scarce and no distinct style seems to have developed there.

A few gunsmiths were working along the Susquehanna River north of Harrisburg; for example, Leonard Reedy worked in Gratztown from 1820 until 1835. The style of his guns suggests that he learned his trade in Berks County, and he continued that style as long as he made rifles.

York County

It is apparent that the erection of each county was attended by certain problems that were created by its geographical location or by the people who lived in the respective areas. The Penns had more than their fair share of trouble in gaining title to the land and organizing the first county west of the Susquehanna. The problems arose principally from the fact that there was no agreement among the Indians concerning ownership of the land and that much of the territory was claimed by Lord Baltimore, the proprietor of Maryland. The following incidents suggest some of the problems that had to be solved prior to the period in which we are interested, early gun production in York County.

Although William Penn received the province of Pennsylvania from the English Crown to liquidate a debt the Crown owed to his father, it is a well-known fact that the Penns bought certain areas of the province from several Indian tribes who claimed previous ownership of the land. Such a forthright procedure was in keeping

View from Bushongo Tavern 5 miles from York Town on the Baltimore road

The Mariner's Musuem, Newport News, Va.

PLATE 50

Log buildings along the road from York to Baltimore. Gunsmiths lived and worked in buildings like these in York County, Pennsylvania, in the eighteenth century.

with Penn's policy in establishing his "Holy Experiment" in Pennsylvania and establishing friendly relations with the Indians for the first half century of the colony's existence.

Penn had a peculiar problem in acquiring the land west of the Susquehanna, for the Indian ownership of this territory was vague and uncertain. The land was claimed by the Five Nations, who had defeated the Susquehanna tribe before Penn's arrival; but the defeated tribes were apparently allowed to continue living there. Penn sent a deputy, Colonel Thomas Dongan, who had formerly been governor of New York, to confer with the chiefs of the Five Nations and secure title to the land. Dongan presumably bought the land from them and delivered a deed to Penn for the same on September 13, 1700. It now appeared that Penn held legal title to the land on both sides of the Susquehanna from the head waters of the river to the Cheaspeake Bay.

The Conestoga Indians were very unhappy about this deal and protested bitterly to Sir William Keith in a conference in 1722. At this time Keith explained that an earlier agreement had been made for the lands on the Susquehanna, but the claim of the Conestoga Indians would be recognized and they would be paid for their land. The matter was finally settled in 1736, when an agreement was reached with twenty-three Indian chiefs for the land on both sides of the Susquehanna "as far as the setting sun." At this time the Penns became proprietors of the land and the Indians relinquished all of their rights to it.

The disposal of the Indian claims was only one step in acquiring this land, for as early as 1684 Penn had been troubled by residents of Maryland squatting on territory that appeared to be within the boundaries of his grant. After Penn's death in 1718, the Marylanders became more aggressive, and by 1722 had made a settlement within ten miles of the present site of York. The boundary dispute continued, and in 1732 Thomas Cressap was apprehended by the Sheriff of Lancaster County and was committed to prison for his offensive part in the dispute. Negotiations were long and bitter until the permanent boundary called the Mason-Dixon line, from the names of the men who established it, was finally drawn in 1784.

In the spring of 1729 John and James Henricks made the first authorized settlement in what is now known as York County. They occupied ground along the banks of the Kreutz Creek and were soon followed by many others, who settled in the same area. Most of the immigrants in the Kreutz Creek area were Germans. They lived simply and frugally in dwellings made of wood. About 1735 John and Martin Shultz built a stone dwelling, and in a few years their example was followed by others.

Some years after the settlement was established at Kreutz Creek, several families from Ireland and Scotland settled in the southeastern part of York County, which was called the "York Barrens." These people, like their neighbors, were interested largely in agriculture and both areas developed into rural agricultural communities.

York County was obviously losing its frontier status and a contingent of Quakers from Chester County moved into the northern part, later called Newberry Township. This area they called the "Red Lands" for the soil and rocks were noticeably a dark red color. Thomas Hall, John McFesson, Joseph Benett, John Rankin, and Ellis

Lewis were the first people to settle here. A descendant of Ellis Lewis laid out the town of Lewisberry, and the main stream which runs through the area was called Benett's Run. This stream was connected with the production of guns and will be discussed later.

Yorktown was not the earliest settlement in the county for, in October, 1741, the proprietors directed Thomas Cookson, deputy surveyor of Lancaster County, to lay out the land east of the Codorus Creek in squares like the plan of Philadelphia. There were to be two streets eighty feet wide to cross each other in the center of the town, with provision for a public building (Courthouse) and a public market. The original plan contained two hundred and fifty-six lots, with sixty foot streets, covering an area of one hundred and two acres. In November, 1741, applications for lots were accepted and twenty-three lots were taken up in that year. No more were sold until March 10-11, 1746, when fifty-four lots were "taken up." In 1748 there were forty residences and three churches in the town. It grew slowly, despite its strategic location with passable roads leading to the north, south, east, and west. On September 24, 1787, the borough was incorporated. The population in 1790 was 2076; in 1800, 2503; in 1820, 3545; and in 1830, it was 4772.

It is evident from the foregoing recital that the area west of the Susquehanna was developed much later than the territory to the east toward Philadelphia. Since it was essentially an agricultural community, it lacked the resources and the markets that Berks, Lancaster, and Northampton Counties enjoyed in Philadelphia. York County was truly an undeveloped frontier area when the furnaces and forges of the older counties were producing charcoal iron for the gun barrels of the early gunsmiths. There was some trading with Baltimore, to the south; but early York County lacked the trades that were flourishing in the eastern part of Pennsylvania.

There was a demand for guns, however, in this frontier community, and some gunsmiths probably came with the first groups of settlers. The earliest reference to the subject of gun making is found in Gibson's *History of York County*, published by F. A. Battey in Chicago, 1886. Unfortunately, this is a secondary source of information, but the later production of guns in that area suggests that Gibson's statement might be founded on documented facts:

> "The first important article of manufacture in this vicinity (Lewisberry) was the flint lock gun, for the making of which the town became famous. The business was begun as early as 1760, and many were made there during the Revolution, for the army, by order of the Committee of Safety of York County.
> "There were a number of gun barrel factories along Bennett's Run; among the persons engaged in the business were Samuel Grove, John Rankin, George Blymire, and John Foster. Until 1830 the flintlock gun was made; after that date the present invention came into vogue. (Percussion ignition.) Dr. Lewis and Isaac Lloyd first made the new patent here.
> "William Hammond was an expert workman."

The reference in Gibson's *History of York County* to the gunsmiths who worked along Benett's Run before the Revolution suggests that rifles were made in York County in the transition era. A few early rifles with round barrels and wooden patch box covers have been found in York County, but these two features would hardly be adequate to identify the guns as products of York County gunsmiths.

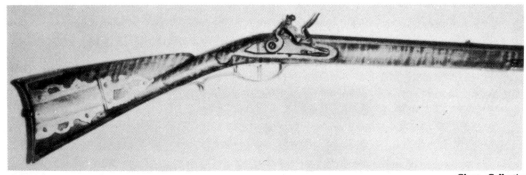

Clegg Collection

PLATE 51

Rifle with flint lock, full stock of curly maple, brass mountings, octagonal barrel with A. W. engraved on the top facet of the barrel. The long narrow wrist of the rifle extending into the butt suggests that it was made in the early part of the Golden Age of gun making in Pennsylvania. The finial of the patch box suggests production in York County, and the initials A. W. might be for Abraham Welshantz.

Although gunsmiths were working in many areas of York County in the Golden Age, it is certain that a number of craftsmen worked in centers like Yorktown, Lewisberry, Hanover, and Littlestown. George Shreyer is known to have bought a lot in Hanover in 1775 and a number of gunsmiths appear in a tax assessment list for Yorktown in the year 1779.

For fifty years following the Revolution, these craftsmen produced rifles that were the finest manufactured in Pennsylvania. Their workmanship was superior in a number of ways; indeed, their patch boxes are particularly outstanding in design and workmanship. A close examination of their design reveals the fact that they were unusually large. They were wide at the butt plate and often reached into the small of the stock. They were frequently pierced, both the finial and the side plates. The finials usually had two or three piercings and the brass work might be described as resembling a drooping feather, although there were many other motifs. Jacob

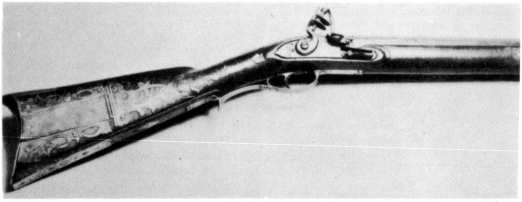

Joe Kindig, Jr.

PLATE 52

Rifle with flint lock, full stock of curly maple, brass mountings, and octagonal barrel 54 inches long with M. Frey engraved in script letters on the top facet of the barrel.

The delicate pattern of the patch box, the exquisite carving on the cheek side of the butt and the fifty-four inch octagonal barrel make this rifle unique. The products of M. Frey are quite rare and in the writer's opinion this rifle is one of the most desirable ones to own of all made in Pennsylvania.

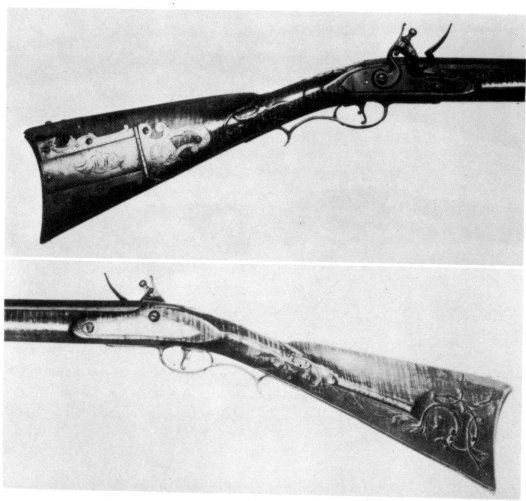

Joseph Aiken

PLATE 53

Rifle with flint lock, full stock of curly maple, brass mountings, and octagonal barrel with H. Pickel engraved in script letters on the top facet of the barrel.

This rifle is particularly interesting because it is the only rifle of Pickel's work known to the writer and the owner, and rarely does one find a lone example to be of the quality of this rifle. The delicate pattern of the carving, the contour of the lock-bolt plate, and the graceful lines of the patch box are notably attractive. The "hand made" lock with its round pan instead of an angular one is another of its interesting features.

Sell used a man's head as a motif on rare occasions in his finial and Frederick Sell occasionally used a bird. There were a number of piercings in each side plate, which was a consistent feature with the finial and the wood of the stock provided an interesting contrast with the brasswork. The C scrolls used in the side plates and the finials were rich in form and were exquisitely engraved so that the outline of the patch box, the piercings, and the engraving were an integrated mass of decorative detail.

The moulded ridge of the cheek piece was attractively carved, and there was a profusion of Rococo C scrolls carved in bas-relief in the front and rear of the cheek piece. The design in front of the cheek piece was often carried over into the right

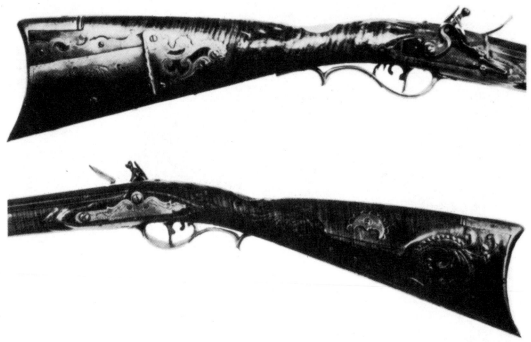

Herman Dean

PLATE 54

Rifle with flint lock, full stock of curly maple, brass mountings, silver inlays, and octagonal barrel with M. Edwards engraved on the top facet of the barrel.

The finial of the patch box on this rifle is obviously the "drooping feather" pattern used by a number of rifle makers in the York County area. The C and S scrolls in the carved portion of the stock are cleverly executed. The wire inlay is an unusual feature of a Pennsylvania rifle. Edwards was obviously a fine gunsmith.

side of the stock and provided an appropriate panel, where the patch-box finial terminated. There was frequently a carved design around the breech tang and a moulded edge along the ramrod. The raised panel for the lock and lock-bolt plate terminated in the rear with a tear drop, as was found on guns in other areas. The toe-plates were unusually long, frequently engraved and were fastened with tacks or screws. The lock-bolt plates were flush with the stock, the rear screw is positioned in the middle of an area that resembles two wings of a bird; and the illusion of a bird is further heightened by an engraved pattern resembling wings. Most of the lock-bolt plates are engraved in some manner, if the spread wing effect was not carried out by the gunsmith. The bottom edge of many of the lock plates is straight or slightly convex. A number of craftsmen used a half-moon inlay on the cheek rest and some added a decorative detail in a number of parts of the stock with wire inlay. The stocks are usually long and slender; many of the gunsmiths obviously selected fine curl for their products.

In 1800 Adams County was created out of the western part of York County, which took the fine craftsmen of the Littlestown area from York County. This change of boundaries had no noticeable effect on their workmanship and no style was evolved that could be described as peculiar to Adams County.

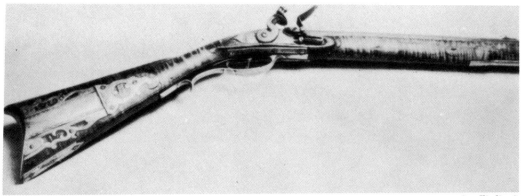

Joe Kindig, Jr.

PLATE 55

Rifle with flint lock, full stock of curly maple, brass mountings, and octagonal barrel 46 inches long with F. Sell engraved in script letters on the top facet of the barrel.

Fredrick Sell was a master in the use of C and S scrolls in his carving and engraving. He rarely repeated a design, yet there are similarities in his work that assist in identifying it. His carved patterns are usually dominated by his use of a large C with long flowing lines and a few small gouge marks. Most of his trigger guards have a line engraved along the edges of the bow.

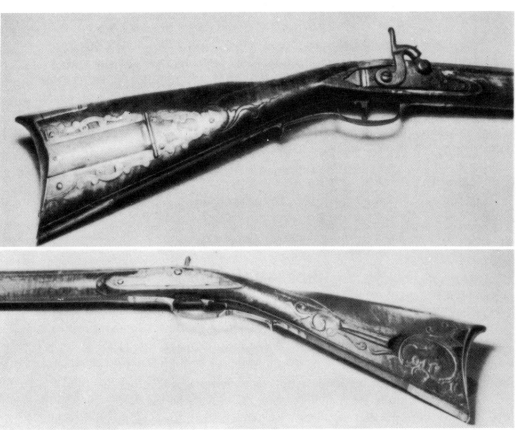

Park Emery

PLATE 56

Rifle with flint lock (now percussion), full stock of curly maple, brass mountings, octagonal barrel with Jacob Sell engraved in script letters on the top facet of the barrel.

The pattern of the patch box, particularly the finial which is a man's head, the engraving and the carving of this rifle indicate that Sell was one of the finest craftsmen to make guns in Pennsylvania.

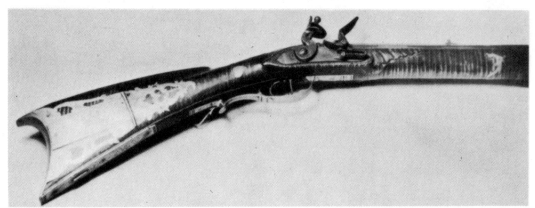

PLATE 57

Rifle with flint lock, full stock of curly maple, brass mountings, and octagonal barrel 36 inches long with J. Meals engraved on the top facet of the barrel.

It is obvious from the radius on the butt plate of this rifle that it was made in the late flintlock era. Meals was an outstanding craftsman in the time that he worked. His designs have a great deal of variation; his engraving is deep and well executed, and his carving in bas-relief is of good quality. His inlays of silver are well designed and cleverly inletted.

This rifle was probably made between 1825 and 1850 in Adams County, Pennsylvania.

There was a general deterioration of workmanship in the percussion era. Stocks were made of plain maple, fewer of the stocks were carved, and the elaborate patch boxes were replaced by simple patterns with separate side plates. A part of the stock between the lid and the side plates of the patch box was exposed. The C scrolls were used less frequently and the work in general fell far below the standards of the Golden Age. According to the Federal Census of 1850, only a few gunsmiths were working in the county and not many more were working in York, which was rapidly becoming an industrial center, where gun parts could easily be bought in hardware stores.

No consistent York County style is known to have existed in the late percussion era.

Cumberland County

It has been pointed out that Dauphin County was near the frontier. It might also be said that Cumberland County was the frontier. An extensive domain, it reached from the Susquehanna to the Ohio line, with the exception of York County, which had been established in 1749. Originally Cumberland County included one-fourth of Pennsylvania, but the portion in which gun collectors are interested coincides with the Cumberland Valley from the Susquehanna River to the Maryland line. The southern portion of this area was formed into Franklin County in 1784.

The first settlers entered the "North Valley" (probably across the river from Harrisburg) about 1731. The population slowly increased and by 1741 several thousand white settlers were living there and a large number of Indians. In 1749 there were 807 taxables in the county, and by 1751 they had increased to 1134.

By earlier standards of settlement the area was filling with white settlers at a very slow rate; and when they pushed beyond the limits of the purchase of 1736, they created a great deal of trouble. The Indians who were being slowly pushed from their hunting grounds, naturally resented the intrusions of the Europeans. Despite the laws of the province, the proclamations of the Governor, and the complaints of the Indians, the Irish, with a few Germans, moved into this forbidden territory. The Indians retaliated by killing their livestock, laying waste their orchards and burning their cabins.

It finally became apparent to the English that the Indian was slowly being pushed into the arms of the French in western Pennsylvania, and that an Indian war would be inevitable. Thomas Penn set aside a part of Cumberland County for the Indians and asked them to return from the western part of the state. The Indians refused, saying that they were afraid and that the land was not convenient for their hunting. The die was cast, but the troubles between the settlers and the Indians simmered for another twenty years before there was war.

As early as 1735 a road was laid out through the county from Harris's Ferry toward the Potomac River. The planning was completed on February 3, 1736, but the route was opposed by many residents. Several men were appointed to review the plans and they reported that the road was crooked and inconvenient for many of the inhabitants. A new and more satisfactory one was proposed and accepted.

A main thoroughfare to the west also passed through the valley, at first used mainly by pack horses. These horses traveled in single lines with a man called a leader in the front and another in the back to supervise the welfare of the horses and the cargo. There were twelve to fifteen horses in a division, and as many as five hundred horses are known to have been in Carlisle at one time. The horse trains would stay there over night and then proceed to the west through Shippensburg, and Fort Loudon.

The County was erected in 1750 and the Court of Common Pleas and the Criminal Court were first held in Shippensburg, the oldest town west of the Susquehanna in Pennsylvania, except York. In 1751, Carlisle was laid out and the court was removed to the new town immediately. It was first held in a temporary log building on the northeast corner of the center square. In 1753, there were only five houses on the site; and the block house, which had been built at an earlier time, was in ruins.

An interesting account of a stockade built in the town in 1753 can be found in Hazards Register, lv, 390.

> "In the same year, 1753, another 'stoccade' of very curious construction was erected, whose western gate was in High street, between Hanover and Pitt street, opposite lot number one hundred. This fortification was thus constructed. Oak logs about seventeen feet in length, were set upright in a ditch, dug to the dept of four feet. Each log was about twelve inches in diameter. In the interior were platforms made of clapboard, and raised four or five feet from the ground. Upon those the men stood and fired through loop-holes. At each corner was a swivel gun, and fired as occasion required, to let the Indians know that such kind of guns were within."

Carlisle was a small village at the start of the French and Indian War, but its strategic location soon caused it to be an important outpost throughout the war. The French did not press their advantage after Braddock's defeat, but the Indians constantly harassed the residents of the town. All work in the fields had to be done under the protection of armed men, and it continued to be a "hot-spot" for many years. In 1758 soldiers were billeted in the homes of the town; and General Forbes advertised for wagons to be sent to the town, where they would be loaded for his western campaign. Wagon trains left the village to establish supply depots every forty miles along his projected line of march. Arms were repaired and a permanent camp and magazine were established in the town, for it was on the direct route from Philadelphia to Fort Pitt.

After the dangers of war and Indian raids ceased to exist, Carlisle slowly became the most important center of population in Cumberland County. Although a number of gunsmiths worked in the borough and the county, a style was not developed there that can be regarded as unique to the area. The lack of a county style might be attributed to the strong influence of York and Lancaster counties on the region.

It is very doubtful if rifles were produced in Cumberland County in the transition era. At least no pre-Revolutionary rifles are known to the writer that can be attributed to the area, despite the fact that at least one gunsmith is known to have worked there. An extract from an order book in the Hamilton Library of Carlisle identifies one gunsmith who worked there as a repairman, if not as a gunsmith.

> Officers are to examine once a day their soldiers, Arms and Ammunition, and confine such soldiers whose Arms are out of order through negligence or waste their ammunition. All arms out of order will be repaired at once. Mr. Butler is the Smith appointed for this purpose.
>
> *Camp near Carlisle, July 3, 1759.*

A number of gunsmiths are known to have worked in Cumberland County in the "Golden Age" but their work does not suggest a common pattern for the area. Henry Lechler moved to Carlisle from Lancaster in the late 1790's, and continued making guns that were partially Lancaster in Character. A later rifle has a patch

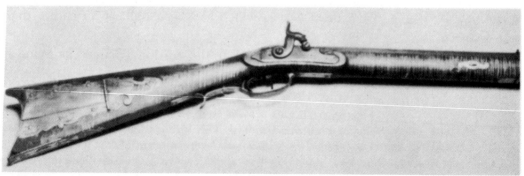

Joe Kindig, Jr.

PLATE 58

Rifle with flint lock (now percussion), full stock of curly maple, brass mountings, silver inlays, octagonal barrel marked H. Lechler in block letters. The patch box of this rifle closely resembles a pattern that was used by a number of gunsmiths in York, Pennsylvania.

box with the "drooping feather" pattern of York County, but despite a high quality of craftsmanship in his products, he did not create a new style in his new residence. Another gunsmith, named Keller, produced rifles in the nineteenth century, a few flintlocks and many with percussion locks; but there is no consistent pattern in his products. There is a Lancaster influence in one of his later guns, but that could arise from the fact that he bought his parts in Lancaster. John Mewhirter and Henry Carlisle lived in Cumberland County, but since their products are very similar to those of Franklin County gunsmiths, they are not included in Cumberland County. It might be pointed out that the Cumberland-Franklin County line runs through the borough of Shippensburg where the latter men lived, which accounts for the similarity of their work to that of Franklin County gunsmiths. Some rifles were produced in the percussion era in Cumberland County but no distinctive style can be found in this late era.

Maryland

The marked superiority of the Pennsylvania rifle naturally led to a demand for it outside the boundaries of the state; rifle-makers are known to have worked in Maryland, New York, Ohio, and North Carolina. Some of the rifles produced in these areas can barely be distinguished from the production of Pennsylvania gunsmiths, while others contained features which led to the development of a new style. The gunmakers of Frederick, Hagerstown, and Emmitsburg, Maryland, made rifles that were stylistic brothers of the Pennsylvania rifle.

There are several reasons for the close resemblance of a rifle produced in Maryland to the Pennsylvania pattern. In the first place, there is evidence that Philip Metzgar worked in Lancaster, Pennsylvania, before he moved to Maryland and, although this change of residence might have influenced to some extent the style of his rifles, it is probable that he continued to use many of his earlier details in his products. Since the three cities previously mentioned are very close to the Maryland-Pennsylvania line, the Pennsylvania influence would be stronger there than in some more distant point in Ohio or New York.

It has also been mentioned that sizable groups of rifle-makers were working in Pennsylvania at Hanover and Littlestown, both of these being near the Maryland line. And, in these Pennsylvania communities, a number of excellent craftsmen were working who might be expected to exert influence on some craftsman in their general locality. As a matter of fact, some of the early Maryland men could have been apprenticed to several of the Pennsylvania gunsmiths.

The scarcity of surviving guns and documentary data of the Maryland region suggest that few, if any, rifles were made there in the transition period. Jacob Metzgar is known to have been working in Frederick in 1788; he could have been working there at an earlier time, although none of his products known to the author suggests such early production.

The eagle engraved on an elliptical inlay on the cheek side of the rifles made in Maryland is a detail which suggests that the guns were made in the early part

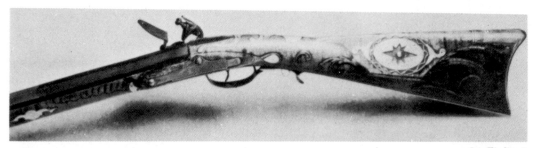

PLATE 59

Rifle with flint lock, full stock of curly maple, brass mountings, silver inlays, and octagonal barrel 42 inches long marked Sheets and Clark.

The appearance of two names on the barrel of a rifle is one of the unique features of this rifle. It is interesting to speculate which part of the rifle was made by the two men involved in its making. The inlay on the cheek piece is unusually clever and attractive, and the star being of wood instead of metal is also a very novel idea. The use of inlay at the breech tang as a substitute for carving was followed by John Armstrong.

of the nineteenth century. It should be noted that rifles made in other areas have similar inlays, and the fact that they are found on Maryland rifles does not imply that they were not used elsewhere. However, men such as John Armstrong did frequently use the eagle motif. Other inlays were placed on carved portions of the stocks or were shaped similar to the carved portions which they replaced. The silver inlays of Maryland makers were executed with much skill and tastefully arranged on the stocks. A small wood screw in the rear portion of the lock-bolt plate holds it to the stock, in case the lock bolt is removed.

A number of patch box patterns were used and certain styles were evolved that are unique to the area. The early patterns had solid finials and side plates, while the later ones were pierced, so that portions of the stock made an interesting contrast to the polished brass. The side plates, inlays, and patch boxes were expertly engraved with patterns that were co-ordinated with the outline of the part.

The long slender shape of the stock is also another identifying feature of the Maryland rifles. The forestock was unusually slender; the wide flare of the butt end provided a pleasing location for a very decorative patch box. The patterns carved in bas-relief on the cheek side of the stock are skillfully executed; many smiths cross-

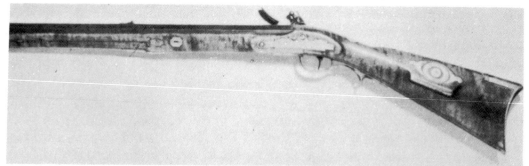

PLATE 60

Rifle with flint lock, full stock of curly maple, brass mountings, silver inlays, octagonal barrel 42½ inches long with M. Sheets on the top facet of the barrel. This rifle has a patch box but its design is not as unusual as the inlay on the cheek side of the butt.

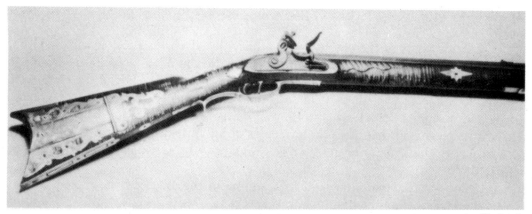

Joe Kindig, Jr.

PLATE 61

Rifle with flint lock, full stock of curly maple, brass mountings, silver inlays and octagonal barrel with D. Marker on the top facet of the barrel. Marker worked in Washington County, Maryland, in the early nineteenth century.

hatched a small panel under the cheek piece. A number of the stocks are made of maple, with excellent curl.

John Armstrong frequently engraved his name on a metal plate, which was inlaid on the top facet of the barrel. He also placed a piece of steel in the projecting end of the butt plate so that it could more easily withstand the abrasion of the soil, while the rifle was being loaded. Other makers are known to have used both of these latter features, also.

The percussion rifles of the area followed the general line of the flint guns of the Golden Age; however, the slow deterioration in style and workmanship which was noted in other areas seems to be evident in Maryland as well. Not a great deal of data is available about the Maryland makers, but the quality of their rifles suggests that this part of the present survey might profitably be expanded by a reader who is familiar with the resources of the region.

Franklin County

Probably no county in Pennsylvania is indebted more to one man than Franklin County is indebted to Benjamin Chambers for his foresight and courage in promoting its welfare. Chambers was born in County Antrim, Ireland, and migrated to the province of Pennsylvania between the years 1726 and 1730. He was twenty-one years old when he built his first house of hewed logs along Falling Creek and covered it with shingles. About 1730, this house was burned by an unprincipled hunter, who is said to have burned it for the nails, no small prize in those days.

On March 30, 1734, the proprietary government encouraged the building of cabins and clearing of land west of the Susquehanna River. Chambers quickly secured a grant of four hundred acres of land at Falling Springs mouth on both sides of the Conochaeque. He first built a saw-mill and within a few years a grist-mill, both of which were influential factors in persuading settlers to move into this virgin territory.

The first settlers of the county were principally of Irish or Scotch ancestry; but soon after the first permanent settlements were made, a number of families of German ancestry moved into the county from southern Lancaster County. The Germans were principally farmers; as soon as land became available, they bought it and erected permanent dwellings. The Germans are also the generic group who made rifles, and it might be presumed that after the problems of an agricultural nature were settled, they turned to the making of guns, or were followed by Germans who were skilled in that trade.

Chambers was active in organizing a militia in the area, and he was appointed one of the first Colonels of the organization. He assisted Forbes in routing his army through the Cumberland Valley, and supplied him with some provisions as he was passing through. Chambers was a man of integrity and was often asked to settle differences between neighbors who could not amicably reach agreements on matters relating to land or personal property. He rendered his country an outstanding service by going to England to assist in settling the dispute over the Pennsylvania-Maryland line. While in Europe, he visited the land of his birth and influenced others to come and live in the new world, particularly the Cumberland Valley. Col. Benjamin Chambers died on February 17, 1788, after a long and brilliant career in the interests of his adopted home.

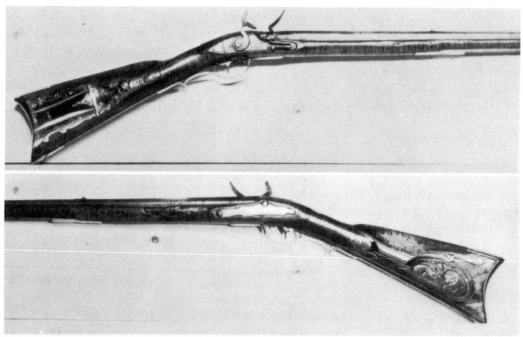

Henry J. Kauffman

PLATE 62

Rifle with flint lock, full stock of curly maple, brass mountings, octagon to round barrel 50 inches long with H. Albright engraved in script letters on the top facet of the barrel.

In 1746 Chambers laid out the town of Chambersburg adjoining his various mill sites. At that time the main artery of traffic through the Cumberland Valley was from north to south and the main axis of the new village conformed to the flow of traffic. After the Revolution, renewed interest in westward expansion increased the movement of goods toward the west; and the town plan was extended beyond the creek, which had been the boundary line of the first town plan. Chambersburg remained a small village until Franklin County was formed and Chambersburg became the county seat.

Franklin County was the thirteenth county erected in the state of Pennsylvania and was established by an act of the assembly on September 9, 1784. It is interesting to note that all the earlier counties (except Washington, 1781) were given English names. It is very likely that the county was named for the great American patriot, Benjamin Franklin.

There is no record of gunsmiths having worked in Franklin County in the transition era, and no guns that might possibly be attributed to makers of that period in the region are known.

In the Golden Age Franklin County not only had a number of fine gunsmiths working within its boundaries, but they also created a style which seems to have been confined to the county and its bordering areas. It might also be mentioned that two men, particularly, worked there who did not conform to the common pattern.

One of these men was Henry Albright, who advertised his products in a Pittsburgh newspaper in 1796. In addition to making rifles, he was engaged in the barrel-making business with a partner named William McCall. The writer owns a rifle made by Albright, which was found in the town of Chambersburg and was probably made while he resided there. This rifle has a daisy finial on the patch box and other details that are evidence of Albright's earlier residence and work in Lancaster, Pennsylvania. John Noll made some superb guns in the county, but did not follow the common pattern. There is a strong possibility that Noll moved there from Lancaster County, although his rifles do not conform to a Lancaster or a Franklin County pattern. Among the men who made rifles in the typical Franklin County style are Abraham Schweitzer, J. Schweitzer, Henry Carlisle, and J. Mewhirter.

The style of the patch box was probably the most consistent feature of Franklin County rifle makers. It was made up of the customary four parts, two side plates, a lid, and a finial. The lid was a rectangle with an elliptical panel engraved frequently in the middle, with a pattern similar to checkering. The panel pattern was elongated by engraving scrolls toward the hinge and the butt of the lid. The side plates were sometimes flush with the lid; however, in most cases, a portion of the stock was exposed between the lid and the side plates. In the latter cases, the inner edge of the side plate was straight, but the other edge tapered toward the top and bottom of the stock, thereby creating a wider portion in the butt end of the side plate. In the middle of the outside edge, a protruding panel was placed to accommodate one of the screws which held it to the stock. There was some variety in the patterns of these small panels. A variety of finials were used, but most smiths used one that

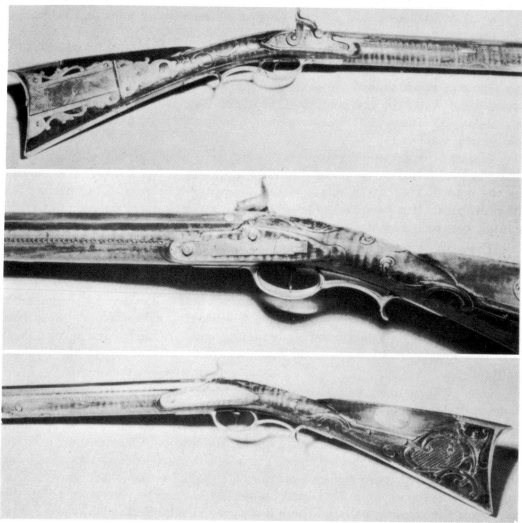

George Ferree

PLATE 63

Rifle with flint lock (now percussion), full stock of curly maple, brass mountings, silver inlay with eagle engraved on it, and octagonal barrel with John Noll engraved in script letters on the top facet of the barrel. Near the breech end of the barrel a silver inlay is inserted with the initials J. N. stamped on it. In front of the inlay is a mark resembling a dagger which could have been Noll's proof mark.

This rifle was made in the late eighteenth or early nineteenth century. The form of the stock is very pleasing; his carving is superb, and his patch box is elegant in all its details. The gouge work on the stock in front of the lock is unique. John Noll was one of Pennsylvania's finest gunsmiths and this rifle is an excellent example of his workmanship.

resembled the capital letter Q. Henry Noll used a form which suggested the head of a bird, and D. Cooley used the popular and attractive horse head finial with the regular lid and side plates.

The lock-bolt plate was flush with the surface of the stock and was usually engraved. There were a few decorative lines engraved around the rear screw and a line or a simple pattern around the entire outer edge. The bottom edge was usually straight. An ellipse engraved with an eagle was very common in the "Golden Age" and there were other inlays to make the rifle attractive.

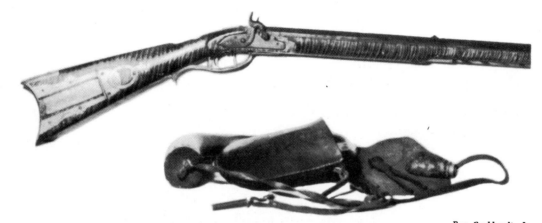

PLATE 64

Rifle with percussion lock, full stock of curly maple, set triggers, brass mountings, octagonal barrel 44 inches long marked H. Carlisle on the top facet of the barrel.
The style of the patch box is very similar to the one used by a number of gunsmiths in Franklin County. The accoutrements were found with the rifle in an attic in Shippensburg, Pa.

The butts were carved on the cheek side in a bas-relief pattern that varies with each maker, although many of them inserted a panel of cross hatching under the cheek ridge and on other areas.

The gunsmiths of the percussion era continued the style that was developed in Franklin County in the Golden Age. The carving of patterns in bas-relief was dropped, although some craftsmen carved designs in the incised technique. The stock became thinner at the butt, which caused a corresponding change in the butt plate. The radius of the butt plate became much sharper and some gunsmiths placed an iron point on the top of the butt plate to protect it from the rough soil when the gun was charged. Many of the trigger guards were also quite narrow.

The four-piece patch box with the Q finial was continued, although it was less attractively engraved than was the case in the Golden Age.

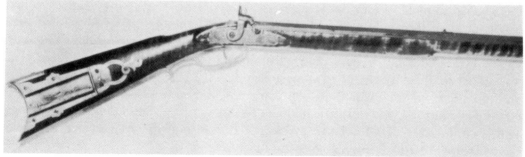

PLATE 65

Rifle with percussion lock, curly maple stock, brass mountings, octagonal barrel 40 inches long with S. H. Shillito on top facet of the barrel. The pattern of the patch box is the typical one used by the gunsmiths of Franklin County in the first half of the nineteenth century. The bow of the trigger guard is unusually large for one trigger.

The inlays of the earlier guns were also continued at the barrel pins and on both sides of the wrist of the stock. Sometimes they were placed between panels on the forestock, which was a reasonable and attractive procedure.

Ornate scroll designs were engraved on the top facet of the barrel by late markers, particularly in the front and rear of both sights. The names were often engraved in script letters particularly those of J. H. Johnson and Jeremiah Senseny.

Bedford County

Although the unique products of Bedford County gunsmiths were known to several collectors, only in recent years has the achievement of these craftsmen gained recognition beyond the general area in which they were made. The obscurity of the county as a gun producing area is indicated by the fact that there is only one entry referring to Bedford County in the index of the *Kentucky Rifle* by Dillin and it does not pertain to description of the rifle. The obscurity of this interesting rifle until recent years can probably be attributed to the physical contour of the county and its isolated position in relation to the large centers of population in eastern Pennsylvania, where most of the Pennsylvania rifles were made.

Bedford County, originally a part of Cumberland County, was formed into a separate unit by an act of the legislature on March 9, 1771. Its southern boundary was the Maryland state line and it extended from the Tuscarora range in the east to the Allegheny mountains in the west. It spread northward to the present location of Centre County. It was later reduced to its present size by forming new counties or parts of counties from it. Its mid-twentieth century size and location are indicated on a map, pages 30 and 31.

An examination of the topography of the county immediately reveals that most of it is rugged and mountainous. A series of ranges sweeps across it from south to northeast, which are not conducive to travel or habitation; however, there are rich valleys of limestone soil, excellent for farming. These areas probably attracted the few German gunsmiths who are believed to have worked in the area.

This forbidding terrain was doubtless one of the restraining factors in the development of the county; in addition, its great distance from the centers of population in the eastern part of the state was a contributing factor. After the Europeans landed in Philadelphia, they would naturally move to the nearest available land best suited to their means of earning a livelihood. For this reason farmers would tend to settle in the rich valleys of Lancaster or Cumberland County and the traders would move beyond, where they could eke out a living by trading with the Indians. In the earliest days the frontier was east of the Susquehanna river, but it slowly moved westward and finally came to Bedford County.

The frontier status of Bedford County also focuses attention on the danger of living a distance from centers of population. Life was naturally precarious in such a location, and the fact that most of the men who lived on the frontier were squatters increased the danger of reprisal by the Indians. The fear of being scalped or of returning to a cabin only to find it in ashes was always present, and, until these two hazards were removed, an area like Bedford was not apt to grow rapidly.

It is assumed that the first settlement in the county was made prior to 1750, but there is no record of the settler or the site. A fort was built near present-day Bedford borough, which was one of a string of forts, reaching from the Blue Mountains in the east to Fort Pitt in the west. These were built as places of refuge to which the white inhabitants could flee in times of Indian raids. A letter written by Joseph Shippen to Richard Peters in 1758 from Raystown (Bedford) indicates that the fort was standing at that time.

> We have a good stockade built here, with several convenient and large stores. Our camps are well secured with a good breast and a small ditch on the outside; and everything goes well. Colonel Burd desires his compliments to you.
> I am, very respectfully, Dear Sir,
> Your obedient and humble servant.
> JOSEPH SHIPPEN

Throughout the last half of the eighteenth century Bedford actively participated in the French and Indian War, the Revolution, and the Whiskey Rebellion. It was a rest station for the trains of pack horses, which moved from Philadelphia to Pittsburgh and slowly grew to a place of importance.

The town of Bedford was laid out in 1766. Its streets were straight and a public square was created in the center, where two main streets crossed. There, a courthouse was built and a public market was maintained where the city dwellers could buy from the farmers who grew produce in the countryside. In 1830 the borough had a population of 879, 7 of whom were engaged in agriculture, 85 in manufacturing and trades, 20 in the learned professions, and the others in various employment. In 1840 its population was only 1036.

The total capital invested in manufacturing in the county in 1840 was $192,039 in projects ranging from potteries to tanneries and distilleries; but there is no mention of gun making.

This brief perspective of the area suggests that rifles were needed there from the time man first set foot within its boundaries; however, no one will ever know when the first rifles were made there. It is likely that at least a repairman lived in the county as early as the Revolution, and there is a legend that Jacob Saylor made rifles for the Committee of Safety. Since no rifles are known that can be attributed to a gunsmith in the county in the transition era, it must be presumed that in this early period there was no Bedford style of rifle.

The surviving rifles from the Golden Age (1775-1825) of rifle making in Pennsylvania indicate that in this period the true Bedford rifle was created. Several rifles with Bedford qualities and flintlocks are known to have been made by Peter White, although a rifle of his, dated 1794, shows no evidence of an embryo Bedford style. Other rifles with flintlocks and Bedford qualities were made by Jacob Stoudenour and Joseph Mills in the first quarter of the nineteenth century. A few other craftsmen are known to have been contemporaries of these men, but few of their rifles have survived; therefore, the major emphasis must be placed on Bedford rifles made in the percussion era.

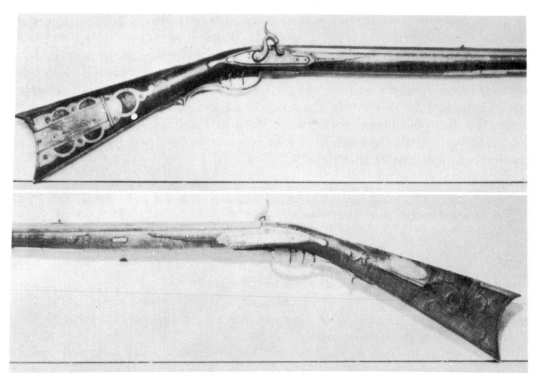

William Bowers

PLATE 66

Rifle with percussion lock, full stock of curly maple, brass mountings, silver inlays, set triggers and octagonal barrel 42 inches long marked W. Defibaugh on the top facet of the barrel. The contour of the stock, the design of the patch box, the style of the lock and hammer, the shape of the lock-bolt plate, and the carved pattern in bas-relief are typical of many rifles made in Bedford County throughout the nineteenth century.

The unique style of the percussion period arouses a great deal of speculation as to how it was originated. One of the reasonable hypotheses is that in the late eighteenth or early nineteenth century a gunsmith, possibly Peter White, moved into the area from an adjoining area, perhaps Franklin County. This gunsmith was a clever craftsman and a prolific producer of guns, who trained a number of apprentices in a style which he had evolved from an earlier one he had learned as an apprentice. In this way a design for a patch box and lock was carried over the mountains and propagated among a number of craftsmen, who eventually developed a reasonably new and distinct style.

This hypothesis is based largely on the fact that some rudimentary evidences of the Bedford pattern can be found in the work of John Armstrong, who made long slender rifles with narrow, plain lock plates. He did engrave his name, however, on some of the lock plates. It is also easy to recognize the "loop and hook" finial of Bedford County patch boxes in the Capital Q form, which was used by makers in Franklin County and the surrounding area.

The isolation of the county from sources of supply in the East may have caused the early smiths to produce their own parts, a practice which they continued throughout the nineteenth century, for they were aware that they had created a rifle peculiar to the region and preferred by the natives to guns made in the eastern

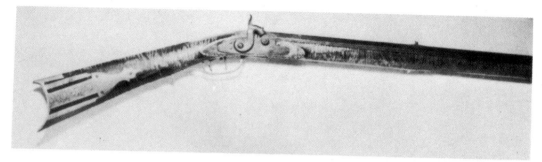

PLATE 67

T. J. Cooper

Rifle with percussion lock, full stock of curly maple, set triggers, brass mountings, octagonal barrel 37 inches long with Peter Smith on the top facet of the barrel. This rifle is typical of the rifles made in Huntingdon County, Pennsylvania.

part of Pennsylvania. The rifle was attractive, accurate, and a true local product; it remained so as long as muzzle-loading rifles were made.

The Bedford rifle is known by a number of distinct characteristics, the foremost one of which is the use of fine curly maple in the stocks. At mid-century, when gunsmiths in the East were using plain maple, or artificially graining their stocks so that they looked like curly maple, the Bedford gunsmiths were using superior wood for their stocks. The procedure was not only true to the traditions of the craft, but produced a stock that was second to none in the beauty of its curly figure.

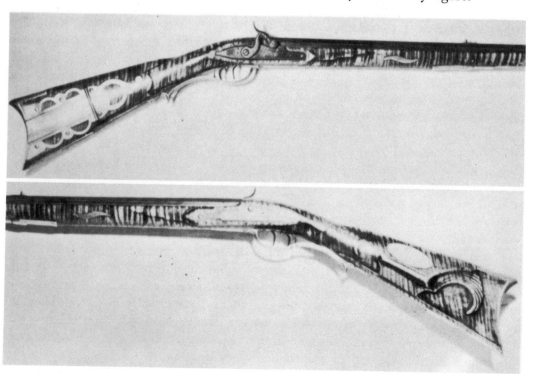

PLATE 68

R. A. Farber

Rifle with percussion lock marked W. B., full stock of curly maple, brass mountings, silver inlays, and octagonal barrel marked W. B. for William Border.

The curl in this stock is obviously an unusual example of wood selection. The carved pattern on the cheek side is different from the traditional style of the Bedford gunsmiths.

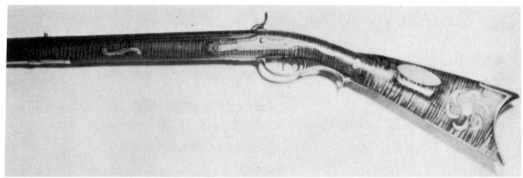

R. A. Farber

PLATE 69

Rifle with percussion lock, full stock of curly maple, brass mountings, silver inlays, set triggers, and octagonal barrel. The inlay on the cheek side of this rifle is quite unusual and the lock-bolt plate is dated Nov. 1, 1849.

The long slender form of the stock contributed an additional aesthetic quality to the form of the rifle. This feature probably arose from the fact that the barrels had a reasonably small caliber; the outer dimension of the barrel was therefore small, and the entire stock was made in proportion to the size of the barrel. The small bore of the barrel did not necessarily dictate such a procedure, for gunsmiths in nearby Huntington County made small-bored barrels which were as large as 1½ inches across the flats.

The small barrel and stock did dictate that the lock be long and slender; it should be noted, however, that the gunsmiths could have resorted to the use of back-action locks, which would have been well suited to their rifles. These locks lacked the distinctive feature of their hand-made locks and reduced the attractiveness of the gun in general. It should also be noted that some Bedford locks had a narrow tail in the rear, while others were rounded; several gunsmiths used locks that were probably made in Birmingham for their less important rifles.

The metalwork of the craftsmen was also outstanding. Their cast brass, trigger guards, butt plates and lock-bolt plates were well made and cleverly fitted. Their patch box finials have been described as a "loop and hook pattern" and the side plates usually were pierced in half circles, with parts of the wooden stock contrasting with the polished brass parts of the patch box. The ramrod pipes and forestock ferrules were also well made.

A few of the Bedford rifles have some decorative details of top quality. Some have silver inlays, placed on portions carved in bas-relief, which are executed in the old tradition of the craft and are nicely engraved. Other rifles have a profusion of inlays which have unimaginative forms, such as hearts and tear-drops. They are not related to the contour of the stock and are lightly engraved. An attractive oval inlay was often used in the cheek side of the butt, engraved with an eagle. Although this cannot be regarded as an exclusive Bedford feature, it was an attractive one. The lock-bolt plates, flat and flush with the stock, often had a screw in the rear tail to fasten it to the stock, and were usually engraved. The lower edge was most often straight and the raised panel, on which the plate was set, conformed to the general size and shape of the plate.

Although the patterns carved in bas-relief on the cheek side of the stock are skillfully executed, the design of the pattern rarely rises above a level of mediocrity. The charm and quality of the Rococo scrolls carved on rifles made in the eastern part of the state is not to be found here, and there is generally little variation in the decorative details of the rifles. Most of the carved patterns are a group of narrow uniform veins, which lack unity and rhythm. A few rifles are known with a checkered design on raised portions of the stock, in front of the lock and the lock-bolt panel, but variations like this are the exception rather than the rule.

We may conclude that a unique rifle was made in Bedford County throughout the nineteenth century. Its outstanding qualities are a long graceful stock and hand-made locks with a unique hammer pattern, all executed with an unusually high quality of workmanship. It was superior to most of the rifles made in Pennsylvania in the percussion era; it cannot, however, be regarded as comparable to the fine rifles made in eastern Pennsylvania in the "Golden Age."

Western Pennsylvania

The western area in this final survey of gun production in Pennsylvania includes the following counties: Allegheny, Armstrong, Beaver, Blair, Butler, Cambria, Clarion, Fayette, Indiana, Jefferson, Somerset, Venango, and Westmoreland. The exact time of the earliest settlement in this region is not known; however, after the

Pennsylvania Historical and Museum Commission
PLATE 70
The old "Block House" in downtown Pittsburgh is an interesting relic of frontier life in the area.

1720's the pressure of European settling in the eastern part of the state forced the Indians to move into the regions around the headwaters of the Ohio River in Pennsylvania and Ohio. The Indians were followed by traders, the traders by squatters, and the squatters by permanent settlers.

The Iroquois title to this territory was recognized by the Indian inhabitants and the English, but Virginia, Pennsylvania, and the French all claimed it by reason of exploration or grant. The French moved into the territory in 1754 and built Fort Duquesne at the junction of the Allegheny and the Monongahela Rivers. The attempts of the British to gain possession of the county were at first flagrant failures, particularly Washington's defeat at Fort Necessity and Braddock's annihilation at the Battle of the Monongahela. General Forbes finally won the struggle for the British when he captured the smouldering ruins of Fort Duquesne, which had been set afire by the retreating French.

The newly stabilized atmosphere of the region encouraged trading; and firms like Baynton, Wharton and Morgan built a large storehouse there, in 1766. This firm operated in areas between Philadelphia and Pittsburgh and sent traders from their base in Pittsburgh as far as "Illinois County." The Fort Pitt Day Book of the company, now in the library of the Historical Society of Western Pennsylvania, mentions the names of three gunsmiths with whom they transacted business in the mid 1760's.

The growth of the region was temporarily slowed throughout the Revolution and in 1783, the German traveler, Johann David Schoepf, wrote a description of the principal settlement as he found it at that time:

> "Pittsburgh numbers at this time perhaps 60 wooden houses and cabins, in which live something more than 100 families, for by the outbreak of the last war the growth of the place, beginning to be rapid, was hindered. The first stone house was built this summer, but soon many good buildings may be seen, because the place reasonably expects to grow large and considerable with the passing of time. . . . . Of public houses of worship or justice there are none yet. . . . . However little to be regarded the place is now, from its advantageous site it must be that Pittsburgh will in the future become an important depot for the inland trade."

Within a very short period of time Schoepf's prophetic vision became a reality. In 1784, the Penns had their manor laid out to embrace the land between the Monongahela and Allegheny Rivers to the present site of Grant and Eleventh Streets. Many artizans and merchants came to live in this frontier town on the outer perimeter of civilization, the last opportunity for the traveler to the West to buy his clothing, guns, and canoe. The following announcement appeared in the April 25, 1789 issue of the *Pittsburgh Gazette:*

INVITATION TO IMMIGRANTS

This county offers at present the most unbounded encouragement to the artificer and laborer. Every office except the President of the United States is open to the most indigent immigrant, if he possesses talent, industry, and virtue to assist his progress. The reward which the mechanic meets with is greater than any former period. One pair of shoes which cost 11s. 3d. will buy 180 pounds of wheat, which will furnish 120 pounds of flour, the shoes will also procure more than 60 pounds of good beef or pork. . . . . We want people, we want sober and diligent tradesmen; hatters, button makers, rope makers, weavers, etc.

The early issues of the *Pittsburgh Gazette* contain many advertisements placed by craftsmen and merchants who were eager to sell their products of iron, tin, copper, and brass. About 1785, Jacob Ferree left Lancaster County and moved to a site on Peter's Creek, where he made rifles and gunpowder. In 1801 he moved to a farm of 330 acres in Moon Township, where the city of Coraopolis is now located.

The soldiers who briefly visited the country at the time of the Whiskey Insurrection were impressed with the opportunities of the region and returned to it or advised friends to settle there. In 1794, the borough of Pittsburgh was incorporated and by 1816, the city came into existence. Within a span of forty years the settlement grew from a village of 60 wooden houses to a thriving and aggressive city.

Although the surrounding area was dominated by the economic pulse of Pittsburgh, the mineral and agricultural resources of the region stimulated growth in many smaller population centers. The Ohio Company wished to secure a direct portage route from the Potomac to the Ohio and laid out a road across the southern part of the region, which later became the National Road. This passes through Fayette County, which was organized in 1813. Brownsville was a thriving community on highway and river routes and became an important industrial center in

Kauffman Photo

PLATE 71

This log house is about a hundred years old and is located near the city of Somerset, Pennsylvania. Gunsmiths lived and worked in similar structures in the early part of the nineteenth century.

the early nineteenth century. At Haydentown, Albert Gallatin (with Melchoir Baker) established a gun factory in 1799, where they manufactured arms for the Federal government. In 1801, when Gallatin was appointed Secretary of the Treasury, his interest in gun making ceased and Baker continued in the business alone.

Washington County was formed in 1781 and the town of Washington became another important site on the National Road because the mineral and agricultural resources of this county were abundant. It became another center of business activity. Many gunsmiths worked there in the nineteenth century, which makes it a significant area to those interested in gun making.

By 1846, Blair County was established and George and Andrew Kopp were making fine guns there for a decade or two. By the middle of the century, gunsmiths were dotted all over western Pennsylvania; their products are now eagerly sought by collectors in the area.

It is unfortunate, although necessary, that the discussion of the production of rifles in western Pennsylvania must cover such a large area, when the production in the central and eastern parts could be given a detailed treatment on a county basis. The most obvious reason for this procedure is the fact that little documented data concerning the makers of western Pennsylvania was available before this survey was started. Many of the gunsmiths whose names were known were assigned to certain areas because their products were found there or their residence was established by a word of mouth procedure. These means of identification have now been replaced by a careful search of virtually all of the tax assessment lists which are extant; many of the previous conclusions have been confirmed and some have been found to be incorrect. For example, the famous gunsmith, Peter White, is thought to have worked first in northern Maryland near John Armstrong, or one of his contemporaries. From there it was suggested that he moved to Bedford County, and that he finally took up residence in the area of Uniontown. His early residence was not documented in this survey; however, the tax records of Bedford County show that a man named Peter White lived there in 1815, although the records which the writer examined there do not list him as a gunsmith. White is listed as a gunsmith in the tax assessment lists for Union Township, Fayette County, Pennsylvania, for the years 1820 and 1834; it is very probable that additional data about him can be found in Bedford and Fayette Counties. Many other names, like Schreckengost and Dunmeyer, have been documented; it is hoped that local studies will be made of these men and that their products will be called to the attention of the collecting fraternity in more detail than is possible in this survey.

The area approach for the gunsmiths of western Pennsylvania is further supported by the fact that some stylistic details can be regarded as peculiar to the region rather than to specific counties in the region. The presence of these characteristics can be attributed to the fact that Pittsburgh took the lead in producing guns and gun parts. In the early nineteenth century (1817), Bosler & Co. advertised the sale of gun mountings, and in 1818 the tin and coppersmith, George Miltenberger, advertised similar merchandise. The extensive advertisement of Benjamin Darlington in the November 29, 1816, issue of the *Pittsburgh Gazette* includes Ketland and German gun locks. Probably by 1825-1830, gun parts were available from a variety of sources in the Pittsburgh area. The aggressive spirit of the merchants and the craftsmen of the area is reflected in the statement from the Business Directory of Pittsburgh (1826), which indicates that guns with percussion locks were being made there at that time. This date precedes the earliest documented date for percussion guns in Lancaster County.

The availability of gun parts in hardware stores does not imply that personal details of workmanship were not used by the individual gunsmiths of the area; however, it is apparent that there are limitations to what different craftsmen can do with a few patch-box patterns.

The documented evidence of gunsmiths working west of the mountains before the Revolution suggests the possibility of rifles having been made there in the transition period of gun making in Pennsylvania. Frontier conditions, however, made it impractical to work on one gun for a week or ten days; it is more probable that these men repaired the English, French and eastern Pennsylvania guns that were used in the area. The records of the Fort Pitt Day Book of Baynton, Wharton and Morgan support the theory of repair rather than production.

The number of gunsmiths living in western Pennsylvania in the Golden Age of gun making indicates that rifles were made there in the late eighteenth and early nineteenth centuries. The eighteenth century rifles had 40-44 inch octagonal barrels with a caliber of approximately 50. Octagon-to-round barrels were rarely used on

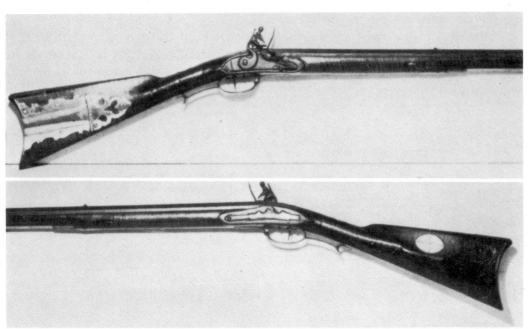

J. T. Herron

PLATE 72

Rifle with flint lock, full stock of curly maple, brass mountings, octagonal barrel 44 inches long marked I (or J) Ferree on the top facet of the barrel. This rifle is one of the few examples known in the Pittsburgh area that was made there in the eighteenth century. Although it was probably made by Jacob Ferree, there is little in its style that suggests his earlier residence in Lancaster County.

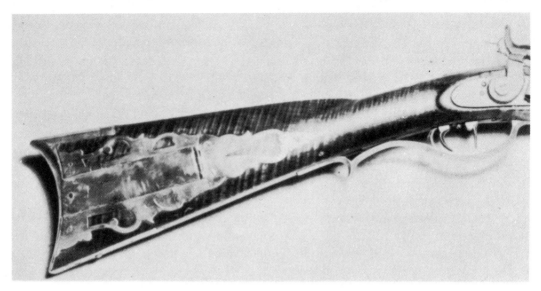

PLATE 73

Patch box design found on a great many guns made in the Pittsburgh area. Some are profusely engraved and some are entirely plain. This one is on a rifle marked S. McCosh on the top facet of the barrel.

western Pennsylvania guns. The stocks were slender, the wrists small, and the wood had an excellent curl. The trigger guard was long and shallow; the butt plate had some radius, although not as sharp as in the nineteenth century. The four-piece brass patch box was used with some piercings in the finials but no particular pattern can be described as common to the area.

The rifles of the early nineteenth century followed the general pattern of those of the late eighteenth century, although the octagonal barrel became a bit shorter and the caliber became slightly smaller. The most notable feature of these rifles is a four-piece brass patch box, which was used by a number of makers. This patch

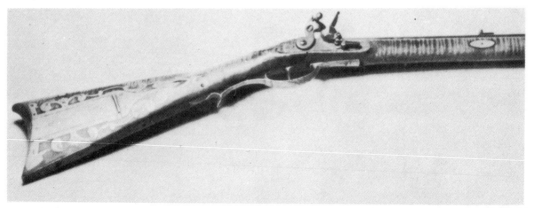

PLATE 74

Joe Kindig, Jr.

Rifle with flint lock, full stock of curly maple, brass mountings, silver inlays, octagonal barrel 41 inches long with T. Allison on the top facet of the barrel.

The quality of the carving on the cheek side of the stock, the number of piercings in the patch box, and the clever engraving on the patch box indicate that Allison was a fine craftsman. It is one of the finest guns made by a gunsmith in western Pennsylvania.

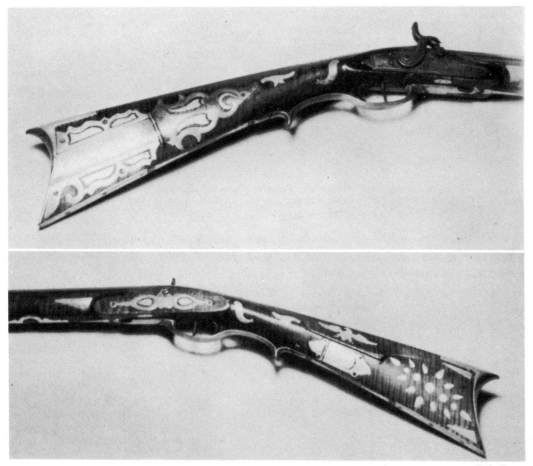

Park Emery

PLATE 75

Rifle with percussion lock, stock of curly maple, brass mountings, silver inlays, octagonal barrel with Jonathan Dunmeyer engraved in script letters on the top facet of the barrel.

This rifle with its extravagant inlays of silver was doubtless a costly gun when Dunmeyer made it. The small box with a cover on the cheek side was probably used for percussion caps. The silver eagle inlaid above the box is an unusually fine example of design and workmanship.

box which is illustrated in Plate 73, was attractive and well-suited to the size and shape of the butt end of the stock. There was a pierced, elongated heart motif in the finial; and there were usually two piercings in each of the side plates, a small one near the hinge end and a large one toward the butt end. On some rifles the patch boxes were plain; on others they were extravagantly engraved.

The fine craftsmanship and the typical patch box pattern of the late flintlock period were carried into the percussion era. The octagonal barrels became a little shorter and the caliber was sometimes reduced, as small as 25. The slender forestock and barrel, combined with the flaring butt and the pierced patch box, created an attractive rifle. Some of these were mounted in German silver, which made them more decorative and much more costly. Some makers profusely inlaid the wrists and the forestock with pieces of silver. A rifle by Jonathan Dunmeyer of Sommerset has a long brass patch box, with piercings which are partially filled with silver. The

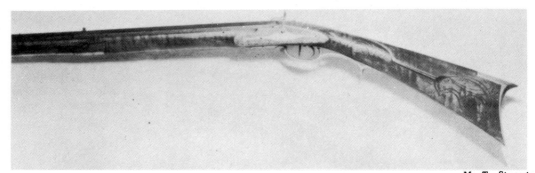

M. T. Stewart

PLATE 76

The form of the stock, the style of carving, and the shape of the lock-bolt plate on this rifle was used by gunsmiths in Somerset County in the last half of the nineteenth century. This one was made by one of the Dunmeyers.

lock-bolt plate is treated in a similar manner and there are many other inlays of silver on the wrist and forestock of the gun. The silhouette of an eagle makes an attractive inlay on the cheek side of the butt.

In the later percussion era the early style of the patch boxes with the heart motif in the finial was changed, so that a piece of the stock was exposed between the lid of the patch box and the side plates. All the long patch boxes, which reached

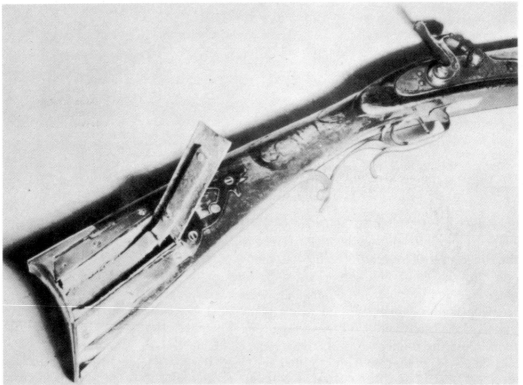

Henry J. Kauffman

PLATE 77

This spring arrangement is frequently found on the lids of patch boxes made by gunsmiths in Western Pennsylvania. This friction action between the two pieces of metal replaced the spring and catch used by most gunsmiths in eastern Pennsylvania.

to the butt plate, were finally replaced by the round or oval pattern, which was used throughout the State. There were at least four different sizes of the new styles. An extra long model was used by Ringle in Indiana County. The Schreckengosts tried to camouflage this simple form by enclosing it within added bands of metal, which, unfortunately, did not seem to enhance it very much. The half-stock pattern arrived about the same time as the round and oval patch boxes; and the combination suggests some deterioration in design of gun making, although full stocks were probably made to order as long as muzzle-loading rifles were made.

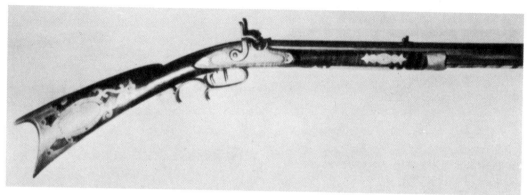

PLATE 78

Western Pennsylvania Historical Society

Rifle with percussion lock, half stock of curly maple, patch box of brass, butt plate, trigger guard, and inlays of silver, set triggers, octagonal barrel 40 inches long with S. G. Schreckengost deeply engraved on the top facet of the barrel. This rifle is a typical Schreckengost product.

The final chapter of rifle production in Pennsylvania took place in the rifle factories of the Great Western Gun Works, and the Enterprise Gun Works and its successors. A description of the New No. 5 rifle by the Great Western Gun Works in their 1879 catalogue indicates the type of rifle that was made at that time:

> Fine wrought iron barrel, fine steel side action, lock best steel, double or set trigger with set screw, American black walnut stock, oil finish barrel, splendidly rifled all the way through, and finished inside just like any of the finest target guns, correctly sighted, to range from 50 to 500 yards, and a white metal front sight. The cylinder or drum has a vent screw, so that powder may be inserted from the breech in case a ball is put down without powder, or in case of dirt in the breech, it fails to prime. Brass mounting, including patch box on side of butt, a bullet mold casting round bullets, an extension wiper screw on rod, and a cloth cover, sent free. The whole gun is hand-made, and well put together by the best gunsmiths, thoroughly inspected before leaving the factory and warranted by us. The sizes made are 26, 28, 30, 33, 36, and 40 inch barrels, 60, 75, 100, 135, 175 round balls to the pound. The weight of the whole gun from 6½ to 10 pounds. The range from 50 to 500 yards. The best sizes for boys are 26 to 30 inch barrels and 6 to 8 pounds weight, unless for target use, when it should be 9 pounds weight. A good average size for general use is 180 balls, 33 inches, 9 pounds weight; for large game, 30 to 33 inches, 60 bore, 9 pounds; for target use 33 to 36 inch, 60 to 75 bore, 9 to 10 pounds. Any size of rifle will be made to order on 1 week's notice and a deposit of at least $1.00 to insure taking when done.

The same company manufactured a rifle called a "Horseback Rifle," which might well be what is known today as a "Plains Rifle." It was in many ways similar to the one described, except that it had a 26 to 30 inch barrel, swivels and sling, round barrel, and was available with silver plate mountings. They were particularly sought by "hunters on horseback or in wagons, as well as on foot."

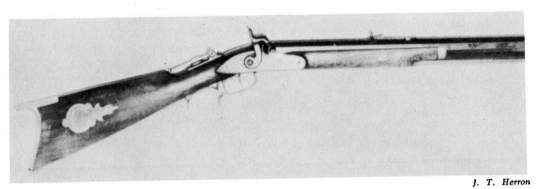

J. T. Herron

PLATE 79

Rifle with percussion lock, half stock of walnut wood, brass mountings, set triggers, octagonal barrel 33 inches long with Great Western Gun Works on top facet of the barrel.

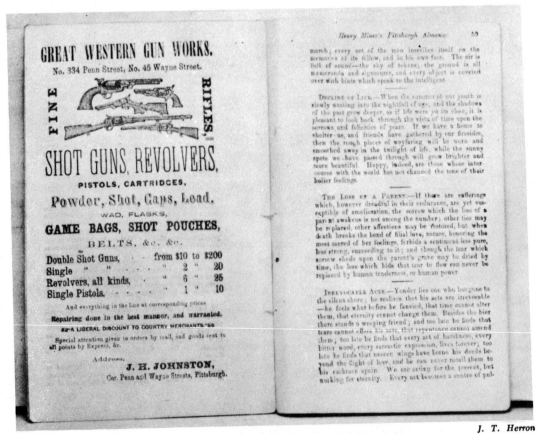

J. T. Herron

PLATE 80

Advertisement of the Great Western Gun Works in a Pittsburgh, Pa., almanac for 1867.

All of the manufacturers made the usual line of double guns, shot guns, with single and double barrels, and one made duck guns with smooth musket barrels. The manufacturers were also merchants and, in addition to their own products, sold Colt revolvers, Flobert rifles, Remington breech-loading guns, Colt's new hammerless double-barrel shotguns, handcuffs, hunting bags, cartridge belts, gun-makers tools, barrels, fishing baskets, pocket flasks, Singer's high front wheel bicycles, and other items that were needed in the sporting world of that day.

A few men, like Fisher and Post, stuck to their workbenches and made muzzle-loading guns into the twentieth century; but, by the end of the nineteenth century, the muzzle loader became a relic or, at best, a piece from by-gone days for a museum.

Chapter 4

Other Guns

Muskets

THE FAME OF Pennsylvania gunsmiths rests to a large degree on their production of rifles; however, it would be an unfortunate omission if their other products did not receive some attention in this survey. This supplementary addition does not presume to include mention of all the oddities and curious weapons which occasionally are found in collections, but will be confined to general areas such as muskets, multiple barrel guns; pistols and fowling pieces.

Before dealing specifically with muskets, the reader should be aware that some of the guns made in Pennsylvania in the eighteenth century are usually called a semi-military type. These smoothbore guns have several qualities of the musket and certain characteristics commonly found in fowling pieces. The exterior form of the barrel is round or octagon-to-round and the length varies from 40 inches to 48 inches. They rarely have rear sights but frequently have a sight on the front end of the barrel.

In the author's collection is such a gun, with an octagon-to-round barrel, 48 inches in length, without a sight, and with a flat spot under the barrel that might have been provision for a bayonet lug. Barrels rarely have proof marks and the finish on them seems to be the work of a provincial gunsmith rather than European

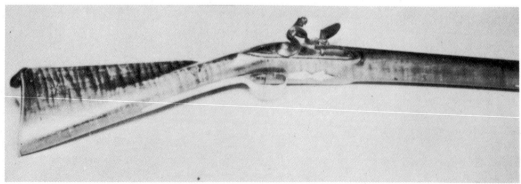

Henry J. Kauffman

PLATE 81

Semi-military gun with flint lock and full stock of curly maple. This gun resembles a musket in size and weight, but there is no provision for using a bayonet on it.

90

professional. Some of these guns are stocked in walnut; but fruit wood and maple are also used, which suggests an American origin. Some have small wrists and high combs like an English Brown Bess, but lack other characteristics of that famous arm. The hardware is usually brass throughout and closely resembles what is found on eighteenth century Pennsylvania fowling pieces. It appears that this gun was made to kill either men or game, and it probably did either very successfully.

The picture of musket-making in Pennsylvania in the eighteenth century is quite nebulous, but because of ordnance records and better survival of arms, the nineteenth century can be discussed with more certainty.

Every schoolboy knows about the problems the Committees of Safety encountered in their attempts to have arms manufactured in America throughout the Revolution. Some correspondence between the Committees and the gunsmiths has been preserved; but few, if any, guns have been found that can be attributed to the men named in the correspondence. A typical example of this situation is found in a letter written to Joel Ferree, who is recorded as a gunsmith in Lancaster County as early as 1758:

> Resolved that a messenger be sent to Joel Ferree of Lancaster County with a letter from the Committee requesting him immediately to complete the Guns wrote for as patterns, and to know how many he can furnish of the same kind and at what price.
> *Minutes of the Provincial Council of Pennsylvania, 1852 Vol. X, page 290.*

Fortunately, the author knows of two muskets which were made in Pennsylvania in the eighteenth century. One of these guns is on display at the location of the Lancaster County Historical Society. The lock of this gun is signed by Wm. Henry, who was armourer to Braddock on his ill-fated expedition to Western Pennsylvania, and was a gunsmith in Lancaster. Stylistically, it is a copy, or closely related, to the British Brown Bess of the period. It has a round barrel, a walnut stock, a long tapering wrist and a high comb. It is difficult to name a specific date when this gun was made, but there seems to be complete agreement among in-

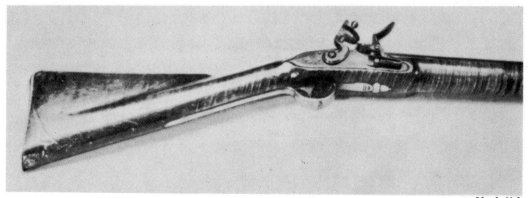

Lloyd Nolt

PLATE 82

This gun was probably made in the late eighteenth century to be used as a musket or a fowling piece. The wrist is small and long and is obviously styled from a Brown Bess, however the stock of curly maple suggests production in Pennsylvania in the late eighteenth century.

formed collectors that this musket was made by Henry about the time of the American Revolution.

Doubtless other signed guns and many unsigned ones have survived that were used in the American Revolution. Very few are alike; and many are equipped with odd pieces of hardware, which indicates that they were made of parts from more than one gun. An attractive gun is illustrated that appears to have been made after the Revolution, but in the eighteenth century.

Pennsylvania gunsmiths seem to have had their share of contract musket making from the 1795 model until the conclusion of the Civil War. Men like Evans and Wickham seem to have been primarily musket makers, while Tryon, of Philadelphia, was producing both types over a long period of time. Dickert and Graeff, in Lancaster, are known to have made a few muskets, and a military-type pistol has survived that was made by Peter Brong of the same city. A complete and detailed record of musket making in Pennsylvania can be found in books devoted to the history of Military Arms.

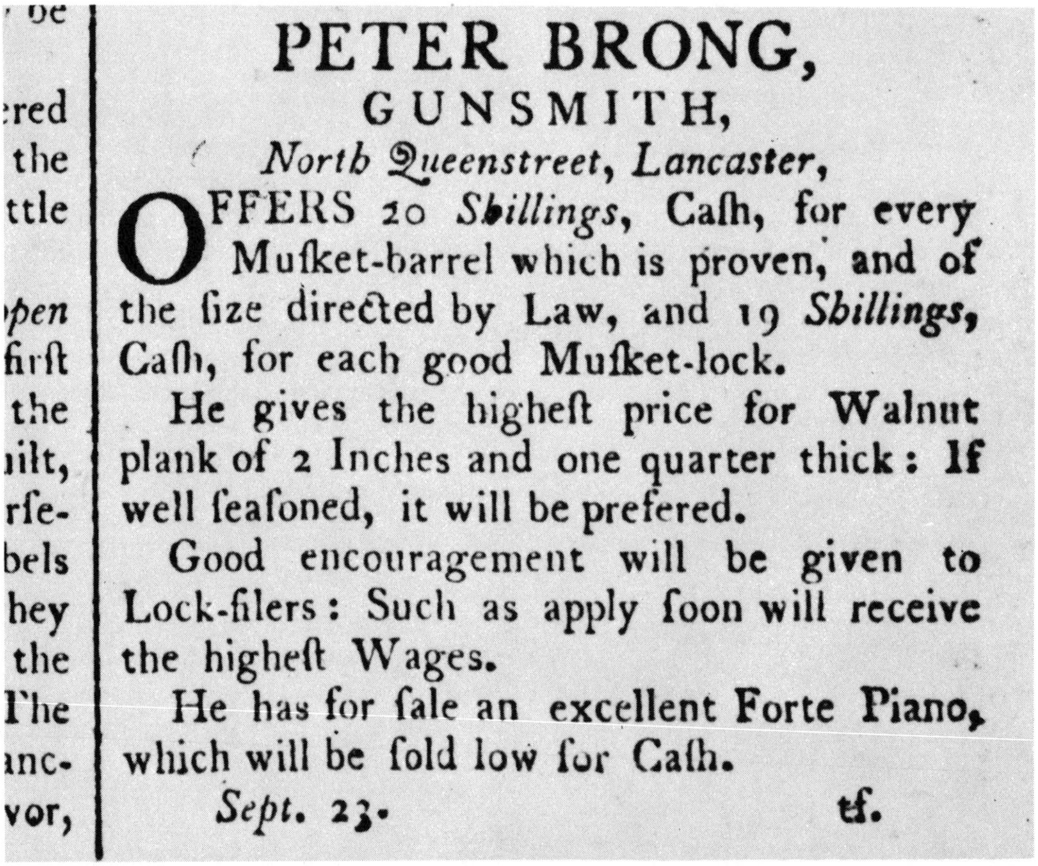

PETER BRONG,
GUNSMITH,
North Queenstreet, Lancaster,

OFFERS 20 *Shillings*, Cash, for every Musket-barrel which is proven, and of the size directed by Law, and 19 *Shillings*, Cash, for each good Musket-lock.

He gives the highest price for Walnut plank of 2 Inches and one quarter thick: If well seasoned, it will be prefered.

Good encouragement will be given to Lock-filers: Such as apply soon will receive the highest Wages.

He has for sale an excellent Forte Piano, which will be sold low for Cash.

Sept. 23.   tf.

Lancaster County Historical Society

PLATE 83

This newspaper advertisement of Peter Brong appeared in the *Lancaster Intelligencer and Weekly Advertiser* on September 23, 1801. It is evident that Lancaster gunsmiths made muskets in addition to their well-established business of rifle making.

Pistols

In comparison with the rifle and the musket, the pistol was a "late-comer" in the arms production of Pennsylvania gunsmiths. In the mid-eighteenth century a few wealthy gentlemen probably owned pistols; but the demand could easily be met by imports from England, where pistols had reached a high stage of development at that time. The pistols they bought were about 12 to 15 inches long over-all; they were full-stocked with walnut wood, and had round, or partially round barrels, which were fastened by pins to the stocks. The mountings were of silver or brass with a respousse treatment in the lock-bolt plate and the mask butt cap. The face of the lock plate and the hammer were slightly rounded and were sometimes engraved with appropriate scrolls or other patterns.

It was this type of pistol that American officers are believed to have carried in the Revolution. A pair of pistols of this general type is said to have belonged to George Washington and is now in the West Point Museum.

A pair of such pistols, made by Fredrick Zorger of York, Pennsylvania, is exhibited in the Winterthur Museum, at Winterthur, Delaware. They are stocked in walnut, have silver mountings, and a very delicate pierced pattern in the lock-bolt plate. The round barrels taper in the traditional manner and have "Yorktown" engraved on the top near the breech. The plain handmade locks are quite incongruous to the balance of the workmanship, but they give added weight to their Pennsylvania pedigree. Fredrick Zorger is known to have lived in York at the time

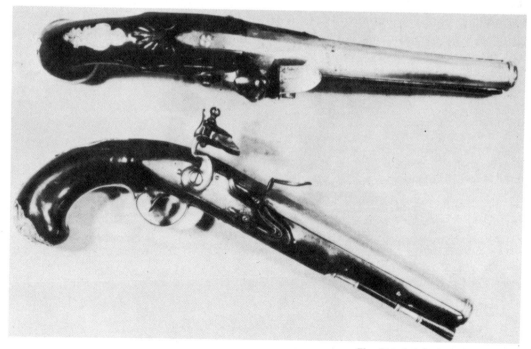

The Historical Society of Pennsylvania

PLATE 84

Pair of pistols with flint locks marked Wm. Henry, full stocks of walnut, silver mountings, mask butt caps, and brass (cannon) barrels with Nazareth engraved on the top facet of the barrel.

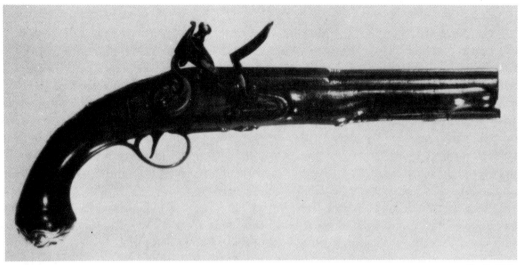

S. E. *Dyke*

PLATE 85

Pistol with flint lock, full stock of walnut, silver mountings, octagonal-to-round rifled barrel. Although the general appearance of this pistol suggests a sophisticated English style, it has some provincial details which indicate it was made in Pennsylvania.

Continental Congress met there, and these pistols are thought to have been made for one of the visiting dignitaries.

Another interesting early pair of pistols is owned by the Historical Society of Pennsylvania in Philadelphia. These also are stocked in walnut, have brass cannon barrels and silver mountings. There is some bas-relief carving around the breech tang, and they have mask butt plates. The front surfaces of the hammer and the lock plate are slightly convex. "W. Henry" is engraved on the lock plate, and "Nazareth" on the top of the barrel near the breech.

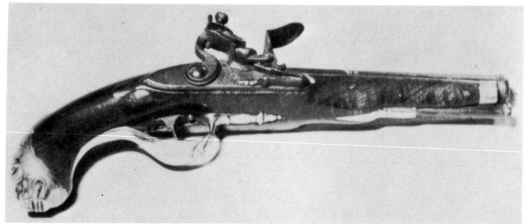

S. E. *Dyke*

PLATE 86

Pistol with flint lock, walnut stock, brass mountings, and octagonal-to-round barrel, 7 inches long with Wm. Antes engraved in script letters on the top facet of the barrel.

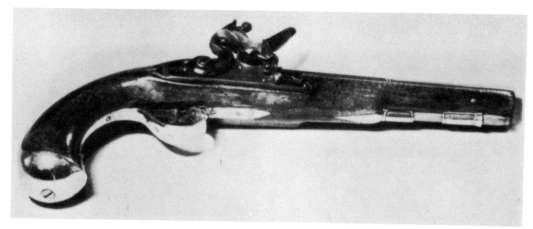

PLATE 87

S. E. Dyke

Pistol with flint lock, maple stock, brass mountings, and octagonal-to-round barrel 8½ inches long with H. Mauger engraved on the top facet of the barrel in script letters.

This pistol was probably made by Mauger in the last quarter of the eighteenth century. The brass barrel is unusually thick and the caliber is about 30.

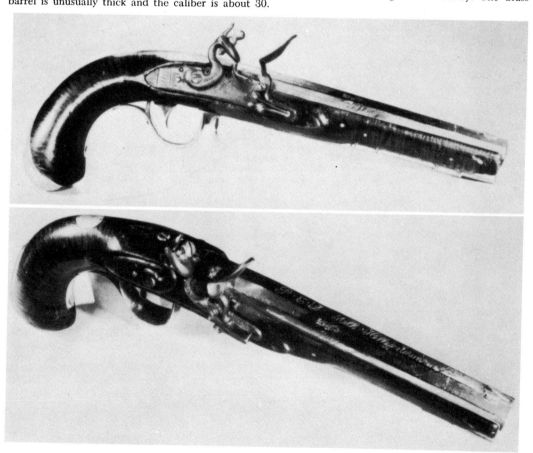

PLATE 88

C. M. Smith

Pistol with flint lock, maple stock, brass mountings, silver thumb-piece, and octagonal brass barrel with P. & D. Moll, Hellertown on the top facet of the barrel.

This is a typical product of the Molls at Hellertown. Sometimes they are found in pairs, but they are becoming very rare.

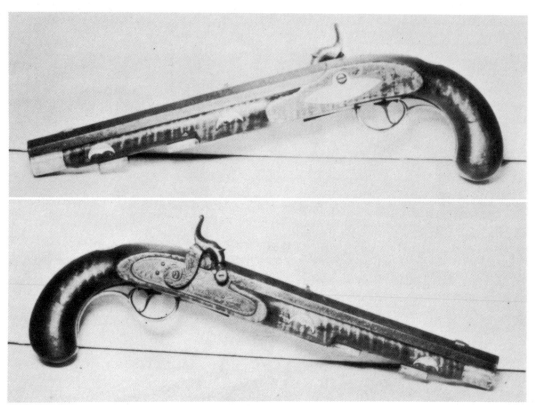

J. T. ·Cooper

PLATE 89

Pistol with percussion lock, full stock of curly maple, brass and mountings, and octagonal barrel marked J. L. in script letters on the top facet of the barrel.

Although this pistol was made in the percussion era, its form is very similar to pistols made in the late flintlock era. Long is known to have used this form of the lock-bolt plate on most of his rifles.

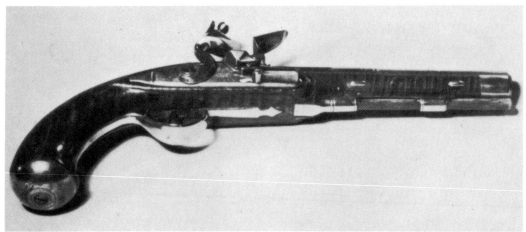

S. E. Dyke

PLATE 90

Pistol with flint lock and John Armstrong engraved in script letters on the lock plate, full stock of curly maple, brass mountings, brass inlay, octagonal-to-round barrel with John Armstrong engraved in script letters on the top facet of the barrel.

The signature of the maker on the barrel and the lock of this pistol is one of its attractive features. The pierced lock-bolt plate and the brass inlay around the breech tang are also decorative details of unusual merit.

A similar pistol in the Dyke Collection has an octagon-to-round barrel which is rifled; it is stocked in walnut, and has silver mountings. The face of the lock and the hammer are flat and "Cowmeadows" is engraved on it. There are doubtless many others, but these five are representative of the early pistols that were made in Pennsylvania.

Although one early example is known, by J. P. Beck, it was not until late in the eighteenth century that the Kentucky pistol assumed its true provincial form. The change probably occurred when the country gunsmiths tried to make an arm that was compatible with the rifle that they were making. Curly maple was substituted for walnut, full-octagonal rifled barrels and all brass mountings were used, with a very simple rounded butt plate. The small pistol locks and lock-bolt plates were scaled-down models of those that were used on rifles. The ferrule on the fore-stock was often dropped and the ramrod pipes were usually of very simple pattern. The barrels were sometimes of brass and were always heavier than their British cousins. The Molls of Hellertown were famous for their octagonal brass barrels.

The signed pistols which are found in collections suggest that most of them were made in the late eighteenth and early nineteenth centuries. Men like Henry Albright, the Molls, John Derr, Haeffer, Rupp, Mauger, and others were working at about

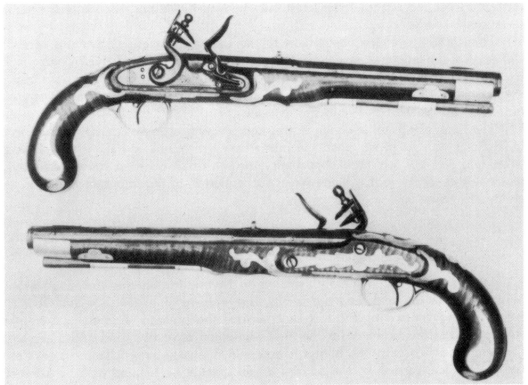

Wees White

PLATE 91

Pair of pistols with flint locks, full stocks marked P. W., of curly maple, silver mountings, silver inlays, octagonal barrels with P. W. on the top facet of the barrels. These pistols are unique in their style and condition. They are outstanding examples of Pennsylvania pistols with stocks of curly maple and inlays of silver.

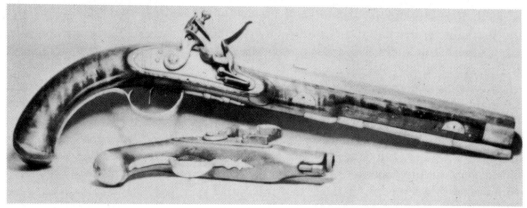

Henry J. Kauffman and John Charles

PLATE 92

Two pistols with flint locks, brass mounted. These two pistols are probably examples of the biggest and smallest pistols made in Pennsylvania.

that time. Some percussion pistols were made, but little change was made in the pattern of the stock. The later pistols usually had simple mountings, were very sparsely engraved, and, as a rule, were less attractive than their predecessors. A pistol by Joe Long is one of the latest ones known, but it has essentially the same form used in earlier times.

There were, of course, exceptions to the common pattern. A few are carved; and some of the late ones have silver inlays, which are quite attractive. A pair made by Peter White have a lot of "jewelry" on them, and there are similar ones by lesser-known makers. Some are large—one in the author's collection is 17 inches over-all— but others are as short as five inches over-all.

The Kentucky pistol is a unique arm and is a very attractive one for the collector to acquire. Most of the good specimens have gravitated into a few outstanding collections and there is little opportunity for the small collector to buy one at a reasonably small figure. Everyone seems to be alerted to the importance and desirability of owning one.

Multiple Barrel

After guns became generally available in Europe for hunting and numbers of hunters took to the fields and the woods, the problem of having a second shot at game that was missed by the first shot became the concern of hunters. A simple solution solved this problem for the men who could have two guns and a servant. One gun was carried by the hunter, who could discharge it at a moment's notice; the second one, carried by the servant, could quickly be handed to his master, if a second shot were necessary. At such times, the servant took the discharged gun and quickly reloaded it.

The second shot dilemma was later solved by a number of gunsmiths who made multiple-barrel guns. Most of them were guns with two barrels and were called

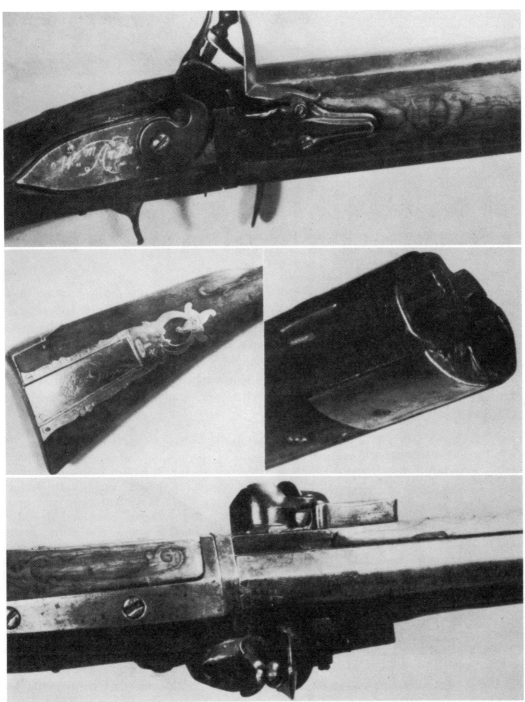

PLATE 93

Double rifle with flint lock, octagonal barrels, brass mountings, walnut stock, Wm. Antes engraved on the lock plate.

The walnut stock, the flat butt plate, and the style of the patch box are evidences that this is one of the earliest double rifles made in Pennsylvania. The barrels swing on a swivel so that they can be alternately fired by the one lock. The figure carved in the stock in front of the lock is thought to be an Indian. Similar figures appear on other rifles made in Pennsylvania. The trigger guard is obviously missing.

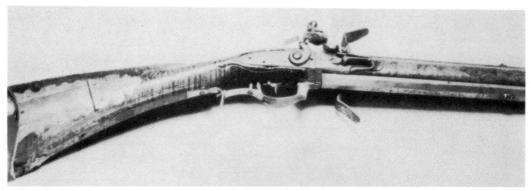

Joe Kindig, Jr.

PLATE 94

Double rifle with original flint lock, stock of curly maple with fine designs carved in bas-relief, brass mountings, octagonal barrels 39 inches long marked John Moll in script letters.

Double rifles with stocks carved in bas-relief are extremely scarce. Berks and Northampton Counties seem to be where most of the men lived who made early double rifles.

double guns. It appears that this term was applied from the earliest times until the late nineteenth century, when Pittsburgh manufacturers continued to use it in their titles but referred to them as "over-and-under" in their descriptive literature.

Just when the first double gun was made in Pennsylvania will doubtless never be known; however, one gun is known that might well have been made in the 1770's. Comparison with a gun dated in that era indicates that it was made about that time. This gun is owned by the Kansas State Historical Society, and they report the following specifications for the gun:

William Antes Double Barrel Sporting Gun (sic.)
(Flintlock) Condition fair. Stock is of two pieces, rear being 16″, forward section being of equal length with the barrels which is 40″, over-all length of the gun is 56″. Weight 13 lbs. Barrels are of octagonal shape with straight (rifled) bore. It is approximately 50 caliber. Plain brass butt plate and brass patch box engraved with scroll and floral design. Carved head and shoulders of person located near each lock on forestock. The name "Wm Antes" is engraved in old script on the plate near the breech and again on the top of only one barrel near the lock. Each barrel has own separate lock which is fired by a single trigger after the desired barrel is turned into position. The trigger guard is missing. Given to the Society in 1917 by E. C. Fox of Fort Hayes, Kansas.

A survey of the products of Pennsylvania gunsmiths indicates that double guns were made for a period of one hundred years. Leonard Reedy, a famous Dauphin County gunsmith, made one in 1826 and charged $40.00 for it. A fine early one made by John Moll is in the Kindig Collection; one in the Dyke Collection is marked A. A. and attributed to Adam Angstadt; and a number are known that were made by Daniel Boyer in Orwigsburg, Pennsylvania.

In the percussion era the form of these guns changed a bit. Some continued to have the swivel feature, while in others the barrels were stationary and the gun was equipped with two locks. The rib of wood was also frequently dropped and the barrels were held together by a brass strip, which was brazed to them where they were joined. The substitution of a smooth barrel for a rifled one was also favored

Herman Dean

PLATE 95

Rifle with two barrels (side-by-side), with percussion locks, full stock of curly maple, brass mountings, set triggers, octagonal barrels marked Thos. Oldham.

Although the swivel double barrel rifle was a common product of Pennsylvania gunsmiths, this type of rifle was not a common product and only a few can be found in collections of Pennsylvania rifles.

and it is quite common to find late ones with the two types of barrels. Bores became smaller, as they did on most muzzle-loading guns; and the barrels became shorter.

One of the last and most prolific makers of multiple-barrel guns was named Jacob Harder, who worked at Lock Haven, Pennsylvania. Harder is reported to have employed eight gunsmiths at one time; and, in addition to making double guns, he made double, double (four barrels) guns and a number of single guns. His neighbor, Joe Long, is also known to have made at least one fine double gun.

The death knell for double muzzle-loading guns was probably struck in the Pittsburgh area. Brown and Hirth advertise them in their catalogue, where they are described as follows:

> Double rifles, over and under iron barrels, well put together, patent breech, set triggers, curly maple stock, brass mounting, patch box, well finished . . $35.00

This advertisement indicates that the term "over-and-under" was used at that time; and a Great Western Gun Works advertisement calls them double barrel guns in the title of their advertisement, but over-and-under in their description of the guns.

J. T. Herron

PLATE 96

Double rifle with percussion lock, set triggers, curly maple stock, checquered wrist, plain brass mountings, octagonal barrels 31 inches long which swivel at the breech. The brilliantly colored ramrod is a replacement.

J. H. Harder made many double guns, at least quite a large number have survived.

Fowling Pieces

It has been previously pointed out that the eighteenth century, semi-military, smoothbore guns made in Pennsylvania could be used as a musket or as a fowling piece. This hybrid gun was very useful to men who needed a cheap versatile gun and could not afford the more expensive rifles. The rich men of Philadelphia and the inland towns placed their orders for rifles with Pennsylvania gunsmiths, but the absence of early fowlers suggests that they were imported from England. The dependence of wealthy Americans on England for luxury items indicates that they probably bought their fowling pieces there, for English craftsmen were making the finest ones in the world at that time.

The mid-eighteenth century English fowling piece was superior to all others. After the invention of the flintlock about 1630 and its subsequent refinement, gun-smithing in England not only came abreast of other European craftsmen, but surpassed them in the making of fine fowling pieces. Their guns had long slender barrels; they were gracefully stocked in walnut wood; they had small efficient flint locks; the mountings were delicate and beautifully engraved, and the over-all weight of the gun was only five to six pounds. A barrel by John Smart, of London, weighed only 2 pounds 4¼ ounces. The improvement of arms created the sport of "shooting on the wing" and the invention, in the late 18th century, of forming shot by dropping it a great distance, rather than by tumbling it or casting it in molds, made it an attractive sport to all who could afford it.

The demand for guns was great in Pennsylvania from the time of settlement until after the Revolution, and it is not likely that many true fowling pieces were made here until the pressure was off in the 1780's. When gunsmiths did get started making fowlers, they had the fine English specimens to copy and there is a marked resemblence between the two guns. The earliest documented evidence of fowlers being made in Pennsylvania is an advertisement of Thomas Palmer which appeared in the March 7, 1773 edition of the *Pennsylvania Gazette*. It is also interesting to note that Palmer was making rifles in Philadelphia at that time. There are extremely few data available about gun production in Philadelphia in the eighteenth century.

THOMAS PALMER Gun Smith

At his shop, the North Side of Market-street, between Fourth and Fifth-streets,

Has for Sale, a quantity of well made rifles, of different lengths and sizes of bores, which he will insure to the Purchasers, to be as good and handsomely fitted up as any in America; he likewise makes Fowling Pieces, of different sizes, such as have been approved by Gentlemen of this City. All persons that will please to favor him with their custom, shall be served with Dispatch and Care.

N. B. He repairs old Guns in the most careful Manner.

The Pennsylvania fowler of the late eighteenth century had a long barrel in the earlier English tradition; the barrel was part round and part octagonal; the stock was slender and graceful; the mountings were engraved, and the earlier shield

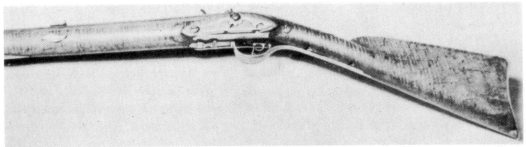

PLATE 97

Fowling piece with flint lock, full stock of curly maple, brass mountings, and octagonal to round barrel 47 inches long with H. Pflieger engraved in script letters on the top facet of the barrel.

The trigger on this gun is evidence of its fine craftsmanship, and the lock-bolt plate with four piercings is a very unusual feature of the gun. Although pierced lock-bolt plates were used over most of Pennsylvania, they are rare and a very attractive feature on any gun.

thumbpiece of the English guns was replaced by a simple circle or ellipse on which the owner's initials were engraved. There is a rumor that these thumbpieces and inlay were made of coins. The writer has an example in his collection of a coin, elongated into an ellipse, and still retaining the milled edge of the coin. Beautiful fowlers have been made by men like J. P. Beck, Peter Berry, Adam Ernst, George Eyster, Martin Frey, Henry Pickel, Issac Hains, Fredrick Sell and others, which are fine specimens of the gun maker's art. The carving on the cheek side of the butts is equal to the finest found on rifles, and the workmanship is superior throughout.

The fowling pieces of the later percussion period are less attractive than the earlier type. Melchoir Fordney continues the early traditions of craftsmanship in his fowling pieces; but men like the Drepperds, the Gumpfs, and others made plain guns which were functionally good but unattractive in appearance. The work finally degenerated into the single- and double-barrel shotguns of the late percussion and early breech-loading period.

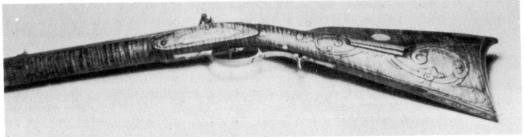

PLATE 98

Fowling piece with flint lock, full stock of curly maple, brass mountings, silver inlay on the cheek piece, and octagonal-to-round barrel 44 inches long with F. Sell engraved in script letters on the top facet of the barrel.

The constant use of a large C scroll in the carving of Fredrick Sell suggests that he frequently used the same design, but a close examination of his work shows that there are always some small variations in his over-all patterns. The carving on the stock is evidence of Sell's superior ability as a carver, and his lock-bolt plate is also engraved in his usual superb manner.

Match Guns

Because match guns were used primarily at shooting matches, some consideration might be given to the historical background of these interesting events, many being held today in various parts of America. A few excerpts from *The Citizen and His Shooting Festivals* by Gutav Freytag will give some insight into the size and importance of these affairs, as they were held in Europe from the time of the longbow, through the popularity of the crossbow, and long after firearms replaced both these early weapons of warfare and sport.

It has been a German custom, older than Christianity, to celebrate the awakening of life and nature in May. This has always been a martial feast, in which the fundamental idea of the old heathen faith, the victory of the awakening divinities of nature over the demons of winter, was dramatically represented. In the rising cities it was the warlike youth of the freeborn citizens who led the May sports, and in the Hohenstaufen time these sports assumed the form of fashionable knightly festivals.

During this century (14th) there was a great change in the life and constitution of the German cities; the patrician youth with their knightly customs were no longer the representatives of the power of the burgher class, the commonalty of the city already began to feel themselves masters, and their weapon, the cross bow, gained the prizes.

About the year 1400, firearms began to be heard at the prize shooting festivals. At Augsburg, in 1429, hand guns and muskets were used, and guns with small lead balls. In 1426 the first prize shooting with arquebuses and muskets was held; afterwards the hand gun in its various forms prevailed. The practical Swiss were among the first to give preference to firearms. As early as 1472, at the great prize shooting at Zurich, only guns were announced; after that, at important festivals, both weapons had prizes assigned, but at smaller ones frequently only firearms. The gun of the prize-shooter, up to 1600, was the smooth hand-gun for one ounce balls, with a straight or crooked stock,—all grooves were forbidden.

The preparation of the city began some months before the feast. The lodgings were prepared for the guests; the safety of the city was provided for; the goldsmiths worked in silver the prize cups and vases, and struck also medals and show specimens; the tailors stitched incessantly at new festival dresses for halberdiers, pages of honor, and motely personages; the shield painters drew arms, garlands, and ciphers, on more than a hundred standards.
On the morning of the festival the "Pritchmeister" with the city band went through the streets, calling strangers to a meeting at the shooting-ground. The givers of the festival marched in solemn procession, the "Pritchmeister" in front; behind, the markers, equally in new dresses and the colours of the city, their marking rods in their hands; then the trumpeters and fifers, next the dignitaries and marksmen of the city, followed by a train of young boys of the city, all dressed in festive attire.

This delightful description of old shooting matches tells of all the work and frivolity that was connected with them. The competition was keen and the honors were great for the best marksman. At the end he was escorted to a platform, with trumpets blaring, where the prize was handed to him by a beautiful maiden. This reward he carried to his home city. He was feted and honored there for bringing distinction to his homeland. The unfortunate poor marksman of the meet was given a small pig as a prize and marched through the crowd, carrying a banner of sack cloth.

There was ample entertainment and activity for non-shooters at these meets. Local merchants displayed their wares and the booths of pewterers were among the favorites for many years. There was bowling on the green, for which modest prizes were sometimes awarded by merchants or local wealthy citizens. Gambling booths went unnoticed by the police and spirited boys tried to climb a greased pole to get a cock that was fastened to the top.

It is extremely doubtful if any such extravagant affairs were ever operated in Pennsylvania, although many of the early residents doubtless had attended them in Europe. The earliest reference to a proposed match (found by the author) is a letter written by a Moravian missionary, named Feisberger, from a Moravian mission at Friedenshutten, near Wyalusing on the upper Susquehanna River. The letter is dated February 11, 1766.

> Three white people from Shomoko wanted to start a shooting match here; however, the Indians referred them to us and we refused it, telling them that we did not like such things here.

There is much talk about old-time shooting matches in Pennsylvania, but the author has not been able to find any information about them in the eighteenth century. Nor are there any guns of the eighteenth century that appear to have been made for match shooting. The absence of match guns does not preclude the possibility of match shooting, however, for it is likely that some was done with the ordinary rifle or smoothbore gun.

One of the distingushing features of a Pennsylvania match gun is an unusually heavy barrel. It is obvious that these massive barrels could not be formed by welding; so it must be presumed that the bore was drilled through a solid bar of metal, and later rifled in the traditional method of performing the latter operation. Some of these barrels weigh as much as twenty to thirty pounds and the forestock must be supported on a bench when used for match shooting. This procedure of supporting the gun has led some people to refer to the type as "bench rifles."

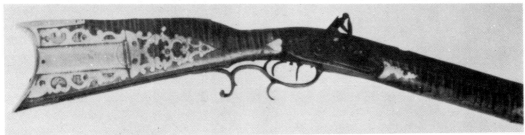

S. E. Dyke

PLATE 99

Rifle with flint lock, full stock of curly maple, brass mountings, silver inlays, set triggers, and octagonal barrel.

The massive size of the barrel of this rifle indicates it was made for match shooting. This is doubtless one of the most handsome match rifles made by a Pennsylvania gunsmith. The numerous piercings in the patch box make it comparable to the fine patch boxes on sporting rifles.

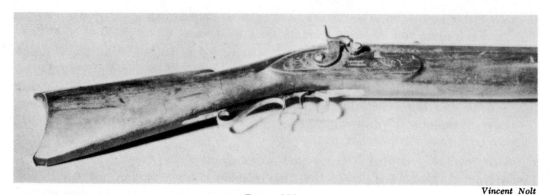

Vincent Nolt

PLATE 100

Match rifle with percussion lock marked J. Fordney, Lancaster. The plain maple stock has brass mountings and is unusually big to accommodate the heavy barrel. The rifle weighs twenty pounds.

Except for their oversize barrels the pattern of match guns usually follows that of contemporary rifles. The mountings are made of brass and usually include a patch box. The workmanship is usually of average quality, although some match guns are shown which are beautiful specimens of the gun maker's art. Match guns are eagerly sought by some "shooters" but because of their graceless form many collectors do not own one.

Chapter 5

Locks of
Pennsylvania Rifles

NO PART OF THE Pennsylvania rifle has puzzled the collecting fraternity more than have the locks, and unfortunately not much has been done to clarify matters. Many locks do not have on them the name to assist in identifying the lock maker. If a name is found on the lock, it frequently is presumed to be the name of the gunsmith who made the gun; and the confusion is often heightened by the fact that the original lock has been changed to a percussion lock, or that a percussion lock was substituted for an earlier flintlock. Even the appearance of the same name on both the lock plate and the barrel is not proof that the gunsmith did not buy a plain lock and engrave his name on it. It is, however, an attractive feature to have the same name on the lock and the barrel, and the possibility is that the gunsmith made both if the name of the one man appears on the lock and the barrel.

Although the ability to identify the gun-lock maker is important and interesting, it might be pointed out that of all the parts of a gun the lock is the part least likely to have been made by the gunsmith. This condition is due to the fact that by the time guns were being made in Pennsylvania, the European gun trade was becoming specialized and there could have been a steady flow of ready-made locks from places like Birmingham and London. Also of secondary importance is the fact that the steel needed in making locks was a scarce item in the colonies and required in its working a skill that iron did not require. The small size of the lock also favored importation, for it could be transported in large quantities more easily than could stocks or barrels. Although these statements might seem to minimize the importance of the gun-lock maker, the fact remains that the lock is an integral part of a gun and that its maker and condition can substantially raise or lower the attractiveness of a gun.

Before the check list of gun-lock makers is examined, some consideration may profitably be given to the evolution of gun-lock mechanisms prior to their use on the Kentucky rifle. The guns made in Pennsylvania during the eighteenth century were equipped with the most refined and efficient type of flintlock known to the trade. It was reasonably small, was simple in construction, was attractive in appearance, and underwent practically no major change until it was discarded for percussion ignition about 1830.

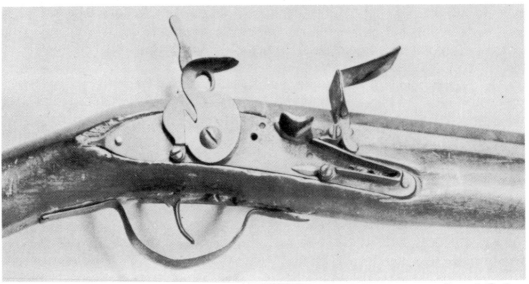

PLATE 101

The lock of this late seventeenth century New England gun has a "dog" safety catch which is rarely found on guns made in America. The lock is seven inches long and has three screws to hold it in place.

Full appreciation of the details of the flintlock might be facilitated by a backward look to the dog lock which preceded it and was used on earlier guns in America that were made in New England. The invention from which the form and function of the dog lock evolved was the combining of the steel and the pan so that the combination, called the frizzen, worked automatically instead of manually. This change caused the hammer and the frizzen to be above and very near the pan when the gun was loaded. Thus it was difficult to prime or charge the pan, and the only alternative was to move the hammer. The hammer could not be safely moved to a full-cock position, for then it could easily be tipped and the gun discharged at a very inopportune time. The solution was the creation of a position called the half-cock or safety, which prevented the hammer from crowding the pan and also made accidental firing virtually impossible.

To hold the hammer in safety or half-cock position, a hook or "dog" was attached to the outside of the lock plate, positively engaging the hammer in a semi-released position. After the gun was fully charged, the hammer was drawn into full cock position and the dog was automatically disengaged. Because this contrivance (the dog) was large, cumbersome, and time consuming to make, lock makers soon eliminated it by filing a notch on the tumbler to hold the hammer in half-cock position. For awhile both the dog catch and the safety notch were used, but the efficiency of the safety notch and its ease of construction made the use of the dog catch unnecessary.

The evolution of the safety notch in the tumbler brought the flintlock mechanism into its simplest form. The first notch, or safety, was filed at such an acute angle that when the sear was engaged, it could only with difficulty be removed by pressure upon the trigger. The second notch, or full cock, was in the shape of a right angle and offered little resistance to such pressure; this arrangement permitted the gun to be fired by applying only a slight pressure. Because of excessive wear on old guns these two notches often look similar, but originally they were quite different.

It was this simple flintlock that was used on the first guns made in Pennsylvania. The inside of the locks had only four parts: the sear, the tumbler, the sear spring, and the main spring. The later addition of a bridle from the tumbler to the sear improved lock operation and promoted evenness of wear on the parts. On the outside of the lock plate were the hammer, pan, frizzen, and frizzen spring. Later a bridle was added from the pan to the frizzen spring screw to increase rigidity and minimize uneven wear.

The simplicity of early Pennsylvania guns was very attractive, although the engraved lock plates were slightly incongruous with the simple arms on which they were placed. The lock plates were pleasantly rectangular in shape, and the rear terminated in an attractive tail pattern. The face of the lock plate was flat or slightly convex and was often engraved with the Rococo scrolls which were then popular abroad. The pan was round on the bottom with a matching frizzen, and the frizzen spring was often engraved or filed with decorative patterns that were compatible with the design on the lock plate. The hammer had the shape of a capital S, had a rounded face, and was appropriately engraved. The bottom edge of the lock plate was straight or slightly concave to conform with the pattern of the stock, as was customary in early locks.

It should be emphasized that the early locks imported from Europe were used on Pennsylvania guns which were similar to European guns. The simple form of the guns, their lack of profuse ornamentation, and their curly maple stocks were frequently the only means of identifying their Pennsylvania manufacture. However, as the Pennsylvania pattern started to evolve, the pattern of the locks also changed. Some of the early engraved locks continued to be used, but throughout the second-half of the eighteenth century a flintlock frequently described as "hand-made" was used.

Kauffman Photo

PLATE 102

Locks with engraved lock plates like this one were used on Pennsylvania rifles about the middle of the eighteenth century. Some of the lock plates were flat and others were convex like this one. Some were made by Ketland and signed on the inside of the plate.

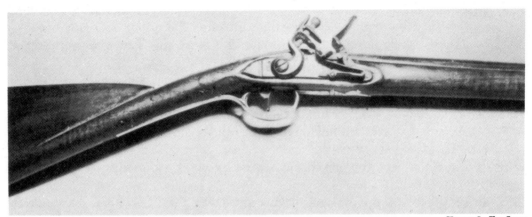

Henry J. Kauffman

PLATE 103
Typical "hand-made" flintlock used on rifles and fowling pieces in Pennsylvania throughout the second-half of the eighteenth century.

"Hand-made" is a vague term which has come into common usage for a number of reasons. In the first place, these locks are remarkably compatible with many of the guns on which they are used, and it seems reasonable to assume that "hand-made" locks should be used on "hand-made" guns. Most of these locks are long and slender with no ornamentation other than a few concave grooves filed across the lock near the tail or rear of the lock plate. The slight variations in the size and arrangement of these grooves might lead an observer to conclude that they were filed by hand. Rarely engraved they seem to be perfect examples of provincial lock making. That their pattern differs from that of the English locks which preceded and succeeded them also suggests local manufacture. That they were unsigned, except for some initials inside the lock plate, conforms with the general practice of the early gunsmiths not to sign their guns.

Attention should be focused on the fact that throughout the last-half of the eighteenth century quite a few Ketland locks were also used on the guns made in Pennsylvania. Although these locks are simple in form and often lack ornamentation, they are definitely different from the so-called "hand-made" pattern. They can be identified by the appearance of the name on the outside or the inside of the lock plate.

The use of European locks, probably English, in the early part of the eighteenth century can be easily understood, for there could have been an easy flow of locks from England to an English colony in America. It is also an established fact that Penn's colony was rapidly filling with people from central Europe, among whom were some gunsmiths. Now considerable weight is given to the idea that the so-called "hand-made" locks were made in central Europe, perhaps Germany. The German gunsmiths in Pennsylvania would obviously prefer importations from the Continent rather than from England, and there is much evidence that they brought small articles with them from the homeland and imported others after their arrival in America. Gun locks were small and could easily have been imported in quantities large enough to satisfy the German gunsmiths.

Perhaps the most conclusive evidence of the German origin of these locks can be found in a newspaper advertisement which appeared in the Lancaster Journal July 1, 1797.

PHILIP SCHAEFFER
North Queen Street, Lancaster, next door to the house in which John Miller Esq. late sheriff formerly lived.
Has just received
An additional and general assortment of ironmongery, cutlery, sadlery and brass wares, also painters coulors, clock and window glass, lamp, linseed, and best boiled oils,—the first quality of American and English gunpowder, shat and bar lead, American and English vices, best English and German gun locks, also James River twist tobacco by the cask or single pound.
All of which he will sell at the most reduced price.

On January 13, 1798, Schaeffer ran a similar advertisement, but "Ketland locks" was substituted for "English locks." This advertisement does prove that German gun locks were used in Lancaster; but it obviously does not prove that the "hand-made" pattern was German. However, it might be said that the circumstantial evidence indicates that the plain-type of lock plate was made in Germany.

It is also interesting to note that as late as 1816 an advertisement in a Pittsburgh newspaper includes German gun locks.

HARDWARE JUST RECEIVED
KETLAND Gun-locks by the dozen
German   do do   do
German looking glasses
Brass Andirons, assorted sizes
Iron and brass head shovel and tongs
One case gilt and plated buttons, assorted
Likewise on hand a general assortment of
CUTLERY AND SADLERY, Assorted
WHOLESALE AND RETAIL, BY
Benjamin Darlington
Third Street, two doors from Market
Pittsburgh, Nov. 29, 1816
(*The Pittsburgh Gazette,* Nov. 29, 1816)

Although the plain type of lock plate was used by some gunsmiths in the nineteenth century, most of the guns which were made after the turn of the century had locks that were made in England or in America. The late use of earlier patterns can be explained by the fact that gunsmiths who worked in the fringe areas were less sensitive to change and fashion than were those who worked in urban areas like Lancaster, Reading, and York. At this time English names such as Robbins, Allport, and Parker, were appearing on flintlock plates that were smaller and had a different shape from that of their predecessors. Little could be changed at the front of the lock, where a projection was necessary to support the mainspring. The narrow tail, which most eighteenth century locks had at the rear, was made wider and was finally discarded for a rounded end which was easier to make and easier to fit into the lock mortise. The locks with the wide tails were engraved in geometric patterns resembling a series of arrow points. The locks with the rounded ends

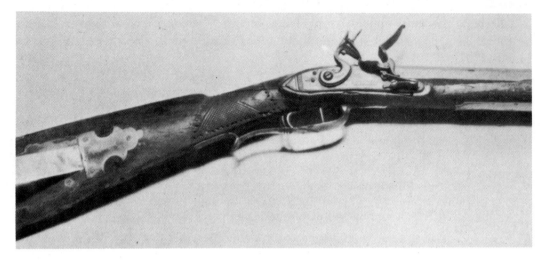

PLATE 104
Typical flintlock used on Pennsylvania rifles after 1800.

had scrolls or hunting scenes engraved behind the hammer. Between the hammer and the pan, floral motifs were often engraved, and straight lines sometimes radiated from the pan or the lock screw. In this area the maker's name usually appears and often the city in which he worked, as James Golcher, Philadelphia. The pans were usually round, although the famous water-proof pan came into popularity about this time. In this pan the splash shield, which normally would funnel the water into the pan, was separated from the pan so that the water would run down over the lock plate instead of collecting in the pan. Also, a roller was often introduced into the frizzen spring to make it more effective, and in all cases the size of the frizzen spring was reduced. The hammer continued in its typical S form,

Devilbliss Collection

PLATE 105
Lock of the late flint era with the name P. A. & S. Small engraved on the front of the lock plate. The Small Company has been engaged in the hardware business in York, Pa., from the late flintlock era until today.

although it was made sharper at the breast and was engraved to match the pattern on the lock plate. From the breast of the hammer to the lower jaw there was finally introduced a support which made it practically break-proof. On the tumbler a finger and arm arrangement replaced the earlier friction movement of the main spring.

The turn of the century also marks the entry of Lancaster craftsmen into the business of making gun locks. Though some were probably working there in the eighteenth century, there is no record of such activity. The earliest record known to the author is an advertisement which appeared in a Lancaster newspaper on August 23, 1808.

GUN LOCK MANUFACTORY
Daniel Sweitzer, & Co.

Respectfully inform their friends and the public in general, that they have commenced the
Gun Lock Making Business
In the borough of Lancaster, West of the court-house, on the street leading to Millerstown,

Where they make and Repair Musket Locks, Rifles, do. with single and double rollers; also plain gun and pistol locks, in the best and neatest manner, and on reasonable terms.
WANTED
Two or three journeymen, who understand filing at the above business. Good workmen will meet with good encouragement and constant employment, by applying at the factory.

N. B. Orders from a distance, post paid, will be punctually attended to.

The Sweitzer lock plates had the narrow tail of the earlier style and had simple patterns engraved on the front of the plate. The edges were nicely beveled. The name Sweitzer was engraved on the front of the plate and sometimes Lancaster was added. This company cannot have been in business very long, for its locks are rarely found on Kentucky Rifles. The locks were of good quality and well suited to the guns on which they were used.

Within the next ten years Anthony Trippert, John Trippert, Philip Metzgar, and George Moyer are known to have started in the business of making gun locks. The Moyer and Metzgar locks were probably not signed, for the writer has never seen a lock with either of these names on it. It is difficult to assign any locks to Andrew Trippert, although many of the locks signed Trippert may have been made by him. It might be mentioned here, parenthetically, that this name has been spelled Trippert, Trippart, Tripperd, Treppert, Dreppert, and Drepperd. In all cases it is the same family name which seems to have been distinguished by the three men: Andrew and John, Senior, and John, Junior.

The most famous of the three men was John, Senior, who was working as a gun-lock maker as early as 1820 and is known to have been a Lancaster gunsmith in the mid-forties. He died in 1864. He was a prolific gun-lock maker, for large numbers of his locks are found on guns, most of which were made by Lancaster gunsmiths. The excellent quality of his locks, however, would warrant a wide distribution, and they might have easily been used on guns made some distance from Lancaster. They might also have been used to replace earlier flintlocks that were "worn out."

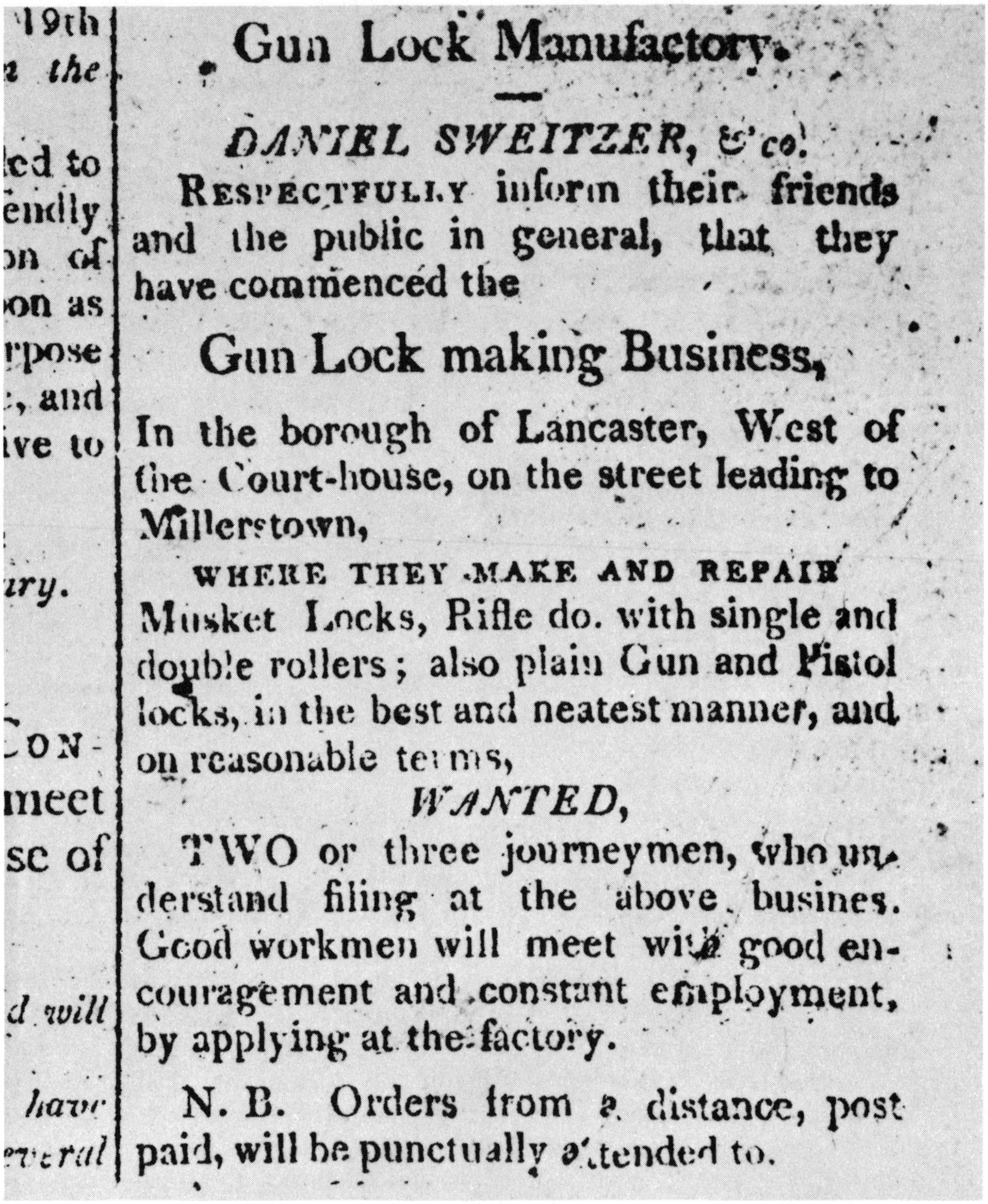

Gun Lock Manufactory.

DANIEL SWEITZER, & co.

RESPECTFULLY inform their friends and the public in general, that they have commenced the

Gun Lock making Business,

In the borough of Lancaster, West of the Court-house, on the street leading to Millerstown,

WHERE THEY MAKE AND REPAIR Musket Locks, Rifle do. with single and double rollers; also plain Gun and Pistol locks, in the best and neatest manner, and on reasonable terms,

WANTED,

TWO or three journeymen, who understand filing at the above busines. Good workmen will meet with good encouragement and constant employment, by applying at the factory.

N. B. Orders from a distance, post paid, will be punctually attended to.

PLATE 106
Advertisement of Daniel Sweitzer & Co. in a Lancaster newspaper in 1808. They made fine locks during their short stay in the lock business.

John Drepperd, Jr., also was a gunsmith and lock maker and some guns bearing his name on the lock and the top facet of the barrel are extant. His guns are of good quality and are usually marked John Drepperd, Lancaster. He is known to have made at least one mule-ear lock, an interesting variation of the common percussion lock. The hammer operates laterally instead of vertically. The Drepperd

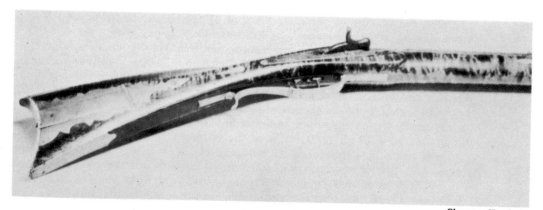

PLATE 107

Clarence Haushauer

Rifle with side-hammer percussion lock, full stock of curly maple, brass mountings, octagonal barrel 42 inches long marked A. Morrison on the top facet of the barrel.

The long narrow lock on this gun seems to have been made for a side hammer. Most locks with side hammers have the regular form of a percussion lock, but are adapted to side action by placing the main spring on the outside of the lock plate. These locks are often called "Mule ear locks."

name spelled with T terminals usually appears on flintlocks, while the D terminals usually appear on percussion locks.

Though the production of gun locks in America is an interesting subject, and an important one, most gun collectors recognize the fact that Pennsylvania guns have locks which were made in England. The following statement about lock production was written for this publication by Howard Blackmore, an outstanding authority on arms production in England.

It was not until the end of the 17th century that the Birmingham gun-makers were able to obtain the contract work of making military firearms for the Board of Ordnance in London. At the beginning of the 18th century, how-ever, a pattern of manufacture began to develop whereby the London gun-makers concentrated on the rough stocking and setting up of guns from parts supplied by Birmingham makers. The change took place gradually, of course, and for sometime many of the bigger London makers like Humphrey Pickfatt continued to supply complete firearms. However, the London workmen could not compete with the industrial resources of Birmingham when it came to the wholesale manufacture of plain cheap firearm parts needed for the Army, Navy, and the East India Company.

Gunsmiths working in Birmingham at this time were Joseph Parmer, John Tittensor, Thomas Probin, R. Weston, W. Smith, T. Hunt, T. Moore, Jacob Austin, Samuel Vaughn, and Andrew Stevens. An ordnance official was sent to Birmingham to show them how to make their locks fit a standard pattern. From then on, orders began to build up, a separate proof house was built and an Ordnance viewer stationed there to view and prove gun materials as they were received. When finally approved, they were sent to the store houses in the Tower of London for issue as necessary to the London stockmakers.

This work soon assumed vast proportions so that many gunmakers were able to establish factories employing many workmen and giving work to many out-workers. They were family businesses passed down from father to son. When Joseph Farmer, for instance died in 1741, his son James took over the business and his daughter Mary married another gunmaker Samuel Galton.

By the middle of the century, the gunmakers of the Birmingham area which included the smaller neighboring town of Wednesbury, Darlston, and Solihul, were able to produce thousands of locks and barrels per year.

As an example of their production the following gunmakers shared an Ordnance contract in 1766, for 20,000 locks and 20,000 barrels—Farmer and Galton, John Watley and Son, Joseph Oughton and Son, William Grice and Son, Haskins and Vernon, Edge and Son, John Short and Co., and Barker and Harris.

Although this supply of firearm parts to the Ordnance was a great stimulant to the trade, it was uncertain business and depended on the warlike state of the nation. In 1770 all contracts from the ordnance were cancelled, only to be renewed again in a hurry on the outbreak of the War of American Independence. The gunmakers, therefore, were only too ready to take other customers. In 1769 they produced over 30,000 gun barrels and locks for the East India Company. There was also a considerable export trade in the supply of arms and ammunition to the American Indians. This continued during the war. In 1776 a typical export is revealed in the license granted to Richard Lever, a merchant, for the despatch to West Florida of 5 tons of gunpowder, 5 tons of lead balls, and 1000 Indian Trading guns for trade in the Mississippi region. In the same year, Graham Johnson & Co., sent to Pensacola 1000 Guns and 500 locks for John Stuart, the Superintendent for Indian Affairs.

These guns and locks were of inferior workmanship and it is interesting to note that the Birmingham gunmakers became so used to this type of work that when contractors tried to place orders for Government work again, they met with a demand for a rise in pay and it was reported that only a certain number of workmen were capable of making the better quality Tower locks. A series of quarrels broke out between the large gun contractors and the many small journeymen lockmakers. In 1778, 95 of the latter sent in a petition to the Board of Ordnance complaining of the price being paid to them by their masters. The masters, in their turn, complained that the Board kept them waiting for their money.

The Ordnance in desperation placed its orders abroad and the Birmingham makers were given no further encouragement. After the war, for sometime London gunmakers like Henry Nock and Durrs Egg were able to fulfill the Board's requirements and the word LONDON on a lock or barrel became a trade mark of world renown. The Birmingham gunmakers were not above placing their rival town's name on their own productions, and as some justification some of them set up branches in London where they factored Birmingham wares. Ketland and Company with a warehouse in the city of London could thus truthfully describe themselves as of London and Birmingham.

At the beginning of the nineteenth century, the Napoleonic Wars caused all differences to be forgotten. New proof houses and view rooms were built in Birmingham and a staff of Ordnance viewers took up residence under a superintendent. Proper agreements were made and the rules of proof revised to the satisfaction of both sides. The locks and barrels were still made almost entirely by hand and the various forging, filing, boring, and polishing operations took place in dozens of small workshops. The cost of a standard musket lock was made up as follows:

For filing	4. 7d.
For forging	1. 3d.
Contractors profit	8d.

This short treatise about the making of arms in Birmingham and London might lead the casual reader to think that it contains little information that can be definitely connected with the making of locks on Kentucky rifles. The researcher's dependence on records relating to English military history is unfortunate, but such public records have been preserved; and the ledgers of merchants who exported locks to Pennsylvania have been lost or discarded a long time ago. It is probably a fact that the lock makers who made military locks in Birmingham and London also made locks which were exported to America. Despite some specialization, it was probably the urgencies of war or the lesser demands of peace that determined which type of lock the lock maker made. Both locks were made of similar metals, by craftsmen using identical tools, on identical workbenches. The Ketland production of both types indicates that such a dual function existed.

An interesting fact of Mr. Blackmore's story is his mention that gun locks were made by out-workers. It appears that these people bought, or were supplied with, metal from which locks or lock parts could be made. They took this metal to their homes, where they had a small workbench with a vise, and fabricated locks or lock parts from the metal. After they had finished their work, they took their products to the manufacturer or to a merchant, who gave them their compensation and another supply of metal.

The most important and most frustrating part of Mr. Blackmore's report is his disclosure of the fact that the name of the city engraved on the lock plate is no guarantee that the lock was made there. He has pointed out that after the magic of the word London was established in international trade circles, some of the Birmingham makers placed London on their locks. Other Birmingham makers maintained a London facade for their up-country products by having a warehouse or an office in London. The second group were slightly more honest than were those who engraved London on their locks, but the fact remains that most of the locks were made in Birmingham.

This exposure of the guile of the Birmingham merchants does not imply that no gun-lock makers worked in London. However, a researcher in London, employed by the writer, has found that only a few such craftsmen were employed there. And when the writer visited Birmingham several years ago, he found that a great many were employed there and in the environs. Obviously there is a discrepancy between the names of the cities that are engraved on lock plates and the

PLATE 108

Henry J. Kauffman

Two lock plates made of brass. The one on the left is marked Pennsylvania Rifle Works and the one on the right Jas. Golcher, Philadelphia.

The projection under the hammer of the Golcher lock suggests that the pan was sawed off this one to make a percussion lock out of it.

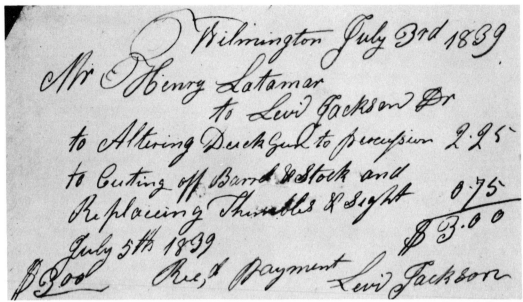

PLATE 109

Henry J. Kauffman

This bill focuses attention on the fact that when a gun was changed to percussion by a gunsmith, sometimes he cut off the barrel and the stock and replaced the thimbles and sight.

number of men found working at the trade in the respective cities. Was a "London Warranted" lock made in London or Birmingham? Mr. Blackmore has partially answered the question. Though later research may reveal another answer, at the moment it appears that most English gun locks were made in Birmingham.

As early as 1826 percussion locks were being used in Pittsburgh, and by 1830 they came into common usage, and many flintlocks were altered to percussion. The conversion involved simply removing the flint appendages on the outside of the lock plate and replacing them with a percussion hammer. A tube or nipple was threaded into the barrel and seated on the concave depression left by the pan in the top of the lock plate. Thus the lock plate was a useful support to the nipple, which was being constantly pounded by the hammer. Two filled holes for the frizzen spring and one for the frizzen are the usual evidences that a lock was at one time a flint. Some conversions were so cleverly done that it is difficult to detect the repairs, though they are usually easy to see on the inside of the lock plate.

From the newspaper advertisement which Jacob Fordney placed in the *Columbia Spy* on June 23, 1830, it is evident that altering guns was an important part of his business.

GUN AND RIFLE MAKING
JACOB FORDNEY

Respectfully informs the inhabitants of Columbia, and its vicinity that he has commenced the above business, at the stand formerly occupied by Wm. M'Clure in Front Street, one door south of LeFever's Hotel, where he will be happy to receive and execute all orders in his line.

Guns altered to percussion principle, and all other kinds of Repairing done in the best manner, and on shortest notice.

By strict attention to business, moderate charges, and excellence of work, he hopes to merit and receive a share of public patronage.

Most of the locks used after this time were percussion, although it is natural to expect some old timers to continue making flint guns. For example, Melchoir Fordney (Jacob's brother) seems to have made very few percussion guns before he died in 1845. Most of the percussion locks were similar in shape and decoration to the late flintlocks, some of the late and cheap percussion models, however, being very plain or poorly engraved. A local old timer told the writer that in his youth, he bought percussion locks from one of the big chain stores handling that type of merchandise.

Some very fine locks were also made for use on the elegant guns of the percussion era. Some lock plates were profusely engraved with hunting scenes and the inside mechanisms were precision products of the highest quality. Some percussion lock plates were made of brass, as were a few flints; but the percussion type is more common.

Finally, it should be pointed out that an important lock-producing area developed in Bedford County, where a typical Bedford County gun was made throughout the nineteenth century. Although a few flintlocks were made in the early part of the century, the peak of production was reached about mid-century, when rather a large number of men were working there.

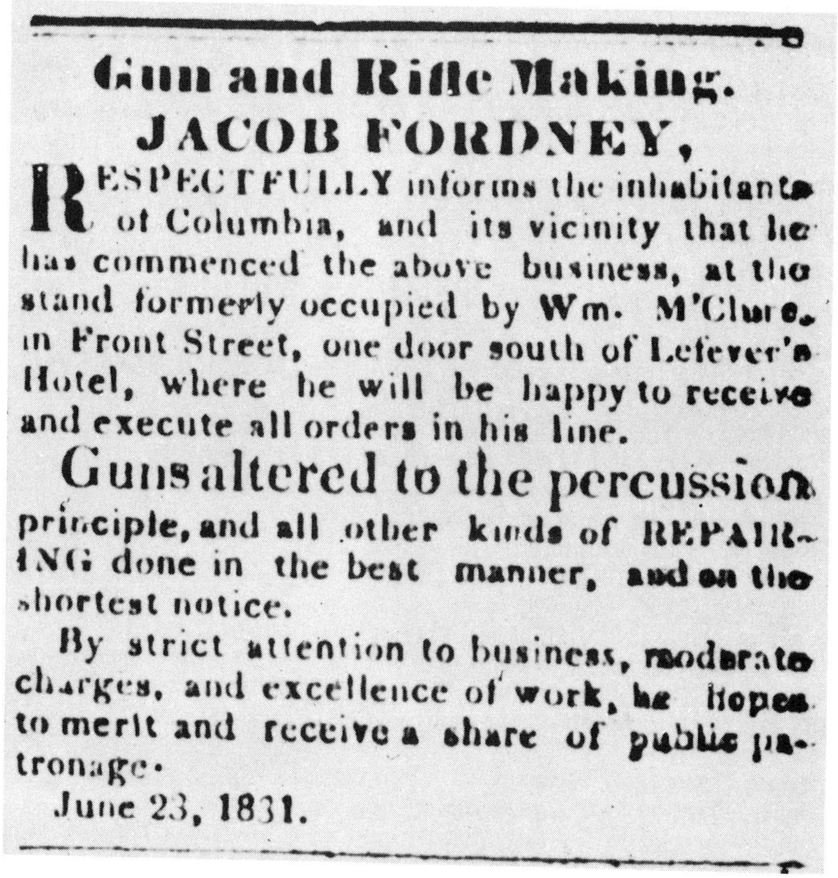

Gun and Rifle Making.
JACOB FORDNEY,

RESPECTFULLY informs the inhabitants of Columbia, and its vicinity that he has commenced the above business, at the stand formerly occupied by Wm. M'Clure, in Front Street, one door south of Lefever's Hotel, where he will be happy to receive and execute all orders in his line.

Guns altered to the percussion principle, and all other kinds of REPAIRING done in the best manner, and on the shortest notice.

By strict attention to business, moderate charges, and excellence of work, he hopes to merit and receive a share of public patronage.

June 23, 1831.

PLATE 110
Newspaper advertisement of Jacob Fordney.

The demand for Bedford locks arose from the design of the gun made there
While other Pennsylvania gun makers were making a gun that often used a very
large lock, the Bedford makers were producing a gun that was long and slender,
particularly in the breech area. This pattern required a very narrow lock which
the local gunsmiths made to fit their guns.

The design of the plate is obviously an adaptation of the earlier hand-made
lock which was widely used in Pennsylvania. The face of the plate was plain,
except that the maker's initials frequently appeared there. One or two slashes were
usually filed across the plate behind the hammer, and the back of the plate terminated in a point which is a bit wider than the point on the early locks. The thumb-
piece on the hammer is always large and seems to have been forged from the blank
from which the hammer was made.

The last phase of lock production in Pennsylvania probably occurred in
Lancaster and Pittsburgh, where rifle factories were located. In the early part of
his career, which started in 1834, Henry Leman made a few flintlocks which are
found on his interesting trade guns. Although most of his gun locks are of the common percussion type, he made some fancy locks for his presentation pieces. Leman
made a great many gun locks, signing most of them with his name in block letters
on the face of the lock plate.

Many other names of Pennsylvania gunsmiths and hardware merchants are
found on gun locks. It is quite difficult in most cases to determine whether these
people made their locks or bought locks and had their names engraved on them.
Specific details about some of these men will be found in the listing of gun-lock
makers which follows.

Directory of Lock Makers

Adams, Alex; Steelhouse Lane, Birmingham, England. 1829, 1830, 1831, 1833,
  1835, 1839, 1841, 1846, 1850
Adams, George; Whittall Street, Birmingham, England. 1831, 1833, 1835, 1841
Adams, Walter; Up. Priory, Birmingham, England. 1846
Adcock, Wm.; Aston Street, Birmingham, England. 1846
Allen & Co.; Birmingham, England. 1821-1830
Allen, Edward; Birmingham, England. 1770
Allen, George; Weaman Street, Birmingham, England. 1829, 1831, 1835, 1841,
  1846, 1850
Allport, Samuel; Birmingham, England. 1825, 1846
*Angstadt, Adam and Son
Armstrong, John; Emmitsburg, Maryland. 1800, 1825
Aston, Joseph; Upper Priory, Birmingham, England. 1829, 1830, 1831, 1833,
  1835, 1841
Aston, Richard; 15 Weaman Row, Birmingham, England. 1850
Baker, Thomas; 34 St. James Street, London, England. 1848
Ball, Henry; 23 Weaman Street, Birmingham, England. 1850

* To all gunsmiths, Adam Angstadt and son are conducting the business of making gun
locks in Kutztown. They sell locks singly or by the dozen. *Reading Adler,* Aug. 14, 1810.

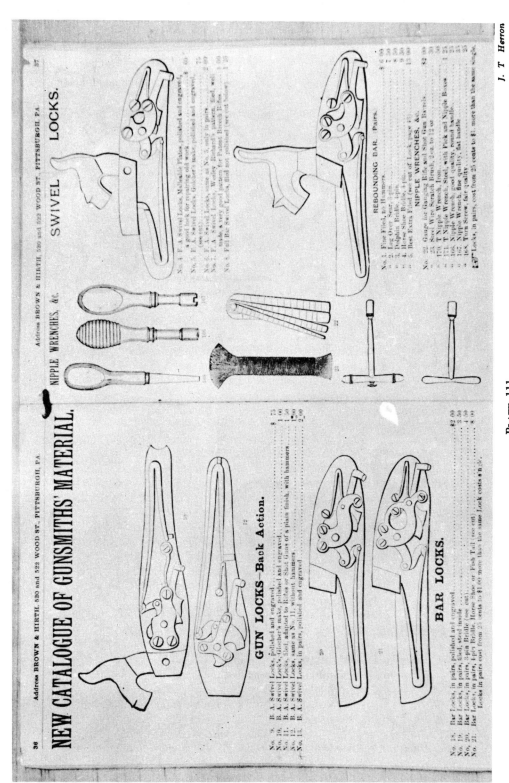

PLATE 111

Locks and odd tools from the 1886 catalogue of Brown & Hirth of Pittsburgh, Pa.

Barton, James; Fleet Street, Birmingham, England. 1829, 1830, 1831
Barton, Joseph; No. 31 Court, Lancaster Street, Birmingham, England. 1850
Baylis, Lewis; Whittall Street, Birmingham, England. 1835, 1841
Bettridge, William; No. 3 Court, Whittall Street, Birmingham, England. 1850
Biddle, R. & W. C.; Philadelphia, Pennsylvania. 1847-61
Billingsley, John; New John St., Birmingham, England. 1841. 104 Dartmouth
    Street, Birmingham, England. 1850
Bird, C. & Co.; Philadelphia, Pennsylvania. 1814
Bird Charles & Co.; 170 High Street, corner of Fifth, Philadelphia, Pa. 1814
Bolus, Thomas; Birmingham, England. 1767
Bosby, John; No. 16 Court, Bath Street, Birmingham, England. 1850
Bown, James & Son; Pittsburgh, Pennsylvania. 1848
Bown & Tetley; Pittsburgh, Pennsylvania. 1855
Bradford, J. Loveday St., Birmingham, England. 1846
Breedon, Samuel; Washwood, Birmingham, England. 1850
Brighton, Joseph; 7 Court, Lancaster St., Birmingham, England. 1835
Britton, B.; Price Street, Birmingham, England. 1846
Brittonn and Waddams; Graham Street, Birmingham, England.
Brown, George; Price Street, Birmingham, England. 1846
Buchmiller, Robert; Lancaster, Pennsylvania. 1861
Bushell, Thomas; Duddeston Street, Birmingham, England. 1846
Challener, Henry; Weaman Street, Birmingham, England. 1846
Chamberlain, Thomas; Weaman Street, Birmingham, England. 1839
Chambers, Thomas; 2 Court, John St., Birmingham, England. 1835, 1839
Clive, William; Legge Street, Birmingham, England. 1839
Coney, John; Stafford Street, Birmingham, England. 1846
Constable, Samuel; Birmingham, England. 1770.
Cooper, and Co.; Legge St., Birmingham, England. 1846, 1847
Cooper, J. M.; Pittsburgh, Pennsylvania. 1839, 1859
Cooper, William; Price Street, Birmingham, England. 1839
Creswell, William; 6 Weaman Street, Birmingham, England. 1850
Cutler, R. and Sons; Weaman Street, Birmingham, England. 1846
Darlington, Benjamin; Pittsburgh, Pa. 1816
Davies, Peter; No. 3 Court, Whittall Place, Birmingham, England. 1850
Davis, John; Lozells, Birmingham, England. 1849
Davis, Joseph; 9 Chamber Street, London, England. 1847, 1848
Davis, Peter; Price Street, Birmingham, England. 1839
Davis & Son; Church La., Handsworth, Birmingham, England. 1846
Davis, Thomas; 1 Court, Loveday St., Birmingham, England. 1833
Dickson, W. H.; State Street, Erie, Pennsylvania. 1873-74
Docker, Thomas; Birmingham, England. 1770, 1767
Duce, John I.; Lambeth Street, London, England. 1848
Drepperd, John; Lancaster, Pennsylvania. 1820-1840
Dudley, Jeffrey; 88 Stainforth Street, Birmingham, England. 1750
Duke, Robert; Weaman Street, Birmingham, England. 1839
Dunlap, Robert, Jr.; Pittsburgh, Pennsylvania. 1837-58
Eagles and Grattidge; Snow Hill, Birmingham, England. 1846
Ebb, William; Legge Street, Birmingham, England. 1829, 1830, 1831
Eccleston, Joseph; Weaman Street, Birmingham, England. 1847, 1850
Edge, D.; Weaman Street, Birmingham, England. 1846, 1847, 1850
Edge, Richard; Wednesbury, England. 1757
Edge, Simeon; Weaman Street, Birmingham, England. 1839, 1841, 1850
Edmonds, Thomas; Bushkill Center, Pennsylvania. 1860
Edwards, Francis; Birmingham, England. 1770, 1767

Edwards, W. and Co.; Bath Street, Birmingham, England. 1847

Ellis, William; Whittall Street, Birmingham, England. 1847

Essex, William; Lancaster St., Birmingham, England. 1841

Evans, Benjamin; 5 Blew St., Birmingham, England. 1833, 1845

Evans, Jesse; No. 32 Court, Lancaster St., Birmingham, England. 1850

Evans, John; 6 Court, Stainforth St., Birmingham, England. 1835, 1850

Fehr, George; Bushkill Center, Pennsylvania.

Fehr, Michael; Bushkill Center, Pennsylvania. 1860

Fenner, B.; Bushkill Center, Pennsylvania. 1860

Field & Langstroth; Philadelphia, Pennsylvania.

Food, Thomas; Little Shadewell Street, Birmingham, England. 1850

Foster, George; 7 Baggott Street, Birmingham, England. 1850

Foster, Thomas; No. 30 Court, Lancaster Street, Birmingham, England. 1850

Fisher, William; Newton Street, Birmingham, England. 1829, 1830, 1831, 1833

Fordney, Jacob; Lancaster, Pennsylvania. 1830, 1860

Francis, James; 60 Ashsted Street, Birmingham, England. 1850

Frazer, John; Loveday St., Birmingham, England. 1846, 1850

Freeth and Jennings; Livery Street, Birmingham, England. 1829, 1830, 1831, 1833

Golcher, James; 74 Slaney Street, Birmingham, England. 1835

Golcher, James; G. T. Road above 2nd, Philadelphia, Pa. 1846-1852

Gough, Thomas; Jones Place, Newland Street, Birmingham, England. 1850

Gratton, William; Hurst Street, Birmingham, England. 1829, 1830, 1831, 1850

Graves, William; Howe Street, Birmingham, England. 1835, 1839

Graves, William; Horse Fair, Birmingham, England. 1839. Weaman Street, Birmingham, England. 1841

Green, James; Ashted Row, Birmingham, England. 1841, 1846

Green, John; Newton Street, Birmingham, England. 1846, 1850

Grice, William; Birmingham, England. 1767.

Griffith, Thomas; Ashsted Rd., Birmingham, England. 1847

Griffiths, William; Hurst Street, Birmingham, England 1829, 1830, 1831, 1850

Guest, Henry; Legge Street, Birmingham, England. 1829, 1830, 1831

Hadley, Edward; New John Street, Birmingham, England. 1841, 1850

Hales, Charles; Vauxhall St., Birmingham, England. 1847

Harper, James; Prospect Row, Birmingham, England. 1835, 1841, 1847, 1850

Harper, Joseph; 9 Court, Lancaster St., Birmingham, England. 1835

Harper, S.; Whittall St., Birmingham, England. 1847, 1850

Harper, Samuel; 1 and 2 Newton Street, Birmingham, England. 1850

Hargrove, Samuel; 90 Bath Street, Birmingham, England. 1835, 1838, 1841

Harris, B. D.; Mary-Ann St., Birmingham, England. 1829, 1830, 1831

Harris, Bernard; Livery Street, Birmingham, England. 1850

Hart, Henry; New Canal Street, Birmingham, England. 1847

Hatt, John; 76 South Birmingham, England. 1850

Hawkins, Henry; No. 6 Court, John Street, Birmingham, England. 1850

Heath, John; Bart St., West, Birmingham, England. 1839

Hedge, Simeon; Tanter St., Birmingham, England. 1829, 1831

Hill, William; Upper Tower St., Birmingham, England. 1847

Hines, Edward; Birmingham, England.

Holland, Benjamin; Hospital Street, Birmingham, England. 1850

Holland, Francis; Bradford Street, Birmingham, England. 1847

Holland, John; Steelhouse Lane, Birmingham, England. 1846

Holland, Simeon; Weaman Street, Birmingham, England. 1829, 1830, 1831

Holland, Thomas; Ashted Row, Birmingham, England. 1847

Hollis and Co., Weaman Row, Birmingham, England. 1847

Hollis, W. E.; Whittall St., Birmingham, England. 1847

Horton, Thomas; Birmingham, England. 1767
Howell, Wm. T.; Philadelphia, Pennsylvania. 1847
Humpage, Enoch; Phillip Street, Aston Road, Birmingham, England. 1850
Hunt, Joseph; Birmingham, England. 1767
Hunt, William; Stainforth St., Birmingham, England. 1839
Jeavons, and Co.; Stainforth Street, Birmingham, England. 1847
Jennings, W.; Great Charles Street, Birmingham, England. 1829, 1830, 1831, 1833
Jevon, John; Wednesbury, England. 1818
Jinks, Samuel; Weaman Street, Birmingham, England. 1841, 1850
Jones, John; Weaman Street, Birmingham, England. 1829, 1830, 1831, 1835
Josebury, Frederick; Lichfield St., Birmingham, England. 1839. Mott Street, Birmingham, England. 1841, 1850
Joseph, John; 121 Lancaster Street, Birmingham, England. 1850
Kelker & Bro.; Harrisburg, Pennsylvania. 1861
°Ketland, Thomas; Birmingham, England.
King, W.; Bath Street, Birmingham, England. 1847
Konigmacher, & Co.; Philadelphia, Pennsylvania. 1807-14
Lander, Charles; Weaman Street, Birmingham, England. 1829, 1830, 1831, 1835, 1841
Lauffman, P. H.; Pittsburgh, Pennsylvania. 1850-76
Lees, Thomas; Wednesbury, England. 1783
Leonard, D.; Aston Road, Birmingham, England. 1847
Logan & Kennedy; Pittsburgh, Pennsylvania. 1831-47
Lowe, Thomas; Birmingham, England. 1767
McCosh, S.; Pittsburgh, Pennsylvania. 1850
Manton, Joseph; London, England. 1825
Marklew, John; No. 1 Court, Lichfield Street, Birmingham, England. 1850
Martin & Smith; Philadelphia, Pennsylvania. 1847-55
Maslin, M. M.; Philadelphia, Pennsylvania. 1847
Maybury, Charles; St. Mary's Row, Birmingham, England, 1847
Moyer, George; Lancaster, Pennsylvania. 1843-61
Merricks, Barney; Loveday Street, Birmingham, England. 1829, 1830, 1831
Metzger, Philip; Lancaster Borough Tax List. 1816
Millington, Thos.; 12 Market Street, Birmingham, England. 1850
Mills, John; Great Brook Street, Birmingham, England. 1829, 1830, 1831
Mills, John; Ashsted Row, Birmingham, England. 1829, 1830, 1831
Moor, John; Birmingham, England. 1767
Moore and Hamis; Loveday Street, Birmingham, England. 1847
Moore, Henszey & Co.; Philadelphia, Pennsylvania. 1855-61
Morton, Thomas; 29 St. Ann Street, Birmingham, England. 1835

° Ketland is the name most frequently connected with English guns and locks used in Pennsylvania in the eighteenth century. The writer was greatly surprised when he visited Birmingham and found only a passing interest in the Ketland business activities, and that biographical data had to be "dug" from original sources in the archives of the public library.

Although the business is thought to have been started by William Ketland about 1750, the first records found by the writer listed Thomas Ketland as one of the "gun lock makers, forgers, finishers and filers" living on Litchfield Street in Birmingham in 1767. In 1775 he continued his trade on Litchfield Street but in 1780 he lived on Katherine Street; and in 1781 he moved to Weaman's Row where most of the men connected with the gun trade seemed to be operating at that time. In 1787 his name appears for the last time, and it is reported that by 1789 he and his brother, John, were living in Philadelphia. They are listed as merchants in the business directories of Philadelphia, but there is no evidence that they made guns there.

A firm of Ketland and Walker continued to do business in Birmingham after 1790 until 1800; however, the relationship of this Ketland to the others is not known.

George, Moyer; Lancaster Borough Tax List. 1819, 1821
Neave, T & C.; Cincinnati, Ohio. 1837-44
Needham, H.; Cannon Street, Birmingham, England. 1833, 1835, 1841
Negus, James; Wednesbury, England. 1782
Nightingale, Thos.; 51 Buckingham Street, Birmingham, England. 1850
Nixon, William; Duddeston Street, Birmingham, England. 1847
Norris, John; Birmingham, England. 1829, 1830, 1831
Ochs, Charles; Bushkill Center, Pennsylvania. 1860
Osborne, Charles; Lichfield Street, Birmingham, England. 1847
Parker, Joseph; 13 Newton Street, Birmingham, England. 1850
Parker, William; London, England. 1825
Parks, Benjamin; Weaman Street, Birmingham, England. 1846, 1847, 1849, 1850
Parks, Samuel; 62 Lichfield Street, Birmingham, England. 1835
Parsons, Thomas & Son; Bath Street, Birmingham, England
Pearsall, Thomas; 25½ Whittall Street, Birmingham, England. 1850
Perks, Samuel; 87 Lichfield Street, Birmingham, England. 1850
Peters, John; New Summer, Birmingham, England. 1841, 1846
Peters, John; Cecil Street, Birmingham, England. 1847
Peters, William; Cecil Street, Birmingham, England. 1846, 1847
Phillips, T. & S.; Weaman Row, Birmingham, England. 1847
Portlock, John; Moland Street, Birmingham, England. 1829, 1831, 1846, 1847
Powell, W. and Son; Carr's Lane, Birmingham, England
Pritchard, Wm.; Union Street, Birmingham, England. 1847
Randall, Joseph C.; Philadelphia, Pennsylvania. 1847-61
Redfern, Thomas; Whittall Street, Birmingham, England. 1847
Reynolds, J.; Weaman Street, Birmingham, England. 1841
Richards, Westley; High Street, Birmingham, England. 1847
Robinson, John; John St., Birmingham, England. 1829, 1830, 1831
Rollins, T.; St. Charles Street, Birmingham, England. 1841
Rooke, George; Bath Street, Birmingham, England
Round, Joseph; Wednesbury, England. 1818
Russel, John; Windsor Street, Birmingham, England. 1829, 1830, 1831
Sargant Brothers; Edmund Street, Birmingham, England. 1847
Sheldon, Joseph; Vaughton Street, Birmingham, England. 1847
Shenton, Wm. & Sons; Wednesbury, England. 1818
Sherwood & Frith; 12 Wellclo Square, London, England. 1848
Siddons, C. and D.; Loveday Street, Birmingham, England. 1847, 1850
Siddons, Charles and William; Weaman Street, Birmingham, England. 1829, 1830, 1831, 1846, 1847, 1850
Simkins, Wm.; 91½ Steelhouse Lane, Birmingham, England. 1850
Skeet, J.; Russell Street, Birmingham, England.
Small, P. A. & S.; York, Pennsylvania. 1820-
Smith, C. J.; Whittall Street, Birmingham, England. 1846
Smith, J.; Price Street, Birmingham, England. 1846, 1847
Smith, J. and Son; Russell Street, Birmingham, England. 1846, 1847
Smith, Sam; 34 Newcastle Street, London, England. 1848
Smith, William; 110 Lancaster Street, Birmingham, England. 1833, 1841
Sowers & Smith; Philadelphia, Pennsylvania. 1855
Spang and Wallace; 94 N. 3d. Street, Philadelphia, Pennsylvania
Spittle, James; Wednesbury, England. 1782
Spittle, Jonah; Blue Ball, Wednesbury, England. 1818
Stanton, J.; Price Street, Birmingham, England. 1847
Steiner, A. B.; Bushkill Center, Pennsylvania. 1860
Stokes, Aguilla; Woodcock, Street, Birmingham, England. 1829, 1830, 1831

Sturk, Edward; Vauxhall Street, Birmingham, England. 1846, 1850

Swinbourne & Son; Russell Street, Birmingham, England. 1847

Taylor & Davenport; 21 Loveday Street, Birmingham, England. 1850

Thursfield, Benjamin; No. 3 Court, Canal Street, Birmingham, England. 1850

Tipping & Co.; Constitution Hill, Birmingham, England. 1847

Tryon, E. K.; Philadelphia, Pennsylvania. 1825-

Tongue, William; Birmingham, England. 1770, 1767

Townsend, J.; Sand Street, Birmingham, England. 1847

Trippart, John; Lancaster Borough Tax List. 1820

Trueman, James; Legge Street, Birmingham, England. 1839

Truitt, & Co.; Philadelphia, Pennsylvania. 1847-61

Waldron, H.; Ashsted Row, Birmingham, England. 1829, 1830, 1831, 1850

Waters; Steelhouse Lane, Birmingham, England. 1767

Watson, Benjamin; Steelhouse Lane, Birmingham, England. 1829, 1830, 1831, 1850

Watson, Benjamin; 14 Steelhouse Lane, Birmingham, England. 1850

Watson, Isaac; Wednesbury, England. 1741

Watson, Isaac; Shadewell St., Birmingham, England.

Watt, J. W.; Washington ab Logan (West Philadelphia), Philadelphia, Pa. 1855

Watton, Henry; Slaney Street, Birmingham, England. 1847

Webley, Phillip; Weaman Street, Birmingham, England. 1839, 1841, 1850

Welch, John; Birmingham, England. 1767

Welch, W; Tower Street, Birmingham, England. 1841

West and Sills; Fisher Street, Birmingham, England. 1839

Whalley, Richard; 33 Lench Street, Birmingham, England. 1850

Whitehouse, Isaac; Steelhouse Lane, Birmingham, England. 1825, 1829, 1830, 1833

Whitehouse, Jacob; Weaman Street, Birmingham, England. 1839

Whitehouse, Wm.; Bath Street, Birmingham, England. 1846, 1849

Whitemore & Wolff; Pittsburgh, Pennsylvania. 1836-52

Whitmore, Wolf & Co.; Pittsburgh, Pennsylvania. 1852-58

Whitmore, Wolf, Duff & Co.; Pittsburgh, Pennsylvania. 1858-72

Williams, Jas.; 73 Weaman Street, Birmingham, England. 1849

Williams, J. and T.; 50 Whittall Street, Birmingham, England. 1835

Wilson, Joseph; Charles Street, Birmingham, England. 1847

Wolff & Lane; Pittsburgh, Pennsylvania. 1850-58

Worley, Richard; Sand Street, Birmingham, England. 1839
    Lench Street, Birmingham, England. 1841
    Loveday Street, Birmingham, England. 1846, 1850

Yates, Josiah; Steelhouse Lane, Birmingham, England. 1841

Chapter 6

Accoutrements

THE MID-TWENTIETH CENTURY reader of this chapter dealing with accoutrements used in Pennsylvania in the eighteenth and nineteenth centuries should be aware that this word has had different meanings at different times. The 1933 edition of the Oxford English Dictionary explains that accoutrements are, "Apparel, outfit, equipment. Milt. The equipment of a soldier other than arms and dress." It is obvious from this definition that in modern times, arms and accoutrements are in two distinct categories; contemporary writers usually discuss each in separate chapters.

There is also a suggestion that the word has applications beyond the military sphere. This is recognized in the eighteenth century Encyclopedia Perthensis, Perth, Scotland, which defines accoutrement as, "Dress, equipage, furniture, relating to the person; trappings, ornament." An interesting ecclesiastical use of the word is found in a 1751 English reference which states, "Rich and glittering accoutrements, wherewith the Church of Rome hath surrounded her devotions." Shakespeare, in 1596, involved then in romance: "To me she's married, not unto my cloathes; could I reapire what she will weare in me, as I can change these poor accoutrements, t'were well for Kate and better for myself."

It is also obvious from the wide use of the term that at an earlier time the word included all the trappings, or equipment, including weapons. Insofar as the guns of Pennsylvania have been treated in detail in other chapters of the book, this discussion of accoutrements will follow the modern concept of the subject and describe the equipment of a gunner other than his arms and dress.

It is interesting to note the changing concepts of the word accoutrements, and it is equally important to note that the accoutrements of a particular period were not the same for all guns. There was obviously some need for uniformity in accoutrements for guns with flint ignitions, but the functions of different flint guns created variations in matters relating to powder storage and loading. There were also changing needs in the nineteenth century, when guns with percussion ignition were used.

The following letter from the Emmet Collection in the New York Public Library lists the accoutrements which were needed for a gun in the eighteenth century:

To Schrimpton Hutchinson Esq.

Sir,

You are hereby ordered and directed, to compleat yourself with ARMS and ACCOUTREMENTS, by the 12th instant, upon failure thereof, you are liable to a Fine of SIX POUNDS, agreeable to Law.

Articles of Equipment

A good Fire-arm with a steel or Iron Ram-Rod and a Spring to retain the same. A Worm, Priming Wire and Brush, and a Bayonet fitted to your Gun, a Scabbard and Belt therefor, and a Cutting Sword, or a Tomahawk or a Hatchet, a Pouch containing a Cartridge Box, that will hold fifteen Rounds of Cartridges at least, a hundred Buckshot, A Jack-Knife and Tow for Wadding, six Flints and one pound of Powder, forty Leaden Bullets to your Gun, a Knapsack, and Blanket, a Canteen or Wooden Bottle sufficient to hold one Quart.

It is fortunate that such an interesting document is available to describe the accoutrements deemed necessary at that time. It is obvious that the iron ramrod with a spring, the bayonet, the cartridge box, and the sword were not appurtenances that the average man with a rifle carried to hunt game for his larder. Some accoutrements not listed above, but usually regarded as essential for a hunter, are a knife, bullet mold, ladle, linen and grease for patches, and two powder horns.

Gunpowder

The expendability of gunpowder might create some question as to its inclusion with accoutrements, but since it obviously is not an arm, it must be part of the equipment. The powder used in ancient long guns was called serpentine. It was unusually fine; but, when tamped in a gun barrel, was not as effective as the later type of black powder, called "corned powder." Corned powder was made up of many small grains separated by air spaces through which the flames from the first powder to be ignited could pass freely, until the entire charge of powder was ignited. The following information on the making of black powder has been supplied by the Eleutherian Mills-Hagley Foundation. This was the procedure of the DuPont mills in the early 1800's and was probably the general procedure of most powder makers of the period.

MAKING BLACK POWDER

A. *Proportions*

The proportions of the three ingredients vary, but a frequently used formula calls for three-quarters saltpetre, one-eighth sulfur, and one-eighth charcoal. The ingredients when refined are ready for mixing. If the sulphur and charcoal are not in powder form, they may be pulverized together in rotating barrels by the tumbling action of iron balls, or under heavy pulverizing wheels.

B. *The Stamping Mill*

The three ingredients are first mixed together according to formula with a spatula with water. Lumps are removed by use of a sieve and a roller. The mixture is then placed in a battery of mortars; water is added and the pestles are put in motion. The stamping continues for about 14 hours.

C. *Grinding*

Instead of the stamping-mill process the materials may be mixed in grinding or incorporating mills. These mills consisted of two vertical rolling millstones or cast-iron wheels set upon a bed-plate. The two vertical wheels turn on the bed-plate, mixing or incorporating the powder ingredients by their great weight and abrasive action.

D. *Pressing*

As it comes from the wheel mill the powder is a mealy, moist "powdercake." To get rid of moisture and to increase its density it is taken to a press mill where it is placed in a mechanical or hydraulic press and subjected to heavy pressure. When taken out it has the appearance and feel of a piece of slate.

E. *Granulating*

This "presscake" is then broken up into small pieces by being run through a series of zinc rollers (late innovation—earlier broken by mallet) and then passed through a series of sieves or screens to obtain the right size of grain. The powder dust and under-sized grains are returned to the press mill and added to the next batch of powder.

F. *Drying*

The powder still contains too much moisture so it is dried by the sun on outdoor tables or on racks in a heated building known as a dry house. To obtain thorough drying it is stirred or turned over periodically.

G. *Glazing*

Sporting and other high quality powders were further dried by being rotated in a glazing barrel for a number of hours. The tumbling action of the powder created heat, rounded off the grains, and imparted a lustre to the finished powder. A later innovation was the adding of a small quantity of graphite to the powder in the glazing barrel. This coated the grains, making them more resistant to dampness, and it enhanced the glossy sheen of the powder.

H. *Packing*

The final step consists of running the powder through a reel sieve to get rid of dust created in the glazing operation. It is then packed in canisters, kegs, or barrels and stored in a magazine.

There were, of course, many powder plants operating prior to the DuPont operation on the Brandywine. A story in the September 1958 issue of *Muzzle Blasts* by Don Berkbile gives a lengthy and interesting account of such activity in Pennsylvania. He tells that after the Royal Proclamation prohibiting the exportation of powder to America, a mill was set up near Philadelphia by Oswell Eve. Within six months two more mills were in operation; and during the war a number of mills were built beyond the Philadelphia area, one as far distant as Dauphin County. All of these mills had difficulty in securing adequate supplies of saltpeter; and the needs of the time were met only because considerable powder was imported from France, where powder manufacturing had reached a high stage of development.

Many small mills were operating in Pennsylvania in the early part of the nineteenth century. The Federal census of 1810 lists about two hundred mills in America, and it must be presumed that a good portion of them were located in Pennsylvania. Among them was the well-known establishment of the Ferrees in the western part of the state. Jacob Ferree had worked in a powder plant before he moved to his Peter's Creek site about 1784. It is not known when he started production there, but the earliest advertisement at hand, at the moment, is from the *Pittsburgh Gazette,* September 14, 1799.

> POWDER. THE subscriber has for sale, the best RIFLE POWDER—he can supply Merchants and others, at reasonable prices, at his Powder Mill on Peter's Creek. Jacob Ferree, Allegheny County, Mifflin Township, September 13, 1799.

This advertisement indicates that Jacob Ferree was the owner and operator of the mill; the next advertisement indicates that after his death in 1807 his sons Joel and Isaac took over its operation. Their advertisement appeared in the *Pittsburgh Gazette,* March 1, 1809.

Park Emery

PLATE 112

Powder flasks in which gun powder was sold by merchants like Tryon, Grubb and Kreider. Also possibly by hardware merchants in smaller cities and towns.

GUN POWDER. The subscribers have on hand, and intend constantly to keep, at their POWDER MILL, on Peter's Creek, two miles from Elizabethtown, a supply of their best manufactured RIFLE POWDER, which they will sell low for cash or on short credit.

From the long experience of the Powder, in most parts of western country, and its high repute among our greatest gunners, we flatter ourselves with the hope of receiving a part of the public patronage.

February 28, 1809   Joel & Isaac Ferree

A later notice advertised that the Ferrees had appointed a Pittsburgh merchant to be their sole agent for powder sales in the city. This practice was followed by George Beck, another powder manufacturer of the area, who had agents in such places as Ligonier and Black-Legs. Philemon Waters made and sold powder at the low end of Monture's Island, on the north side of the Ohio.

Later in the nineteenth century, the number of powder makers dwindled; and powder making became the business of a few large manufacturers, who sold their products through a network of small outlets such as the local hardware store. The preference for cartridges after the Civil War marked the "beginning of the end" for the use of muzzle loaders and black powder.

Flints

The most expendable products, next to gun powder, were the flints used to ignite the powder and fire the gun. There were good and bad flints, as explained in a *Dictionary of Arts and Manufactures* by Andrew Ure, New York, 1841. "The best are somewhat convex, approaching to globular; those which are irregular, knobbed, branched, and tuberose, are generally full of imperfections. Good nodules seldom weigh more than twenty pounds; when less than two, they are not worth working. They should have a greasy lustre, and be particularly smooth and fine grained. The colour may vary from honey-yellow to blackish-brown, but it should be uniform throughout the lump, and the translucency should be so great as to render letters legible through a slice about one-fiftieth of an inch thick, laid down upon paper. The fracture should be perfectly smooth, uniform, and slightly conchoidal; the last property being essential to the cutting of perfect gun-flints."

The same article continues, "Five parts may be distinguished in a gun-flint: 1. The sloping facet or bevel part, which is impelled against the hammer of the lock. Its thickness should be from two to three-twelfths of an inch, for if it were thicker it be too likely to break, and if more obtuse, the scintillations would be less vivid. 2. The sides, or lateral edges are always somewhat irregular. 3. The back, or thick part opposite the tapering edge. 4. The under surface, is smooth and rather concave. 5. The upper face, which has a small square plane between the tapering edges and back for entering into the upper claw of the cock."

To describe the entire operation of making a flint would require many pages, but a competent "flintknapper" could make a flint in less than a minute. A good craftsman could manufacture more than 1000 chips a day, which would "work up" into probably 500 gun flints.

Possibly there were sporadic attempts to make gun flints in America, but most of the early ones which have been found came from Europe. Flint is mined today at Brandon, England, very much as it has been for the past 300 years. The flint material is dark in color and is considered excellent rough material by the few men who are engaged in the business. Flint of a lighter color is mined nearby and is called "Norwich flint." This is usable but not as desirable as the darker variety.

Park Emery

PLATE 113

Cannister was used by the country storekeeper to hold gunpowder which was sold retail in small quantities. It is about twelve inches high.

Flints were made in sizes suitable for the guns in which they were to be used, a pistol naturally requiring a smaller flint than a rifle or a fowling piece. It was held in the hammer between a fold of leather or lead. Whether the slant was turned up or down is uncertain; however, the question is strictly an academic one, for it is known that after the flint ceased to function in its first position it was turned "upside down." A good flint could be used for 50 to 60 firings.

Powder Horns and Flasks

The early use of powder horns in Europe suggests that some were probably brought to Pennsylvania by the first settlers. A local supply was created as soon as the first cattle were slaughtered for food.

The use of horn over a span of centuries for carrying a reserve supply of powder can easily be explained by its availability, utility, and attractiveness in its function. Not many objects of such importance were so inexpensive or so easy to

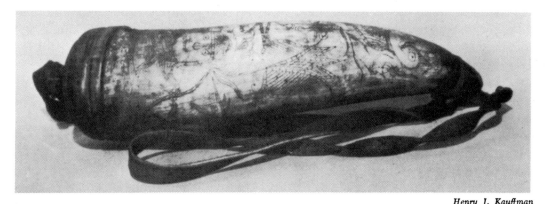

PLATE 114

This powder horn is engraved with motifs found on other "objects of art" made in Pennsylvania. It was made for John Weirich in 1809.

PLATE 115

acquire. The inner portion of the horn was not very difficult to remove; and after a hole was cut into the small end, and the large end was plugged, a satisfactory container for powder was created. They were made in a variety of sizes and shapes. This suggests that they could be carried or used in a stationary position.

Horn was a tough, durable material. It could withstand the abuse of rough usage in the forests, and it would not easily break if dropped on a rock. The assembled horn was not completely waterproof, but was adequate to keep the powder dry. The evidence of wear on many horns shows that they were used over a long span of years.

Their color was one of their most attractive features. The values ranged from white to black, with a variety of soft yellow-brown predominating. Some horns were

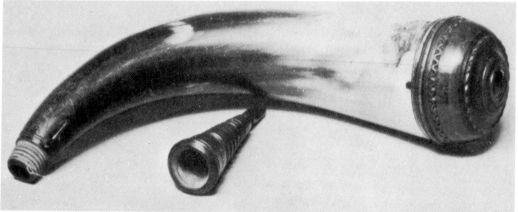

Kenneth Mundis

PLATE 116

Powder horn with a separate funnel end which could be removed to facilitate filling the horn. The separate end, the pleasing gradation in color, and the carved pattern on the plug of the large end of the horn make such horns attractive to collect.

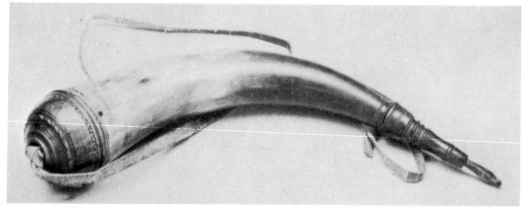

Henry J. Kauffman

PLATE 117

The carving on the end-cap of this powder horn is typical of the fine horns which are attributed to makers living in York County, Pennsylvania. The two lines on the big end of the horn can also be seen on this one.

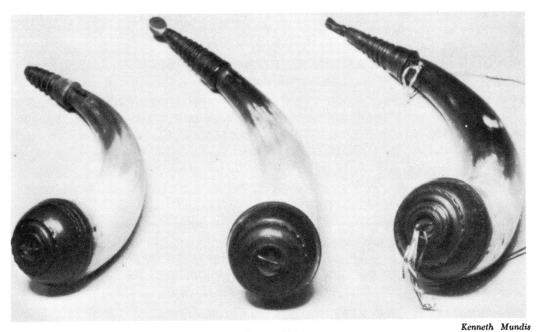

Kenneth Mundis

PLATE 118

Most of the horns that are attributed to one, or more makers in York County, Pennsylvania are graceful in form and attractive in their range of color values.

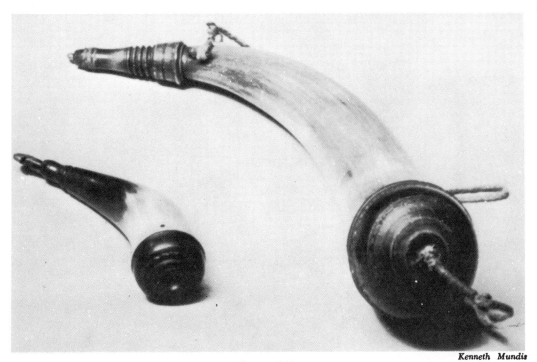

Kenneth Mundis

PLATE 119

Cow horns attributed to craftsmen who worked in York County. The large one is the size most frequently found and the small one is probably unique.

uniformly dark or light, while others had a speckled or striped pattern. More striking contrasts were obtained by some craftsmen who, by removing portions of the outer light layer, exposed the inner dark layer.

The apex of the work on horns was reached by the men who engraved designs on them. The provincial horns have simple, folk art patterns, such as tulips and unicorns, which are found on other products of the folk artist. Many are dated and some have the owner's name appropriately engraved in a panel left for such a purpose. Some of the famous map horns were made in Pennsylvania, a number of which have plans of early Philadelphia on them, and one is known to have Pittsburgh territory engraved on it.

Equally important as the engraved horns is a Pennsylvania type that is thought to have been made in York County. This hypothesis is based on the geographical areas in which they are found today. There are slight variations in the type, but they are usually of a pleasing curved shape with a slight twist in them which seems to conform to the portion of the body which they touched when suspended over the shoulder on a leather thong. The small end does not have the simple terminal of most horns, but has an external thread cut on it to which is attached a larger turned piece of horn. This arrangement permits the removal of the small end and facilitates the filling of the horn. Near the edge of the big end of the horn two lines, usually appear. The slight difference in depth and width of the lines suggests that this operation was performed on a lathe so that a cut could be made on a horn with slight irregularities in contour and thickness. The turned ends are usually made of a fruit wood with an interesting arrangement of turned lines and other patterns carved with a chisel. A metal staple is appropriately placed on both ends to receive the thong.

Park Emery

PLATE 120

Double powder horns like this one are very rare. It is possible that regular powder was carried in one end and priming powder in the other end.

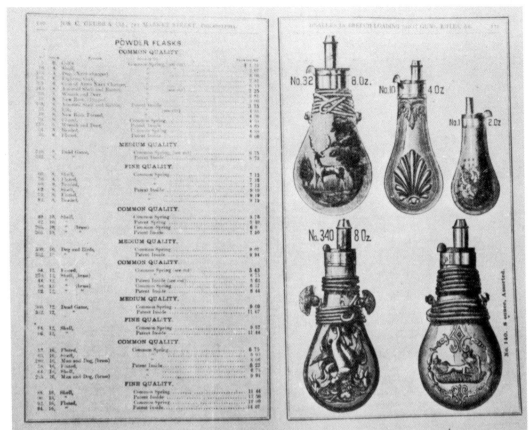

J. T. Herron

PLATE 121
Powder flasks and their prices from the 1885 catalogue of Jos. C. Grubb & Co., Philadelphia, Pa.

Before leaving the subject of horns, the reader should be alerted to the fact that two sizes of horns were used in the period of the flintlock. The larger horn was filled with coarse powder for the barrel; the smaller horn contained a fine powder that was placed in the pan for ignition.

The invention of the percussion lock eliminated the need for the smaller horn and the more recent large horns were not as attractive as the ones used in the earlier times. Only a few were engraved and less attention was given to details on the large end of wood, which obviously became a product of the Industrial Revolution. The horn lost its charm and became a simple functional object, sold through trade channels like Tryon of Philadelphia, and the Great Western Gun Works of Pittsburgh.

The decline in quality and popularity of the powder horn in the early nineteenth century can be attributed to the introduction of the metal powder flask. Flasks were made of tin, copper, zinc, brass, and German silver with ornate decorative patterns stamped on each side. In addition to being new, colorful, and practical, they could be easily carried in a coat pocket. In the 1830's merchants like Tryon in Philadelphia were stocking them, and not many years later they could be bought in the hardware stores of most cities.

PLATE 122   *Park Emery*

This is an exceptionally fine example of a gunner's hunting pouch. It is made of black leather with white binding on the edges and red felt shows through the heart and diamond motifs on the lid.

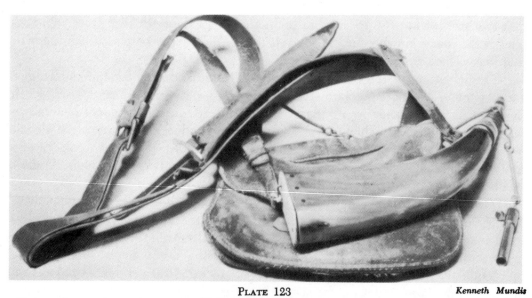

PLATE 123   *Kenneth Mundis*

Hunting bag with its accessories including a flat powder horn with a separate end which can be removed to fill the horn. Flat horns with such ends are very rare.

Hunting Bags

Because hunting bags were used in Europe prior to the English and German settlements in Pennsylvania, it must be presumed that they were used here in the earliest times. Most of the bags were simple, functional objects made of leather with one or two compartments. A flap was attached to the top edge to protect the contents from the rain or prevent their spilling out when the bag was slightly tilted. A shoulder strap, attached to each end of the top edge, supported the bag when it was carried into the field. The exterior appurtenances to the hunting bags varied. Most of them had a horn attached to the shoulder strap; a few had knife sockets and crude hunting knives. In the flintlock era a pick and brush were also attached to the shoulder strap, to pick open the touch hole and brush foul powder from the pan. A few had powder measures also.

The two inner compartments of the bag were used to carry bullets, or buckshot, leather or linen for patches, flints, and a small bullet mold. They might also have carried their small powder horn in the bag. It is interesting to note here that

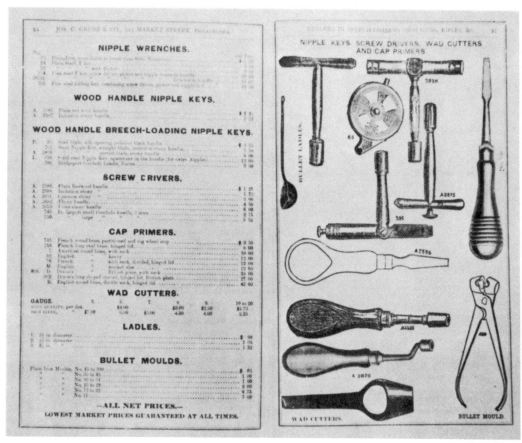

J. T. Herron

PLATE 124

Two pages of accoutrements from the 1885 catalogue of Jos. C. Grubb & Co., Philadelphia, Pa.

an entry in the *Fort Pitt Day Book* of Baynton, Morgan, and Wharton tells that in 1765 Moses Henry bought 21 yards of linen and 21 pounds of lead. There is no proof that he used the linen for patches, but the coincidence is certainly suggestive of such a procedure.

The bags of the percussion-lock era were essentially the same as those of the earlier period, but contained percussion caps instead of flints and patches. The pick and brush were also replaced by the simple tools which men carried at the time.

Chapter 7

The Gunsmith

IT MAY BE SAFELY SAID that little is known about the trade operations of the gunsmith of the eighteenth and nineteenth centuries in America. True, a few "old timers" lived and worked in the twentieth century, but it is to be doubted that they made their barrels or locks in the early traditions of the craft; and in all cases their precious bit of knowledge about the trade seems to have slipped away with their passing. By piecing together information gleaned from inventories of estates, from bills of sale, from correspondence about old guns, and by studying the few tools and machines that have escaped the scales of junk dealers, some hypotheses can be formed about the trade and trade techniques. Restoration projects like Williamsburg in Virginia, Old Sturbridge Village in Connecticut, and Old Salem in North Carolina, have culled as many tools as could be found; but it is doubtful whether the combined resources of all their possessions would be adequate to produce a gun. Barrel anvils and boring benches are particularly scarce, although each restoration has managed to acquire a rifling bench.

That this scarcity of tools and data exists in Europe, where people have been sensitive to the preservation of old crafts is also true. Extensive displays like the National Folk Art Museum at Arnhem, Holland, St. Fagans in Wales, and Pueblo Espanol in Barcelona, Spain, have nothing to offer in this line, although they have exhibits and demonstrations in such crafts as ceramics, textiles, and glass blowing.

The obscurity of details of the trade in America is particularly mysterious in view of the great numbers of men engaged in it. The Federal census of 1850 lists the occupations of all males over 15 years of age, and 3,843 gunsmiths were reported at that time. To estimate that probably an equal number of men were engaged in the craft before and after the census was taken would result in a total of 6,000 to 7,000 men who worked at the trade in America during a span of about two hundred years.

The recent surge of interest in American arms, and in Pennsylvania guns in particular, and the resultant stimulation of research on the subject have made considerable new data available to the collecting fraternity. About seven years ago the writer located the intestate inventory of John Philip Beck, who lived in Lebanon Township, Dauphin County, Pennsylvania. At his death in 1812 the executors of his estate listed among his possessions many common mechanic's tools, such as a grinding wheel, saws, vises, shears, tongs, scales, etc. The list also included a number of tools that a gunsmith would use, such as crucibles (for melting brass), engraving tools, implements for drawing rifles, irons for cutting screws, cherries, etc.

The discovery of Beck's tools led to other research and other discoveries, one of the most interesting being the inventory of Matthius Roessor who died in Lancaster, Pennsylvania, in 1771. His worldly effects included important objects such as a barrel anvil, a boring machine, a rifling machine, crucibles, bick irons, calipers, etc. Other research has brought to light the floor plan of a gunsmith's shop, prices for repairs to guns by the famous gunsmith of Philadelphia, John Nicholson, and finally a business ledger of a famous Dauphin County gunsmith, named Leonard Reedy. Details from these, and other resources will be used to describe the training and trade of the gunsmith when guns were made by hand.

The first aspect to be considered is the training of the embryo gunsmith, that is, his apprenticeship. A legal document, called an indenture, was signed by the master and the apprentice and was recorded in the courthouse so that each participant was legally held to his bond. It should be mentioned here that many of the children who were apprenticed to craftsmen were orphans or illegitimate children. For all apprentices two copies of the indenture were made, one to be held by the

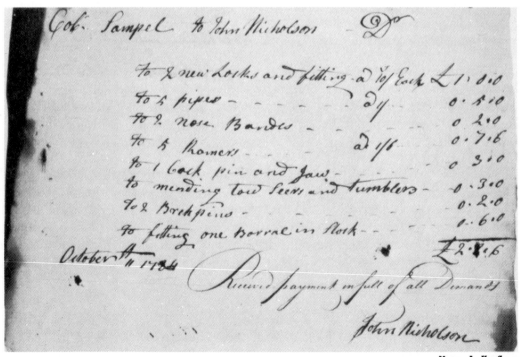

Henry J. Kauffman

PLATE 125

Although John Nicholson is not known to have made any Pennsylvania rifles, this receipted bill provides some information about the cost for gun repairs in 1784.

master and the other by the apprentice. When the apprentice period was concluded, the apprentice received the second copy as evidence that he had fulfilled the requirements of his agreement.

Throughout Europe and America in the eighteenth century the apprentice period was usually seven years and terminated when the youth became twenty-one years of age. However, the period of apprenticeship was probably shortened after parts like gun barrels and locks could be bought from a hardware merchant. Although there is no doubt that some youths continued to learn all aspects of the trade in the nineteenth century, newspaper adveriements of the period indicate that the age of specialization was rapidly advancing, for there were frequent requests for lock filers, barrel welders, and stockers. The following advertisement of Phillip Schaeffer in the January 1, 1796 issue of the *Lancaster* (Pennsylvania) *Journal* indicates the trend at that time.

> N. B. A person who understands the business of making gun barrels, will meet with encouragement and highest wages, by applying to said Schaeffer.

It might also be pointed out that another Schaeffer advertisement of the same year included brass gun mountings, English and German gun locks.

A record of indentures in the office of the mayor of Philadelphia shows a shortening of the seven-year training period for craftsmen. In the early 1770's a cooper learned his trade in three years, a leather breeches maker was bound for two years, a goldsmith was apprenticed for thirteen, and a blacksmith had to serve only a year and eight months to learn his trade. The only record relating to a gunsmith, in the period, is that of a servant indentured to John Nicholson for three years. The fact that the man was a servant suggests that he was probably getting maintenance for his services and he was not an accredited gunsmith when his indenture was terminated.

Since the first draft of this chapter about the gunsmith was written, the author's attention was directed to the indenture of Abia Smith to Joel Ferree, both of whom lived in Findley Township, Allegheny County, Pennsylvania. An apprentice agreement from any trade is a rarity today and to have located one of a Pennsylvania gunsmith is a most fortunate experience.

The indenture obviously confirms the hypothesis of a shorter learning period in the nineteenth century, and it also includes an agreement permitting the apprentice to leave his learning for nine days to assist in harvesting grain. The harvesting of grain by hand was a time-consuming labor; and it is known that all hands were needed, including those of women and children. The contents of the indenture follows:

> This indenture made this 9th day of May A. D. 1836 by and between Abia Smith, son of John Smith, of Findley Township, by and with the advice and consent of his Father of one part; and Joe Free of the Township of Findley in the County of Allegheny of the other part. Witness the said Abia by and with the consent of his said Father hath bound and put himself by the signing and

Courtesy Mrs. Ellen Watt

PLATE 126
Indenture of Abia Smith, who was apprenticed to Joel Ferree on the 9th of May A. D. 1836.

sealing these presents doth bind and put himself apprenticed to the said Joel Ferree, Gunsmith, after the manner of an apprentice to dwell with and since the said Joel Ferree, his executors, administrators, and assigns, from day of the Date hereof and during and until the full end of two years and four months thence next ensuing and full end. During all of which term the said apprentice his Master shall . . . . and that Honestly and Faithfully all the things as a dutiful apprentice aught to do. And, the said Joe Ferree his executors, administrators, and assigns are bound to teach, instruct, or cause to be instructed the said apprentice the Art and Mystery, or trade of the Gunsmith with all its various branches. To find him decent clothing both common and to go to church, board and wash and in every respect find said apprentice in comfortable lodging and to give the apprentice Nine days free to himself in Harvest. It is especially understood that the term of service is to expire the 9th day of September in the year A. D. 1838. The said parties have herewith bound themselves their heirs and assigns & every one of their family by these present and duly witnessed.

Attest   T J Hairl

Abia Smith
Joel Ferree
John Smith

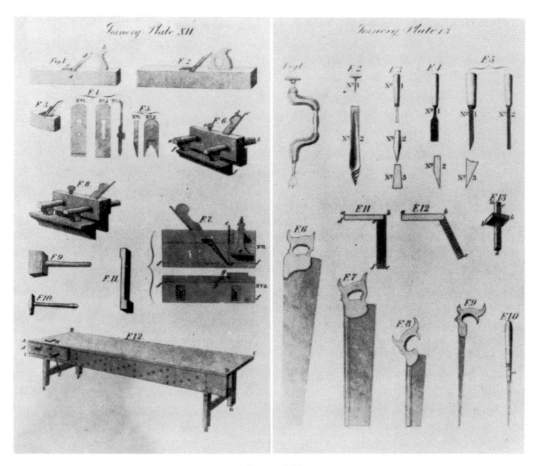

PLATE 127
Joinery tools similar to those used by a gunsmith in the middle of the nineteenth century. Illustrations from *The Mechanic's Companion* by Peter Nicholson, published by John Lochen in Philadelphia, 1845.

The indentures of the eighteenth and nineteenth centuries obviously required that the master teach his apprentice the "Art and Mystery of his Trade." The first responsibilities of the youth were necessarily simple ones, such as cleaning the shop, sharpening tools, starting the forge fire, pumping the bellows, or polishing gun parts. These simple tasks bored many of the apprentices, particularly if the master kept him at chores that were characterized by their drudgery rather than by importance in learning the trade. Some of the youths ran away from their masters, as one did from Christian Klein, a gunsmith working in Lancaster, Pennsylvania, in 1795.

EIGHT DOLLARS REWARD

Ran away the 15th instant, from the subscriber living in Lancaster, indentured servant lad named John McCan.—is about 19 years of age, 5 feet, 6 or 7 inches tall, of a dark complexion, and has a long nose. He speaks both English and German, but English best: and is by trade a gunsmith. He had on when he went away a good hat, a light coloured cassimer coatie, and a nankin waistcoat and breeches.

Whoever apprehends the said Runaway so that the Master may get him, shall receive the above reward and reasonable ·charges if brought home, from

Christian Klein, Gunsmith

Lancaster Journal, September 16, 1795.

Although newspapers of the eighteenth century contain many advertisements for run-away apprentices, one must presume that in most cases a satisfactory arrangement existed between the master and his apprentice and that he "Faithfully his master served." As the apprentice gained more knowledge and skill in his work, he was given more difficult operations to perform until he was competent in all the exacting demands of his chosen trade. Some of the most important techniques will be fully explained in the second part of this discussion.

In spite of many intangible compensations to the youth while learning his trade, in the eighteenth century many a young man looked forward to the end when he would receive an important gift from his master. Because the youth had little opportunity, if any, to acquire money to start him on his way when he became a journeyman, it was customary for the master to give him a "set of tools and a suit of clothes" at the end of his training period. The importance of both of these items to a young craftsman is so obvious that the subject need not be discussed more fully.

One can presume that the set of tools included only the hand tools which a gunsmith could carry from shop to shop, as a machinist carries his tools from factory to factory today. It is interesting, however, to examine the complete list of tools found in the shop of Matthius Roessor after his death in 1771. It should be pointed out that the forge is not mentioned because it was actually a part of the real estate and was sold to the person who bought the house and shop. The set of tools which the apprentice received probably included many of the hand tools found in the following list.

2 bellows
rifling engine
old stocks of wood
one anvil
one beck iron
5 prs. tongs
a polishing leath
wheel bearing bits and floats
forging tools
barrel anvil
one vise
6 vises
2 small hacks
2 saw frames
12 smooth files
2 vise claps & 3 Wedges
2 rasps
8 bench hammers
1 ax and hatchet
2 saw frames
12 large screw plates and britchen tools
1 small screw plate
6 pairs plyers
7 pairs compasses
1 pair large stillyards
2 draw knives
4 ramer bits
4 old guns
1 saw

stocking tools
drill stock
tumbler tool
2 pairs old shears
boaring mill
boaring rods
2 pairs nippers
1 compass saw
1 square
3 saw plates
6 double trickers
20 cherrys
1 pair bullet molds
2 spring hooks
2 picks to casting tools and sand
1 grindstone and frame spelter and
   block tin division plate
punches and reemers
barrel gauge
old iron
1 half-finished gun
1 new gun lock
1 smooth rifle
1 powder proff
needsfoot oil
2 soddern irons
9 planes
half finished pistols and barrels

Despite the fact that some Pennsylvania gunsmiths were born in Germany and that certainly many of them were of German descent, there is no record of their following the German custom of making a "meisterstuck," or masterpiece, at the conclusion of their training period as was done in Germany. It is possible, however, that some of the fine and unique guns are a result of such a practice here. An interesting account of the procedure was written by William Howitt, after he returned from Germany, in his book *The Rural Life of Germany*, which was published in Philadelphia by Carey and Hart in 1843.

> The apprentice on the expiration of his term, must then proceed with a certificate from his guild, on his Wanderschaft, or journey, for three or more years to perfect himself. His years of learning were called Lehrjare, or learning years; those of his travel were his Wanderjare, or wandering years. On his return, he must, if he wished to become a master, make a chef d'oeuvre, which must be submitted to the masters of the guild, and only on their approval of it could he receive his freedom, and right to exercise his calling in a free city.

Some isolated, though interesting, facets of the apprentice and his training have been found which might logically be included here because of their intimate relationship with the production of the Pennsylvania rifle. It is obvious to any person interested in the subject that the court records of the master-apprentice agreements should have survived and be available for study. Unfortunately, the author has been

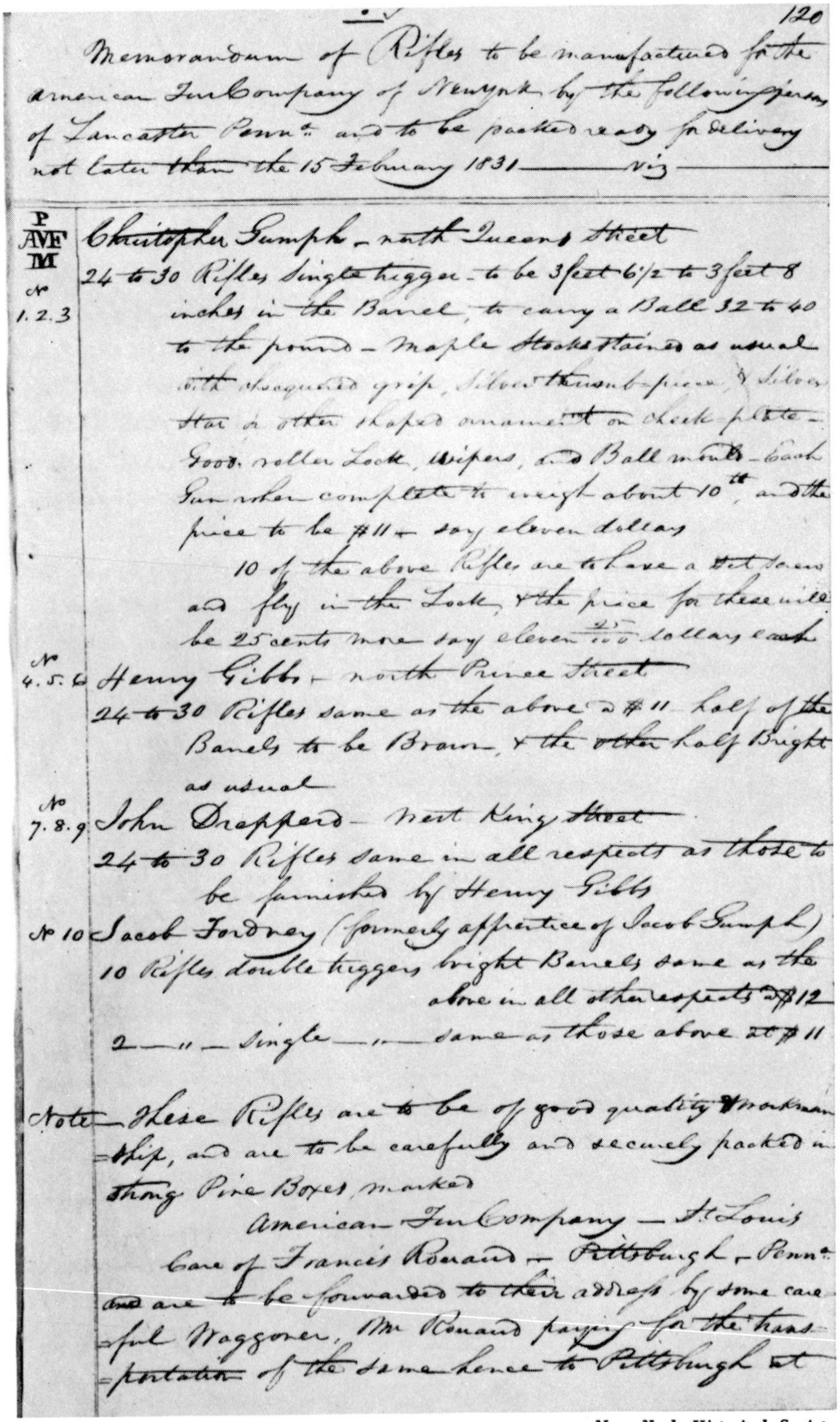

120

Memorandum of Rifles to be manufactured for the
american Fur Company of New York, by the following persons
of Lancaster Pennt. and to be packed ready for delivery
not later than the 15 February 1831 — Viz —

P
AVF
M
No
1. 2. 3

Christopher Gumpf — north Queen street
24 to 30 Rifles single trigger — to be 3 feet 6½ to 3 feet 8
        inches in the Barrel, to carry a Ball 32 to 40
        to the pound — Maple Stocks stained as usual
        with chequered grip, Silver thumb piece, & Silver
        Star or other shaped ornament on cheek plate —
        Good, roller Lock, wipers, and Ball moulds — each
        Gun when complete to weigh about 10 lb, and the
        price to be $11 — say eleven dollars
            10 of the above Rifles are to have a set screw
        and fly in the Lock, & the price for these will
        be 25 cents more say eleven 25/100 dollars each

No
4. 5. 6
Henry Gibbs — north Prince street
24 to 30 Rifles same as the above at $11 half of the
        Barrels to be Brown, & the other half Bright
        as usual

No
7. 8. 9
John Drepperd — West King street
24 to 30 Rifles same in all respects as those to
        be furnished by Henry Gibbs

No 10
Jacob Fordney (formerly apprentice of Jacob Gumpf)
10 Rifles double triggers bright Barrels same as the
                above in all other respects at $12
 2 — " — Single — " — same as those above at $11

Note
These Rifles are to be of good quality & workman
-ship, and are to be carefully and securely packed in
strong Pine Boxes, marked
            American Fur Company — St Louis
            Care of Francis Renaud — Pittsburgh — Pennt
and are to be forwarded to their address by some care-
-ful Waggoner, Mr Renaud paying for the trans-
-portation of the same hence to Pittsburgh at

New York Historical Society

PLATE 128

A page from the transactions of the American Fur Company with gunsmiths in Lancaster, Pennsylvania in 1831. This record not only describes the type of rifle made for the American Fur Company, but also mentions the names of four gunsmiths who made them. It is also interesting to note that Jacob Fordney was apprenticed to Jacob Gumpf. This is the only master-apprentice relationship known to the writer to be documented in Lancaster County, Pennsylvania.

able to find only scattered examples of these records, and in no case, except the one which mentions John Nicholson in Philadelphia, has data been available about known makers of guns.

However, authorities on the subject, relate two craftsmen to each other in this master-apprentice relationship by comparing the details of their work. It is not uncommon to find two rifles with a marked resemblance in carving or engraving which suggests that the maker of one gun was the master and the other maker was the apprentice. For example, the engraving on a rifle made by Henry Eberman, of Lancaster, Pennsylvania, shows that he was definitely influenced by Melchoir Fordney of the same city. Unfortunately, little of Jacob Gumpf's work has survived; and such a comparison cannot be made between him and his apprentice, Jacob Fordney.

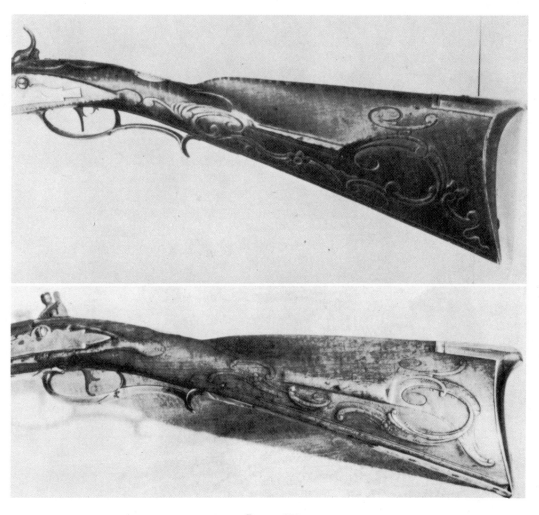

PLATE 129

Although the carved patterns on these two guns are not identical, their similarity suggests that there was some connection between the makers. The rifle with the percussion lock is signed J. Ernst on the top facet of its octagonal barrel. The fowling piece with the flint lock has been identified as a product of George Eyster. The lockbolt plate on this gun is not original.

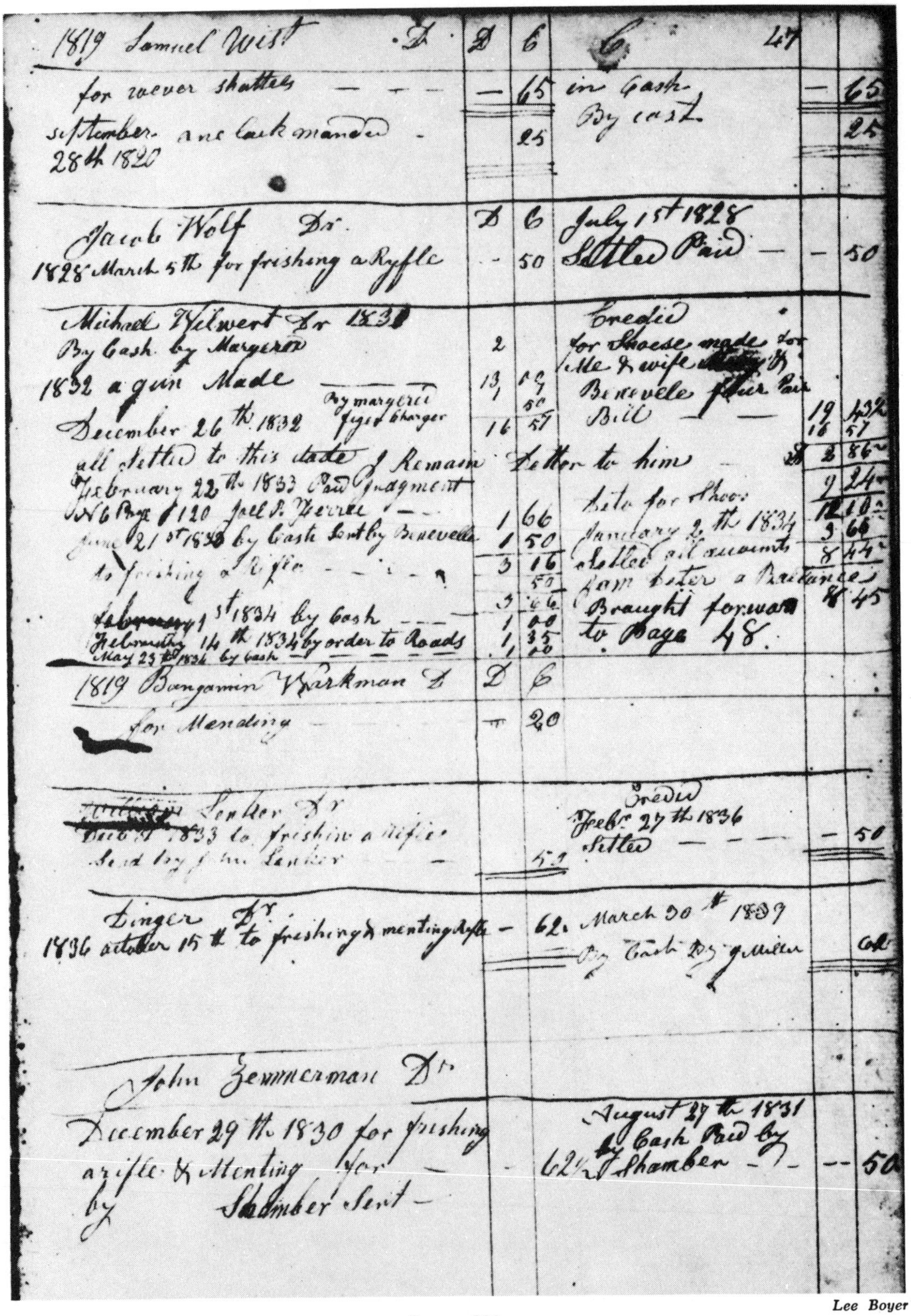
1819 Samuel Wist Dr 47

for weaver shattles — 65 in Cash — 65

September one cask mended 25 By cash 25

28th 1820

Jacob Wolf Dr. July 1st 1828

1828 March 5th for freshing a Ryfle 50 Settled Paid — 50

Michael Wilwert Dr 1831 Credit

By Cash by Margeret 2 for Shoese made for

1832 a gun Made 13

December 26th 1832 16 57 Bill 19 43

all settled to this date I Remain better to him

February 22th 1833 Paid Judgment

January 2th 1834

settled all accounts

Braught forward to Page 48.

February 1st 1834 by Cash

February 14th 1834 by order to Roads

May 23th 1834 by cash

1819 Bengamin Workman Dr

for Mending 20

Lenker Dr Credit

1833 to freshing a rifle Febr 27th 1836

Settled — 50

Dinger Dr. March 30th 1839

1836 october 15th to freshing & menting Ryfle — 62

John Zemmerman Dr

December 29th 1830 for freshing August 27th 1831

a rifle & Menting for — 62½ by Cash Paid by Shamber — 50

by Shamber Sent —

Lee Boyer

PLATE 130

A page from the business ledger of Leonard Reedy, who lived in Gratz, Dauphin County, Pennsylvania. A number of entries on this page are for "Frishing a rifle," which means to renew the grooves which have been partially worn.

Another very interesting facet of the apprentice and his training in keeping accounts is the discovery of a ledger recording the business transactions of Leonard Reedy, a Pennsylvania riflemaker. This ledger lacks the precision of twentieth century bookkeeping, but its charm lies in its simply organized way of recording the transactions of this famous craftsman. From the first to the last pages of the book are many examples of problems, such as computing interest; the changing of money from the English pound to the American dollar; the methods for computing contents of round liquid containers, like barrels; and the writing of forms for notes, deeds, wills, etc. This information was very useful to Leonard Reedy, for in addition to being the town gunsmith he was also the justice of the peace and was almost daily engaged in executing legal documents of some type. He wrote vendues for sales, secured power of attorney for various people, and probably wrote many letters for people who were unable to write in this small community. Though his spelling might be described as phonetic and his grammar lacked polish, his training as an apprentice proved to be invaluable to him.

An additional need for arithmetical computation occurred in the business of the day, usually called barter. In his ledger are numerous examples of exchanges like the one on page 47, where he made a gun for, "shoes for Me & wife & Benevle, four pair."

Reedy had some unorthodox uses for his ledger. In the back of it he recorded the birth and baptismal dates of his children, and two pages are devoted to the cost of "keeping house" for the year 1825. The following is a random listing of activities that he included among his gun business transactions.

Sharpening a coffee mill	A tumbler schrue
Making a shuttel	To make a rope wheel
Stock a rifle	Spinning wheel iron mended
Mend a lock	Mending a compass
Frish a rifle	Stealing a frissen
Clean a gun	A rat trap
Make a mainspring	Making a smooth rifle
Ramrote mate	Stealing a hammer
One touch hole, a wiper and a ramrott	Writing a deed
One mainspring and swevel	A cock scrue
Writing a vendue	To make a sight
Writing a power of attorney	Mounting a sythe

The above listing does not give a true proportion of time which he spent on making guns, although it does focus attention on the fact that he was doubtless the town's handyman. He did an extensive business in sharpening coffee mills, and he probably made a hundred weaver's shuttles. He must have been taught English, for most of his exercises are written in English, but his German ancestry is obvious, for his earliest entries are in German. His later entries were made in English with a heavy Germanic flavor.

Another interesting outcome of the apprenticeship occurred when it was at the same time a father-son relationship. If the son followed his father's trade, he could continue living at home and receive the sympathetic direction of his parents for a long period of time. There was also the possibility in such arrangements that the son could take over the business of the father after the latter was unable or unwilling to continue with it. To acquire easily an established business in this way was an unusual opportunuity for any youth. It is possible that apprentices other than sons of master also had the opportunity to take over their master's business.

It is interesting to note that the children of gunsmiths often intermarried, as was probably true also in other trades. Peter Gonter of Lancaster, Pennsylvania, is known to have married the daughter of Wolfgang Haga of Reading, Peter Resor of Lancaster is known to have married the daughter of a gunsmith named Welshantz in York, and Peter Resor's sister married Jacob Kraft, a gunsmith of Revolutionary fame in Lancaster.

This brief survey of details about the apprenticeship does not constitute a thorough study of the subject, but relates some of the facets as they were concerned with the learning of making guns.

The Gunshop

To consider the arrangement and architecture of the gunshop seems to be the next logical step in the problem of gun making. However, no buildings have survived intact and complete, so that again a piecemeal assemblage of ideas from different sources is necessary. It is likely that the European practice of building a house and a shop under one roof was at first followed in America. In Lancaster, York, and Reading the shops, with their forges, were either in the basement of the residence or attached to a rear wall. There was less need for the European demands for safety and frugality, but departures from old customs do not occur rapidly.

On the other hand, if such a combination was used at first, it is likely that the prospering smith of Pennsylvania soon found that a separate building was a more desirable arrangement. In Carlisle and Lancaster are two buildings which are reputed to have been used as gunshops. It is interesting to note that both of these buildings are built of stone, and that they are about the same size, having about the same proportions of width to length. It is extremely important to notice, too, that the interior architectural plan of a gunshop which has been discovered in the Moravian Archives in Bethlehem, Pennsylvania, was of about the same proportions as these two buildings, and with a little adjustment would fit the plan of either of them.

The use of stone in the exterior walls of these buildings can be easily understood, for it was a plentiful commodity, it was cheap, it was attractive, and it was fireproof. The hearth could have been built of stone or brick on the inside of one of the gable ends, or a completely independent stack could have been built where the Moravian plan indicates that one was built. The roof was probably made of slate, which was durable and completely impervious to the sparks that might fall from the chimney.

The floor of the gunshop might be made of gravel, bricks, or flat stones. A floor made of clay mixed with gravel, and pounded solid by constant pressure

PLATE 131

This building is thought to have been the gunshop of Martin Meylin. The building is on property which Meylin owned; it was built in the eighteenth century; and it is an appropriate size and shape for a gunshop; but there is no evidence of its having windows or a forge, both of which were conventional parts of a shop.

from the shoe soles of the workmen would be a very satisfactory material for the floor of a smithshop. Such a floor could be later made more attractive by overlaying it with bricks or stones. The need for a fireproof floor in a smithshop is obvious, and such a one might have been used in the Moravian plan, while a floor of planks would have been more comfortable and satisfactory for the room where the gun stockers worked.

The interior architectural arrangement of the Moravian shop suggests a facility for large-scale production rather than a small shop for a single gunsmith. The room in which the forge is located was the "smith's room," a term which implies that more than one man worked there. The theory that a number of smiths worked at welding barrels is substantiated by Greener in his *Gunnery in 1858,* in which he illustrates a barrel being welded by three men. They are grouped around a barrel anvil and alternately strike the barrel until each weld is completed.

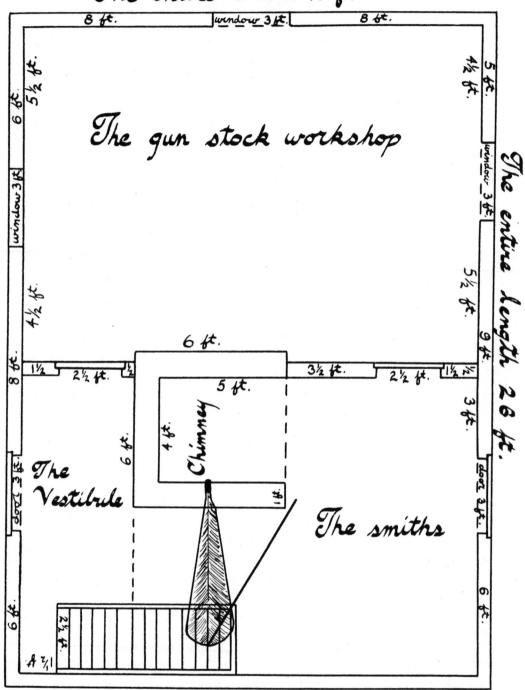

Moravian Archives, Bethlehem, Pa.

PLATE 132

The floor plan of a gunshop could be for a shop in Europe or in Pennsylvania. There was probably little difference in them in mid-eighteenth century.

It is interesting to note that the inside width of the forge was four feet and the outside was six. The hearth was obviously bigger than that of the average blacksmith's forge. If the bellows were in the same scale as the remainder of the shop, they would have been at least six feet long.

The appearance of the vestibule and a partition between the smith's room and the stocking room indicates that the plan was not crudely or indifferently developed. The vestibule kept some of the cold winter air out of the work rooms and provided a separate entry to each of the rooms on the first floor. It was probably also an entry to the apartment on the second floor, through the stairs along the wall. Perhaps the vestibule also served as a small sales room where the merchant-craftsman could show a gun to a prospective customer. At a later time any surplus guns which were in stock could be displayed there, so that a customer could make a selection from a number of guns.

The number and location of the windows suggest that the plan was made no later than the last half of the eighteenth century. The small size of the windows are reminiscent of the poor lighting of buildings in the late mediaeval times and their location in the center of the walls was a typical Georgian custom. The smith's room must have been very poorly lighted with only one window; and the vestibule did not have any windows, though, of course, the upper part of the vestibule door may have been divided into nine or twelve lights with thin mullions between them.

The later shops in which gunsmiths really did little more than assemble guns, were probably smaller than this one and may not have had a forge. Barrels, locks, and brass mountings could be bought; so there was little need for extensive space or a coal-fired forge. A workbench with a vise for woodwork and probably a lathe for turning and polishing was needed, however. The mid-nineteenth century gun shop probably looked like the smithshop that is illustrated in *The Mechanic's Companion,* compiled by Peter Nicholson and published in Philadelphia by John Lochen in 1845.

Documentary evidence shows that by the time of the Revolution another structure called a boring and grinding mill came upon the Pennsylvania scene of gunsmithing. In 1774 Jacob Dickert and John Henry bought a tract of land in Manheim Township, Lancaster County, and built a boring and grinding mill on it. This mill was doubtless a successful business venture, for when Henry died in 1779, Dickert bought the second interest in it from Henry's widow and owned it until the 1790's when he resold it to the man from whom they had originally bought the land.

An interesting part of the purchase agreement was that the mill could be used only for gun-barrel work and could never be converted into a grist-mill. This agreement was doubtless inserted because of the common practice of converting grist-mills to boring mills; and probably the reverse was true at times when the owner of the tract did not want any competition with the grist-mill which he had built along the same creek. A famous mill near Lancaster, the Stoneroad mill is thought to have been converted from grist to boring and grinding at the time of the Revolution; and a grist-mill standing along Mill Creek, south of Lancaster was definitely a boring and grinding mill in the late eighteenth and early nineteenth

PLATE 133

Interior plan of a nineteenth century smith's shop as illustrated in The Mechanic's Companion by Peter Nicholson, published by John Locken in 1845. A gunsmith's shop of the same time had similar tools and machines.

centuries. This latter mill was owned by James Bryan, who was called a gunbarrel-smith when he bought the mill and when he sold it. Although the mill is in a dilapidated condition now, it is probably the only structure connected with gun making in the eighteenth century, standing today in Lancaster County, Pennsylvania.

There is also an interesting account of a combination boring and grinding mill in the *Proceedings of the Northumberland County Historical Society,* Volume VII, 1935, pp. 70-76. The most significant portion is quoted here.

> . . . . Catherine Smith, widow of Peter Smith, commenced building a grist mill and saw mill at the mouth of White Deer Creek in 1774 which she completed a year later . . . . In 1779 Widow Smith's mill was burned by the red men at the time of the massacre at Fort Freeland . . . . In her petition to the general Assembly at Philadelphia in 1785 to recover her property, Catherine Smith sets forth that she built a gun-boring mill in 1776, where a great many gun barrels were bored for the patriot army. The Indian invasions of the West Branch valley soon after coming on, the flour mill, hemp mill, saw mill, and boring mill became a frontier fort, and in July 1779, to use her very modern expression, "The Indians burned the whole works." According to her descendant she returned to Lancaster County with some of her family, visiting among relatives, and did not come up the river again until late in 1783. . . . . among those who endorsed Catherine Smith's petition to the Assembly was General James Potter of Potters Fort, and Colonel John Kelly of Kelly X. Roads.

Photo Courtesy of J. Luther Heisey

PLATE 134

This grist-mill was at one time the barrel mill owned by "gunbarrelsmith" James Bryan in the late eighteenth century. It is the only building standing in Lancaster County which is known to have been part of the gun industry in the eighteenth century.

PLATE 135

Many important incidents in the History of York, Pa., have been recorded by the famous folk artist, Lewis Miller. This sketch shows the burning "boremill" on the edge of the town and tells the names of the gunsmiths who were working in the town at the time.

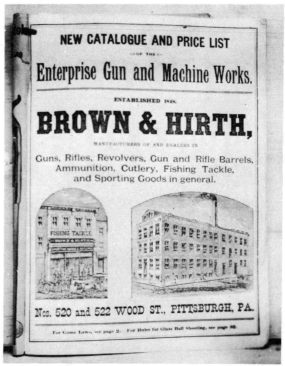

J. T. Herron

PLATE 136

A page from the 1886 catalogue of Brown & Hirth of Pittsburgh, Pa., showing the factory and retail store.

In York County the existence of a boring mill has been perpetuated by the famous folk artist, Lewis Miller, who drew a picture of the burning mill. In addition he tells, "Fire, the Bore Mill, burnt in 1800, it was a little more than a mile from town near the little Bridge on the Baltimore Pike, now, this mill was useful to our gunsmiths in York. Their names, Philip Heckert, Conrad Welshants, Joseph Welshans, Jacob Letter, Jacob Doll, Henry Pickel, George Brenise, Frederick Zorger."

The evidence of the Dickert mill in Lancaster, the Smith mill at White Deer Creek, and the Lewis Miller sketch of a mill at York suggests that each area had at least one mill that was devoted to this specialized type of production. A boring mill also known to have been located at the Boulton site of the Henry gun manufacturing plant, and Henry Leman of Lancaster is reputed to have had the first boring mill that was operated by a steam engine.

It is not known exactly when barrel welding was added to the activities of boring and grinding, but Henry and George Landis in volume seven of the *Pennsylvania German Folklore Society Publications* tell about these new, three-function mills. They tell that the Wyomissing Creek flows northward and empties into the Schuylkill River opposite the city of Reading. Along the banks of this creek, formerly known as "Schmutz Deich" or dirty ditch, were nine dams within a distance of three miles. The first one was built in 1755 and the last one ceased operations in 1906.

Their account of the shops and their mechanisms is in part, as follows:

> Each shop had its own dam and water wheels, the latter having a diameter of fourteen feet for the forge hammer and another six feet diameter for providing the air blast. The water wheels were made of wood; they were four feet wide and of the overshot type. Grinding was done by water power. The grind stones being five feet in diameter and sixteen inches wide, running fifty revolutions per minute. The main shop usually had a forty square foot floor plan and there was another shop twenty feet by fifteen feet. . . . .

PLATE 137

The rifle factory of Henry E. Leman as it appeared in the 1870's in Lancaster, Pennsylvania.

Forging along the "Schmutz Deich" was done with a trip hammer. Not all of these were alike in details. Usually there was a wooden belt wheel on the water wheel axle on which ran a wide strong belt. On the wheel shaft end were about five spurs or projecting strips which pressed upon the pivoted hammer or bar, raising the hammer end quickly as the trip end was forced downward against a long spring. As the trip left the hammer bar the force of the spring helped to give power to the hammer blow. The hammer was seldom changed, instead handled shapers were used to conform to the anvil being used at the time. The anvil base was of iron, fastened permanently to the heavy timber foundation.

While the water wheels along the Wyomissing were "turning out" gun barrels for individual craftsmen, some factories were producing complete guns for the "trade." The Leman factory at Lancaster and the Henry establishment at Boutlon are outstanding examples of mass production of guns in eastern Pennsylvania. The Enterprise Gun Works was established in Pittsburgh in 1848 and subsequently became the property of James Bown & Sons and later of Brown and Hirth. The buildings of Leman and the Enterprise Works are illustrated and are typical factory buildings of the late nineteenth century. When places like these closed their doors, the muzzle-loading industry no longer existed.

Gun Making

Most of the treatises on gun making explain about barrel making first, for a gun was obviously built around a barrel. A review of the published information about the making of gun barrels in the eighteenth and nineteenth centuries reveals an abundance of data on the subject. Although barrel making was a very fascinating process, the early absorption of the work by specialists seems to indicate a minimum demand for this information; and a greater demand for written instructions about stock making, which was the work of every individual gunsmith as long as muzzle-loaders were made. It is difficult to explain the discrepancy between the supply and demand for information in these two facets of gun making

The explanation of how a muzzle-loading rifle was made might be also prefaced by the statement that there was little change in the procedures in barrel making from 1644, when Alonzo Martinez de Espinar described the operation, until the final production of barrels along "Schmutz Deich" in Berks County, Pennsylvania, in the last half of the nineteenth century. Except for the substitution of water power for hand power, the materials and procedures stayed about the same.

A barrel was made of a ruler of metal, called a skelp, which was of appropriate width, thickness, and length, for the desired barrel. The center section of the skelp was placed over a forge fire and heated to a white welding heat. It was then placed over a groove in a barrel anvil and welded around a small piece of iron called a bick iron, or mandrel. Because only a short section could be welded at a time, the bick iron was removed and the skelp replaced in the forge after each welding operation. This heating and welding continued until the skelp was converted into a metal tube with a small hole in the center.

PLATE 138

The grooves of the barrel anvil varied in size so that only one anvil was needed to make barrels of different diameters.

This procedure was followed because it was impossible to drill a hole through a solid bar of iron; however, is was possible to enlarge the undersized hole left by the bick iron, to the desired caliber of the barrel. A skelp as long as two pistol barrels was welded and later cut in half, thus insuring uniformity in the bore and equal quality of workmanship in the welding of both barrels. Such precautions were particularly important if a pair of duelling pistols was being produced.

Attention should doubtless be called to the fact that in the last half of the nineteenth century muzzle-loaded barrels were made of cast steel and the hole was drilled in them. Brown & Hirth of Pittsburgh described their "Celebrated Kentucky Muzzle Loading Rifle" as follows.

> No. 7. Same style as no. 5, with cast steel barrel, cut with increased twist, imitation patent muzzle, fine curly maple stock, plated mountings, double bullet molds for casting long and round bullets, and finished in superior style . . $32.00

A few Pennsylvania rifles had brass barrels which, it must be presumed, were drilled, for it is impossible to weld brass in the way that iron can be welded. A brass tube could have been silver soldered from muzzle to breech, but not with the strength needed to have it serve as a gun barrel. Brass being less resistant to drilling than iron, all of the brass pistol and rifle barrels must have been drilled on a lathe or some specialized machine which was built to bore such barrels.

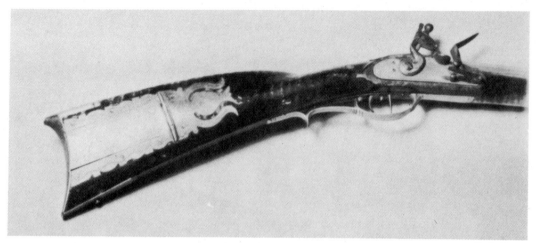

Park Emery

PLATE 139

Few Pennsylvania rifles have decorative motifs that are found on "objects of art" made in Pennsylvania such as manuscripts, decorated chests, etc. This one has a tulip finial on the patch box and an octagonal brass barrel, which is equally rare.

Boring the barrel followed the welding; both operations were performed in the earliest time by the gunsmith, and in later times by the barrel specialists who welded, bored, and ground the barrels. The boring was a critical procedure, for the shooting quality of the gun depended a great deal on the precision of the boring. And, if there were defects on the interior of the barrel, they had to be discovered early so that precious time was not lost on a barrel with an irreparable flaw.

The barrel was first clamped to a flat carriage which was mounted in a recess of a wide bench top, with provision for the carriage to move backward and forward. In order to bore the barrel, both the carriage and the barrel were pressed

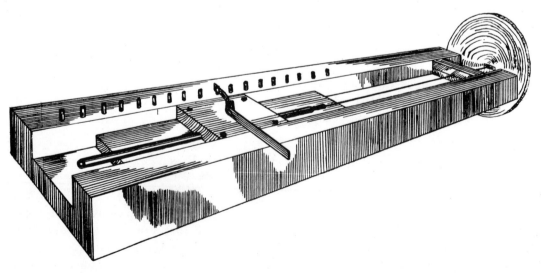

PLATE 140

Typical boring machine used by Pennsylvania gunsmiths. The flywheel could be motivated by hand or water power.

against the rotary motion of the bit until it cut its way though the barrel. Larger drills were subsequently used until the bore reached the desired diameter. Each drill had a cutting action, except the last one which was simply rectangular in shape, the sharp corners of the rectangular one reamed the bore to a brilliant smooth finish.

The inside of the barrel had to be examined frequently during the boring operation to determine if any low, black spots appeared, spots which were frequently removed by tapping the outside of the barrel over the low spot on the inside. If the bore was not perfect after a number of such trials, it was discarded.

The final test of the smooth bore was to determine if it were straight. To do this a taut silk thread was stretched along the inner wall of the barrel. If it touched the metal throughout its length, the barrel was straight; if otherwise, the barrel was tapped with a copper hammer until the desired uniformity was obtained.

In the earliest times the boring machine was turned by hand by the gunsmith, or more likely his apprentice. It is interesting to note that Greener shows in his *Gunnery in 1858,* a Birmingham boring machine with a large wheel and a knob by which a man was to turn the wheel. By that time most boring machines in Pennsylvania were probably being turned by water power.

Grinding, which followed the boring operation in barrel making, is described in the previously-mentioned Landis article as it was performed in Pennsylvania.

> Finishing the barrel by grinding out the hammer dents and giving it the desired shape was done upon a large and wide grind stone which was not less than a foot wide and about five feet in diameter. A centered plug was fitted into the bore at the ends and a circle scribed on the end of the barrel which indicated the outside of the barrel when finished. The barrel was then set in a frame with two center points so that it could be turned freely. This iron frame was attached to a wooden block which was moved in and out between guides and the frame moved from side to side in guides. In this way the barrel was pressed against the revolving stone and moved across it until one face was ground down to the circle scribed on the end. However, the ends were ground down to the circle first and the middle section was ground down even with the ends. Then the barrel was turned halfway around and the opposite face completed; and then the faces on either side. After that the four faces between were ground to make a regular eight sided barrel.

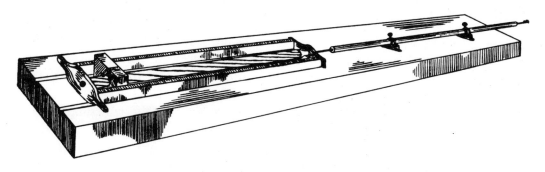

PLATE 141

Typical rifling machine used by Pennsylvania gunsmiths in the eighteenth century. Most of the parts of this one are made of wood. Later types were made of metal.

Greener shows a similar grindstone of about the same width, but certainly not with a diameter of five feet. The cross marks of the grindstone were usually left on the underside of the barrel, but the top facets were draw filed and carefully finished so that no tool marks remained.

From this point the barrel needed only a breech plug, barrel lugs, and sights to make it usable in a smooth-bore gun. And it should be emphasized that although a great many smooth-bore guns were made and used in Pennsylvania, the rifle was the gun on which care and work were lavished to make it an accurate fire-arm.

A rifling bench was used to cut grooves on the inside of the rifle barrel. The top of the bench was made of a heavy, wide plank about eight feet to ten feet long. On one end of the plank two eyes were attached with set screws in the top of each for clamping the barrel rigidly in place. On the other end of the plank a sliding frame was installed, about twelve to fifteen inches wide and 42 to 48 inches long; in the center of the frame was a cylinder of wood, about six inches in diameter, with a free turning handle on one end. Ribs were attached to the surface of the cylinder in the same spiral form as the shape of the grooves in the barrel was intended to be.

A forward thrust of the handle caused the cylinder to move forward through the index plate, which was permanently fastened to the bench top. A cutting tool on the end of the rod, which was attached to the cylinder followed the spiral motion of the cylinder and cut a groove on the inside of the barrel. Subsequent thrusts brought the groove to the desired depth, after which the barrel was given a partial turn and the operation repeated until all the grooves were cut to the correct depth.

In the earliest time rifling, like boring, was done by each gunsmith in his shop. There is no mention that rifling was done in the barrel production shops of the nineteenth century; consequently, for a number of reasons, it must be presumed that the gunsmith himself continued this operation. Despite the fact that rifling a barrel was hard work, it could be conveniently done in a small shop; and the gunsmith could save the money he would have to pay to have the work done elsewhere. It was work that a clever apprentice could quickly learn to do, particularly when a master craftsman was nearby to help him if he came to an impasse. Besides some customers probably wanted custom rifling by the gunsmith rather than a production job at a barrel mill.

That some men were listed as barrel riflers in the tax assessment lists indicates they were particularly apt at such work, or preferred it to making a complete gun. Such men could do both custom work for gunsmiths and production work if occasion demanded it. The number of barrel rifling machines which have survived indicates that a large number of gunsmiths did their own rifling; however, the invention of power-driven rifling machines in the last half of the nineteenth century probably made idle most of the hand operated machines in the gun shops.

Fitting the breech plug was the last major step in barrel making. The thread in the breech end of the barrel was started by using a long tapered object with a male thread on it, called a tap. Taps were made of steel and had to be hardened so that they could cut away metal to allow the breech plug to turn into the barrel. After the first pass was made with the long tapered tap, one with less taper was used, and finally one with practically no taper cut the thread to its full depth. After the breech plug was threaded and fitted to the barrel, a hole was bored through the tang for the tang screw. In the earliest guns this hole was threaded and the tang screw turned up from the bottom of the gun. In all nineteenth century guns the tang screw was inserted in the top and terminated in the trigger plate on the bottom of the gun.

Virtually no information about lock making is available in the English language. The easy importation of locks reduced the quantity that were made here, although

Kauffman Photo

PLATE 142

Rifling benches and part of the arms collection at the Pennsylvania Farm Musuem of Landis Valley, Pennsylvania.

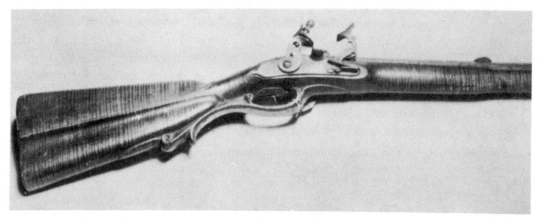

PLATE 143

Although the stocking of guns in curly maple is regarded by some collectors as an American practice, a few guns of European manufacture are known to exist with similar stocks.

some locks have on them names of Pennsylvania makers like Sweitzer, Drepperd, and Armstrong. The unique design of these lock plates combined with the names of Pennsylvania gunsmiths engraved on them suggests that they were locally made, but no information on the procedures of the craft has been found.

There is evidence in the inventories of early Pennsylvania gunsmiths that they cast their brass mountings in sand; however, by the end of the eighteenth century such parts were in ample supply in hardware stores. There is evidence too, that the stores were supplied by local foundries who cast them in the traditional methods of brass foundry work. The ramrod pipes were made by wrapping a piece of sheet brass or silver around a metal rod and then filing them to the desired shape. The procedure for making a one-piece ferrule for the forestock is a complete mystery at present, in so far as the author is concerned, although some evidence exists to suggest that the heavy, early type was cast in sand.

By the time guns were made in Pennsylvania the art and craft of gun-making was several centuries old and certain traditional practices had been definitely established in European workshops. One of these was the stocking of guns in walnut wood, which was strong, reasonably easy to work, and attractive as a "back drop" for the metallic parts of the gun. It is very likely that the first guns made in Pennsylvania were stocked in walnut; it is obvious, however, that the trend soon turned to maple.

Many gun enthusiasts are apt to identify a gun as a Pennsylvania product if it has a maple stock, but a look into the history of firearms shows that a few European guns were stocked in maple wood. A New England gun stocked in maple wood is almost as rare as a European one; nevertheless, a few early New England guns with maple stocks are known. The fact remains that maple was the favorite wood of the Pennsylvania gunsmiths and was used more extensively there for gun stocks than in any other place in the world.

The gunsmiths certainly had no trouble in securing wood of good quality. Pennsylvania's supply of most hardwoods was ample, and much of it was cut and burned to clear the land for agricultural purposes. The logs could be split into oversize planks, which were then left to dry for as long as seven years. The number of rough gunstocks found in the inventories of gunsmiths indicates that it was common practice to cut out blanks and store them for future use. This smaller piece of wood would dry more rapidly than those in log form, and the gunsmith could discard pieces with age cracks before he started working them into stocks. One item in the inventory of John Philip Beck is "33 pieces of wood hewn for gun stocks." They were valued at "£2/5/0."

The size and design of the stock was influenced by a number of factors. For example, most of the gun stocks made in Berks County, Pennsylvania, were of a pattern called the "Roman Nose," a pattern popular there for at least fifty years. If a customer did not happen to like the pattern, he may have influenced the gunsmith to use another; or he may have gone to another area to have his gun made. There were also more universal styles in stock making, such as the thick butt and the thin butt. The earliest guns had very thick butts, and even in 1780 one would have probably had much difficulty in getting a thin one.

The drop and length of the butt was influenced by the stature of the buyer. A small, short-armed man could not comfortably use the gun that was made for a tall man with long arms. The problem was solved by the gunsmith who had a number of guns for the prospective customer to try or a number of patterns which were good substitutes for guns.

After an appropriate pattern was selected, the gunsmith traced it or drew it free-hand on a smooth side of the plank from which the stock was to be cut. The earlier smoothing of one side permitted a preliminary examination of the grain structure for its attractive pattern or its suitability for a gun stock. A reasonably straight grain was desirable, and it was important that the line of the grain coincide with the main axis of the barrel. A cross-grain section in the forestock would have been very difficult to cut to shape, and very apt to break while it was being cut or after the gun was finished. Any fancy figure which the wood had was placed in the butt end of the stock, where breakage was not likely to occur and where it would be displayed to advantage. Particular attention was focused on the importance of good strong grain in the wrist of the stock, where the wood was thin. Hundreds of guns have been broken at this part, despite the precautions taken by gunsmiths to have the grain at the point strong.

After the blank had been planed to the proper uniform thickness, a center line was drawn on the top edge of the stock to position the barrel for inletting. The channel for the barrel was cut roughly to size by using hand tools such as bits, chisels, planes, and floats. The final fitting of the barrel was made by coating it with a substance such as chalk or oil, which would rub off on the high spots of the stock and indicate where small cuts had to be made.

After properly locating the lock plate, the next procedure was to draw a line around it, or a template, with a thin knife blade. The entire area inclosed by the knife mark had to be recessed as deep as the thickness of the lock plate; and a smaller area had to be recessed to accommodate the mainspring, tumbler, sear, and sear spring. If any of the interior parts of the lock rubbed against the wood, the lock would not function properly.

The trigger plate was located with much caution, for if the lock was to operate properly, the trigger must move against the sear with a positive smooth action. Consideration was also given to the location of the hole for the tang screw, which normally terminates in the trigger plate. Most triggers and trigger plates were made of iron; only very rarely were they made of brass.

After these parts were fitted into place, the stock was reduced to its final shape, and other parts—trigger guards, butt plates, inlays, and patch boxes—are put in place. The inlays were sawed and filed into shape before they were temporarily fastened in place with the pins that were finally used for that purpose. A knife line was drawn around them and the wood removed to allow them to be properly seated in the stock. The patch box was temporarily fastened in place by the screws and nails before a knife line was drawn around the edges. After the plate was recessed, a brace and bit was used to remove most of the excess wood in the patch box cavity. The cavity was later made square by the use of a wood chisel or carving tools.

Although carving the stock may not have been the last work of the gunsmith on the gun stock, it was in this work that the craftsman reached the apex of his achievement. A gun might be distinguished because of its good balance, its fine wood, its beautiful symmetry, or its cleverly engraved brass work; but none of these qualities were as important as a fine design carved in bas-relief on the cheek side of the butt or on other appropriate places. Furthermore, not all gunsmiths who carved guns were superior craftsmen, but the workmanship of men like N. Beyer, J. P. Beck, Jacob Sell, Fredrick Sell, George Eyster, and Martin Frey is among the best that was produced in Pennsylvania.

If a gunstock was to be carved, the wood had to be left oversize where the carving was to be done. Patterns like scrolls, animals, and geometric figures were sketched on the raised area and outlined with a sharp knife blade. The lowest parts of the designs were usually cut flat at the same level as the flat portion adjoining the carved area. The raised bands were rounded and carved into the desired contours. The cuts of a sharp chisel needed little finishing, and there is rarely any evidence of poorly finished work. Carving curly maple was extremely difficult, but one rarely sees a bad split or unintentional cut in the work of early craftsmen.

Not all carving was done in bas-relief, for there was a less time-consuming technique requiring less skill and known as incised carving. In this technique the pattern was cut below the level of the stock instead of being raised in bas-relief. A few guns show a combination of the two techniques.

A few guns have inlays on the top level of designs which were carved in bas-relief. This type of work was done by gunsmiths in Bedford County, Pennsylvania, although few men are known to have done it in other parts of the State. At least one gunsmith is known to have used this technique around a patch box.

This treatise on gun making has not been written for people who want to make guns. It is an attempt, based on many fragments of information and logical hypotheses, to tell how a gun was probably made by the average gunsmith.

Chapter 8

Biographies

ABENDSEN, JOSEPH

S & H, 50 Wayne Avenue, Pittsburgh, Pennsylvania. 1858-1859.

ADAMS, DANIEL

Somerset Township, Somerset County, Pennsylvania. Tax list 1837.

ADAMS, JAMES

Riceville, Bloomfield Township, Crawford County, Pennsylvania. 1879-1880.

ADAMS, TOWER (BLACKMAN)

Washington Township, Washington County, Pennsylvania. Tax lists 1826, 1834, 1859.

AFFLERBACH, WILLIAM

631 N. 2nd Street, Philadelphia, Pennsylvania. 1855-1861.

ALBRECHT, ANDREW

Warwick Township, Lancaster County, Pennsylvania. Tax list 1780.

ALBRECHT, CHARLES

148 Twentieth Street, Pittsburgh, Pennsylvania. 1870-1871.

ALBRIGHT, HENRY

Although no guns are known that can be identified as the product of Andrew Albright, there is evidence that he was a gunsmith, and he cannot be ignored, for there is always a possibility of finding a gun bearing his name. The following information about him has been taken from the *Cemetery Records of the Moravian Church*:

> Andrew Albright, born at Zella, near Suhl, Thuringia, April 2, 1718. His trade was that of a gunsmith. A soldier in his youth, he served in the army of Fredrick the Great, came to America in 1750 going to Christiansspring to live, and taught school in the boys school at Nazareth. Married Elizabeth Orthin 1766, and until 1767 they had charge of the Sun Inn in Bethelem. Came to Lititz in 1767 where he resumed his trade of gunsmith. He had six children: John Andrew, John Henry, Jacob, Susanna, Elizabeth, wife of Philip Bachman, organ builder and Gottfried. He was tenor singer in the church choir.

The relationship, if any, between Andrew and Henry Albright might never be established, but circumstantial evidence points to the fact that Henry was probably the son of Andrew. It is known that sons were frequently apprenticed to, or at least followed, the trade of their father; so it would seem reasonable to assume that there was a father-son relationship between these two men. It is also known that it was a Moravian custom for people to drop their first name and use their second name in social and civil transactions. This substitution could easily have occurred in the Albright family, for, in addition to it being a common custom, there were two Johns in the family; some form of differentiation must have been made between them. There is also the possibility that the first John had died before the second was born; nevertheless, some distinction between the two sons had to be made.

The following data about Henry Albright is copied from the *Cemetery Records of the Moravian Church*.

> Henry Albright was born August 5, 1772 in Lititz. Lived in Nazareth since 1816 after having resided in Lititz, Gnadenhutten, Ohio, Shippensburg, and other places. Married Barbara Hubley March 27, 1794 with whom he had ten children. February 25, 1830 he married Catherine Louisa Beck with whom he had four children.

This short biography focuses attention on the fact that Henry Albright was one of the famous gunsmiths of Lancaster County who moved to greener fields in the West. The first documentary evidence establishing him as a gunsmith is his appearance as a contributor to an account known as "Continental Rifles, Account of when Received and Forwarded, by Order of General Hand, Lancaster, February 7, 1794." The neophyte gunsmith of twenty-two years was associated in the venture with men like Dickert, Gonter, Greaff, Fainot, Brong, and Messersmith in producing arms for the Army of the United States or the Militia of Pennsylvania.

By 1796 he had moved to Chambersburg, as indicated in the following advertisement in the *Pittsburgh Gazette*, August 27, 1796.

> HENRY ALBRIGHT, GUNSMITH, RESPECTFULLY informs his friends and the public in general, that he has removed from Lancaster to Chambersburg, to the house lately occupied by Peter Snider, near the paper mill, where he intends to carry on the Gunsmith Business in all its various branches. He also has a large quantity of guns on hand, which he will sell on reasonable terms for cash or country produce.
>
> Also, said Albright and William McCall carries on the barrel making in all its branches—They have a large quantity on hand, which they will sell on moderate terms. Chambersburg, June 2, 1796.

It is obvious from this advertisement that Albright hoped to do business with gunsmiths from the Pittsburgh area who might be passing through Chambersburg, or who might come to Chambersburg to buy barrels. At that time there were about a half-dozen gunsmiths working in the Pittsburgh region and there was some prospect of doing business with them, unless one of them made barrels for the gunsmiths who lived over the mountains. It has been established that Jacob and Joel Ferree were in the Pittsburgh area at that time; and, because of their earlier training in Lancaster County, it is likely that they were skilled in the art of barrel making.

At any rate, the gun business apparently did not prove to be as good as Albright had hoped, for in 1800 he was living in Shippensburg. His next move was to Gnadenhutten, Ohio.

Gnadenhutten was one of the first settlements in Ohio and the fact that it was established by Moravian missionaries might partially explain why the Moravian Albright moved there. There is no doubt that gunsmiths were urgently needed in Ohio at that time and Albright again tried his luck on a distant frontier. Nothing is known of his activity there, and according to the cemetery record, he had returned to Nazareth by 1816 where he died and was buried.

The Andrew Albright biography tells that he had a son, Jacob, who could well be the gunsmith working in Northumberland County, Pennsylvania, in 1800. Little is known of his activity there, although a few guns have survived which bear his name.

No guns with the signature of Andrew Albright are known to the writer, so no evaluation can be made of his work. This condition is particularly unfortunate for he probably was apprenticed abroad and his earliest guns, at least, would show a European influence in their design and construction. A number of guns are known with the initials A. A. engraved on the top facet of the barrel, but they are attributed to Adam Angstadt, who worked in Kutztown, Pennsylvania, early in the nineteenth century.

The guns of Henry Albright are of a uniformly high quality and are eagerly sought by collectors. Many of them have unusually long barrels of the octagon to round pattern. The one illustrated has a daisy finial on the patch box, which indicates that he learned his trade or worked in Lancaster. Others have an attractive

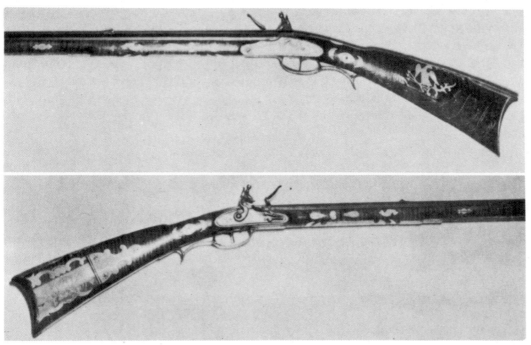

Clegg Collection

PLATE 144

Rifle with flint lock, full stock of curly maple, brass mountings, silver inlays, octagonal brass barrel with J. Albright on the top facet of the barrel.

In addition to signing his rifles on the barrel, J. Albright also carved his initials on the cheek side of the stock of some of his guns. This one is signed at both places.

horse-head finial on the patch boxes, which he could have used in Lancaster, but probably used after he moved to the Chambersburg area or Ohio. Many of his guns have patterns carved in relief on the cheek side of the stock, around the breech tang and in back of the ramrod thimble. The engraved patterns on the brass mountings are equally well done.

Although the work of Jacob Albright is pleasing, it does not compare favorably with that of Henry. He is known to have carved his initials on the cheek sides of a number of his guns, which is an attractive feature, but his incised technique is not as desirable as the relief carving of Henry. One of his guns is known to be profusely inlaid with pieces of sterling silver.

ALBRIGHT, JACOB
Haines Township, Northumberland County, Pennsylvania. Tax list 1800.

ALBRIGHT, ZACHARIAH
Bedford County, Pennsylvania. 1846.

ALEXANDER, DONALD
Elizabeth Township, Allegheny County, Pennsylvania. Census 1800.

ALLEGHENY GUN WORKS (John Fleeger)
78 Diamond, Allegheny, Pennsylvania. 1871-72.

The Allegheny Gun Works was established by John Fleeger in Allegheny in 1831. The city of Allegheny has since been incorporated into Pittsburgh's North Side and has lost its separate identity.

William A. Fleeger, John's son, was admitted into partnership in 1860. In 1879 they advertised that they manufactured both sporting and target rifles and carried a stock of English breech-loading and muzzle-loading shotguns, revolvers, etc. John died about 1882 and the business was continued by William until 1892.

The workmanship of these craftsmen was above average; some fine guns with the Fleeger name on the top facet of the barrels are known in the area.

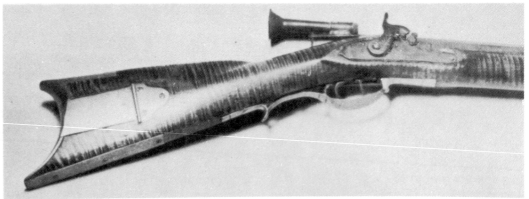

Park Emery

PLATE 145

Rifle with flint lock (now percussion), full stock of curly maple, brass mountings, set triggers, octagonal barrel marked T. Allison in script letters on the top facet of the barrel. This gun weighs about 15 pounds and was obviously made for match shooting. Its style indicates that it was made at the end of the flintlock era.

ALLISON, THOMAS

Pittsburgh, Pennsylvania. 1810.

Respectfully informs his friends and the public, that on the first of April next he will remove to the town of Pittsburgh. In Front street near the post-office where he intends carrying on the Gun-Smith Business in all its different branches. He flatters himself from his knowledge of the business and the strict attention he is determined to pay to it, that he will give satisfaction to those who may please to employ him. He will be constantly supplied with Ferree's best Powder, to supply those who may require it. *Pittsburgh Gazette,* March 30, 1810.

ALLISON, WILLIAM

German Township, Fayette County, Pennsylvania. Tax list 1811.

Menallen Township, Fayette County, Pennsylvania. Tax lists 1816, 1817, 1818, 1819, 1820, 1821, 1822, 1823, 1824, 1825, 1828, 1829, 1830, 1831, 1832, 1833, 1834.

ALLWAY, AXARIAH

Fawn Township, York County, Pennsylvania. Census 1807.

ALTLAND, ANDREW

Dover Township, York County, Pennsylvania.

Andrew Altland was born January 11, 1810, and died May 6, 1878. A tax assessment list for Dover Township, York County, Pennsylvania lists him as a resident and a gunsmith.

ALTLAND, JACOB

Jacob Altland is listed as a gunsmith in the tax assessment list for Dover Township, York County, Pennsylvania in 1820. The intestate inventory of his estate, dated February 15, 1830, includes a number of items related to the trade of gunsmithing:

A lot of gun stocks	
3 new guns, not finished	$15.00
Lot of gunsmith tools	$12.00
Powder and powder horns	$ 2.00
1 rifle pouch and powder horn	$10.00
1 pistol, 1 iron shear, 1 small saw	

Jacob Altland was a fine craftsman. His stocks are beautifully carved in bas-relief patterns on the cheek side of the butt. His patch-box designs are of good quality and are skillfully engraved, as are other mountings of his rifles. The fact that he lived near George Eyster could partially account for the high quality of his rifles.

ALTMAIER, PETER

Lewistown, Mifflin County, Pennsylvania. 1861.

ALTMAN, JONATHAN

Kittanning, Pennsylvania. Tax lists 1867, 1871, 1875, 1880.

AMOS AND BORDER & CO.

Bedford, Pennsylvania.

This business partnership consisted of John Amos and his brother-in-law Daniel Border.

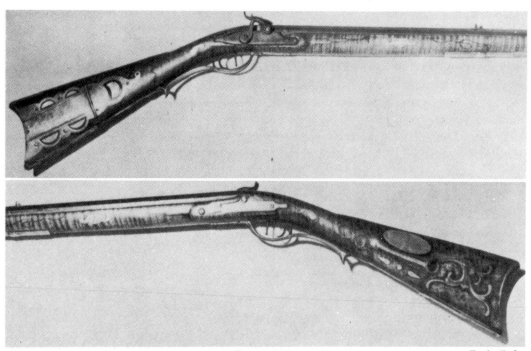

PLATE 146   *F. A. Farber*

Rifle with percussion lock, full stock of curly maple, set triggers, brass mountings, silver inlays, octagonal barrel marked J. Amos. The style and workmanship of this rifle indicates that Amos was one of Bedford County's outstanding craftsmen.

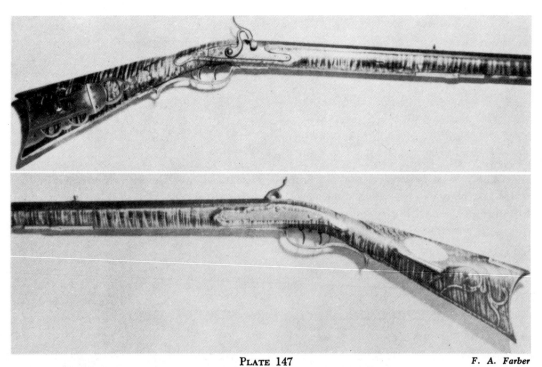

PLATE 147   *F. A. Farber*

Rifle with percussion lock marked A. & B. for Amos and Border, full stock of curly maple, brass mountings, silver inlays, set triggers, and octagonal barrel. Examples of business partnerships like this one of Amos and Border and Co. are rarely found in the gun trade.

AMOS, JOHN

Bedford Township, Bedford County, Pennsylvania. Tax list 1843.

John Amos was one of Bedford County's finest craftsmen. He used sterling for his inlays and some of his guns are carved.

ANDREWS, JACOB (Barrelsmith)

Annville Township, Dauphin County, Pennsylvania. Tax list 1807.

ANGSTADT, ADAM

Maxatawny Township, Berks County, Pennsylvania. Tax list 1800, 1805.

The guns with the initials A. A. on the top facet of the barrel are attributed to this craftsman.

ANGSTADT, JOSEPH

Maxatawny Township, Berks County, Pennsylvania. Tax list 1800.

Kutztown, Berks County, Pennsylvania. Tax list 1817.

ANGSTADT, PETER

Rockland Township, Berks County, Pennsylvania. Tax list 1800.

ANNELY, THOMAS

Philadelphia, Pennsylvania. 1798.

Notice of death of Mrs. Sarah Annely, wife of This. Annely of this city, gunsmith. *Federal (Phila) Gazette*, September 12, 1798.

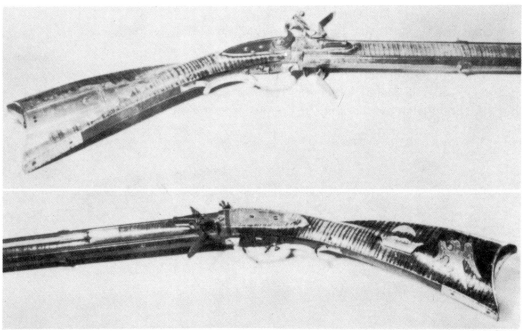

S. E. *Dyke*

PLATE 148

Double rifle with original flint lock, brass mountings, stock of curly maple with original pane along the barrels, octagonal barrels marked A. A. on the top facet. This stock is of very fine curly maple, the eagle inlay on the cheek side is very attractive, and the original flint lock is rarely found on double rifles.

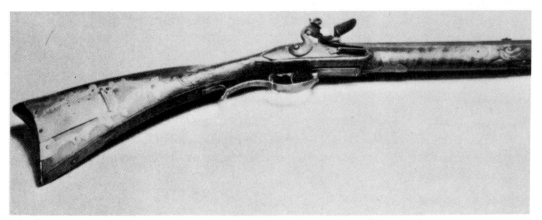

Joe Kindig, Jr.

PLATE 149

Rifle with flint lock, full stock of curly maple, brass mountings, and octagonal barrel 43½ inches long marked P. Angstadt in script letters on the top facet of the barrel.

The outstanding feature of this rifle is the lion which is carved in bas-relief on the cheek side of the butt. Other rifles are known with a similar patch box, however, the small tail on the end of the toe plate seems to be a unique feature.

ANTES, WILLIAM

Mahoning Township, Northumberland County, Pennsylvania. Tax list 1783.

ARMSTRONG, AARON

Borough Township, Beaver County, Pennsylvania. Tax lists 1843, 1845, 1846.

ARMSTRONG, CRAWFORD (Gun-barrel maker)

Pike Street, Marshall's Row, Pittsburgh, Pennsylvania. 1852.

ARMSTRONG, JOHN

Although information about the life of John Armstrong is very meager, a record in the Recorder of Deeds Office of Frederick County, Maryland, indicates that he lived in Emmitsburg, Maryland in the first quarter of the nineteenth century. A

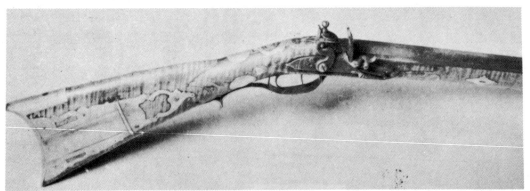

Joe Kindig, Jr.

PLATE 150

Rifle with flint lock, full stock of curly maple, brass mountings, silver inlays, and octagonal barrel 43½ inches long with J. Armstrong engraved in script letters on the top facet of the barrel.

This rifle is a typical Armstrong product. The patch box was one of two patterns which he frequently used, the silver inlay at the breech tang, and the eight pointed star as a barrel pin escutcheon were also some of his favorite details.

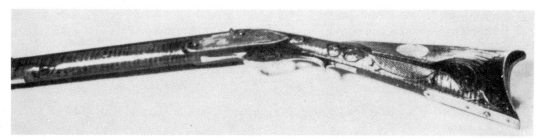

S. E. *Dyke*

PLATE 151

Armstrong's carving was consistent with the other fine decorative details on his rifles. He cleverly varied his C scrolls, and the cross-hatching under the cheek piece is a feature of most of his carved rifles.

History of Emmitsburg, Maryland, written by John A. Helman, gives the following information about him and his associates:

> John Armstrong was an early settler of the Town. His name appears on the plat as owner of No. 1 and No. 2 lots. His reputation as a gunsmith was good and he made rifles and shot guns. When he died his business was continued by his former apprentice, Nathaniel Rowe who retained Armstrong's reputation. Rowe's brother Samuel worked with him for a time before moving west.

In this statement there is no mention of other Armstrong gunsmiths, but a gun bearing the name of Samuel Armstrong is known. The similarity of the decorative datails of the Samuel Armstrong gun to those of John Armstrong would support a hypothesis of a brother or father-son relationship.

The guns of John Armstrong are outstanding in a number of ways. His products can usually be identified by either of two patch box designs which he used. Variations of the two patterns were used by other craftsmen of the area, but none are exactly like Armstrong's. His carving is of high quality, and the designs of his silver inlays are similar to his carved designs. His guns are long and slender, and show evidence of superior workmanship throughout.

His locks are a particularly distinctive part of his products, for they were probably made by him, as many are signed J. A. on the outer surface of the lock plate. They are long and slender with bevels around the edges and with lines filed across at the tail end. He seems to have used a "store" lock on his cheaper guns.

The writer has never seen a shotgun, or a fowling piece, that Armstrong made, but in a Lancaster collection there is known to be a fine pistol that is signed on the barrel and the lock.

ARTZ, CHARLES
Pittsburgh, Pennsylvania. 1826.

ATLEY, CONRAD
Bedford Township, Bedford County, Pennsylvania. Tax list 1800.

AUBER, DANIEL
George Township, Fayette County, Pennsylvania. Tax list 1804.

AYERS, ROBERT, JR.
French Creek Township, Venango County, Pennsylvania. Tax list 1828.

AYERS, WILLIAM

French Creek Township, Venango County, Pennsylvania. Tax list 1828.

Franklin Borough, Venango County, Pennsylvania. Tax lists 1833, 1838, 1840, deceased 1845.

BAER, JOHN

Chanceford Township, York County, Pennsylvania. Census list 1807.

BAKER, ANDREW

Andrew Baker was a gunsmith by trade, and during a number of years conducted a shop at Newry, where, with care, skill and patience he fashioned a certain kind of muzzle-loading gun, greatly favored by hunters, and other firearms made use of at that time. He established a reputation for fine workmanship and completeness. He was a man of pronounced temperance views and a devoted member of the Lutheran church. *20th Century of Altoona & Blair County, Pennsylvania.* J. C. Sell, Chicago, 1911. Federal Census 1850.

BAKER, JACOB.S. (Gunsmith)

Jacob S. Baker's Rifle Manufactory, No. 516, North Front Street, Philadelphia.

Respectfully informs his friends and the public, that he still continues the above business in all its various branches—he is enabled at all times to render a satisfaction to those who may favour him with their orders.

All orders for Rifles, Pistols, Fowling Pieces and Muskets, will be punctually attended to.—The above articles repaired at a low rate. *Whitely's Philadelphia Directory,* 1820; advertising pages.

BAKER, GEORGE

Lampeter Township, Lancaster County, Pennsylvania. Tax list 1786.

George Township, Fayette County, Pennsylvania. Tax lists 1802, 1803, 1805, 1808, 1809, 1810, 1816, d. 1821.

BAKER, JOSEPH

Blair Township, Blair County, Pennsylvania. Tax lists 1859, 1860, 1861.

BAKER, JOSHUA

Lancaster, Pennsylvania. 1753.

Joshua Baker's will is recorded in Will Book B., Vol. 1, Page 57, and is dated May 7, 1753. In his will he is called a gunsmith, but an earlier legal document in the Lancaster County Court House calls him a gunbarrelsmith.

BAKER, MELCHOIR

George Township, Fayette County, Pennsylvania. Tax lists 1799, 1800, 1802, 1803, 1804, 1805, 1806.

BAKER, NICHOLAS

George Township, Fayette County, Pennsylvania. Tax lists 1799, 1800, 1802, 1803, 1804.

BAILEY, ROBERT

Yorktown, Pennsylvania. Deed 2 B 171—1/7/1777.

BALSLEY, CHRISTIAN

Dickinson Township, Cumberland County, Pennsylvania. 1781, 1782.

BANNACKER, GEORGE

Philadelphia, Pennsylvania. *New Trade Directory of Philadelphia,* 1800.

BARBER, SAMUEL

Hempfield Township, Lancaster County, Pennsylvania. Census list 1800.

BARNHILL, ROBERT

Horsemen's Pistols, To be sold by Robert Barnhill, No. 68, North Second Street. Also, a large assortment of English Cocking pieces and Squirrell guns, Riffles, Double barrel guns, Pocket pistols, with secret triggers, without ditto, Pistols with spring bayonets, Officers fusses with bayonets complete, powder proofs, gun powder, patent and common shot, agate and common gun flints, powder flasks and shot pouches, Rifle locks, with double rollers, common ditto, Spanish segars, Hyson and Souchong tea, &c. *Pa. Packet (Dunlap & Claypoole's Am. Daily Advertiser)* no. 5180. Nov. 17, 1795.

BARNS, LUTHER

441 North Third Street, Philadelphia, Pennsylvania. *New Trade Directory of Philadelphia,* 1800.

BATCHELOR, W. R.

Miller's Court, Philadelphia, Pennsylvania. 1814.

BATEMAN, THOMAS

Butler Street, Lawrenceville, Pennsylvania. 1847.

BATES, FRANCIS

Mulberry Street, Pittsburgh, Pennsylvania. 1857-58.

BAUM, SAMUEL

East Buffalo Township, Northumberland County, Pennsylvania. Census list 1800. Mahoning Township, Columbia County, Pennsylvania. Tax list 1821.

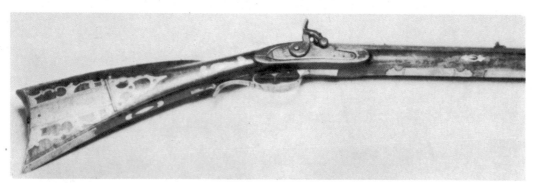

Benson McDowell

PLATE 152

Rifle with flint lock (now percussion), full stock of maple, brass mountings, silver inlays, octagonal barrel 44 inches long with S. Baum, New Berlin, engraved in script letters on the top facet of the barrel. This is a very attractive rifle, the deep red color of the stock makes a nice contrast with the inlays of silver. Although Baum probably worked over a span of twenty to thirty years, his rifles might be regarded as rare.

BAUNELL, WILLIAM
Allegheny Township, Somerset County, Pennsylvania. Tax list 1853.

BAYER, HENRY (Gunbarrel maker)
Pine Creek, Pittsburgh, Pennsylvania. 1837.

BEAR, GEORGE
Derry Township, Westmoreland County, Pennsylvania. Tax lists 1809, 1810, 1811, 1820.

BEAR, ISAAC
Marquaretta Furnace, York County, Pennsylvania. 1861

BECK, CHRISTIAN
Bethel Township, Lebanon County, Pennsylvania. Tax list 1808, 1810.

BECK, JOHN PHILIP
John Philip Beck was born in 1752 and died in Lebanon Township, Dauphin County, Pennsylvania, in 1811. He seems to have lived his entire life in this one

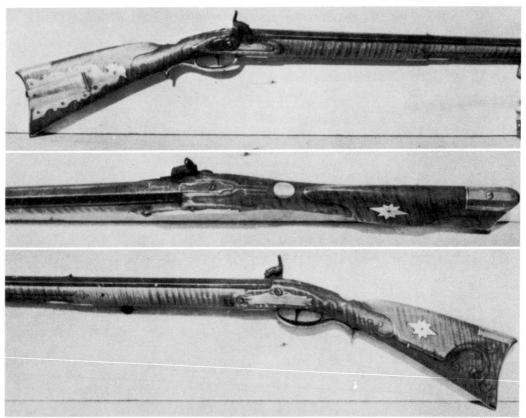

Clegg Collection

PLATE 153

Rifle with flint lock (now percussion), full stock of curly maple, brass mountings, and octagonal barrel marked C. Beck in script letters on the top facet of the barrel.

C. Beck was a contemporary of J. P. Beck and N. Beyer, all of whom worked in the same area. Their carved patterns have elements in common and the patch box on this gun was used by both C. & J. P. Beck. This patch box is not engraved but a few are known that are engraved.

place and doubtless was the most important gunsmith to have worked in the area.

Some of Beck's rifles have sliding wooden patch box covers with a molded pattern on the top, which is a more refined style than those made in the transition era of gunsmithing in Pennsylvania. The straight top and bottom edges of his butts suggest some Lancaster County influence, which is very possible, for Lebanon Township was part of Lancaster County before Dauphin was formed in 1785. He used at least three patterns of four-piece brass patch boxes. One pattern had a flower motif in the finial but was not pierced; another had a similar pattern but was pierced, and another had a finial which slightly resembles the head of a rooster. Some of the last patterns were left plain and some were engraved. This pattern was also shared with his son, C. Beck.

His carved guns are of high quality and often have beautiful grain in their stocks. He seems to have created a distinctive style, readily recognized by collectors who are familiar with his products. He is one of the very few makers of the eighteenth century who used two initials and his last name. Most of his contemporaries used only one initial and their last names.

BECK, JOHN VALENTINE
B. July 25, 1731, Henneberg, Germany. D. March 7, 1791, Bethania, N. C.
Valentine Beck, who will establish himself as a gunsmith arrived in Bethabara from Pennsylvania. *Moravian Archives,* Winston Salem, N. C.

BECK, W. M. (Armourer)
Allen Street, Lawrenceville, Pennsylvania. 1856-57.

BEE, BENJAMIN
Horton's, Indiana County, Pennsylvania. 1861.

BEER, GEORGE
Derry Township, Westmoreland County, Pennsylvania. Tax lists 1809-1819.

BEERSTECHER, FREDERICK
Lewisburg, Union County, Pennsylvania. 1861.

BELL, JOHN
Carlisle, Pennsylvania. Tax lists 1800-1823, 1828, 1844.

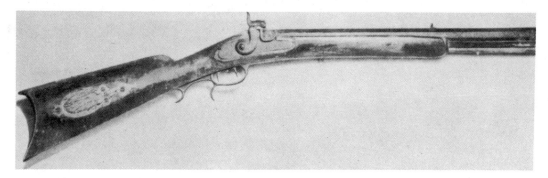

PLATE 154
Rifle with percussion lock, half stock of maple, brass mountings, octagonal barrel with Beerstecher, Lewisburg, Pa., on the top facet of the barrel.

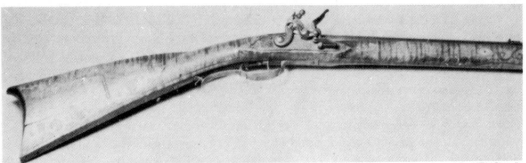

Joe Kindig, Jr.

PLATE 155

Rifle with flint lock, full stock of curly maple, brass mountings, and octagonal barrel with P. Bellis engraved in the top facet of the barrel.

The style of the patch box on this gun suggests a close connection with S. Miller who might be called one of Bellis' distant neighbors. His use of two rivets in the patch box lid also suggests that he was influenced by John Bonawitz of Womelsdorf, Pennsylvania. The rifle was probably made in the first quarter of the nineteenth century.

BELLIS, PETER

Lykens Township, Dauphin County, Pennsylvania. Tax lists 1831, 1834.

BENDER, CHRISTIAN

Lancaster, Pennsylvania. Tax list 1785.

The tax list for Lancaster in 1785 indicates that Christian Bender worked for, or lived with Michael Bender. Both men were gunsmiths.

BENDER, JACOB

Allegheny Township, Cambria County, Pennsylvania. Tax lists 1808, 1810, 1811, 1812, 1813, 1815, 1816.

BENDER, JOHN

The earliest evidence that John Bender was a gunsmith in Lancaster, Pennsylvania, is found in a letter written to the Ordnance Department of United States in 1809. The letter was a request for money long overdue to a group of Lancaster gunsmiths consisting of Jacob Dickert, George Miller, Christopher Gumpf, John Bender, and Peter Gonter.

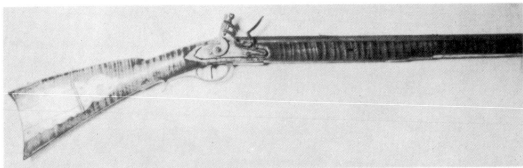

Monroe Hufford

PLATE 156

Rifle with flint lock, full stock of curly maple, brass mountings, octagonal barrel marked J. Bender in script letters on the top facet of the barrel. The lock on this gun was made by Dreppert. The horse head finial on the patch box was used by a few other gunsmiths in Lancaster county; however it is not a common feature of rifles made in Lancaster County. The products of J. Bender are very rare.

In the tax assessment lists Bender is listed as a gunsmith of Lancaster, Pennsylvania, in 1812, 1813, 1814, and 1815. The list of 1812 discloses also that Jacob Haeffer was working for him. It is possible that Bender's military contracts had continued that long and that Haeffer was helping to do the work.

Bender's association with the outstanding gunsmiths of Lancaster might indicate that he was a fine craftsman, and that his work was probably on a par with his associates. Only one rifle which bears his name is known to the writer and its only distinctive feature is a horsehead finial on the patch box. The lock is signed Dreppert, one of the rare spellings of that name.

BENDER, MICHAEL
Lancaster, Pennsylvania. Tax list 1785.

BENFER, AMOS
Benfer, Snyder County, Pennsylvania.
The demand for handmade, muzzle-loading guns seems to have almost disappeared in Benfer's time, so he devoted part of his time to farming and worked as a carpenter. He was born in 1841 and died in 1916.

BERGER, BARNHART
N. W. Ward, Reading, Pennsylvania. United States Census 1850.

BERINGER, JOHN
1448 North 5th, Philadelphia, Pennsylvania. 1861.

BERLIN, ABRAHAM (Barrelsmith)
Easton, Pennsylvania. Tax list 1782.

BERLIN, ISAAC
Abbottstown, Pennsylvania, Berwick Township, Adams County. Tax lists 1800 and '05.

BERNDS, PHILIP
Trumbaursville, Bucks County, Pennsylvania. 1861.

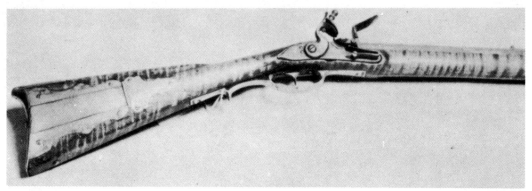

Joe Kindig, Jr.

PLATE 157

Rifle with flint lock, full stock of curly maple, brass mountings, and octagonal barrel 42 inches long marked I. Berlin in script letters on the top facet.

Although this gun is carved, the products of I. Berlin are so rare that no statement can be made about the general quality of his products. This rifle was probably made in the last decade of the eighteenth century.

BERRY, PETER

Peter Berry is listed as a gunsmith in the tax assessment lists of Heidelberg Township, Dauphin County, from 1786 until his death in 1796.

His products are of a uniform high quality in style and workmanship. The pattern of his patch-box finials is attractive and constant. There is usually one piercing in the finial and one in each side plate. The engraving is also quite good.

The carved pattern on the cheek side of his stocks is in the form of a capital C and resembles an illuminated letter from a mediaeval manuscript.

The style of his lock-bolt plates is also very constant. Some of his guns have a narrow metal plate inlaid in the ridge of the cheek piece.

BIDDLE, GEORGE

Bullskin Township, Fayette County, Pennsylvania. Tax lists 1816, 1823.

BIDDLE, R. & W. C. (Hardware)

47 Market Street, Philadelphia, Pennsylvania. 1855.

BIDDLE, R. & W. C. & Co.

131 Market Street, Philadelphia, Pennsylvania. 1861.

BISBING, AMOS S.

Tannersville, Monroe County, Pennsylvania. 1861.

BISHIP, M.

Linesville, Crawford County, Pennsylvania. 1879-80.

BISHOP, ALEXANDER

Center Township, Union County, Pennsylvania. Federal Census 1850.

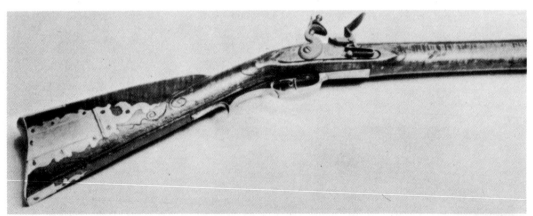

Joe Kindig, Jr.

PLATE 158

Rifle with flint lock, full stock of curly maple, brass mountings, and octagonal barrel with J. B. in an intaglio stamp on a side facet of the barrel.

Bonawitz worked in the late eighteenth century and his guns are typical of that period. His carving is of high quality and his products are fine throughout. The style of his patch boxes is consistent and he usually used two rivets to hold the stud which engaged the catch for keeping it closed. The patch box release is usually located on the butt plate. His products are rare and a very desirable asset to any collection.

BLACK, HENRY

German Township, Fayette County, Pennsylvania. Tax lists 1807, 1808, 1809, 1810, 1816.

BLACK, HENRY, JR.

German Township, Fayette County, Pennsylvania. Tax lists 1811, 1812, 1813, 1814, 1815.

BLACK, JAMES

Duncannon, Perry County, Pennsylvania. 1861.

BLAIR, WILLIAM

Brothers Valley Township, Somerset County, Pennsylvania. Tax list 1823.

BLAUTZ, JOHN

Brickerville, Lancaster County, Pennsylvania. 1861.

BOBB, ANTHONY

Reading, Pennsylvania. *Pennsylvania Archives,* 3d series Vol. 18, page 532. Tax list 1781.

BONAWITZ, JOHN

John Bonawitz is listed as a resident of Middletown (now Womelsdorf) Berks County, Pennsylvania, from 1792 until 1810; however, he is listed as a gunsmith only in 1792 and 1800.

Although a number of unsigned guns are attributed to him, only one with his name on the barrel is known to the writer. This gun has given the clue to his place of residence, for "Womelsdorf" is engraved on the lid of the patch box. Some other guns are signed by him with an intaglio stamp (I. B.) on the side facet of the barrel opposite the lock. This method of signing was probably used by other craftsmen in Berks County, although Andrew Figthorn is the only one known to the writer.

Bonawitz was unquestionably one of the best gunsmiths to have worked in Berks County. The design of his patch boxes is excellent and they are cleverly engraved. His carved stocks are of excellent quality, and their style, too, suggests that the maker lived in Berks County.

BONNET, A.

Clarion Borough, Clarion County, Pennsylvania. Tax lists 1868, 1871, 1875.

BOONE, SAMUEL

Ran away from the Gun-Lock Factory, Frederick-Town, a servant man . . .
                                                              Samuel Boone.
Maryland Journal, (Baltimore), Page 1, Col. 2, September 1, 1778.

BOOTH & CO.

80 South Second Street, Philadelphia, Pennsylvania. *New Trade Directory of Philadelphia,* 1800.

BOOTH, WILLIAM

85 South Front Street, Philadelphia, Pennsylvania. 1798.
88 South Second Street, Philadelphia, Pennsylvania. 1814.

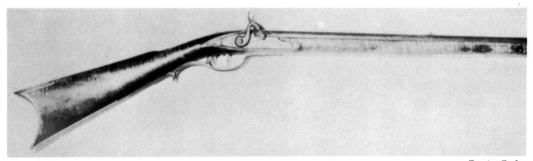

R. A. Farber

PLATE 159

Rifle with percussion lock, curly maple full stock, set triggers, brass mountings, silver inlays, octagonal barrel, marked D. B. for Daniel Border. The style of the rifle suggests production in the mid-nineteenth century. The curl in the stock is a superior type and the silver inlays are used with discretion.

BORDER, DANIEL

Bedford Township, Bedford County, Pennsylvania. Tax lists 1849, 1854.

Daniel Border lived in the town of Bedford and was one of the outstanding craftsmen of the mid-nineteenth century. He was also a silversmith and worked on apparatus to demonstrate perpetual motion.

He visited the Colt Factory, and Col. Colt introduced him to the employees as a master gunsmith.

His guns are among the best made in Bedford County.

BORDER, ENOS

Bedford Township, Bedford County, Pennsylvania. Tax list 1843.

BORDER, JOHN

Bedford Township, Bedford County, Pennsylvania. Tax list 1861. Federal Census 1850.

No guns with patch boxes by this man are known, but some plain guns marked J. B. are attributed to him. He used the typical Bedford County lock, which he signed J. B.

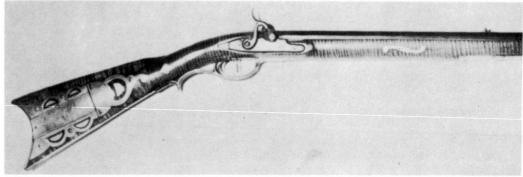

M. T. Stewart

PLATE 160

Rifle with percussion lock, curly maple full stock, brass mountings, set triggers, octagonal barrel 39 inches long, marked D. B. on the barrel and the lock for Daniel Border.

This gun has a typical Bedford-style lock and is an excellent example of the line and balance in Bedford Guns.

BORDER, SAMUEL

Bedford Borough, Bedford County, Pennsylvania. Tax list 1841.

Conemaugh Township, Somerset County, Pennsylvania. Tax lists 1843, 1845, 1850, 1853.

It appears that Samuel Border started his gunsmithing activity in Bedford and later moved to Somerset County. He is known to have made a few fine guns in the typical Bedford style.

BORDER, WILLIAM

East St. Clair Township, Bedford County, Pennsylvania. Tax list 1850.

William Border was the father of John and Daniel. He was a fine craftsman. Some of his guns have inlays of silver and are skillfully carved.

BOSLER, JOSEPH

New Fourth Street, Philadelphia, Pennsylvania. *New Trade Directory of Philadelphia,* 1800.

BOUSHINGER, HENRY

Brothers Valley Township, Somerset County, Pennsylvania. Tax lists 1805, 1806, 1808, 1810, 1812, 1813.

BOWERS, JOHN

Jonestown, Pennsylvania. 1860.

BOWMAN, PETER

Worchester, Montgomery County, Pennsylvania. 1861.

BOWN, ALBERT

Albert Bown, dealer in HARDWARE, RIFLES, GUNS, REVOLVERS, PISTOLS, ETC. Stencils cut to order. Rifles and general repairing done with dispatch. Rifles made to order. West end of Neshannock Bridge, New Castle, Pennsylvania. *Wiggens Directory of Beaver, Shenango and Mahonong Valleys,* 1869.

BOWN, E. F., OF JAMES BOWN & SON

Directory of Pittsburgh and Allegheny Cities, 1874-75.

BOWN, JAMES & SON

James Bown & Son, Guns, Pistols, Hardware, Cutlery.

136 & 138 Wood Street, Pittsburgh, Pennsylvania. 1874-75.

BOWN, JAMES

James Bown, successor to Bown & Tetley, Manufacturer and Importer of GUNS, RIFLES, PISTOLS, HARDWARE, GUNSMITHS MATERIALS, CUTLERY &c. No. 136 Wood Street, Pittsburgh, Pennsylvania. Agents for Colt's Pistols and Rifles. *The Pittsburgh Commercial,* March 6, 1865.

BOWN & TETLEY

Bown & Tetley Rifles are cheap and well made. Emigrants would do well to give us a call. We keep a large stock of our manufacture always on hand. All guns warranted. *The Daily Morning Post,* Pittsburgh, Pennsylvania, March 13, 1855.

PLATE 161

James Bown

BOWN & TETLEY RIFLE MANUFACTURERS
    136 Wood Street, Pittsburgh, Pennsylvania. 1859-60-61.

BOWN, W. H., OF JAMES BOWN & SON
    Directory of Pittsburgh and Allegheny Cities, 1874-75.

BOWSHINGER, HENRY
    Brothers Valley Township, Somerset County, Pennsylvania. Tax lists 1820, 1823.

BOYD, WILLIAM
    Harrisburg, Pennsylvania. Tax list 1811.

BOYER, D.
    In a search for a document in which his trade is indicated, D. Boyer is an elusive gunsmith. There is, however, in the Western Pennsylvania Historical Society

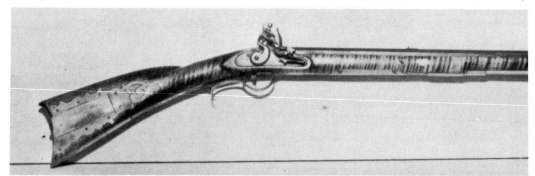

Western Pennsylvania Historical Society

PLATE 162

Rifle with flint lock, curly maple stock, octagonal barrel 42 inches long. "D. Boyer, Orwigsburg" is engraved on the lid of the patch box.

collection in Pittsburgh, Pennsylvania, a gun with "David Boyer, Orwigsburg," engraved in script letters on the lid of the patch box.

From this clue the natural procedure was to examine the records of Schuylkill County, and the following is the result: David Boyer's name first appears in the assessment records of the Borough of Orwigsburg in the year 1837. He owned a house and a lot but no description of his occupation is included. At later dates he acquired six valuable units of real estate, mostly with improvements on them; some of these are described as being located in the sprawling country side of North Manheim Township, adjoining the borough. Records indicate that Orwigsburg prospered at mid-century, for it was the county seat, was not far from the Philadelphia-Sunbury turnpike, and was near the busy water course of the Schuylkill Canal. In this prosperity Boyer seems to have shared.

Since no will or administrative record appears in the court house, some form of intestacy must be presumed, or he may have moved from the county.

David Boyer is thought to have been a second generation gunsmith, although no documentary data on an earlier one exists. That some guns of an earlier period are attributed to a craftsman named Boyer is the main source of information in this matter. Both the earlier Boyer and David were specialists in the making of over-and-under guns. Both makers made fine guns that were typical of their period and are eagerly sought by collectors.

An examination of the records concerning men who were liable for military service in the Civil War indicates that a George Boyer lived in Orwigsburg at that time and was called a gunsmith. A descendant of David Boyer informed the writer that a son of David assisted his father in the business of gunsmithing. It is likely that this son was named George; however, no guns that bear his name are known in the central Pennsylvania area.

BOYER, GEORGE

Orwigsburg, Pennsylvania. 1862.

George Boyer was 22 years old and a gunsmith in Orwigsburg, Pennsylvania, when he was listed in the enrollment of men liable for military service for the Civil War in 1862.

BOYER, BENJAMIN

Hamburg, Berks County, Pennsylvania. United States Census 1850.

BOYER, HENRY

Lebanon Township, Dauphin County, Pennsylvania. Tax list 1807, 1842.

BOYER, NICHOLAS

Lebanon Township, Dauphin County, Pennsylvania. Tax list 1807, 1842.

BRANDT, JACOB

Union Township, Fayette County, Pennsylvania. Tax lists 1835, 1840.

BRANT, JACOB F.

Haddon's *History of Uniontown*, 1913, informs us that Jacob F. Brant worked as a gunsmith in the town from 1835 to 1851. In 1835 he advertised that he "makes

M. T. Stewart

PLATE 163

Rifle with percussion lock, full stock of curly maple, brass mountings, octagonal barrel 41 inches long with J. Brandt, Lancaster, engraved in script letters on the top facet of the barrel. The chequered wrist and the form of the stock are typical features of Lancaster rifles of the percussion era.

a patent gun to put two loads in at once, and be discharged, separately, one after the other until all are discharged." He was also an active dealer in real estate while living in Uniontown.

In 1852 he moved to Pittsburgh, where he became a partner in a gun business with Samuel McCosh. Their business was known as the "Pittsburgh Gun Works." They separated in 1855 and Brant established his own business at 46 St. Clair Street. He moved to 4 Fifth Street in 1859 and remained at that site until 1865. During his later years he kept "A General Intelligence Office" in addition to his gun shop. It is probable that the guns marked J. F. B. were made by Jacob F. Brant.

BRANDT, JOHN
Lancaster Borough, Pennsylvania. Tax list 1834.

BRASHERS, ROBERT A.
Franklin Borough, Venango County, Pennsylvania. Tax lists 1834, 1837, 1838, 1841, 1842, 1844, 1852, 1856.

BREIGLE, JACOB
Union Township, Bedford County, Pennsylvania. Tax list 1860.
Breigle is known to have made one fine double barrell, full-stocked gun, signed Jacob Breigle—Bedford County, Pennsylvania. His other guns are average quality.

BRENISE, GEORGE
York, Pennsylvania. *York Recorder,* January 19, 1819.

BRENBERGER, FREDERICK (Gunbarrel Maker)
Martin Township, Lancaster County, Pennsylvania. Tax lists 1813, 1815.

BRENEISSEN, GEORGE
York, Pennsylvania. Census 1800.

BRIGGS, WILLIAM
Egypt near Arch, Norristown, Montgomery County, Pennsylvania. 1861.

BRINDLE, JOHN F.

Sarah below Bedford (Kensington), Philadelphia, Pennsylvania. 1855.

BRITZ, ADAM

Heidelberg Township, York County, Pennsylvania. Census List 1807. Tax list 1809-1810.

Britz was probably a repairman, for he is listed as a gunsmith only three times. In previous and later listings he is called a locksmith.

BRONG, PETER

The earliest evidence that Peter Brong was a gunsmith in Lancaster, Pennsylvania, is found in an accounting of rifles entitled, *"Continental Rifles, Account of when received—and when forwarded by order of Genl. Hand, Lancaster, February 7, 1794."*

The fact that Brong's name appears for the first time as a gunsmith in this document and that he contributed only 5 guns while the veteran Jacob Dickert contributed 173 does not prove that Brong was then an embryo craftsman, but the evidence strongly supports such a hypothesis. It seems safe to assume that Brong became a journeyman gunsmith in Lancaster about 1790.

Brong was also a member of the Lancaster cartel which made arms for the

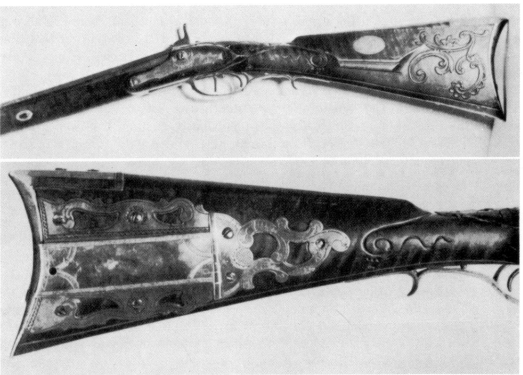

Reaves Goehring

PLATE 164

Rifle with flint lock (now percussion), full stock of curly maple, brass mountings, set triggers, silver inlays, octagonal barrel with P. Brong in block letters on the top facet of the barrel. The carving on the cheek side of this rifle is an interesting combination of C scrolls. This is a fine example of workmanship by a Lancaster gunsmith whose products are very rare.

Ordnance Department of the United States in the first decade of the nineteenth century. He was associated particularly with Abraham Henry and John Guest in this venture. Their correspondence, as recorded in *United States Ordnance* by James E. Hicks, is very interesting because most of it deals with the manufacture of pistols, which were not so common a product of Lancaster gunsmiths as rifles and muskets.

Brong is listed as a gunsmith in the tax assessment lists of Lancaster, Pennsylvania, in 1800, 1802, 1803, 1814 and 1816. It is interesting to note that in 1800 Jacob Haeffer, Jr., was employed by Brong as a locksmith and Jacob Haeffer, Sr., was listed as a single freeman, gunsmith. Brong's advertisement in the *Lancaster Intelligencer and Weekly Advertiser*, September 23, 1801 indicates that he employed lock filers in connection with this production of military arms. Brong died in 1817.

> Peter Brong, Gunsmith, North Queen Street, Lancaster, offers 20 shilling, Cash for every Musket-barrel which is proven, and of the size directed by Law, and 19 shillings Cash for each good Musket-lock. He gives the highest price for walnut plank of 2 inches and one quarter thick; If well seasoned, it will be preferred. Good encouragement will be given to lock filers; such as soon apply will receive the highest Wages. He has for sale an excellent forte piano.

The quality of Brong's work is very difficult to evaluate, since only a few specimens are known to exist. Several better-than-average rifles with incised carved designs are in existence and one rifle is known with workmanship of a superior quality. The later rifle has an attractive patch box, not a typical Lancaster pattern, and the relief carving on the cheek side of the gun is excellent. There is also an elliptical silver plate, inlaid on the cheek side where most Lancastrians at that time were using eight pointed stars, although one Dickert gun is known with a similar inlay at the same place.

It is important to note that recently a Brong pistol that was made for military use has been found. The signature is the same that appears on his rifles and probably on the contract arms which have been previously mentioned as appearing in *UNITED STATES ORDNANCE* by James E. Hicks. Any of Brong's products would be a valuable addition to a collection of American arms.

BROOKS, FRANCIS (Gunsmith)

Francis Brooks, Gunsmith, Magazine, Backwork and machine Pistol Maker.

Returns his most sincere thanks to his friends, and the public, for their past favours, and now informs them that he carries on the business as usual, in all its various branches, at his manufactory, No. 87, bank side South, Front street between Chestnut and Walnut streets, Philadelphia, and also at his Shop, No. 86, Water street, where he has ready for sale a most fashionable assortment of Jewellery, Cutlery and hardware, received from the last vessels from Europe, which will be disposed of on the most equitable terms, and he flatters himself, his abilities as a workman are well known to his employers, to whom he looks up for a continuance of the encouragement he has already so amply experienced, to secure the same will be his utmost ambition.

The highest price for old Gold and Silver, &c. &c.

A Youth of reputable Parents is wanted as an Apprentice. *Federal Gazette*, no. 924 (marked 927) September 21, 1791.

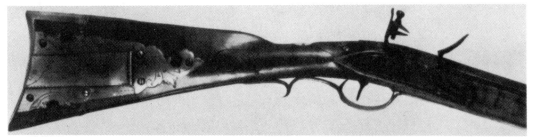

PLATE 165

Joe Kindig, Jr.

Rifle with flint lock, full stock of curly maple, brass mountings, and octagonal barrel with J. Brooks on the top facet of the barrel.

BRONOUP, JAMES

Philadelphia Tax list 1779, *Pennsylvania Archives*, 3 series, Vol. 15, page 101.

BROOKS, JOHN

Lancaster, Pennsylvania. Tax list 1800.
Harrisburg, Pennsylvania. Tax lists 1814, 1817.

BROSWELL, JOSEPH

West Brownsville, Washington County, Pennsylvania. 1861.

BROWN, DAVID

Lancaster, Pennsylvania. Tax list 1840.

BROWN, JOHN

Smith Township, Washington County, Pennsylvania. Tax list 1831.

BROWN, JOHN B.

Pittsburgh, Pennsylvania. *The Pittsburgh Gazette*, April 19, 1824.

BROWN, JOHN F.

515 North Third Street, Philadelphia, Pennsylvania. 1855.

BROWN AND HIRTH

520 Wood Street, Pittsburgh, Pennsylvania. 1885.

BROWN, W. H. (Gun & Hardware Mt.)

If advertising is a criterion of a man's business activity, William H. Brown must have been a busy man from 1838 to 1841. The following excerpts from Pittsburgh newspapers focus attention on his production of guns at that time and his mercantile interests, which were largely confined to the hardware business. His business was obviously a forerunner of other similar businesses which were located in the city of Pittsburgh in the last half of the nineteenth century. Guns bearing his name are quite rare, although the writer recently acquired one that was found in an attic in York, Pennsylvania.

The Democrat & Workingman's Advocate, Jan. 12, 1838:
> WM. H. BROWN, HAS THE pleasure to acquaint his friends and the public, that he has extensively supplied his establishment, No. 126 Wood Street,

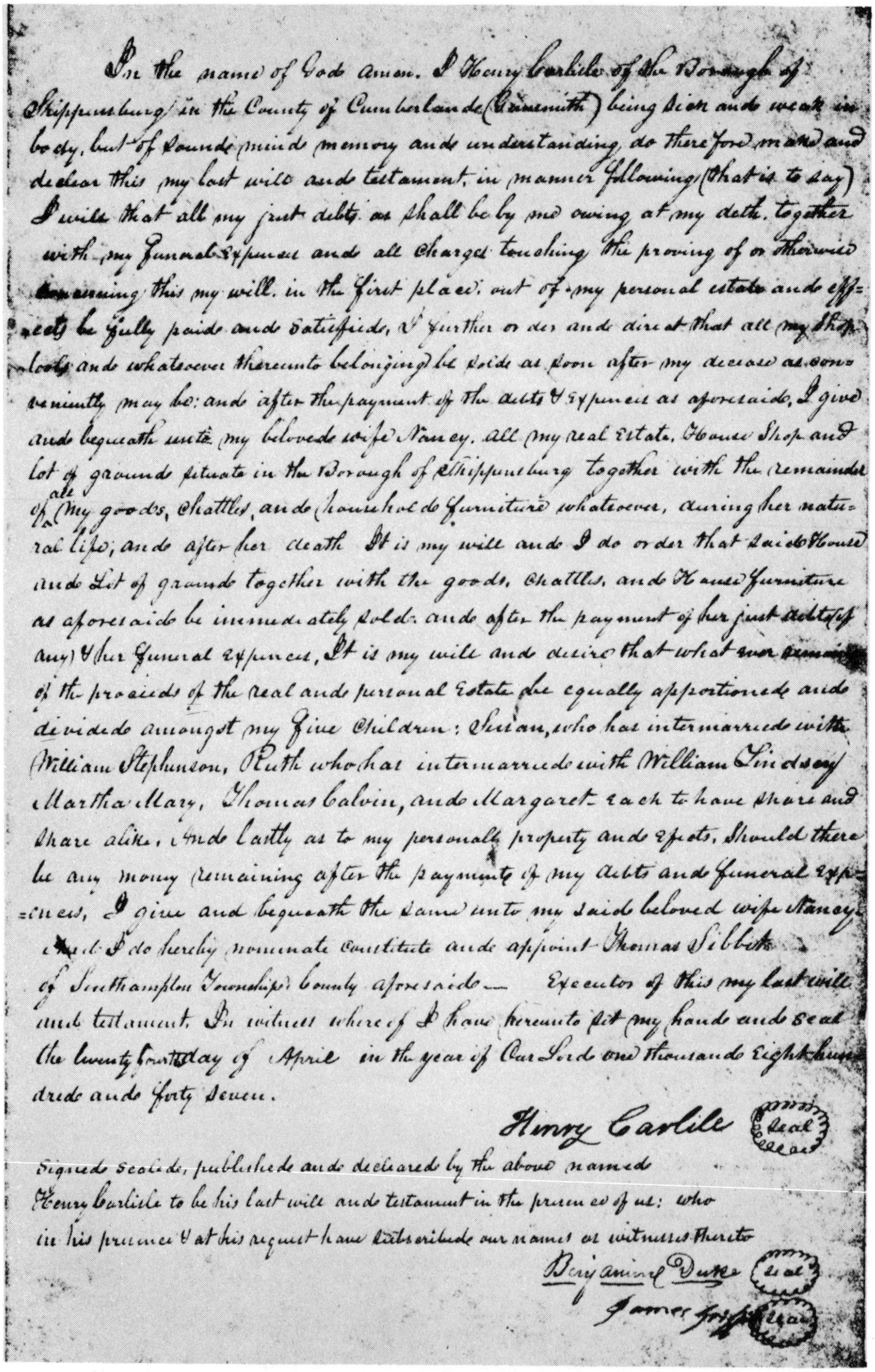

In the name of God Amen. I Henry Carlile of the Borough of Shippensburg, in the County of Cumberland (Gunsmith) being sick and weak in body, but of sound mind memory and understanding, do therefore make and declare this, my last will and testament, in manner following (that is to say) I will that all my just debts as shall be by me owing at my death, together with my funeral Expences and all charges touching the proving of or otherwise concerning this my will, in the first place, out of my personal estate and effects be fully paid and satisfied. I further order and direct that all my Shop tools and whatsoever thereunto belonging be sold as soon after my decease as conveniently may be: and after the payment of the debts & Expences as aforesaid, I give and bequeath unto my beloved wife Nancy. all my real Estate, House Shop and lot of ground situate in the Borough of Shippensburg together with the remainder of all my goods, Chattles, and household furniture whatsoever, during her natural life; and after her death It is my will and I do order that said House and Lot of ground together with the goods, Chattles, and House furniture as aforesaid be immediately sold. and after the payment of her just debts if any & her funeral Expences, It is my will and desire that whatsoever remains of the proceeds of the real and personal Estate be equally apportioned and divided amongst my five Children: Susan, who has intermarried with William Stephenson, Ruth who has intermarried with William Lindsey Martha Mary, Thomas Calvin, and Margaret each to have share and share alike. And lastly as to my personal property and effects, Should there be any money remaining after the payments of my debts and funeral Expences, I give and bequeath the same unto my said beloved wife Nancy. And I do hereby nominate constitute and appoint Thomas Sibbets of Southampton Township, County aforesaid — Executor of this my last will and testament. In witness whereof I have hereunto set my hands and seal the twenty fourth day of April in the year of Our Lord one thousand Eight hundred and forty seven.

                                        Henry Carlile (seal)

Signed sealed, published and declared by the above named
Henry Carlile to be his last will and testament in the presence of us: who
in his presence & at his request have subscribed our names as witnesses thereto
                                        Benjamin Duke (seal)
                                        James ___ (seal)

PLATE 166

with a great variety of articles in his line, from Philadelphia, of the choicest quality, selected by himself, and comprised in part as follows;—Double barrel Guns, of patent breech of Damascus wire, and stub and twist barrels and of Electrum and Steel Mountings—an apartment of Single barreled Fowling Pieces, from the finest to the common kind—every description of Holster, Dueling, Belt, and Pocket Pistols—all kinds of Bowie and Pocket Knives—DuPont's best F.F.F. Powder in papers and Cannisters—Percussion Caps, Shot, and Lead—Powder Flasks and Horns, Game Bags and pouches, Cleaning aparatus complete, and implements of every sort in his line. He has also Fishing Rods and Canes, Lines, Hooks, and Tackles of all kinds; in short he invites the choicest Sportsmen to call and examine his present stock.

He has made arrangements to be kept supplied with RIFLE BARRELS, and gun mountings, which he will furnish to Gunsmiths, on better terms than they can procure them in this city.

Guns to be let out on reasonable terms.

The Daily Advocate & Advertiser, October 19, 1838:
TO GUN SMITHS. For sale 50 doz. Rifle Barrels, at the reduced price of $30.00 per doz., also materials, gun mountings, gun locks and all articles used by gun manufacturers, of all qualities and at lower prices than they can be had at any other establishment in the city. Constantly on hand an assortment of Pennybacker's superior Rifle barrels, powder and shot, &c. W. H. BROWN, Gun Smith, 5th St., one door from Market St.

The Pittsburgh Daily Advocate & Advertiser, Oct. 18, 1839:
A CARD. THE undersigned would respectfully call the attention of his friends and the public generally, to his superior assortment of Rifles, double and single barrel Shot Guns, Powder Flasks, Shot Belts, Game Bags, Fishing tackle, and all articles necessary for sportsmen. His rifles are of his own manufacture, and warranted equal if not superior in material, workmanship, style of finish, &c, to any brought from the eastern cities: In addition to the above named articles, he keeps constantly on hand a good assortment of warranted Roger's cutlery of the best quality, and the most extensive assortment of pistols to be found in the city.
W. H. BROWN, No. 7 Fifth St. Oct. 19.

The Pittsburgh Daily Advocate & Advertiser, Oct. 29, 1839:
W. H. BROWN, Manufacturer of Guns and Pistols, and DEALER IN SPORTING TACKLES, NO. 7, Fifth Street, Pittsburgh.

The Pittsburgh Daily Advocate & Advertiser, Oct. 5, 1840:
1200 RIFLE BARRELS, just received and for sale cheap by WM. H. BROWN, Corner of Diamond and Market Sts. Oct. 3.

The American Manufacturer, April 10, 1841:
GUNSMITHS. 5 JOURNEYMEN GUNSMITHS wanted immediately. None but good workmen need apply. WM. H. BROWN, Corner Diamond & Market St. Dec. 5, 1840.

The American Manufacturer, Aug. 28, 1841:
W. H. BROWN'S NEW HARDWARE STORE AND GUNSMITHING ESTABLISHMENT. Corner of the Diamond and Market Street. Pittsburgh, July 24, 1841.

The American Manufacturer, April 3, 1841:

NEW HARDWARE STORE. Corner of the Diamond and Market Street. W. H. BROWN WOULD respectfully inform the public that he has opened a New Hardware Store at the above named place, where he will keep constantly on hand a full and complete assortment of articles in the line. He has just returned from the East with an entire new and fresh stock of goods; consisting in part of table and pocket cutlery, edge tools of all kinds; locks of every description; hand, tenon, and circle saws; house, tea and cow bells; Britania and German Silver table and tea spoons, Etc, Etc. Also, Farming utensils, such as hoes, rakes, hay and manure forks, shovels and spades, of the most approved patterns and made by the most approved makers; he is determined to sell every article in the line at the lowest market prices, and hopes by unremitted perseverence and attention, to merit a share of public patronage.

Gunsmithing is still carried on by the subscriber, and those wishing to purchase anything in that line will always find a complete assortment at his establishment; such as rifle barrels, gun materials of all description, sheet brass, German silver, brass mountings, Etc. Etc. Also, sporting tackle, such as fishing rods, lines and hooks; game bags and shot belts; powder flasks, powder and shot. He would here ask purchasers of guns and rifles to consider the advantage they will gain by purchasing of the subscriber, as he is regularly brought up in the business and warrants every gun purchased from him to shoot well, whereas those purchasing at other hardware stores, purchase from those that know no more about the article they are selling than the purchaser does; consequently it will be mere accident if he should get a good article. The strictest attention will at all times be given to the above business, and every effort made to please those who favor him with their patronage. Terms in all cases cash. W. H. BROWN Hardware Merchant and Gun Smith, Corner of Market and the Diamond. June 6, 1840.

BRUBAKER, JOHN

Earl Township, Lancaster County, Pennsylvania. Tax list 1820.

BRYAN, JAMES

Lampeter Township, Lancaster County, Pennsylvania. Tax list 1801.

Although Bryan is a very obscure maker of guns, it has been established that he owned a boring mill in the eighteenth century that is standing today. The first patent on this property was executed by John Thomas, and Richard Penn to Andrew Shultz in 1734. Andrew Shultz subsequently sold the property to his son, John Shultz, from whom Bryan acquired it.

In the records of Bryan's purchase and sale of the property he was called a gunbarrelsmith and the mill was called a boring mill. His agreement involved the right to dam Mill Creek upon the land of Tobias Gryder, which apparently was necessary to get enough "head" to run the water wheel. Sometime after Bryan's possession of the mill, it was converted into a grist mill.

BRYCE, JOHN

All Sorts of Musket Balls made and sold by John Bryce, the fourth Door from Market street, in Front-street, on the most reasonable terms. *Pennsylvania Evening Post*, no. 60. June 10, 1775.

BUCHANAN, GEORGE
Blair County, Pennsylvania. Federal Census 1850.

BUCHANAN, SAMUEL
Halifax, Dauphin County, Pennsylvania. Tax list 1814.

BUCHMILLER, ROBERT
57 North Queen Street, Lancaster, Lancaster County, Pennsylvania. 1861.

BURG, (BURGE) WILLIAM
Freeport, Pennsylvania. Tax lists 1876, 1877, 1878.

BURLY, WILLIAM
Morris Township, Washington County, Pennsylvania. Tax lists 1854, 1855.

BURNS, JAMES
136 Lombard Street, Philadelphia, Pennsylvania. 1814.

BUTLER,
Pittsburgh, Pennsylvania. 1765.
The Fort Pitt Day Book of Baynton, Wharton & Morgan contains entries which indicate that Butler was a gunsmith there in 1765.
One entry is as follows, "Cash due to Butler/ye Gunsmith—1-6-6".

BUTLER, RICHARD
Pittsburgh, Pennsylvania. 1767.
Entry in the *Fort Pitt Day Book* of Baynton, Wharton & Morgan. June 13, 1767. John Finney Due to Summary Acco. Viz. To Richard Butler, Gunsmith 15/.

BUTLER, THOMAS
Lancaster, Pennsylvania. 1754. West Pennsborough Township, Cumberland County, Pennsylvania. Tax lists 1771, 1779, 1786, 1789.

BUTLER, THOMAS (Armourer)
Water-street Armoury, July 19, 1772
Wanted two or three Gunlock Filers, and a good Stocker or two, who, by applying as above, shall be properly encouraged by Thomas Butler, chief armourer of the United States.
N.B. Those who live at a distance, will do well to write first. *Pennsylvania Evening Post,* no. 380. July 19, 1777.
Continental Armoury, August 18, 1777
Wanted, a quantity of Walnut Plank. Any person, who has plank for sale, by applying to Thomas Butler, esq; at said armoury, shall have ready money and a good price for the same. *Pennsylvania Evening Post,* no. 393. August 19, 1777.

BUTLER, WILLIAM
Pittsburgh, Pennsylvania. 1766.
The following entry is in the *Fort Pitt Day Book* of Baynton, Wharton & Morgan. Oct. 13th, 1766. William Butler for cleaning a Rifle.

BUTTERFIELD, BENJAMIN
Yrab Oxford, Philadelphia, Pennsylvania. 1831.
F road opp Marlboro (Kensington), Philadelphia, Pennsylvania. 1847.

BUTTERFIELD, J. S.
    1528 Frankford Avenue, Philadelphia, Pennsylvania. 1861.

BUTTERFIELD, SARAH, WIDOW OF BENJAMIN F.
    Road opp. Marlborough, Philadelphia, Pennsylvania. 1855.

BYERS, JAMES
    Wanted to hire immediately, to work at the brass gun foundry in Southwark, two Brass Founders, or Whitesmiths, that are capable of turning, filing, hammering, &c. on heavy work. Inquire of   James Byers.
    N.N. None need apply but those who have the characters of honest sober son, and being friends to the United States. *Pennsylvania Evening Post*, no. 361. June 5, 1777.

CABLE, WILLIAM
    Lawrenceville, Pennsylvania. 1847.

CALDERWOOD, WILLIAM
    Germantown Road, Philadelphia, Pennsylvania. 1814.

CALDERWOOD, WILLIAM, gunsmith of Liberty.
    Between the Street and Strawberry Alley. *Pittsburgh Directory* of 1819.

CANNON, JAMES
    Mt. Morris, Greene County, Pennsylvania. 1876.

CARLISLE, HENRY
    Shippensburg, Pennsylvania. Tax lists 1826, 1832, 1835, 1844.

CARNMAN, D.
    Aaronsburg, Centre County, Pennsylvania. 1861.

CARNY, JAMES N.
    McAllisterville, Juniata County, Pennsylvania. 1861.

CARR, CHARLES
    106 Fourth Street, Philadelphia, Pennsylvania. 1855.

CARRELL, LAWRANCE
    Philadelphia, Pennsylvania. Federal Census of 1790.

CAVE, CHRIST
    Philadelphia, Pennsylvania. Tax list 1779. *Pennsylvania Archives*, 3 series, Vol. 14, page 750.

CHAMBERS, JOSEPH
    Washington County, Pennsylvania. *Pennsylvania Archives*, 9th series, Vol. 6, page 4231.

CHAPIN, LUTHER
    Watman's Ct., Philadelphia, Pennsylvania. 1847.

CHEYNEY, CHARLES
    Birmingham, Pennsylvania. 1839.

CHERINGTON, THOMAS
    Ashland, Pennsylvania. 1860.

CHERRINGTON, WILLIAM
    Missemer's Mills, Lebanon County, Pennsylvania. 1861.

CHERRY, JOHN
    Hempfield Township, Westmoreland County, Pennsylvania. Tax lists 1802, 1803, 1806, 1809, 1810, 1812, 1813.

CLARK, JAMES
    Hopewell Township, Bedford County, Pennsylvania. Tax list 1821.

CLARK, JOHN
    Reading, Pennsylvania. 1804. *Reading Adler,* June 19, 1804.
    Shippensburg, Pennsylvania. Tax lists 1811, 1814.

CLARK, WILLIAM
    Philadelphia, Pennsylvania. Tax list 1783. *Pennsylvania Archives,* 3 series, Vol. 16, page 747.

CLAUSE, GEORGE
    Woodbury Township, Bedford County, Pennsylvania. Tax list 1855. United States Census 1850.

CLAUSE, HENRY (Reiffel Smith)
    Heidelberg Township, Lehigh County, Pennsylvania. Tax list 1821.

CLAUSE, HENRY
    South Woodbury Township, Bedford County, Pennsylvania. United States Census 1850.

CLEWELL, JESSE
    Bustleton, Philadelphia County, Pennsylvania. 1861.

CLINE, JACOB
    Saltsburg, Indiana County, Pennsylvania. 1861.

CLIPPINGER, JOSEPH
    Washington Township, Franklin County, Pennsylvania. Tax lists 1821, 1826, 1828.

CLOUSE, VALENTINE
    South Woodbury Township, Bedford County, Pennsylvania.
    Clouse worked in the twentieth century and was known by residents now living in Bedford County. He was the son of George Clouse. He made a neat, small gun of excellent quality. Few had patch boxes. One gun is known to be marked, "Shot a deer, 450 yards. V. F. C." He charged $15.00 for a rifle.

COATES, JAMES
    Back, 47 Tammany, Philadelphia, Pennsylvania. 1814.

COCHRAN, LANDON
    Brownsville Township, Fayette County, Pennsylvania. Tax lists 1818, 1826.

COCHREN, ROBERT
    458 North Third Street, Philadelphia, Pennsylvania. 1814.

COLDREIN, JNO.
    German Township, Fayette County, Pennsylvania. Tax lists 1822, 1823, 1825, 1831, 1835, 1836, 1837.

COLVIN, DAVIS
    Green Grove, Luzerne County, Pennsylvania. 1861.

CONRAD, SAMUEL
    Brothers Valley Township, Somerset County, Pennsylvania. Tax list 1832.
    Berlin Township, Somerset County, Pennsylvania. Tax lists 1837, 1840.
    Brothers Valley Township, Somerset County, Pennsylvania. Tax lists 1833, 1834.
    Berlin Borough, Somerset County, Pennsylvania. Tax lists 1843, 1850, 1853.

CONSTABLE, R.
    88 South 2nd Street, Philadelphia, Pennsylvania. 1847.

COOK, JACOB
    Caernarvon Township, Lancaster County, Pennsylvania. Tax lists 1813, 1809, 1811, 1812.

COOK, THOMAS
    Still House Alley, Philadelphia, Pennsylvania. 1814.

COOLEY, DAVID
    David Cooley was born February 7, 1790, in Huntington Township, York County, Pennsylvania. He is thought to have worked in Cranberry Valley, Tyrone

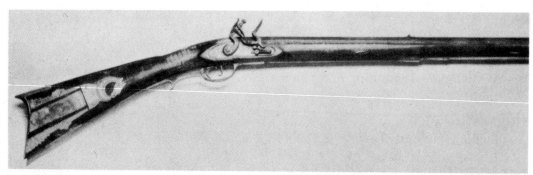

Monroe Hufford

PLATE 167

Rifle with flint lock, full stock of curly maple, set triggers, brass mountings, octagonal barrel with D. Cooley on the top facet of the barrel.

Township, Adams County, Pennsylvania. His products are typical of the late flint and early percussion period. He selected choice wood for his stocks and decorated some of them with a number of silver inlays. He is also known to have carved some of his stocks.

He died on July 14, 1856, and is buried in the graveyard of the Upper Bermudian Lutheran Church in Huntington Township, Adams County, Pennsylvania.

COOPER, J. M. (Wholesale Hardware Mt.)
    58 Wood Street, Pittsburgh, Pennsylvania. 1841.

COOPER, J. M. & Co. (Pistol Works)
    Corner First & Short, Pittsburgh, Pennsylvania. 1863-64.

COOPER & LAVELY (Pistol Manufacturers)
    Factory Corner First & Short, Pittsburgh, Pennsylvania. 1861-62.

CORBLEY, D.
    York County, Pennsylvania.

CORNAY, FRANCIS
    89 South Water Street, Philadelphia, Pennsylvania. 1814.

CORNET, CHARLES
    93 South Water Street, Philadelphia, Pennsylvania. 1814.

CORRELL, GEORGE
    Kunkletown, Monroe County, Pennsylvania. 1861.

COULAUX, JULIEN
    93 South Water Street, Philadelphia, Pennsylvania. 1798.

COUTTY, SAMUEL
    Philadelphia, Pennsylvania. Tax list 1783. *Pennsylvania Archives*, 3 series, Vol. 16, page 747.
    (Adv. of estate of Samuel Coutty, deceased.) *Federal (Philadelphia) Gazette*, no. 1967. February 11, 1795.

COVER, JOHN
    Connellsville, Fayette County, Pennsylvania. 1861.

COVER, JOHN
    Main & Spring Streets, Connellsville, Fayette County, Pennsylvania. 1859

COWDAN, JAMES F.
    Chandlerville, Chester County, Pennsylvania. 1861.

COWELL, EBENEZER
    Philadelphia, Pennsylvania. Tax list 1780. *Pennsylvania Archives*, 3d series, Vol. 15, page 338.

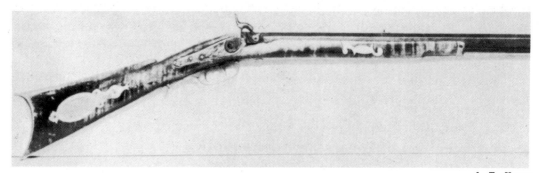

J. T. Herron

PLATE 168

Rifle with back action percussion lock, curly maple half stock, brass mountings, set triggers, elliptical patch box, octagonal barrel 36 inches long with G. W. C. on top facet of the barrel.

CRAFT, D. S.

Brush Valley, Indiana County, Pennsylvania. 1861.

CRAFT, GEORGE WASHINGTON

Craft Creek, Morris Township, Washington County, Pennsylvania.

Craft served his apprenticeship under Abe Williams of Craft Creek near Prosperity, Washington County, Pennsylvania. He produced half-stock percussion rifles from 1860 to 1875.

CRAIG, JOSEPH

House, Hand near Liberty. *Pittsburgh and Allegheny Directory*, 1857-58.

CRAIG AND MUSGRAVE

50 Wayne Street, Pittsburgh, Pennsylvania. *Directory of Pittsburgh and Allegheny Cities*, 1861-62.

CRAIG, WILLIAM

Manufacturer of and Dealer in Guns, Pistols, Cartridges, Ammunition, etc. No. 56 Federal Street, Allegheny, Pennsylvania. *The Pittsburgh Commercial*, November 1, 1850. *Harris' Business Directory of Pittsburgh and Allegheny*, 1847.

CRAIG, WILLIAM

WM. CRAIG, Gunsmith, having removed from 124 Liberty Street, to third street, one door above the St. Charles Hotel, will continue to manufacture and keep on hand, all kinds of Guns and Pistols. Repairing done with neatness and dispatch in all kinds of guns and pistols. *The Daily Commercial Journal*, Pittsburgh, January 2, 1850.

CRAIG, WILLIAM

Rochester Borough, Beaver County, Pennsylvania. Tax lists 1867, 1869.

CRAIG, WILLIAM & JOSEPH

CO-PARTNERSHIP—the undersigned have formed a co-partnership for the purpose of carrying the business of Gunsmiths. They will occupy the old stand of William Craig on St. Clair Street, opposite the centre of the Exchange Hotel. Guns of all descriptions will be made to order, and every attention given to repairs. William Craig, Joseph Craig. *The Daily Commercial Journal*, Pittsburgh, Pennsylvania. March 2, 1846.

CRAIG, WILLIAM & SON
Foxburg, Clarion County, Pennsylvania. 1877.

CRINER, A.
Cross Creek Village, Washington County, Pennsylvania. 1861.

CRISSY, (CRISSEY) ELIAS
Quemahoning Township, Somerset County, Pennsylvania. Tax lists 1859, 1867.

CRISWELL, SAMUEL
Carlisle, Pennsylvania. Tax list 1782.
Guns made and mended by Samuel Criswell in Carlisle. *Kline's Carlisle Weekly Gazette*, August 20, 1794.

CROLL, DANIEL (Gun Stocker)
Providence Township, Montgomery County, Pennsylvania. Census report 1800.

CRONER, ABRAHAM
Cross Creek Township, Washington County, Pennsylvania. Tax lists 1845, 1856.

CROSSLAND, JOHN
North Union Township, Fayette County, Pennsylvania. Tax list 1858.

CROSSLAND, JOHN
Union Borough, Fayette County, Pennsylvania. Tax lists 1871, 1883.

CUMMINGS, WILLIAM
107 Charlotte Street, Philadelphia, Pennsylvania. 1855.

CUNKLE, GEORGE
North Third near Walnut, Harrisburg, Dauphin County, Pennsylvania. 1840-1861.

CUNNINGHAM, ALEXANDER
German Township, Fayette County, Pennsylvania. Tax lists 1802, 1803, 1804, 1805 (1807-"gone away")

CURRY, WILLIAM
Carlisle, Pennsylvania. Tax list 1779.

CUSTER, NICHOLAS
Providence Township, Montgomery County, Pennsylvania. Census list 1800.

DALBY, ALEXANDER
Millsboro, Washington County, Pennsylvania. Tax lists 1858, 1859, 1865.

DALBY, ENOCH
Millsboro, Washington County, Pennsylvania. Tax lists 1841, 1844, 1865.
Enoch Dalby is known to have made some percussion half-stock rifles with silver sights.

DALBY, JAMES
    Millsboro, Washington County, Pennsylvania. Tax list 1865.

DARLINGTON, BENJAMIN (Merchant)
    Pittsburgh, Pennsylvania. 1816.
    The Pittsburgh Gazette, November 29, 1816:
            HARDWARE JUST RECEIVED
    KETLAND Gun-locks by the dozen
    German   do   do
    German looking glasses
    Brass andirons, assorted sizes
    Iron and brass head shovel and tongs
    One case gilt and plated buttons, assorted
    Likewise on hand a general assortment of
    CUTLERY AND SADDLERY, assorted
    WHOLESALE AND RETAIL
    Benjamin Darlington,
    Third Street, two doors from Market
    Pittsburgh, November 29, 1816

DAUGHERTY, ABSALOM
    Annville, Lebanon County, Pennsylvania. Tax list 1842.

DEBENDER, GEORGE
    337 South Street, Philadelphia, Pennsylvania. 1855.

DEBOLT, HENRY
    Monongahela Township, Greene County, Pennsylvania. Tax list 1869.
    Mapletown, Greene County, Pennsylvania. 1876.

DEFIBAUGH, DANIEL
    West Providence Township, Bedford County, Pennsylvania. Tax list 1846.

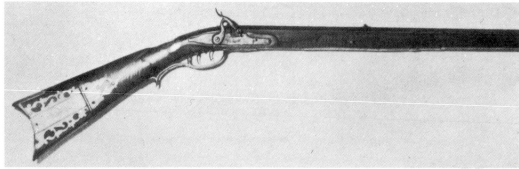

M. T. Stewart

PLATE 169

Rifle with percussion lock, full stock of curly maple, brass mountings, and octagonal barrel with W. Defibaugh on the top facet of the barrel. The design of the patch box on this rifle is very interesting for it does not conform to the pattern generally used by gunsmiths in Bedford County, Pennsylvania.

DEFIBAUGH, DAVID

Bedford Township, Bedford County, Pennsylvania. Tax list 1864.

David Defibaugh was a son of William. He made a number of double-barrel guns with half stocks. After he dropped his gunsmithing activity, he became a jeweler in Everett, Pennsylvania.

DEFIBAUGH, L.

Bedford Borough, Bedford County, Pennsylvania. Tax list 1871.

DEFIBAUGH, MILTON

Monroe Township, Bedford County, Pennsylvania.

Milton Defibaugh was a late nineteenth century gunsmith. He charged twenty silver dollars for his rifles.

DEFIBAUGH, WILLIAM

Monroe Township, Bedford County, Pennsylvania. Tax list 1852. United States Census 1850.

William Defibaugh was one of Bedford County's prolific and fine craftsmen. His guns were very slender and he used a beautifully proportioned lock and hammer.

DeHAVEN, PETER

Wanted immediately, a number of hands who understand any of the branches of the Gunsmith's business. Stockers in particular will meet with good encouragement, by applying to Peter DeHaven, at the public manufactory at French Creek, or James Carter, in Third Street, near Arch Street. *Pennsylvania Evening Post*, no. 318, February 22, 1777.

DEHUFF, HENRY

Lancaster, Pennsylvania. Tax list 1800.

DEHUFF, JOHN

Washington Township, Washington County, Pennsylvania. Tax list 1796, 1803.

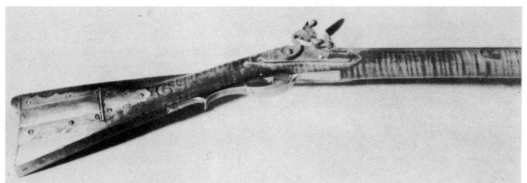

Reaves Goehring

PLATE 170

Rifle with flint lock, curly maple stock, brass mountings, octagonal barrel 44 inches long, and H. Dehuff engraved in script letters on top facet of barrel. The daisy finial on the patch box and the shallow curve of the butt plate suggest eighteenth century production in Lancaster.

DEHUFF, JOHN

Lancaster, Pennsylvania. Tax lists 1813, 1816.

There was probably a father and son relationship in these two men.

DEISINGER, WENDELL

North Second ab Dauphin, Philadelphia, Pennsylvania. 1861.

DELANEY, NELSON

8 North Fifth Street, Reading, Pennsylvania. 1860.

Nelson Delaney appears to have worked in Reading, Pennsylvania, throughout most of the last half of the nineteenth century. He is listed as a gunsmith in a Pennsylvania Business Directory of 1860 and two groups of his rifles were offered for sale in the 1885 catalogue of Jos. C. Grubb in Philadelphia, Pennsylvania.

The one group had bores ranging from 165 to 185 and were described as having "Plain Iron Barrel, Plug and Nipple Percussion, Side Action Lock, Double Trigger, Oiled Finish Walnut Stock, with Brass Mountings." The second group had the following specifications: Plain Iron Barrel, Tang Patent Breech Percussion, Bar Locks, Double trigger, Oiled Finish Walnut Stock, with Bolt and Escutcheons, Brass Mountings. Moulds and wipers were supplied with all rifles.

DEMSEY, JOHN

Conemaugh Township, Cambria County, Pennsylvania. Tax list 1852.

Summerhill Township, Cambria County, Pennsylvania. Tax lists 1853, 1854.

DEMSEY, MATHEW

Conemaugh Township, Cambria County, Pennsylvania. Tax lists 1834, 1835.

DEMUTH, J.

A name on the top facet of an octagonal barrel usually indicates that the gun was made by the person whose name appears there, but sometimes such a conclusion must be made with reservations. The name, John Demuth, appears on the barrel of a gun in the arms display of Old Sturbridge Village, but the writer is sure that John Demuth was not a gunsmith.

The name, John Demuth, is connected with the Demuth family, who owned a tobacco shop on East King Street, in Lancaster, Pennsylvania, from the late eigh-

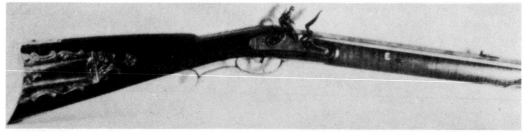

Old Sturbridge Village

PLATE 171

Rifle with flint lock, full stock of curly maple, brass mountings, octagonal barrel 44 inches long with J. Demuth engraved in script letters on the top facet of the barrel. Although this rifle has little ornamentation, the patch box is a beautiful example of the work done in Lancaster County in the late eighteenth and early nineteenth century.

One lock is known to the writer with J. Demuth, Lancaster, engraved on the lock plate.

teenth century until the present. It was not uncommon for an eighteenth century gunsmith in Lancaster to be engaged in sidelines, such as operating a dry-goods store or a board yard, so it is entirely possible that Demuth sold guns at his tobacco shop. Such guns would have been made in Lancaster and the name John Demuth could easily have been engraved on the barrel. Two other guns are known with the name, John Demuth, engraved on the locks, so it is possible that Demuth also did some retail lock business.

The fact that Demuth did have some interest in the gun business is proved by the presence of his name on a list of men who supplied guns to a cartel operated by General Hand in 1794. A copy of this account can be seen in the Library of the Historical Society of Pennsylvania. The title is *Continental Rifles, Account of when received and when forwarded by order of General Hand, Lancaster, February 7, 1794.*

Although most of the men who contributed rifles to this account were gunsmiths, at least three of the men have not been regarded as such. They are Peter Getz, who was a local silversmith and later an inspector of arms, Joseph Simon, who was an Indian trader, and John DeMuth.

There is no evidence in the legal records of the Lancaster County Courthouse that Demuth was a gunsmith. In no transactions is he so designated, and the intestate inventory of his estate does not include any tools or equipment that suggest he was a craftsman of any kind. The conclusion that John Demuth was not a gunsmith could be incorrect; however, there is no documentary evidence at the moment to prove such a vocation.

DENNIS, WILLIAM
Wilkes-Barre, Pennsylvania. 1818.
To Gunsmiths, The subscriber, residing in Wilkes-Barre, Pennsylvania, wants to engage immediately one or two journeymen to make rifles. One to stock and one to breech cut and finish barrels fit for stocking, or such as can make all parts except the barrels, locks, and castings. Good wages will be given to good and steady workmen, if they come in two or three weeks.—William Dennis, Linglestown, May 15, 1818. *Harrisburg Republican*, Friday, May 22, 1818.

DERR, CHRISTIAN
Oley Township, Berks County, Pennsylvania. 1805.

DERR, JOHANNES
Berks County, Pennsylvania. *Reading Adler*, October 27, 1818.

DERR, PETER
Tulpohocken, Pennsylvania. 1860.

DERRINGER, HENRY
374 North Front Street, Philadelphia, Pennsylvania. 1814. Philadelphia, Pennsylvania. 1831.
RIFLE MANUFACTORY, a general assortment of Rifles, Pistols, Guns, Swords, etc., on hand for the Southern and Western Trade. *American Advertising Directory*, 1831.

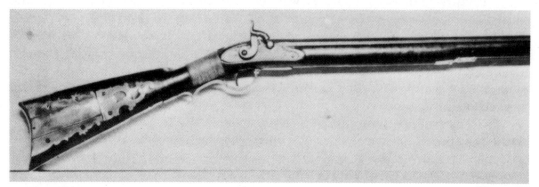

Vincent Nolt

PLATE 172

Rifle with percussion lock, stock of curly maple, brass mountings, octagonal barrel 38 inches long with H. Derringer on the top facet in block letters. A number of Pennsylvania rifles by Derringer have survived, although the design of the patch box on this rifle is more attractive than his common eagle pattern.

Tamarind ab Green, Philadelphia, Pennsylvania. 1847. (Rifle Manuf.)
370 North Front Street, Philadelphia, Pennsylvania. 1855. (Rifle and Pistol Manuf.)

DERRINGER, PHILIP
North Fourth ab Washington, Reading, Berks County, Pennsylvania. 1860, 1861.

DETWEILER, ANDREW
Springfield Furnace, Blair County, Pennsylvania. 1861.

DETWILER, ANTHONY
Bloomfield Township, Bedford County, Pennsylvania. Tax list 1870.

DEVORE, BENJAMIN
Stony Creek Township, Somerset County, Pennsylvania. Tax list 1840.

Monroe Hufford

PLATE 173

Rifle with flint lock, full stock of curly maple, brass mountings, octagon-to-round barrel 42 inches long with John Derr in block letters on the top facet of the barrel.

The pattern of the patch box on this rifle was also used by Mauger on a number of his products. It is likely that Derr was also engaged in another occupation, for not many of his rifles are found in collections in Pennsylvania.

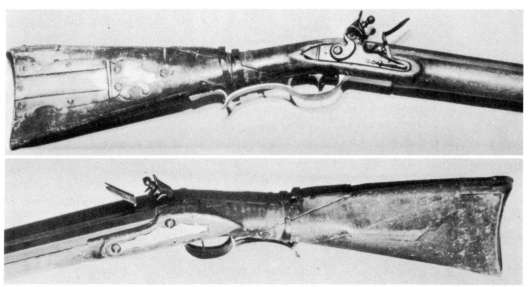

PLATE 174

Reaves Goehring

Rifle with flint lock, full stock of maple, brass mountings, octagonal barrel 42 inches long marked J. Dickert on the top facet of the barrel.
This rifle is one of the earliest products of Dickert. The butt plate is almost flat and is about two inches thick. The patch box with a daisy finial is engraved but not as profusely as those made in the late eighteenth century by Lancaster gunsmiths.

DICKERT, JACOB

Gunsmiths have achieved positions of importance in the history of firearm manufacture for a variety of reasons. Some lived in critical times such as the Revolution or the War of 1812; others produced large quantities of guns; some made guns of outstanding quality; and a few made guns over a long span of years. It is interesting to note that Jacob Dickert qualifies for recognition in all of these ways, and therefore must be regarded as one of the most important gunsmiths to have worked in Pennsylvania.

Dickert was born at Maintz, Germany, in 1740 and came to America with his parents in 1748. In 1756 the family moved to Lancaster, Pennsylvania, and it is likely that the sixteen-year-old youth was immediately apprenticed to a gunsmith. An apprentice period of seven years would then have terminated for him at the age of twenty-three, instead of at twenty-one, as was customary in Europe and America at that time.

In 1764 he married Johanetta Hofer of York, Pennsylvania; and the following year he became a citizen of His Majesty's Colony in America. That same year a son, named Johannes, was born to the young couple; and in 1765 their daughter Maria was born.

In 1774 Dickert and John Henry bought a plot of land in Manheim Township, on the edge of the borough of Lancaster, and built on it a boring mill to bore gun barrels. This purchase may be regarded as a shrewd move because such equipment would be very useful in supplying barrels for the impending war. The mill was doubtless successful, for when John Henry died in 1779, his half-interest was bought by Dickert. Mrs. Henry was forced to sell her interest in the boring mill so that she could meet the responsibility of educating her children as her husband had directed in his will. Dickert apparently owned and operated the mill until late in the eighteenth century, when he sold it to the person from whom the land had originally been bought.

In 1787 Dickert's daughter married James Gill, a Lancaster dry goods merchant, and for a number of years the names of Dickert and Gill were involved in selling dry goods and guns. Some Dickert and Gill guns are known to exist. When in 1796, Gill died, Dickert advertised in the local newspaper that all outstanding claims against this partnership would be settled.

It is obvious that Dickert was an outstanding and active citizen of his adopted country. He supported the construction of the great turnpike from Lancaster to Philadelphia and was an active member of the Moravian Church, where some of the data about him has been fortunately preserved for posterity to read.

Dickert died in 1822 after a very long and productive career in Lancaster. He was called a gunsmith at his death, which usually implies that a man was active in his trade until the time of his death, although such a conclusion is not entirely safe to make at all times.

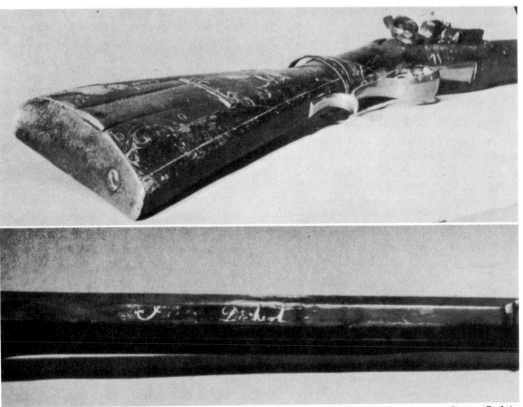

Reaves Goehring

PLATE 175

Rifle with flint lock, brass mountings, and octagonal barrel with J. Dickert on the top facet of the barrel.

This rifle has a four-piece patch box with a daisy finial and a very thick butt. All of these features suggest that the rifle was made by Dickert about the time of the American Revolution.

An advertisement in a Lancaster newspaper in 1795 tells that Dickert could supply articles in the gunsmith line and that customers could depend on satisfaction, for he had forty years experience as a gunsmith. Although there is a discrepancy of one year between this statement and the records of the Moravian Church, it is obvious that he started his career about 1755. Extremely few of Dickert's earliest products are known to exist, but one that probably qualifies for such a category is known to the writer. Dickert's ownership of the boring mill placed him in a position of importance throughout the Revolution, and an undocumented source tells that a number of his guns were used at the battle of Kings Mountain. This dramatic battle may have been fought with American rifles against English rifles designed by Ferguson, who was killed in the battle.

Dickert's interest in making military arms seems to have continued throughout much of his life, for in 1794 he is credited with rifles in the "Hand Account of Continental Rifles." To this account he contributed 173 rifles in one four-month period and 143 in another period of the same length. It must be presumed that Dickert was employing journeymen gunsmiths in order to have been able to produce so many rifles in so short a time.

In the early nineteenth century, 1800-1810, Dickert was active in a cartel which was producing arms for the United States Government. The men associated with Dickert were Henry Dehuff, Peter Gonter, George Miller, Christopher Gumpf, and John Bender. They were making military rifles with silver stars and thumb pieces for eleven dollars, "the common type for ten dollars and a half." They also made Charleville (type) muskets like the pattern from the United States Armory at Springfield, and in one of the letters to the Lancaster craftsmen the gunsmiths were solicited to supply milled yarn half stockings, bells for cows, horses and sheep for the Indian stores. A few muskets that Dickert made in this period are known to exist.

Dickert's fame also rests on his production of sporting rifles, which he seems to have made from the beginning to the end of his career. Most of his eighteenth century rifles have long barrels and patch boxes with the typical daisy finial used by other Lancaster gunsmiths, although each gunsmith had a pattern that was slightly different from the designs of other makers.

The designs are engraved in the usual deep Lancaster style and are attractively placed so that some portions of the brass surface are plain, while others are fully decorated. In the early nineteenth century Dickert used another patch box pattern that was also used by his contemporaries, Gonter and Brong. He seems to have made guns throughout the late years of his life, despite that fact that in 1800 he attained the age of sixty, when many men ceased production. There is a sharp demand for his guns, and no collection of Lancaster rifles is complete without one.

DICKEY, DAVID
Middletown Township, Cumberland County, Pennsylvania. Tax list 1780. *Pennsylvania Archives*, 3 series, Vol. 20, page 336.

DIESINGER, W.
1500 North Second Street, Philadelphia, Pennsylvania. 1855.

DIEBERGER, HENRICH (Gunsmith)

Henrich Dieberger, der Bachsenschmidt, 1st aus der Zweyten-strasse in die Market-strasse gezogen, in das zweyte Haus vom Schwarzen Bären; allwo er das Bächsenschmidts-Handwerk in allen dessen Theilen, wie gewöhnlich, fortsetzt. Alle Herren, und andere, welche ihn mit ihrer Kundschaft zu begünstigen belieben, können vergewissert seyn, dass ihre Arbeit auf das sauberste und mit der grossten Beschleunigung soll gemacht werden. Er macht auch Lancetten mit Springfedern, und Instrumenten zum Schröpfen und Zähnausziehen. Er verkauft gleichfalls allerhand Pistolen. *Staatsbote,* no. 447. August 14, 1770.

KAUFFMAN TRANSLATION

Henry Dieberger, the gunsmith, has moved from 2d St. to Market St. in the second house from the Black Bears; where he practices as formerly, the gunsmith's trade in all its branches. All gentlemen and others who will favour him with their custom may be assured that their work will be done in the neatest manner and with the greatest dispatch. He makes also lancets with springs, and instruments for cupping and drawing teeth. He likewise sells all kinds of pistols.

DIETZ, JOHN

Somerset County, Pennsylvania. Tax list 1800.

DILLON, JAMES

Bedford Borough, Bedford County, Pennsylvania. Tax list 1844.

DIMOND, DANIEL

Pershing, Cambria County, Pennsylvania. 1861.

DINGLER, WILLIAM

Rear 337 North Third Street, Philadelphia, Pennsylvania. 1855.

DINSMAN, JOHN

404 North Third Street, Philadelphia, Pennsylvania. 1814.

DOLL, DANIEL (Single Man)

York Borough, Pennsylvania. Census list 1800.

A man named Daniel Doll (single man) is listed in the 1799 tax assessment list of Yorktown as a gunsmith. No rifles which bear his name are known in the region.

DOLL, JACOB

Jacob Doll is known to have worked at the trade of gunsmithing in York, Pennsylvania, as early as 1794. In that year he bought from Charles Barnitz (Deed # 2L495) lot #142 in the general plan of the borough; it was located on the west side of Water Street and extended fifty-seven feet, six inches, to the Codorus Creek. In 1838 Jacob Doll sold the same lot to the York and Maryland Railroad to accommodate the tracks that were presumably being built at that time. The railroad is located on Water Street, although the modern name for it is Pershing Avenue. After Doll sold this property, he moved to West Manchester Township, York County,

Joe Kindig, Jr.

PLATE 176

Rifle with flint lock marked J. Doll in script letters, full stock of curly maple, brass mountings, and octagonal barrel 43½ inches long marked J. Doll in script letters on the top facet of the barrel.

Although this stock is carved in the incised technique, and Doll engraved his name on the lock plate, the rifle does not establish Doll as an outstanding craftsman.

where he died in 1847. The inventory of his estate includes one vise valued at $2.00 and a lot of gunsmith's tools consisting of files, pinchers, hammers, etc., valued at $5.00. His rifles are of average quality.

DORNER, (DONER) JOHN

Antis Township, Huntington County, Pennsylvania. Tax lists 1859, 1867, 1870.

DONHAM, L. N.

Monongahela Township, Green County, Pennsylvania. 1876.

DOUGLAYS, DAVID

Frankstown Township, Blair County, Pennsylvania. Federal Census 1850. Tax lists 1866, 1867.

DOUGLAS, JOSEPH

Huntington County, Pennsylvania. Federal Census of 1850.

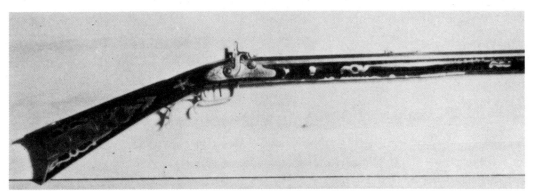

Lloyd D. Norris

PLATE 177

Rifle with percussion lock, full stock of curly maple, brass mountings, brass inlays, set triggers, octagonal barrel 41 inches long with J. Douglas on the top facet of the barrel.

The curl of the stock on this gun is particularly good and the engraved patch box indicates that Douglas was a fine engraver.

Lloyd Nolt

PLATE 177A

Fowling piece with original flint lock marked Drepperd, full stock of plain maple, brass mountings, octagon-to-round barrel marked Drepperd on top facet of the barrel. The chequered wrist was a feature of many guns made by Lancaster gunsmiths. The engraved trigger guard and toe-plate resemble the work of Melchoir Fordney, also of Lancaster.

DOUTHERT, JOHN

Conemaugh Township, Indiana County, Pennsylvania. Tax lists 1826, 1827, 1828. Douthert is listed as a blacksmith in the tax lists of 1823, 1824 and 1825.

DOWNWARD, THOMAS

George Township, Fayette County, Pennsylvania. Tax lists 1799, 1800, 1802, 1803, 1804.

DRAKE, DOLFUS

Everett Borough, Bedford County, Pennsylvania. Tax list 1880. Drake was the last of the Bedford County gunsmiths. He died a few years ago at the age of 103. He was an excellent shot and is known to have gotten 19 out of 25 turkeys that were offered at a shooting match.

DREPPERD, JOHN

Lancaster, Pennsylvania. Tax lists 1834, 1840.

DREPPERD, JOHN JR.

Lancaster, Pennsylvania.
Business Directory of Lancaster, Pennsylvania. 1843.

DRIESBACH, J.

Mifflinburg Union County, Pennsylvania. Federal census 1850.

DREIRBACK, JOHN

Mifflinburg, Union County, Pennsylvania. 1861.

DUNBAR, ALEXANDER

Providence Township, Montgomery County, Pennsylvania. Census list 1800.

DUNHAM, JOB

New Geneva, Fayette County, Pennsylvania. 1861.

DUNHAM, LEWIS

Monongahela Township, Green County, Pennsylvania. Tax lists 1869, 1875, 1876.

Lewis Dunham is probably the same man as L. N. Dunham, grandson of Barney Engle from whom it is thought he learned his trade. He made good guns and worked at the trade until late in the nineteenth century.

DUNKLE, GEORGE

Shippensburgh Township, Cumberland County, Pennsylvania. Tax list 1828.
Letterkenny Township, Franklin County, Pennsylvania. Tax list 1835.

DUNLAP, ROBERT, JR. (Hardware Dealer)

93 Market Street, Pittsburgh, Pennsylvania. *Harris' General Business Directory of the Cities of Pittsburgh and Allegheny*, 1841.

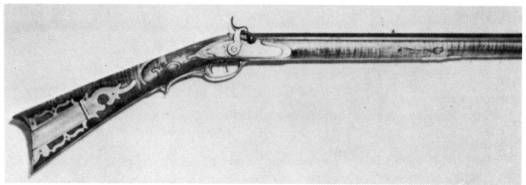

M. T. Stewart

PLATE 178

Rifle with percussion lock, full stock of curly maple, brass mountings, set triggers, octagonal barrel 36 inches long with Dunmeyer on the top facet of the barrel. Because of the scarcity of signed Dunmeyer rifles it is impossible to determine which of the three gunsmiths by that name made this rifle.

DUNMEYER, DAVID

Somerset Township, Somerset County, Pennsylvania. Tax lists 1856, 1872.

DUNMEYER, JONATHAN

Somerset Township, Somerset County, Pennsylvania. Tax lists 1852, 1853, 1856, 1861, 1872, d. 1885.

In an appraisal of Dunmeyer's estate an item of "Gun tools and other stuff" was valued at $9.00.

C. M. Knupp, another Somerset County gunsmith bought two barrels when Dunmeyer's personal possessions were sold at a public vendue.

DUNMYERE, (DUNMYER) PETER

Conemaugh Township, Cambria County, Pennsylvania. Tax lists 1826, 1828, 1832.

Somerset Township, Somerset County, Pennsylvania. Tax lists 1844, 1849, 1852, 1853, 1856, 1859.

DUNSETH, ANDREW

Cincinnati, Ohio. 1800. *Western Cincinnati Spy*, December 3, 1800.

Dunseth & Sutton

Sutton & Dunseth, Gunsmiths Request all persons indebted to them to make payment on or before the 1st of March, otherwise their accounts will be put in proper officers' hands for recovery. Pittsburgh, January 29, 1799.

N.B. Those who have left old guns to repair are requested to call for them soon or they will be sold for the repairs. *The Pittsburgh Gazette*, February 2, 1799.

Dunwick, William (Gunsmith)

Eight Dollars Reward—Thereas some time said one William Dunwick, Gunsmith, came to the subscriber and borrowed sundry Smith's tools, among which was a new forging anvil, and bick iron; just before he absconded a young man was seen to take the said tools away in a wheel barrow.

Duvice, (Devece) John

Springhill Township, Fayette County, Pennsylvania. Tax lists 1818, 1819.

Ealer, Lewis

556 North 10th Street, Philadelphia, Pennsylvania. 1855.

Earley, Amos

West Hanover, Pennsylvania. *Boyd's Business Directory*, 1860.

Earnest, Jacob

Hempfield Township, Westmoreland County, Pennsylvania. Tax lists 1827, 1829, 1830.

Earnest, Jacob

Salem Cross Roads, Westmoreland County, Pennsylvania. 1861.

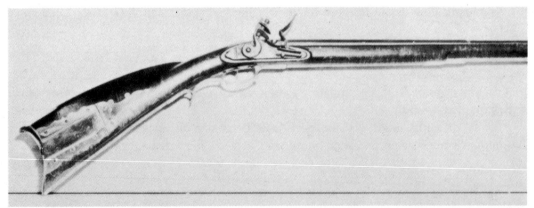

Henry J. Kauffman

PLATE 179

Rifle with flint lock, brass mountings, full stock of curly maple, octagon-to-round barrel with H. Eckler engraved in script letters on the top facet of the barrel. The barrel on this rifle is much thicker than most octagon-to-round barrels. The drop of the stock and the pronounced "Roman nose" of the butt are also departures from the normal pattern.

Although Eckler is listed as a gunsmith in 1860, this gun was made before that time, possibly by Eckler's father.

EBERMAN, HENRY

Lancaster, Pennsylvania. Tax lists 1820, 1822, 1829, 1834, 1840.

Eberman is one of the very few gunsmiths listed as a freeman through their careers as gunsmiths.

A few guns are known that bear his name, one of which is better than average quality. The engraving is well done and there is some carving on the forestock.

ECKLER, HENRY

Pine Grove, Pennsylvania. 1860.

Eckler is listed as a deceased soldier from Pine Grove, Schuylkill County, Pennsylvania, in the enrollment of men who were liable for military service in 1862. He had been a member of the 96th Regiment, Company b.

EDDIE, JAMES

Noble near Third, Philadelphia, Pennsylvania. 1814.

EDMOND, JACOB

Aaronsburg, Centre County, Pennsylvania. 1861.

EDWARDS, MICHAEL

Yorktown, Pennsylvania. Deed 5 G 423.

Affidavit—That I was a resident of Yorktown, now Boro of York, where I was born August 10, 1767. Until Spring of 1801 was apprenticed to Conrad Welshans, a gunmaker when I left York. During my minority, Mr. Welshans and myself were both members of a Fire Company in Yorktown, which was organized long before I was a member. I helped to repair the engine of the Fire Company. Jacob and Conrad Welshans helped.

EDWARDS, MICHAEL, JR.

Washington Township, Washington County, Pennsylvania. Tax lists 1807 1808, 1826.

EICHOLTZ, JOHN

Lancaster, Pennsylvania. Tax list 1840.

EICHOLTZ & BROS.

59 North Queen Street, Lancaster, Lancaster County, Pennsylvania. 1861.

ELDER, JOHN

Conemaugh Township, Indiana County, Pennsylvania. Tax lists 1826, 1827, 1828.

ELLIOT, MICHAEL

Morris Township, Washington County, Pennsylvania. Tax lists 1854, 1856.

ELLS, JOSIAH (Revolving Pistol Manufacturer)

Short and Second, Pittsburgh, Pennsylvania. *Directory for 1856-57 of Pittsburgh & Allegheny Cities.*

ELLY, C. DAVIS

New Paris Borough, Bedford County, Pennsylvania. Tax list 1884.

No guns are known that were made by Elly. His work was probably of the repair type.

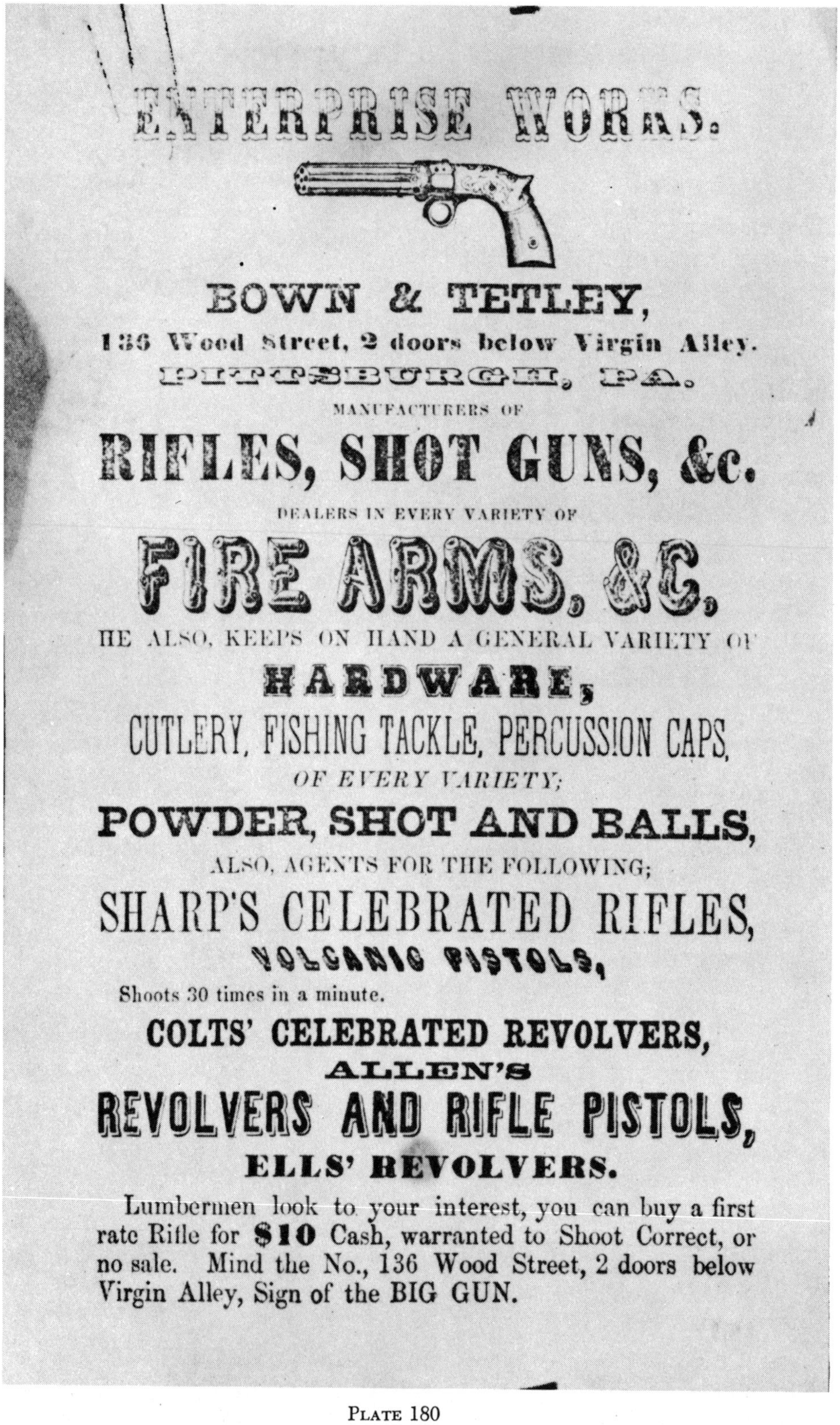

ENTERPRISE WORKS.

BOWN & TETLEY,
136 Wood Street, 2 doors below Virgin Alley.
PITTSBURGH, PA.
MANUFACTURERS OF
RIFLES, SHOT GUNS, &c.
DEALERS IN EVERY VARIETY OF
FIRE ARMS, &C.
HE ALSO, KEEPS ON HAND A GENERAL VARIETY OF
HARDWARE,
CUTLERY, FISHING TACKLE, PERCUSSION CAPS,
OF EVERY VARIETY;
POWDER, SHOT AND BALLS,
ALSO, AGENTS FOR THE FOLLOWING;
SHARP'S CELEBRATED RIFLES,
VOLCANIC PISTOLS,
Shoots 30 times in a minute.
COLTS' CELEBRATED REVOLVERS,
ALLEN'S
REVOLVERS AND RIFLE PISTOLS,
ELLS' REVOLVERS.
Lumbermen look to your interest, you can buy a first
rate Rifle for **$10** Cash, warranted to Shoot Correct, or
no sale. Mind the No., 136 Wood Street, 2 doors below
Virgin Alley, Sign of the BIG GUN.

PLATE 180
Advertisement of the Enterprise Works from the Allegheny Pilot, by E. L. Babbit, Freeport, 1855.

ELTON, A.
Next 43 Zane, Philadelphia, Pennsylvania. 1814.

ELTON, THOMAS
Philadelphia, Pennsylvania. Tax list 1780. *Pennsylvania Archives,* 3 series, Vol. 15, page 303.

ENGLE, BARNEY (BARNET)
Monongahela Township, Greene County, Pennsylvania. Tax lists 1833, 1834, 1835, 1836, 1838, 1848, 1860, 1869, 1875, 1876, 1878.

ENGLE, EZRA
Greene Township, Greene County, Pennsylvania. Tax lists 1817, 1820, 1821, 1835, 1838.

Monongahela Township, Greene County, Pennsylvania. Tax lists 1824, 1829, 1835, 1838.

ENGLE, PETER
Greene Township, Greene County, Pennsylvania. Tax lists 1803, 1809, 1817, 1823.

ENGLES, CHRISTIAN
Monongahela Township, Greene County, Pennsylvania. Tax lists 1824, 1829, 1833.
Morris Township, Washington County, Pennsylvania. Tax list 1845.

ENTERPRISE GUN WORKS
The Enterprise Gun Works was established in 1848 by Bown and Tetley at 136-138 Wood Street, Pittsburgh, Pennsylvania. The company seems to have produced good guns over a long period of time despite the fact that ownership of the business frequently changed hands. The following excerpt from the catalogue of James Bown & Sons is very interesting, for it is the earliest record known to the author of a manufacturer calling his products "Kentucky rifles."

> We wish to notify the public that James Bown and Sons of 121 Wood Street, Pittsburgh, Pa., are the only manufacturers of the CELEBRATED KENTUCKY RIFLES, which name was adopted by the senior member of this firm in 1848;—

The early location of this manufacturer in the busy city of Pittsburgh probably accounts for some of their success. An advertisement in *The* (Pittsburgh) *Morning Post,* March 13, 1855, suggests that many of their customers were people traveling to the newly opened West, who bought their arms in Pittsburgh enroute:

> Bown and Tetley's rifles are cheap and well made. Emigrants would do well to give us a call. We keep a large stock of our manufacture always on hand. All guns are warranted.

By 1862 the business was owned entirely by James Bown; his newspaper advertisement on March 6, 1865 indicates that he was agent for Colt's pistols and rifles, that he sold gunsmiths, materials, and that he imported arms to sell at retail in his store. A Pittsburgh Business Directory of 1874-75 lists the company as "James Bown and Son" and in 1883 the name was changed to "James Bown and Sons." They also had a new location at 520 Wood Street. About 1883 the business was bought by Brown and Hirth, who continued to produce guns of high quality at the best prices in America. In 1889 W. S. Brown, who had a machine shop and factory on Virgin Alley, became the sole owner of the business. The following excerpt is from the 1883 catalogue of James Bown and Sons:

CAUTION TO THE PUBLIC. We wish to notify the public that James Bown & Sons, of 121 WOOD STREET, PITTSBURGH, PA., are the only manufacturers of the CELEBRATED KENTUCKY RIFLES, which name was adopted by the senior member of this firm in 1848; since that time we have improved on the style and workmanship until they are now the BEST SHOOTING Muzzle Loading Rifle made. In consequence of the reputation we have made with these Rifles other dealers are manufacturing what they call KENTUCKY RIFLES, in order to bring grist to their mill; all our rifles have our name stamped on each barrel, and this stamp (a drawing of a deer and the words KILL BUCK). All other not bearing this name and stamp are counterfeit. Our Rifles are the cheapest and the best made in the world for the money.

The muzzle Loading Rifle for accurate shooting from 50 to 300 yards is fully equal to any breech loading rifle made, and for small game is far superior, because you can get them made with such a size ball as is best adapted to the game in the part of the country which you chance to live. In many places there is no large game—hence a breech loading rifle, either a 38-100, 44-100, or 50-100 caliber, would be of no use, because the ball being so large that small game hit with such a size ball as the two latter sizes would be entirely destroyed and not fit to use. Then again, the expense in ammunition is not one-fourth for a Muzzle Loading Rifle, for what it is for a Breech Loading Rifle, and in the country the item of ammunition is looked upon in a business way, especially when in some parts it is very difficult to get cartridges for Breech Loaders. But you can always get powder, lead and caps in the most remote part of the world, and this is why we claim the Muzzle-Loader is better for the money than the Breech-Loader, and especially when you can get such accurate shooters as are made by us. We make all our own barrels, which no other Muzzle-Loading Rifle manufacturer does; therefore we have advantages over those who buy a cheap grade of barrels in order to compete with us. Also, all our locks, triggers, and mountings are made by us; therefore we have all the advantages that can be had in assisting us to make a first-class Rifle, which we have done ever since the year 1848, now over thirty-five years of our firm's existence. We are proud of the success we have made, and can only attribute it to making a good article, and giving the people who order from us the worth of their money; and we shall continue to do so in the future as we have done in the past, soliciting your orders for those goods, assuring you that under all circumstances you will be fairly dealt with.

We wish to call the attention of our customers to the fact that for the past three years we have not been able to fill the orders for our celebrated Kentucky Rifles. We shall do our best this year, and hope to be able to do so; but we may be in the same fix as former years—have more orders than we can fill during the hunting season; therefore we advise those who want our rifles to order early. Their chances will be much better than if they put it off until late in the season; then it takes us from two to three weeks to fill orders for a single Rifle.

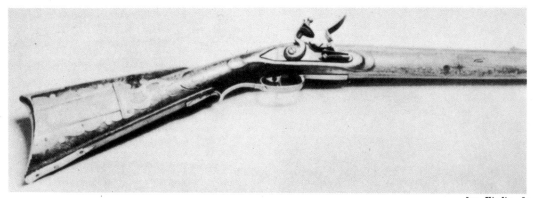

Joe Kindig, Jr.

PLATE 181

Rifle with flint lock, full stock of curly maple, brass mountings, and octagonal barrel 48 inches long with A. Ernst engraved on the top facet of the barrel.

A. Ernst was a master craftsman and there is some evidence that he learned his trade from George Eyster. The design and execution of his carving is outstanding and his patch box is an attractive variation of the style used by many gunsmiths in York County, Pennsylvania.

ERNST, ADAM

Berwick Township, Adams County, Pennsylvania. Tax lists 1805, 1811.

ERNST, JACOB

Paradise Township, York County, Pennsylvania. Census list 1820.

ESHLMAN, JOHN

Bds. 37 Fourth, Pittsburgh, Pennsylvania. 1856-57.

ESTEP, CORNELIUS

Donegal Township, Washington County, Pennsylvania. Tax list 1849, 1850.

EVANS, JAS. E.

86 South Street, Philadelphia, Pennsylvania. 1855.

EVANS, JAMES E.

230 South Street, Philadelphia, Pennsylvania. 1861.

Henry J. Kauffman

PLATE 182

Fowling piece with flint lock, full stock of curly maple, brass mountings, silver and brass inlays, octagonal-to-round barrel 46 inches long with A. Ernst engraved on the top facet of the barrel. The fowling piece with its wire inlay, its silver half moon, and its highly engraved lock-bolt plate is an outstanding example of a Pennsylvania fowling piece.

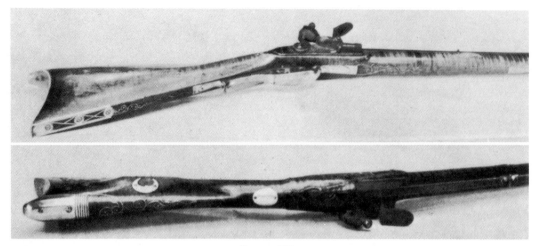

PLATE 183

Fowling piece with flint lock, full stock of curly maple, brass mountings, brass wire inlay, and octagon-to-round barrel 45 inches long with A. Ernst engraved in script letters on the top facet of the barrel.

This fowling piece is made unusually attractive by the brass wire inlays, by the carved patterns on the cheek side of the stock and around the breech tang, and by the half moon inlay of silver. The six grooves filed on the top end of the butt plate are also evidence of careful and imaginative workmanship on the part of the maker.

PLATE 184   *Hill Collection*

Rifle with flint lock (now percussion), full stock of curly maple, brass mountings, and octagonal barrel with J. Ernst engraved in script letters on top facet of the barrel.

This patch box design is usually associated with the work of Frederick Sell and its appearance on this gun by J. Ernst focuses attention on the possibility that Sell worked for Ernst or possibly supplied him with a patch box for one of his fine guns.

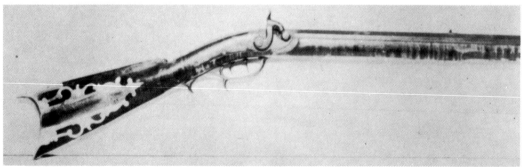

PLATE 185   *J. T. Herron*

Rifle with percussion lock, curly maple stock, plain brass mountings, set triggers, octagonal barrel 44 inches long with C. Estep on top facet of the barrel. The sharp curve of the butt plate and the early design of the patch box are incongruous but original to the rifle. The curved shape of the lock plate is not the typical pattern.

EVANS, DANIEL

Adv. for two guns taken from the shop of D. Evans, Fifth Street, near Market Street, Philadelphia. *Pennsylvania Evening Post*, no. 63, June 17, 1775.

EVANS, OWEN

Providence Township, Montgomery County, Pennsylvania.
Contract for Arms, *Pennsylvania Archives*, 9th series, Vol. 2, page 1318. 1797.

EYSTER, GEO.

It is not known exactly when George Eyster started his gunsmithing activity in York County. The earliest documented evidence of his trade is found in a deed, dated December 14, 1787, in which he was called a gunsmith. This purchase of land carried with it the privilege of erecting a dam (5½ feet perpendicular and no more) on it, which presumably was to be a source of power for the varied demands of his trade. It is very likely that he had a boring mill on the site, for he is not listed as one of the gunsmiths of York who suffered by the burning of a "bore mill" on the edge of town in 1800. In the 1799 tax assessment list for Manchester Township, York County, Pennsylvania, George Eyster, Sr., is taxed as a property holder with two hundred and forty acres, and George Eyster, Jr., is listed as a gunsmith with a property of thirty acres.

George Eyster was unquestionably one of the master craftsmen in York County. The carving on his stocks is superb in design and execution. His engraving is also of a uniform high quality and the pattern of his patch boxes is a distinctive Eyster creation.

FABER, E. & F.

Wanted. Two or Three Blacksmiths, who understand welding Gun Barrels, and one or two hands for boring, finishing, etc., to whom liberal wages, and constant employment will be given. Apply to the subscribers at their Machine Factory, Liberty Street, Pittsburgh. *The Allegheny Democrat*, April 14, 1835.

FAINOT, FREDERICK

Lancaster, Pennsylvania. Tax list 1780.

FAINOT, GEORGE F.

Lancaster, Pennsylvania. 1794.

FARVER, WILLIAM

Hollidaysburg Borough, Blair County, Pennsylvania. Tax lists 1848, 1849.
Newport, Perry County, Pennsylvania. 1861.

FAY, GEORGE

Allegheny Township, Blair County, Pennsylvania. Federal Census 1850.
Gaysport Borough, Pennsylvania. Tax list 1859 (Crossed out in 1860).
Hollidaysburg, Pennsylvania. Tax list 1860 (Crossed out in 1861).
Altoona, Pennsylvania. Tax lists 1862, 1864, 1869, 1874, 1879.

FAY, WILLIAM

Altoona, Pennsylvania. Tax list 1864—Entry marked "Killed in War."

FERREE, ISAAC
    Pittsburgh, Pennsylvania.

FERREE, JACOB
    Strasburg Township, Lancaster County, Pennsylvania. Tax list 1783.

FERREE, JOEL & ISAAC (Gun Powder)
    Mary Ferree, accompanied by her son, Daniel Ferree, and her son-in-law, Isaac Lefevre, came to Pennsylvania in 1712. They bought a parcel of land from Martin Kendig, who had previously acquired a tract of ten thousand acres in the Lancaster area from the proprietor commissioners. This tract was originally part of Chester County; but when Lancaster County was created in 1729, it became a part of the new county.
    Joel Ferree, a descendant of the above-mentioned Mary Ferree, was the first gunsmith of the family and is so recorded in the tax assessment records of Leacock Township, Lancaster County, in 1758. He is known to have been working at the trade at the time of the Revolution, because of the following record taken from the "Minutes of the Provincial Council of Pennsylvania of 1775":

> "Resolved that a messenger be sent to Joel Ferree of Lancaster County with a letter from the Committee requesting him immediately to complete the Guns wrote for as patterns and to know how many he can furnish of the same kind and at what price."

    It is obvious that he was important not only as a craftsman but also as progenitor of a family of gunsmiths, few of whose guns have survived for the collecting fraternity to acquire. His will, which is recorded in the Lancaster County courthouse, gives us important clues about his property and his descendants.
    He directs that the property on which he lived should become the possession of his son, Isaac. In addition, he directs that the property which he owns on Peter's Creek in Allegheny County should become the possession of his son-in-law, Jacob, for the balance of his life; thereafter it should revert to the children of Rachael Ferree, Joel's daughter and Jacob's wife. Rachael died in Lancaster County before Jacob moved to the property on Peter's Creek.
    Jacob Ferree was first married to his cousin, Rachael Ferree, late in the 1770's and was recorded as a gunsmith in Strasburg Township, Lancaster County, in 1783. Little is known about his gunsmithing activity before he moved to the West. He was probably attracted to this region by a new promotion plan for Pittsburgh in 1785, which was advertised widely as an attractive spot for all craftsmen to settle and sell their wares. Joel Ferree II was born in Lancaster County and probably became a partner with his father in the gunsmithing and powder business. The proprietors of the business were simply known as J. & I. Ferree. The 1800 census list for Allegheny County records a Jacob and Joel Ferree as gunsmiths, a probable reference to this father-and-son combination. Jacob Ferree died in 1807; a record of articles sold at his vendue includes some gunsmith tools sold to Isaac Ferree for $50.00, and one rifle sold to Joel Ferree for $17.00.
    Joel Ferree, 1771-1813, the eldest son of Jacob is the famous Col. Ferree of the War of 1812. He commanded the 1st Regiment, Pennsylvania Infantry, which

was mobilized at Dunlap's Plains near Pittsburgh. The regiment consisted of 35 officers and 511 enlisted men. On October 19 the 1st Regiment marched to Upper Sandusky, Ohio, and in December of that year construced a fort, which was called Fort Ferree in honor of the Regiment's leader. When the six month enlistment period of the regiment expired in the spring, they started marching back to Pittsburgh. Col. Ferree became ill on the return trip but was determined to march home with his men. On April 9, 1813, he died in Zanesville, Ohio, and was buried there. Joel Ferree had a son, Joel, who was a gunsmith at Bridgeville, Allegheny County.

Isaac Ferree 1786-1822, a son a Jacob and half-brother of Col. Joel Ferree, was born in western Pennsylvania. His trade is established by the following advertisement, which appeared in the April 8, 1812 issue of the *Pittsburgh Gazette:*

> The subscriber having removed from Pittsburgh, informs all those who had left guns with him to repair, that they are left with Mr. Aron Hart, Gunsmith, Pittsburgh, where they may get them on giving such satisfactory evidence that they are the proper owners.
>
> Isaac Ferree

Isaac had two sons, named Joel Thorton Ferree and George Spencer Ferree, who were gunsmiths. The following agreement, dated September 14, 1838, indicates that they were connected with the trade:

AGREEMENT
Joel Ferree and George S. P. Ferree, both of Clinton, Findley Township, Allegheny County, that said Joel Ferree doth agree to sell to said George S. P. Feree—one set of gun smith tools, consisting of one set of smith tools, four vices, three sets of bench tools and other apparatus belonging to the business, together with the use of the shop now occupied by the said Joel until the first of April, 1839. $178.00

Only a few Ferree products have survived and no broad estimate can be made of their work. The only gun examined by the author was a fine eighteenth century specimen, which shows considerable quality. The patch box is an attractive design and the cheek side of the stock is carved in the incised manner. Although some nineteenth centry Ferree guns should be in collections throughout the country, there has been no public recognition of their work.

FESIG, CONRAD
Reading, Pennsylvania. Tax list 1779, *Pennsylvania Archives*, 3d series, Vol. 18.

FETTER, JOHN
Water, between Ferry Street and Redoubt Alley. *The Pittsburgh Directory* for 1819.

FIGTHORN, ANDREW
There is considerable uncertainty about the makers of Berks County guns, but the ones with an intaglio A. F. mark on a side facet of their octagonal barrels are attributed to one of the Andrew Figthorns, both of whom worked in the Borough of Reading.

In a 1773 tax assessment list an Andrew Figthorn is listed as a laborer. This man could have been the father of the first Figthorn gunsmith, or he could have been the first gunsmith, although it is unlikely that a gunsmith would have been listed at any time as a laborer. By 1781 there was a gunsmith named Andrew Figthorn and this man was unquestionably the older of the two gunsmiths. In the census of 1800 only one gunsmith by the name of Figthorn is listed; in 1822 his death is reported in the *Berks and Schuylkill Journal*.

Andrew Figthorn, the younger, came upon the scene as a gunsmith sometime after 1800 and died in 1827. It must be presumed that both men worked at the trade until their deaths, for both were called gunsmiths in the inventory of their estates.

FILLMAN, WILLIAM

Milton Borough, Northumberland County, Pennsylvania. Tax list 1820, 1826, 1829, 1832, 1833, 1840, 1855, 1861.

FINCH, JOSEPH

Franklin Borough, Venango County, Pennsylvania. Tax list 1850.

FISHEL, JACOB

Hopewell Township, Bedford County, Pennsylvania. Tax lists 1846, 1849, 1858, 1861. Bedford Court House.

FISHER, FRANCIS

Corner Main & Chestnut, Allegheny, Pennsylvania, 1859-60.

FISHER, GEORGE

Washington Township, Washington County, Pennsylvania. Tax lists 1803, 1805.

FISHER, HARRISON (Gun Barrel Maker)

Lower Heidelberg Township, Berks County, Pennsylvania. United States Census 1850.

FISHER, JACOB

Hopewell Township, Bedford County, Pennsylvania. United States Census 1850. Tax list 1846-1858.

FISHER, PAUL

White Deer, Lycoming County, Pennsylvania, 1861.

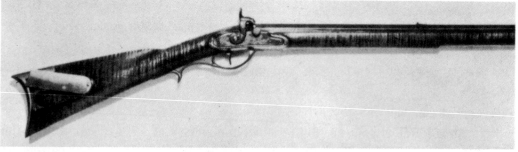

J. T. Herron

PLATE 186

Rifle with percussion lock, full stock of curly maple, brass mountings, octagonal barrel 42 inches long with J. Fleeger engraved in script letters on the top facet of the barrel. Although other western Pennsylvania makers might have used this simple patch box cover, the writer has seen it only on the products of J. Fleeger.

FLECK, VALENTINE
Huntington County, Pennsylvania. Federal Census of 1850.
Memmo, Mifflin County, Pennsylvania. 1861.

FLEEGER, CHRISTIAN
McCandless, Butler County, Pennsylvania. 1861.

FLEEGER, JOHN
Harris' Business Directory of Pittsburgh and Allegheny, 1837, 1841, 1847, 1856-57.
Allegheny Gun Works—John Fleeger, 49 Ohio Street. Mr. Fleeger, proprietor of the Allegheny Gun Works, has carried on the gunsmithing business in Allegheny City since 1831. He occupied a stand on Diamond Street for over thirty years and has been in this present location about two years, where he occupies a building 18 x 27 feet and carries a stock valued at about $5,000.00. He manufactures to order sporting and target rifles, and carries a stock of fine English breech and muzzle loading shotguns, revolvers, cartridges, and ammunition. Manufacturing and repairing is a specialty. Mr. John Fleeger and his son William A. Fleeger are both practical gunsmiths. Fine specimens of this work is on exhibition. *Industries of Pittsburgh, Trade, Commerce & Manufactures, etc.,* for 1879-80.

FLEEGER, PETER
NS of Robinson, between Godrich & Hope, Allegheny, Pennsylvania. *Directory for 1856-57 of Pittsburgh & Allegheny Cities.*

FLEEGER, WILLIAM
Directory of Pittsburgh & Allegheny Cities for 1861-62, 1870-71.
Was associated with his father, John Fleeger, in the Allegheny Gun Works in 1879, 1880, and 1886.

FLEGLE, GEORGE (Armourer)
U. S. Arsenal, Philadelphia, Pennsylvania. 1814.

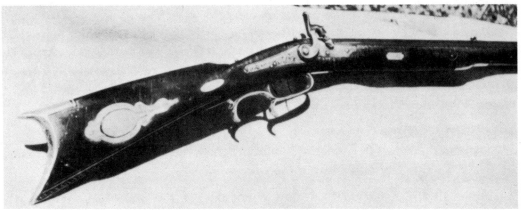

Nixon Collection

PLATE 187

Rifle with percussion lock, half stock made of curly maple, set triggers, brass mountings, silver inlays, octagonal barrel marked C. Flowers on the top facet of the barrel.
This gun is dated 1875 and is a fine example of the style used by gunsmiths in western Pennsylvania at that time.

PLATE 188

Rifle with percussion lock, full stock of curly maple, silver mountings, silver inlays, and octagonal barrel marked C. Flowers on the top facet of the barrel.

FLEHARTY, JAMES

German Township, Fayette County, Pennsylvania. Tax lists 1801, 1803, 1804.

FLOWERS, CHARLES

Some gunsmiths had a reputation for making fine guns in their home community, but were not well-known in other areas. Charles Flowers of Harmony, Pennsylvania, fits into such a category. Flowers was born in 1802 and must have learned the trade of gunsmithing late in his life, for most of his guns are of the Civil War period, or later. It is possible that he learned the trade while he worked at the Arsenal at Pittsburgh during the Civil War.

In 1866 he and his wife bought a plot of ground in the town of Harmony from John Pearce, it being part of a larger tract of land which Pearce had bought from Abraham Zeigler, who, in turn, had bought it from George Rapp in 1814. Harmony was the earliest site where the Harmony Society lived but there was no connection between Flowers and the Society.

His shop was on Wood Street and burned within the memory of many residents of the town. Dr. Stewart, a local physician, recalls when it burned, for he assisted in fighting the fire. He also owns a number of Flowers rifles.

Flowers is thought not to have made any rifles for at least ten years before his death.

A number of Flowers rifles have been examined by the author and all of them are attractive guns. They have a few remnants of early design and craftsmanship, but they were unquestionably made after the Civil War. His octagonal barrels are about thirty-six inches long and he signed them in script or block letters on the top facet of the barrel. Sometimes he used only his initials, C. F. His stocks are usually of plain maple, although the one in the Ball collection is beautifully curled and is profusely inlaid with silver.

FONDERSMITH, GEORGE

Strasburg Township, Lancaster County, Pennsylvania. Tax list 1803.

FONDERSMITH, JOHN

Although the Fondersmith family is not one of the important families who made guns in Pennsylvania, certain facets of their activity are interesting to gun collectors. John Fondersmith, undoubtedly the senior member of the trio, is recorded as a gunsmith in the 1779 tax assessment list of Strasburg Township, Lancaster County, Pennsylvania. His entry into the gun business at such a strategic time might indicate that he was influenced by the urgent need of guns in the Revolution. It is entirely possible that he was in some way connected with his neighbor, Joel Ferree, who is known to have been engaged by the Committee of Safety to produce arms. John Fondersmith's name appears on subsequent tax lists in 1788, 1796 and 1803.

The 1803 tax list for Strasburg Township lists three Fondersmiths as gunsmiths; John, George, and Luis. George and Luis were probably sons of John. Appearing together for a few years, they disappear as gunsmiths by the end of the first decade of the nineteenth century. It is possible that the two sons became merchants or moved into other areas to work.

Fondersmith guns are extremely rare; only a few—and they are of average quality—are known in the Lancaster area.

FONDERSMITH, LUIS

Strasburg Township, Lancaster County, Pennsylvania. Tax list 1803.

FONDERSMITH, WILLIAM

Smith Township, Washington County, Pennsylvania. Tax lists 1856, 1857, 1859.

FORD, JOHN

Harrisburg, Pennsylvania. Tax list 1817.

North Ward, Harrisburg, Pennsylvania. Tax list 1840.

FORDNEY

The will of Jacob Fordney, recorded in the Lancaster County Court House in 1819, tells that he had a number of children, including Melchoir, Jacob, and Elizabeth. Melchoir and Jacob became two of Lancaster's outstanding gunsmiths; and their sister married Jacob Kraft, who was probably the son of an earlier Jacob Kraft, both of whom were gunsmiths. The earlier Kraft was an eighteenth century gunsmith in Lancaster, Pennsylvania, and the son is recorded as a gunsmith in Heidelberg Township, York County, Pennsylvania, in the tax lists of 1813-1814.

Nothing is known about Melchoir's early life in Lancaster, but he is listed as a gunsmith in the tax lists of the borough in 1813. His name continues to appear regularly until his tragic death in 1846. It is obvious from his work that he was trained in the old traditions of the craft. His workmanship was of a superior quality and, while other gunsmiths were producing a style of gun that might be regarded as

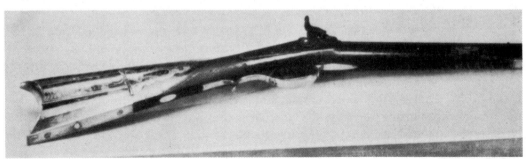

Henry J. Kauffman

PLATE 189

Rifle with back action percussion lock, full stock of curly maple, brass mountings, silver inlays, set triggers, octagonal barrel 40 inches long with J. Fordney, Lancaster, Pa., in block letters on the top facet of the barrel.

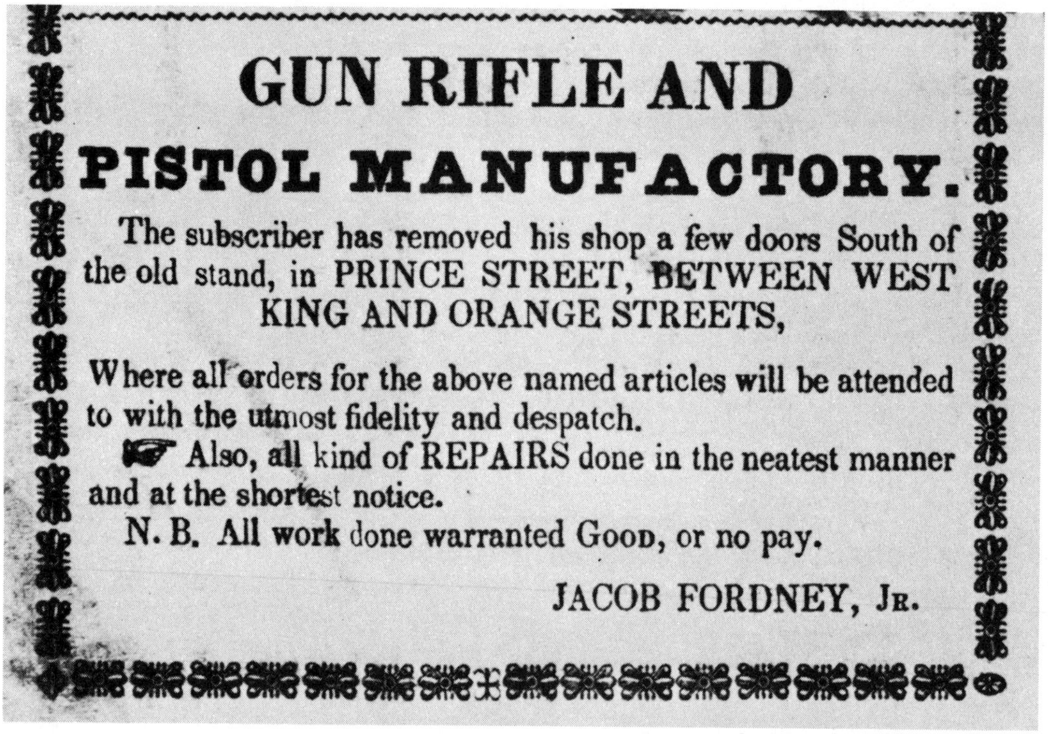

GUN RIFLE AND
PISTOL MANUFACTORY.

The subscriber has removed his shop a few doors South of the old stand, in PRINCE STREET, BETWEEN WEST KING AND ORANGE STREETS,

Where all orders for the above named articles will be attended to with the utmost fidelity and despatch.

☞ Also, all kind of REPAIRS done in the neatest manner and at the shortest notice.

N. B. All work done warranted GOOD, or no pay.

JACOB FORDNEY, JR.

Lancaster County Historical Society

PLATE 190

Advertisement of Jacob Fordney, Jr., in the Lancaster Business Directory of 1843. Fordney's rifles are found in many collections of Pennsylvania rifles but the writer has seen only one of his pistols.

a common Lancaster pattern, Melchoir Fordney was making guns in his unique style. His carving is reminiscent of the work of earlier craftsmen and his engraving is comparable to the best that was done in Pennsylvania. Many of his guns had checkered wrists, some of which were further enhanced by the addition of brass nails between the intersections of the checkering. His carved pattern between the patch box lid and the side plates was another typical Melchoir Fordney detail.

His engraved patterns were cut deeply and profusely and used on the patch boxes, trigger guards, side plates and other brass appendages. Being a contemporary of the Drepperds, he frequently used their locks, which made the gun a one hundred percent Lancaster product.

His tragic death occurred about 9:00 A. M. on Saturday morning, October 17, 1846, when John Haggerty, a neighbor of Fordney, asked for a gun to shoot his horse. Fordney refused but Haggerty picked up a gun and went outside to destroy the animal. Twice the weapon failed to discharge, whereupon Haggerty went into his house to emerge later with the gun and an axe. This time the gun fired, killing the horse, and alerting the neighborhood to some unusual event. Fordney and his housekeeper, named Tripple, came into the street and asked Haggerty for the gun. He gave the gun to Mrs. Tripple and moved toward Fordney with the axe. Fordney fled to his home, but was followed by Haggerty, who mercilessly struck him with the axe and killed him. Haggerty next killed Mrs. Tripple and seriously wounded a child, who recovered from her injuries.

One of the most dramatic trials in the legal history of Lancaster County followed these incidents, wherein Haggerty's counsel tried to save him on evidence of insanity. Throughout the trial Haggerty frequently referred to his horse, which was known to climb trees, and to his goats, which occasionally climbed the trees to be with his horse. The horse caused him trouble so he wanted to kill it, but he was restrained by Fordney; he therefore killed Fordney.

A judge was imported from York County for the case, who charged the jury to deliberate with much care on this important affair. Haggerty was found guilty of murder in the first degree and was hanged in the yard of the jail on July 23, 1847.

"An inventory and Appraisement of the goods and Chattels which were of Melchoir Fordney, late of the City of Lancaster deceased" is recorded in the office of the Recorder of Deeds. It contains the typical tools of a gunsmith of the period such as screw plates, drawing knives, bits and files, a shears and a grindstone. A drilling apparatus is included, which indicates that at some time Fordney drilled his barrels which could be bought in a local hardware store as early as 1796. His total assests were only $171.40.

Most of the collectors in the Lancaster area have been of the opinion that Jacob Fordney was the son of Melchoir, but it is evident from the will of the father that they were brothers. It has also been established from the Lancaster tax list of 1834 that there were two Jacob Fordneys who were gunsmiths at that time. It is impossible to separate them or their work, so the following data could apply to one or both of them.

It might be presumed from the following advertisement from the *Columbia Spy*, June 23, 1830, that one of the Jacob Fordneys was starting the business of gunsmithing at that time.

Gun and Rifle Making

JACOB FORDNEY,

Respectfully informs the inhabitants of Columbia, and its vicinity that he has commenced the above business, at the stand formerly occupied by Mw. McClure in Front Street, one door south of LeFever's Hotel, where he will be happy to receive and execute all orders in his line.

Guns altered to the Percussion principle, and all other kinds of REPAIRING done in the best manner, and on the shortest notice.

By strick attention to business, moderate charges, and excellence of work, he hopes to merit and receive a share of public patronage.

June 23, 1831.

Business must have been brisk for Fordney because by 1835 he had moved to Lancaster and placed the following advertisement in the October 24th issue of the *Pittsburgh Gazette*.

GUN MAKERS WANTED.—Fifteen or twenty good Journeymen Gun Makers will find constant employment and good wages, on application to JACOB FORDNEY, Rifle Manufacturer, Lancaster city, Pa.

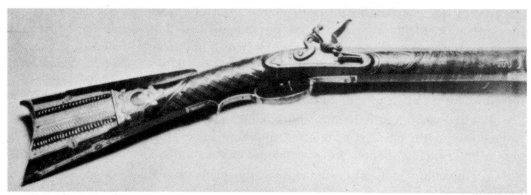

Reaves Goehring

PLATE 191

Rifle with flint lock, full stock of curly maple, brass mountings, set triggers (one missing), octagonal barrel 43 inches long and 1 3/16 inches across the flats at the muzzle. M. Fordney is engraved in script letters on the top facet of the barrel.

The fact that this rifle weighs fifteen pounds suggests that it was made for match shooting. The carving and engraving are fine quality and typical of many of the rifles M. Fordney made. The scarcity of fowling pieces made by M. Fordney indicates that most of his products were rifles. Although he made guns until his death in 1845, the writer has never heard of a gun with a percussion lock made by him.

This advertisement is one of the first evidences of an embryo gun manufacturing business in Lancaster. Although H. E. Leman is usually thought of as the first big manufacturer, it is obvious from this advertisement that Fordney was in the business in a big way at about the same time that Leman started in Lancaster.

Most of the guns marked J. Fordney, Lancaster, Pa., on the top facet of the barrel seem to follow a common style, and one is led to conclude that they were made by one man. All that the writer has seen were percussion ignition which suggests that they were made after 1830. Many of the J. Fordney guns have a keyhole style finial on the patch box and some have a running fox of German silver inlaid on the cheek side of the stock. One is known to exist that has German silver hardware throughout. This one was obviously a presentation piece, for it is superior to the average run of J. Fordney guns.

It is obvious from the style and size of the J. Fordney guns that they were made about the same time as the Gibbs and Gumpf products. These guns were not elegant, but well-made, functional weapons.

Another Fordney, named Casper, is known to have been a Lancaster gunsmith, but none of his products has been seen by the writer, nor is there any known relationship between him and the other Fordneys.

FORESTER, JOHN

Monongahela Township, Greene County, Pennsylvania. Tax list 1824, 1825, 1826, 1838.

FORKER

The progenitor of the Forker family of gunsmiths was Adam Forker, a blacksmith from New Jersey. Two of his sons became gunsmiths; they were John and Samuel. A third son, Adam, was High Constable of Mercer Borough in 1818, but he has not been proven a gunsmith.

John settled in Mercer Borough, Mercer County, in 1816. He was no doubt the oldest son of Adam and worked in Mercer for a considerable length of time as a gunsmith. The Pennsylvania State Business Directory for 1861 lists a man by this name as a gunsmith in Mercer, but there is uncertainty as to whether this is John or a son with the same name. His son Joseph, born in Mercer in 1829, was also a gunsmith but only for a period of eight or nine years. In 1857 Joseph entered another line of business and did no more gunsmithing. Israel Forker, who was a gunsmith in Ravenna, Ohio, in 1853, was possibly also a son of John.

Samuel Forker, another son of Adam, was born in Brownville (sic), Pennsylvania in 1798. He settled in Meadville, Crawford County, in 1823 and carried on the gunsmithing trade. The following article concerning him appeared in the *Pittsburgh Gazette,* March 9th, 1837:

> "Improvement in Fire Arms. Mr. Samuel Forker, of this place, has invented an improvement in fire-arms, by which four loads can be discharged in rapid succession from a single piece. He has a rifle made upon his improved plan, and from experiments thus far, it is likely the invention will prove highly useful. It is very simple and reflects great credit on the ingenuity of the inventor. *Meadville Currier.*"

Samuel was also a County Commissioner in his later years and died in 1860. His son, William H., was born in Meadville in 1828 and was also a gunsmith. He was living there in 1899.

FORKER, JOHN
Philadelphia 1875.

FORKER, JOSEPH
Joseph Forker was born in Mercer, Pennsylvania, on March 6, 1829. He was a gunsmith for a considerable period, but went into another line somewhat prior to 1857. *The Manufactories & Manufacturers of Pennsylvania of the 19th Century,* Philadelphia 1875.

FORKER, SAMUEL
Samuel Forker was born in Brownsville, Pennsylvania, November 25, 1798, and came to Meadville in 1823. *The Daily Pittsburgh Gazette,* March 9, 1837.

FORKER, WILLIAM H.
2nd Floor, 174 Chestnut Street, Meadville, Pennsylvania. 1879-80.

FORMAN, JOHN
562 Frankford Avenue, Philadelphia, Pennsylvania. 1861.

FORREST, CASPER
West King Street, Lancaster, Lancaster County, Pennsylvania. 1861.

FORSYTH, JOSEPH
Somerset Township, Somerset County, Pennsylvania. Tax lists 1802, 1803.

FOSTER, THOMAS

German Township, Fayette County, Pennsylvania. Tax lists 1812, 1813, 1814, 1815, 1816, 1825.

FOSTER, WILLIAM

North Liberty, Mercer County, Pennsylvania. 1861.

FOX, GEORGE

Borough Street, Lawrenceville, Pennsylvania. *Harris' General Business Directory of Pittsburgh and Allegheny*, 1847.

FRAIZIER, FRANCIS

Dunnings, Luzerne County, Pennsylvania. 1861.

FRAZIER, JOHN

Although John Frazier has been listed as a gunsmith many times, there never was any documentary proof of his activity in this line. A recent biography of Frazier by Howard Clark in *The Western Pennsylvania Magazine of History* enumerates Frazier's losses at the Battle of Fort Necessity. Among the items is a "Complete set of Armourer's tools," which shows that he owned them, but does not prove that he made guns. And, if he used them, it may have been in the capacity of a repairman rather than of a gunsmith who made complete guns.

Muskets that bear the name Frazier are known to exist, but a look into the history of English gunsmithing shows that two Fraziers were working in England in the mid-eighteenth century.

The listing in the magazine article mentioned above does include "7 rifled guns, 5 smooth guns, 2 cases neat pistols and furniture, 4 dozen pipe tomahawks, 2 dozen bridle gun locks, 6 dozen plain gun locks, 5 ct. gunpowder, 5 ct. bar lead," and many other items that are interesting to the collecting fraternity. The appearance of rifles on the frontier at this early date is very interesting. Anyone can guess where they were made, but a good calculated guess would point toward Lancaster County, Pennsylvania. The rifles were valued at 6 pounds each, and the smooth bore guns at 4 pounds each.

FRANK, ABRAM

Newberry, Lycoming County, Pennsylvania. 1861.

FRESH, JOSEPH

Cambria Township, Cambria County, Pennsylvania. Tax lists 1845, 1846.

Summerhill Township, Cambria County, Pennsylvania. Tax lists 1850, 1854, 1857, 1858.

Croyle Township, Cambria County, Pennsylvania. Tax lists 1860, 1864, 1867.

FREY, MARTIN

Martin Frey was born in 1769 and baptized in the Reformed Church in York, Pennsylvania, in 1800. The tax list for the borough of York lists him as a single man, gunsmith, in 1799. By 1804 he was married but continued to live in York and work at his trade of gunsmithing. He owned a one-third share in the boring mill which was located on the edge of the town and burned in 1800.

Although guns by Martin Frey are quite scarce, a number are known that identify him as a fine craftsman. His carving is skillfully executed and his patch boxes are of comparable quality. Perhaps his most outstanding contribution to the collecting fraternity is a rifle with a fifty-four inch rifled barrel. It is uncommon for such a long barrel to be rifled, and it is also uncommon for the grooves to have survived so many years of use and abuse.

FRONTFIELD, JOHN

Providence Township, Montgomery County, Pennsylvania. Census report 1800.

FRY, GEORGE

Hopewell Township, Bedford County, Pennsylvania. Tax list 1840.

FRY, JOHN

Ligonier Township, Westmoreland County, Pennsylvania. Tax lists 1843, 1852.

FRY, JOSEPH

Ligonier Township, Westmoreland County, Pennsylvania. 1861. Tax lists 1866, 1876.

FUCH, GEORGE

Huntington County, Pennsylvania. Federal Census of 1850.

FUNDERSMITH, JACOB

Harris' General Business Directory of Pittsburgh and Allegheny, 1847.

GABLE, HENRY

Williamsport, Lycoming County, Pennsylvania. 1861.

GALBREATH, SAMUEL

Newton Township, Cumberland County, Pennsylvania. Census list 1800.
Letterkenny Township, Franklin County, Pennsylvania. Tax list 1804.
SIX CENTS REWARD. Ranaway from the subscriber on the 9th instant an apprentice to the gunsmith business named John M'Ewan, close upon nineteen years of age, about five feet five inches tall, very much pock marked, had on when went away a blue roundabout, half worn, a pair of new shoes, a half roram hat. The above reward, but no charges will be paid to whoever will return said boy. Samuel Galbreath, Gunsmith, Pitt Township, February 17, 1813. *The Commonwealth*, Pittsburgh, February 17, 1813.

GALE, WILLIAM

Chillisiquaque Township, Northumberland County, Pennsylvania. Tax list 1826.

GALL, JOHN

Pine Alley, Washington County, Pennsylvania. 1859, 1861.

GALLOWAY, HENRY

Jefferson Township, Greene County, Pennsylvania. Tax lists 1807, 1808, 1809, 1810, 1819.

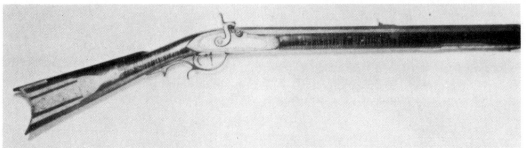

T. J. Cooper

PLATE 192

Rifle with percussion lock, full stock of curly maple, brass mountings, octagonal barrel 37 inches long with J. F. Geherett on the top facet of the barrel.

GANON, THOMAS
   Huntington County, Pennsylvania. Federal Census 1850.

GARRETT, JACOB F.
   Orbisonia, Huntington County, Pennsylvania. 1861.

GARVER, JOHN
   Egypt near Franklin, Norristown, Montgomery County, Pennsylvania. 1861.

GASS, VALENTINE
   Dry Run, Franklin County, Pennsylvania. 1861.

GEIGER, J. V.
   Towanda, Bradford County, Pennsylvania. 1861.

GEHRETT (GARRETT), SAMUEL
   Union Township, Huntington County, Pennsylvania. 1820, 1824, 1825, 1828.

GEIRSH, WILLIAM
   Bushkill Center, Pennsylvania. 1860.

GEORGE, CHARLES
   Maxatawny, Berks County, Pennsylvania. 1860. United States Census 1850.

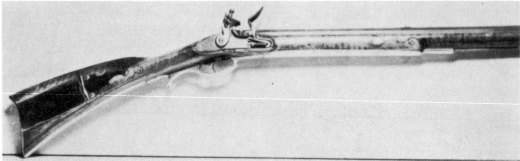

Henry J. Kauffman

PLATE 193

Rifle with flint lock, full stock of curly maple, brass mountings, brass inlays, octagonal barrel 45 inches long with Jacob Georg, 1819, engraved on the top facet of the barrel.
   The two-piece patch box with an Indian head engraved on it and the date on the barrel are features rarely found on Pennsylvania rifles.

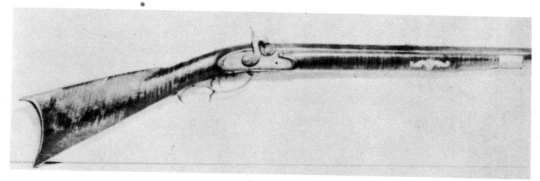

PLATE 194

J. T. Herron

Rifle with percussion lock, curly maple stock, brass mountings, silver inlays, set triggers, octagonal barrel 35½ inches long marked J. S. Gibbons. The fine curl in the maple stock of this gun makes it a particularly attractive product of the Gibbons workshop.

GEORGE, HENRY

Molltown, Berks County, Pennsylvania. 1861. United States Census 1850.

GEORGE, JACOB

Jacob George lived in Greenwich Township, Berks County, Pennsylvania. He is listed as a property owner from 1793 until 1805, but is listed as a gunsmith only in 1805. His work is interesting because he made rifles that exhibited qualities of both Berks and Northampton Counties. The "Roman nose" is quite evident in some of his guns, and most of them are thicker through the wrist horizontally than they are vertically. He also made a number with two-piece patch boxes. The writer has owned two of his guns, which were dated. The one illustrated is dated 1819.

GETZ, JACOB F.

Buck Road near Federal, Philadelphia, Pennsylvania. 1861.

GIBBONS, HENRY

Brownsville Borough, Fayette County, Pennsylvania. Tax lists 1857, 1870.

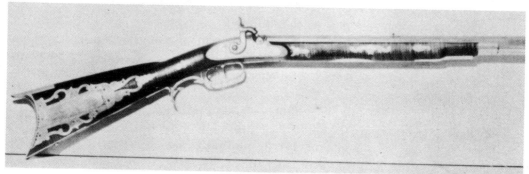

PLATE 195

Western Pennsylvania Historical Society

Rifle with percussion lock, stock of curly maple, silver mountings, silver inlays, set triggers, octagonal barrel 40 inches long with Jos. Gibbons on the top facet of the barrel. Some rifles made in western Pennsylvania after the Civil War have many silver inlays like this one. There is an obvious similarity between the two guns made by Gibbons. The lone inlay on the one is duplicated on the second rifle.

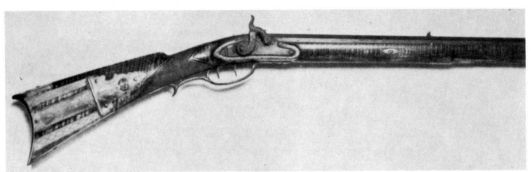

Monroe Hufford

PLATE 196

Rifle with percussion lock, full stock of curly maple, brass mountings, silver inlays, set triggers, octagonal barrel marked A. Gibbson on the top facet of the barrel.

The design of the patch box, the chequering on the wrist, and the form of the stock are characteristics found on rifles made in Lancaster near the middle of the nineteenth century.

GIBBONS, JOSEPH

Brownsville, Fayette County, Pennsylvania. Tax lists 1856, 1870.

Gibbons is noted in Western Pennsylvania for his fine half-stock rifles with silver mountings. His engraving was of an equally high caliber.

GILLMAN, NICHOLAS

Maytown, Lancaster County, Pennsylvania. Tax list 1806.

GIBBS, ABRAM

Lancaster, Pennsylvania.

GIBBS, JOHN

Lancaster, Pennsylvania. Tax list 1819.

GIBBS, HENRY

It is difficult to place the Gibbs family of gunsmiths in their proper relationship, because not much documentary data about them can be found in the Lancaster County Court House. Only one recorded will throws a little positive light on Henry and his children; most of the relationship of the four men must be a matter of conjecture.

In the tax assessment lists of the Borough of Lancaster for 1812 and 1813 Henry Gibbs is called a freeman, gunsmith. Though to name a man as a freeman does not prove he was young at the time, he usually was and the fact that Henry later was married and had a number of children points to the fact that he was probably young and starting to work at his trade at that time. Henry Gibbs, gunsmith, died in 1843, and his children Henry, Abraham, and John Frederick are mentioned as heirs in his will. This information focuses attention upon the possibility that there might have been two gunsmiths named Henry Gibbs, but the style of most H. Gibbs guns indicates that the senior Henry Gibbs could have made most of them. There is no mention of any tools in the will, nor are the occupations of his children mentioned.

In the tax assessment list of 1819 John Gibbs is mentioned as a gunsmith, and it is likely that he was a brother of Henry. The listing of William Gibbs as a free-

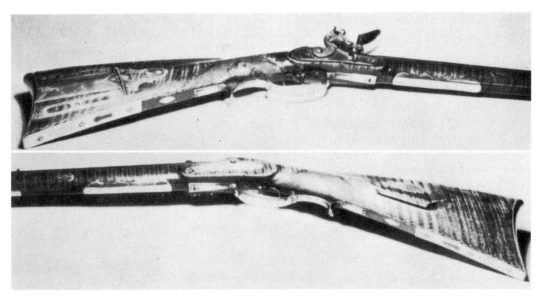

Robert Frey

PLATE 197

Rifle with flintlock, full stock of curly maple, brass mountings, silver inlays, octagonal barrel marked H. Gibbs in script letters. This rifle has unusually fine curl in the stock and the chequering on the wrist is a very unusual pattern. The pattern of the patch box is different from the usual Lancaster pattern. The lower piercing in the toe-plate is filled with ivory or bone. Although most of the rifles Gibbs made are of average quality, this one and another known to the writer are very handsome guns.

man in 1834 suggests that he was probably a third brother of John and Henry, or perhaps a son of John. Abraham's late appearance as a gunsmith in Lancaster points to the fact that he was the son whom Henry mentioned in his will.

Many of Henry Gibb's guns originally had flintlocks, although an original flintlock is very hard to find today. Many have been changed to percussion, and some have been reconverted to flint. The engraved brass hardware, double-set triggers, and checkered wrist that most of his guns have are typical of the Lancaster region from 1820 to 1840. The A. Gibbs illustrated, closely resembles a John Drepperd gun that was probably made about the same time. It should be noted that both of these guns always have had percussion locks.

GIBBS, WILLIAM (Single Freeman)
Lancaster, Pennsylvania. Tax lists 1834, 1840.

GIBSON, THOMAS
12 Saranack Street, Philadelphia, Pennsylvania. 1845, 1847.

GILL, BENJAMIN
Lancaster, Pennsylvania. b. 1790. d. 1860.

GILL, D. B.
Lancaster, Pennsylvania. *The Lancasterian,* May 31, 1848.

DICKERT AND GILL
Notice is hereby given that the partnership of Dickert and Gill is dissolved. All persons having any just demands against said firm are requested to bring forward

their accounts, properly attended for settlement. An to all those indebted to said firm are requested to make speedy payment, as no further indulgence will be given.

Jacob Dickert

Intelligence and Weekly Advertiser, November 10, 1800.

Business partnerships in the eighteenth century were quite rare. This one probably occurred because Gill, a merchant, married Dickert's daughter. In addition to guns, they sold mirrors, dry-goods, and china.

There is at least one gun extant that is signed Dickert and Gill.

GILL, JACOB
Lancaster, Pennsylvania. Tax list 1819.

GILLMAN, DANIEL
Maytown, Lancaster County, Pennsylvania. Tax lists 1782, 1807.

GILLMAN, NICHOLAS
Maytown, Lancaster County, Pennsylvania. Tax list 1806.

GINGERICH, GEORGE
Pleasant Gap, Centre County, Pennsylvania. 1861.

GINTER, C.
Smiths Mills, Clearfield County, Pennsylvania. 1861.

GLASS, HUGH COOK
SIX PENCE Reward: Runaway from the subscriber living in Pittsburgh, on the 18th instant, an apprentice boy named Hugh Cook Glass, about 20 years of age, he is about 5 feet 6 or 7 inches high, marked with small pox, short black hair, darkish complexion, took away with him a continental rifle. It is expected he is going down the river, and will pass for a gunsmith. Whoever takes up said apprentice and delivers him to the subscriber shall have the above reward, without reasonable charges.

Henry Wolf, Gunsmith

Pittsburgh Gazette, April 23, 1795.

GLASS, JOHN
NOTICE. THE subscriber, in the beginning of the year 1797, repaired two rifle guns, one for a certain McClaughlin, the owner of the other not known. The owners of said rifles are hereby required to come forward and pay charges for repairing before the first day of October next, or they will then be sold for to pay that charge. JOHN GLASS, August 13, 1799. *The Pittsburgh Gazette,* August 17, 1799.

GLASS, SAMUEL
Washington Township, Washington County, Pennsylvania. Tax list 1807-08.

GLASS, VALENTINE
Huntington Township, Adams County, Pennsylvania. United States Census 1850.

GOBRECHT
Samuel Gobrecht was listed as a gunsmith in the 1807 tax assessment list of Heidelberg Township, York County, and the 1830 list in Germany Township, Adams

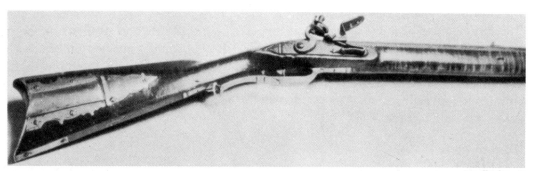

PLATE 198

Rifle with flintlock, full stock of curly maple, brass mountings, and octagonal barrel with S. Gobrecht stamped in block letters on the top facet of the barrel.

County. He died in 1836; only a few items related to the trade of gunsmithing can be found in his will. He refers to his old smith shop and leaves one vise to each of his three sons, Daniel, David, and John. Daniel later renounced his right to be executor of his father's will, so that he could purchase the fulling and carding mill which his father had directed that Daniel should continue to operate, and thereby keep his business intact.

Daniel Gobrecht was born November 22, 1816. It is obvious that he did some gunsmithing, in addition to operating the fulling and carding mill. Because gunsmithing was not a year-round activity for some men, it might be presumed that Daniel worked at both.

The guns of the father and son are so similar that it is very difficult to tell by whom they were made. The later style would naturally be attributed to the son and the earlier style to the father. Their guns have attractive patch boxes and some of their stocks were carved. Neither of these men reached the standard of excellence that some of the other gunsmiths in this area achieved.

GOETZ, FREDERICK

163 North Second Street, Philadelphia, Pennsylvania. 1814.

GOFF, WILLIAM

Second Street, between Wood and Market, Pittsburgh, Pennsylvania. 1826.

GOLCHER, JAMES

158 North Second Street & G. T. Road ab. Second, Philadelphia, Pennsylvania. 1855, 1861.

GOOD, PETER

Alsace Township, Berks County, Pennsylvania. United States Census 1850.

GOODSELL, A.

Coudersport, Potter County, Pennsylvania. 1861.

GONTER, JOHN

Columbia, Pennsylvania. 1810.

John Gonter bespoke an eight day clock with 14″ dial on February 20, 1810. Recorded on page 12 of John Hoff ledger, clockmaker in Lancaster, Pennsylvania.

Reading, Pennsylvania (Gunsmith).

John Gonter, recently from Lancaster, here with informs the residents of Berks and the bordering counties that he has begun the Gunsmith business in his workshop on the west side of Penn Street, the second door, above the sign of the Black Horse, in the city of Reading. He makes every kind of new weapon, repairs old ones, and especially rifles. The work will be good and the price cheap. *Reading Adler*, January 20, 1824.

GONTER, PETER

Peter Gonter, the gunsmith, was born in Lancaster, Pennsylvania, in 1751. His father's name was also Peter and many people have referred to him as a gunsmith, but there are no records indicating such an activity in the Moravian Archives, where considerable information about the Gonters is to be found.

Peter Gonter must have been apprenticed at an early age, for he was busily engaged in a number of activities around Lancaster in the mid-1770's. In 1774 he contributed money toward the relief of Boston and in 1775 he signed a document indicating his opposition to the British Crown and his determination to fight for American independence.

It is not known when he was married, but it is known that he married a girl named Haga, who was the daughter of the well-known Reading gunsmith, Wolfgang Haga. It does not seem possible that Gonter would have met his wife while being apprenticed to a Reading gunsmith, when there were so many good gunsmiths in Lancaster County, to whom he could have been apprenticed. The marriage is not only established by the name, which was an uncommon one at that time, but also by the fact that Gonter is called a son-in-law in Haga's will.

From 1803 to 1807 Gonter was treasurer of the Borough of Lancaster. He also owned a tavern and there are frequent references to soldiers and politicians staying at his tavern on various occasions late in the 1790's.

He must have been a successful business man, for when he died in 1818 he bequeathed to his widow a sizeable estate. He owned two houses on North Queen Street, one of which was probably his tavern, thirty-five shares of bank stock, and plots of ground in East Petersburg, New Ephrata, and Warwick Township.

Although Peter Gonter was in the gun business a long time, his side interests must have absorbed much of his time, for few of his rifles can be found in local collections. In the early nineteenth century he was actively engaged in supplying rifles to the United States Ordnance Department, but it is doubtful if these were signed. In addition to the rifles that he himself manufactured, he appears to have been an agent and secured rifles from other makers for filling the contracts. It is evident that he had ability in business transactions, since much of the correspondence between the Ordnance Department and Lancaster gunsmiths was directed to him.

A few Pennsylvania rifles bearing his name have survived, but most of them lack the daisy patch box and the carved double C scrolls, which are typical of the Lancaster area while he was working there. His patch box pattern with narrow side plates was used by men like Dickert and Eberman. His name is found on the top facet of the barrels and is usually in large block letters. Gonter is known to have made some fine guns, although today any gun bearing his name must be regarded as a rarity.

GOUGHNOUR, DANIEL

Pershing, Cambria County, Pennsylvania. 1861.

GOUTY

For Sale, A Rifle Gunn, Made by Mortemer, Gunmaker to his Majesty, London, to be seen and particulars made known, at Mr. Gouty's, Gunsmith, South Front Street. *Pennsylvania Packet (Dunlap's American Daily Advertiser)* no. 4427. April 3, 1793.

GRAEFF, JOHN

Lancaster Borough, Lancaster County, Pennsylvania. Tax lists 1773, 1793, 1802, 1803, 1808.

GRAEFF, WILLIAM

Reading, Pennsylvania. Patentee of town lot in Reading 1761.

GRAFFELDER, PETER NAPOLEON

NEW ESTABLISHMENT

Importer and manufacturer of Guns, Rifles, Pistols, etc. One door east of S. W. corner Penn & Fifth Streets.

He manufactures:

Elegant double barrel guns, from $35-50-100.

Single barrel guns from $12-20-40.

Double barrel Rifles from $30-40-100.

Single barrel Rifles from $12-25-40.

Cane guns from $20-30-40.

Cut pistols for target firing from $30-50-160.

Air Rifles from $50-100.

Air Canes from $30-50.

All kinds of repairing done on the most liberal terms. *Berks and Schuylkill Journal,* Reading, Pennsylvania. May 28, 1842.

GRAHAM, JOSEPH

Freedom Borough, Beaver County, Pennsylvania. Tax lists 1841, 1842, 1852, 1854.

GRANGER, JOHN

Guthrieville, Chester County, Pennsylvania. 1861.

GREAT WESTERN GUN WORKS

The Great Western Gun Works was doubtless one of the great rifle factories of Pennsylvania. It was founded in 1866 by James H. Johnson; an advertisement in the *Pittsburgh Evening Chronicle* on September 4, 1866 indicates the character of his business at that time:

GREAT WESTERN GUN WORKS, J. H. JOHNSTON, MANUFAC-
TURER AND DEALER IN FINE RIFLES AND SHOT GUNS, ARMY, NAVY,
and Pocket Revolvers, Carbines, and Muskets. All sorts and sizes of Ammunition and Gunmakers materials. Military companies furnished with arms on short
notice. Repairing and jobbing done in the best manner. Shot guns for hire.
Remember the place, COR. PENN AND WAYNE STREETS, PITTSBURGH,
PA.

John A. Johnson, son of James H. Johnson, joined the firm about 1888 and was
manager until 1896. James H. Johnson died in 1915 and the business was continued
by John A. until 1923. They were located at the following addresses in Pittsburgh.

1866-1868, Corner Penn and Wayne Streets.
1868-1874, 179 Smithfield Street.
1874-1877, 285 Liberty Street.
1877-1883, 169 Smithfield Street.
1884-1889, 621 Smithfield (same as above but numbers were changed).
1889-1895, 706 Smithfield Street.
1895-1905, 529 Smithfield Street.
1908-1923, 639 Liberty Street.

A catalogue of the Great Western Gun Works for the year 1879 includes the
following muzzle-loading guns which they were selling at one-third less than ever
offered before. These were wholesale prices and a retail catalogue was available
for those who canvassed for business. Merchandise could be sold for less than retail
price if the merchant desired; however, the company policy was, "positively no
goods sold on credit, and no discount for cash whatever. The prices are net cash.
All cash orders boxed free."

MUZZLE LOADING RIFLES

Plain rifles	$ 8.25-$ 9.50.
Our new No 5 Rifle	$11.50-$12.00.
EXtra fine Rifles	$15.50-$26.00.
Horseback Rifles	$10.00-$11.50.
Double Barrel Rifles	$10.00-$11.50.
Double Rifle and Shot Gun	$22.00-$35.00.
Great Western Rifle and Shot Gun	$40.00.
Single Barrel Shot gun	$ 2.00-$10.50.
Double Barrel Shot Guns	$ 5.00-$ 9.50.
Medium Quality, Fine Twist Double Guns	$10.50-$20.00.
Great Western Double Barrel Duck Guns	$11.00
Fine laminated steel Double Guns	$22.00-$27.00.
Extra Fine Laminate Steel Double Barrel Shot Guns	$30.00-$54.00.
Turkey, Goose, and Deer Guns	$38.00-$55.00.

These listings required the first eight pages of their catalogue, which had a
total of forty-eight pages. The balance of the catalogue was devoted to breech-
loading guns of different styles, shot belts, powder flasks, hunting knives, dog calls,
glass ball traps, archery goods, revolvers, watches and small cannon.

GREENE, LOT

Redstone Township, Fayette County, Pennsylvania. Tax lists 1817, 1818.
Luzerne Township, Fayette County, Pennsylvania. Tax lists 1818-1844.

GRIMES, DAVID (Gun Barrel Maker)

Upper Heidelberg Township, Berks County, Pennsylvania. United States Census 1850.

GROVE

It is recorded in Prowell's *History of York County* that Samuel Grove, Sr., came from Europe and settled for a short time in Lancaster County before moving to Lewisberry in York County, Pennsylvania. Although he is reputed to have been a pre-Revolutionary gunsmith in York County, the earliest reference to him in a tax assessment list as a gunsmith is in 1783. Samuel Grove, Sr., died in 1822.

Samuel Grove, Jr., is called a gunsmith in his will, recorded in Will Book R., 129, and dated October 4, 1834. The following details from his will describe his trade and his home:

> Being sick and weak I bequeath unto my wife Hannah my log house, now occupied as a gunsmith shop and lot situated in the Boro of Lewisberry—adjoining the property of Chas. A. Barnitz on West Front Street. On the north along the said street as far as my Smithshop, then paralleled south with the Barnitz lot until it strikes the line of Wm. Nickols. The house and lot and appurtenances thereunto belonging to me my said wife shall keep during her life provided she remains a widow, said property to be kept in repair for a family to reside in at the expense of my estate, and at her decease, or if she refuses to reside in said house or accept the same.

An interesting inventory of his estate is attached to his will; it includes some items that are rarely found in such inventories. The objects of principal interest are "2 baskets with patterns for casting," which suggests that the mountings on Grove guns were doubtless made in their shop from these patterns. Other items in the inventory support the theory that early gunsmiths made a large portion, if not all, of the parts for their guns. The related items are as follows:

1 Bellows.
1 Anvil.
1 Vise.
5 Hammers.
1 Rifle britzer and looper.
1 Rifle gun.
Lot of gunsmiths tools, including 2 guides and all the racks on the north and west sides of the wall of the shop.
Lot of maple plank.
Gunstocks in the rough.
Old Auger bits.
Old Hand axe.
Turning bench and sundries.
1 Grindstone.

1 lot boring bits and sundries.
1 lot of iron borings.
1 crowbar and grinding frame.
1 Cast anvil and old iron.
Large sledge.
Anvil, hammers, and tongs.
3 shot gun barrels partly finished.

No rifles made by Samuel Grove, Sr., that could be dated in the transition period are known to have survived. The work of both men is similar and is characterized by well-carved stocks, fine patch boxes, and excellent engraving on the mountings. Samuel, Jr., is known to have inlaid on one of his rifles an eagle that is beautifully designed and expertly inletted.

GRUBB, JOSEPH C. (Hardware)
76 Market Street, Philadelphia, Pennsylvania. 1847-1855.
236 Market Street, Philadelphia, Pennsylvania. 1861.

GRUBB, TOBIAS
Northampton Township, Lehigh County, Pennsylvania. Tax list 1821.

GUEST, JOHN
Lancaster Borough, Lancaster County, Pennsylvania. Tax list 1802.

GRUNIGAL, FREDERICK
East Lane near Third, Allegheny, Pennsylvania. 1858-59.

GUGER, JAMES R.
Muncy, Lycoming County, Pennsylvania. 1861.

GUMPF
Despite the fact that nine Gumpfs are listed as gunsmiths in the tax assessment lists of Lancaster, Pennsylvania, covering a span of sixty years, very little factual data can be found about them. One will and one transaction of real estate are recorded under the name in the Lancaster County Court House, but neither

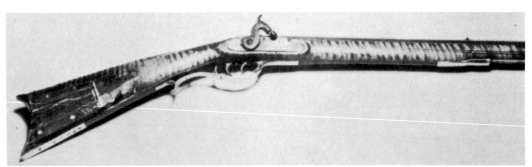

Henry J. Kauffman

PLATE 199

Rifle with percussion lock, full stock of curly maple, brass mountings, octagonal barrel 43 inches long with I. Guest engraved in script letters on the top facet of the barrel. It is possible that this gun was made by the J. Guest who worked in Lancaster, but it probably was made by his son who probably worked in western Pennsylvania in the percussion era.

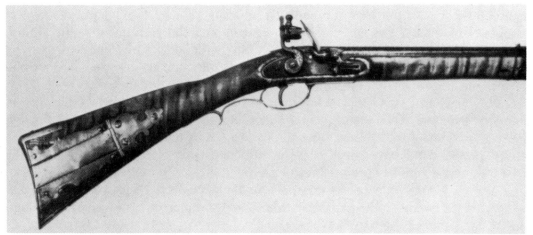

Wilson Collection

PLATE 200

Rifle with flint lock, full stock of curly maple, brass mounted, octagonal barrel 43 inches long marked C. Gumpf on the top facet of the barrel.

C. Gumpf worked over a long span of years and made some attractive rifles in the traditional Lancaster style. This one with a daisy finial on the patch box is a fine specimen of his work. Another one of comparable quality is in the S. E. Dyke collection.

document throws any light on their gunsmithing activity or on the family relationships of the different men.

Stophel Gumpf, whose name appears on the tax assessment list of 1793, was probably the first Gumpf to work as a gunsmith in Lancaster. There is documentary evidence that Christopher was working at the trade in 1794, and the tax lists of 1802 and 1803 list another Gumpf named Christian as a gunsmith.

It is probable that one, or more, of these three men was the father of Henry, Jacob, John, Matthias, and George whose names appear in tax lists in the early 1820's. Andrew and Michael, who appear as Lancaster gunsmiths in 1843, were probably sons of one of the latter group.

Although few rifles bear the names of the early Gumpfs, there is evidence that Christopher was a very productive craftsman. He is listed as a contributor to "Continental Rifles, Account of when received and forwarded, by order of Genl. Hand, Lancaster, February 7, 1794." These rifles were probably made for state militia and were shipped to Middletown, to Northumberland, Luzerne, Mifflin, and Huntington Counties, and to Philadelphia. In this venture Christopher Gumpf was associated with men who worked in Lancaster during the Revolution and helped to give the borough a superior status as rifle making territory. These men were Peter Gonter, Jacob Dickert, and John Graeff. Also included were men of later importance: Henry Albright, Peter Brong, Jacob Messersmith, and Chris. Kline. The C. Gumpf contribution consisted of about a hundred rifles, compared with 314 by Dickert, but it is evident from the tax listings that he was only starting at that time.

In 1809 C. Gumpf appears as one of the contractors making rifles for the Ordnance Department of the United States. His associates at this time were Jacob Dickert, George Miller, John Bender, and Peter Gonter. There probably are some plain rifles bearing the name C. Gumpf in the arms collections of the country, but none are known in the Lancaster area. A sporting rifle by C. Gumpf, the typical Lancaster product of the late eighteenth century and the early nineteenth century, is illustrated. The daisy finial on the patch box, with some variations was used by a number of Lancaster craftsmen, and on some rifles the patch-box lids, lock-bolt plates, and trigger guards are engraved with appropriate designs.

A. Gumpf and G. Gumpf are known to have made some sporting rifles in the late flint-lock era. These have long slender barrels with small bores. The patch boxes show some disintegration from the earlier Lancaster patterns, but are typical, of the period. Some have silver inlays in the cheek side of the butt and along the forestock and a few have mountings of German silver.

Andrew Gumpf is listed as gunsmith in the 1859-1860 Lancaster Business Directory. He is probably the craftsman who made the pair of pistols marked Gumpf on the top facets of the barrels.

GUNTER, PETER
Letterkenny Township, Franklin County, Pennsylvania. Tax list 1821.

HADDEN, JAMES
Philadelphia, Pennsylvania. Tax list 1769. *Pennsylvania Archives,* 3 series, Vol. 14, page 153.

HAEFFER, JACOB
Lancaster Borough, Lancaster County, Pennsylvania. Tax lists 1802, 1803, 1821.

HAFER, JOHN
N. W. corner of Liberty and Marbury Streets, Pittsburgh, Pennsylvania. *Pittsburgh Directory,* 1819.

HAGA, WOLFGANG
Reading, Pennsylvania. Tax lists 1767 to 1781. *Pennsylvania Archives,* 3 series, Vol. 18, page 757. Will probated 1796.

HAGER, JONATHAN
Washington County, Maryland. Hager Land Patent, August 10, 1753.

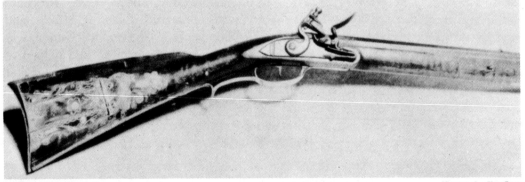

Henry J. Kauffman

PLATE 201
Rifle with flint lock, full stock of curly maple, brass mountings, and octagonal-to-round barrel 48 inches long with J. Haeffer engraved in block letters on the top facet of the barrel.

HAGY, (HAGI) JOHN
Cocalico Township, Lancaster County, Pennsylvania. Tax lists 1800, 1805, 1806.

HAHN, JOHN
Star, Warren County, Pennsylvania. 1861.

HAINS, ISAAC
Lampeter Township, Lancaster County, Pennsylvania. Tax lists 1772, 1783, 1792.

HALDEMAN, P. S.
Georges Township on York Run, Fayette County, Pennsylvania. 1872.

HAMELIN, CHARLES W.
Rye Township, Perry County, Pennsylvania. Federal Census of 1850.

HAMILTON, JAMES (Single Man)
Fawn Township, York County, Pennsylvania. Tax list 1797.

HAMMERLEE, WILLIAM
Cooperstown, Venango County, Pennsylvania. 1861.

HAMPTON, JOHN N.
West Hanover Township, Dauphin County, Pennsylvania. Tax lists 1837, 1840.

HANATTER, JACOB
Allen Township, Cumberland County, Pennsylvania. Tax list 1842.

HANNI, HIERRONIMUS
Reading, Pennsylvania. *Reading Adler*, January 4, 1824.

HANTZ, JACOB
Berwick Township, Adams County, Pennsylvania. Tax list 1805.

HARDER, JACOB
Lock Haven, Pennsylvania. Tax lists 1861, 1864, 1879, 1880.

HARDINGER, PETER
Windsor Township, Berks County, Pennsylvania. Tax list 1780. *Pennsylvania Archives*, 3d series, Vol. 18.

HARNING, L.
Schuylkill Haven, Schuylkill County, Pennsylvania. 1861.

HARRIS, HENRY
Paxton Township, Dauphin County, Pennsylvania. *Pennsylvania Archives*, 3d series, Vol. 17, page 573. Tax list for Paxton Township, Dauphin County.

HARRIS, JOHN
Yorktown, Pennsylvania. Tax list 1799.

HARRIS, SAMUEL
Augusta Township, Northumberland County, Pennsylvania. Tax list 1782.

HARSON (HASSON), SAMUEL.
Rostraver Township, Westmoreland County, Pennsylvania. Tax lists 1811, 1822, 1824.

HART, AARON
Aaron Hart was a gunsmith in Pittsburgh as early as 1810. On January 17, 1812 the following advertisement appeared in the *Pittsburgh Gazette*:

> AARON HART (sic), GUNSMITH. Carries on that business, in all its various branches, at the corner of Front and Wood Streets. He has constantly on hand a variety of Rifles, Fowling Pieces, etc., and can supply those who may require any particular pattern, at the shortest notice. Guns repaired expeditiously and with care.

In April of the same year another gunsmith, Isaac Ferree, left the city and advertised that he had left his stock of repaired guns with Aaron Hart and that the owners could pick them up at Hart's shop. It is obvious that not many did so, for a similar advertisement appeared in the *Pittsburgh Gazette* a year later.

In 1815 Hart was operating a ferry across the Monongahela River, and probably continued his gunsmithing activity as a sideline. About 1819 he entered the shipping business and, no doubt, stopped making guns. He was very successful in his new activity and by 1823 owned at least seven keelboats and an interest in the steamboat, *Pennsylvania*. In 1826 he advertised that he had a quantity of nails, pig lead, whiskey, etc., for sale at his warehouse on Wood Street.

HARTMAN, AARON
Pittsburgh, Pennsylvania.

HARTMAN, PETER
State near Seventh, Erie, Erie County, Pennsylvania. 1861.

HARSHMAN, GEORGE
Connelsville Township, Fayette County, Pennsylvania. Tax lists 1835, 1836, 1837.

HARTSOCK, GEORGE
Springhill Township, Fayette County, Pennsylvania. Tax lists 1802-1824.

HARTZOG, FREDERICK
George Township, Fayette County, Pennsylvania. Tax lists 1806, 1808, 1810.

HARTZOG, DAVID
Springhill Township, Fayette County, Pennsylvania. Tax lists 1823, 1824.

HARTZOG, JACOB
George Township, Fayette County, Pennsylvania. Tax lists 1806, 1808, 1810.

HAWK, NICHOLAS

Gilbert, Pennsylvania. b. March 3, 1782, d. March 23, 1844.

HAWK, PETER S.

Long Valley, Monroe County, Pennsylvania. 1861.

HAWKEN, CHRISTIAN

Washington County, Maryland. 1804.

HAWKEY, HENRY

Hempfield, Township, Westmoreland County, Pennsylvania. Tax lists 1805, 1808, 1810, 1811, 1812, 1813, 1815.

Although there does not seem to be reason for confusing Hawken and Hawkey, the fact that both names never appear together on a tax list might indicate that two names were used or given to one man.

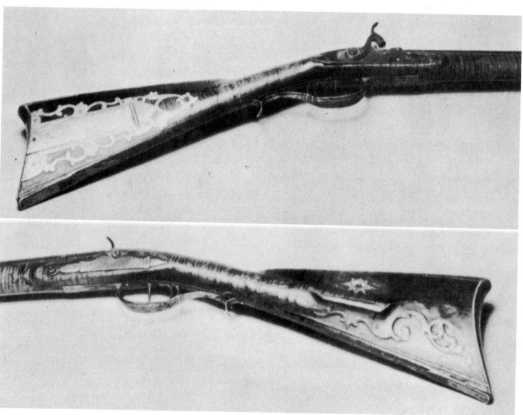

PLATE 202

Carl Pippert

Rifle with flintlock (now percussion), full stock of curly maple, brass mountings and octagonal barrel 42 inches long. This gun is not signed but is similar to another gun which is signed C. Hawken. The delicate brasswork of the patch box and the style of carving indicate that Hawken was an outstanding craftsman.

HAWKEN, HENRY
Hempfield Township, Westmoreland County, Pennsylvania. Tax lists 1804, 1807, 1809, 1814.

HEASLEY, JOSEPH
Hempfield Township, Westmoreland County, Pennsylvania. Tax lists 1815, 1816, 1817.

HECKERT, PHILIP
Philip Heckert was one of the early gunsmiths in York, Pennsylvania. He is listed as such a craftsman in the tax lists of 1779, 1783, and 1799. He died in 1812; and an inventory of his estate, which follows, was filed in the York County Court House on December 12, 1812. This inventory is interesting because it contains a number of bick irons which were used in the forging and welding of gun barrels. Of interest also is the use of the word scelp, the name used for the flat iron blank from which a barrel was forged. Although this word was frequently used in Europe, it is rarely found in the literature relating to gun making in America.

1 anvil	$22.00
1 bick iron	1.50
Lot mandrels	
Smith tongs and sundries	2.00
Hammers	3.00
Vise and sundry smith tools	6.00
Lot of old iron punches	6.00
8 welded rifle barrels	8.00
3 iron grates	6.00
Lot of gunsmith tools	2.00
Lot of gunsmith tools	5.00
Lot of files, chisels, engravers, sundries	2.50
Lot of gun stocks	13.00
2 screw plates	3.00
Gun scelps	8.00
Lot of gun scelps partly welded	8.00

HEED (HEAD), ABRAHAM
Plumstead Township, Bucks County, Pennsylvania. Tax lists 1796-1805.

HEHN, PETER
Maxatawny Township, Berks County, Pennsylvania. Tax list 1805.

HENKELS, DANIEL (Gunsmith and Sword Maker)
261 St. John Street, Philadelphia, Pennsylvania. 1814.

HENNINGER, DANIEL
Augusta Township, Northumberland County, Pennsylvania. Tax list 1841.

HENNINGER, JOHN
Augusta Township, Northumberland County, Pennsylvania. Tax list 1841.

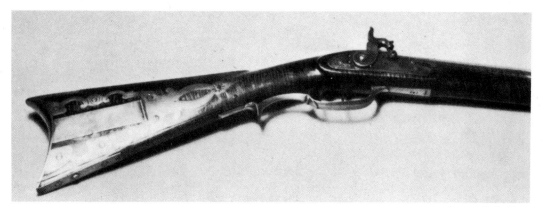

Park Emery

PLATE 203

Rifle with percussion lock, full stock of curly maple, brass mountings, octagonal barrel with H. Hawken on the top facet of the barrel. The design of the patch box on this rifle seems to be entirely original to Hawken and it has no noticeable connection with any of the county styles of Pennsylvania.

HENRY, ABRAM

Lancaster, Pennsylvania. Tax list 1803.

HENRY, JAMES & SON

Bushkill Centre, Northampton County, Pennsylvania. 1861.

HENRY, JOHN

Lancaster Borough, Lancaster County, Pennsylvania. Tax list for Lancaster Borough 1775. *Pennsylvania Archives.* 3d series, Vol. 17, page 458.

HENRY, J. J., GUN FACTORY

Corner Third & Noble Streets, Philadelphia, Pennsylvania. 1814.

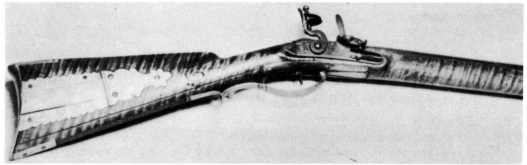

Joe Kindig, Jr.

PLATE 204

Rifle with flint lock, full stock of curly maple, brass mountings, and octagonal barrel marked A. Henry on the top facet of the barrel.

The side plates of the patch box on this rifle are unique and the daisy finial on the patch box is an interesting variation of the daisy pattern used by many gunsmiths in Lancaster County. It is also the only rifle by this maker known to the writer and the owner.

M. T. Stewart

PLATE 205

Rifle with percussion lock, curly maple full stock, plain brass mountings, set triggers, octagonal barrel 40 inches long with J. Henry on the top facet of the barrel.

HENRY, MOSES

The appearance of Moses Henry as a gunsmith in Pittsburgh indicates that he worked in Pennsylvania before moving to Ohio. Some of his gunsmithing activity is recorded in the Fort Pitt Day Book of Baynton, Wharton, and Morgan, who were merchants in Pittsburgh until 1770, when they failed and sold out to Franks & Co. of Lancaster, Pennsylvania.

The following extracts from the Day Book give some insight into his activity in Pittsburgh.

Fort Pitt March 1st 1766
Sundries Due to Moses Henry
for Repairing 1 Rifle & Smooth Bored Gun 1.1.0

Fort Pitt June 16th 1766
Sundry Acct. Due to Moses Henry, Viz.
for stocking & Riffling a Fuzee 20 / & 1 pr. Whippers 4 /   1.4.0
Profit & loss for cleaning 2 Fuzees & 1 Pair of Pistols   15.0
                                                              ———
                                                              1.19.0

Fort Pitt June 17, 1766
John Jennings Due to Moses Henry for Moulds, ——— & pollishing
Pistols   12.0

Fort Pitt Oct. 17th 1767
The Crown, for the Indian Department, Due to Sundry Accounts, Contracted by order of Capt. Murray Since the 1st of June 1766. To Merchants for Sundry Goods & Liquors delivered to Indians between the 1st of June 1766 and the first of September 1767. To Moses Henry for 3 Rifle Guns   25.

Fort Pitt Oct. 24th 1767
Sundry Accounts Due to Moses Henry
Merchandise for Stocking & Repairing Sundry Guns for the use of the Trading Store   2.16

Fort Pitt Nov. 1767
The Crown Due to Moses Henry for a Rifle Gun Rcd. of him for the use of the Crown in May 1767, & Charged in that acco., but not carried to the credit of said Henrys acco.   8

PLATE 206

The Henry Gun Factory at Boulton, Pennsylvania. The building was demolished in the 1940's because it was a safety hazard in the community.

PLATE 207

In this house several generations of the Henry family lived when the factory at Boulton was in operation. It stands on a hillside where the owner could survey most of the activity connected with the factory.

Kauffman Photo

PLATE 208

Only a portion of the dam remains at the Henry Rifle Factory at Boulton, Pennsylvania. The flat stones in the foreground were originally on top of the dam breast to minimize erosion and protect the lower stones from "washing out."

HENRY

Although only a few of their products can be found in contemporary collections of firearms, there is documentary evidence that the Henry family was one of the most outstanding families of gunsmiths to have worked in Pennsylvania. Much of the following data has been taken from *The Life of William Henry* by Francis Jordan, Jr., and a small portion was found in the papers of the American Fur Company which are collected in the library of the New York Historical Society. Tax assessment lists and other scattered sources have been searched to make the story as complete as possible. Finally, the writer visited the Boulton site and was kindly directed by Albert Toth who, as a youngster, played in the rifle factory and scaled the walls of the barrel mill.

William Henry, the first of the Henry gunsmiths, was born in Chester County, Pennsylvania, on May 19, 1729. The untimely death of his father denied him the opportunity for the scholastic training planned for him and, in its stead, at the age of fifteen he was sent to Lancaster, Pennsylvania, where he was apprenticed to the famous gunsmith, Matthias Roessor. Henry was apparently an apt pupil, for at the age of twenty he was making arms in his own shop in Lancaster. In January, 1755, he married Ann Wood and in the same year became armourer to General Braddock on his ill-fated expedition to western Pennsylvania. He later served in the same capacity under General Forbes.

Kauffman Photo

PLATE 209

Only two pillars of stone remain at the old barrel-mill site at Jacobsburg, Pennsylvania. The barrel mill was located a few miles from the factory at Boulton.

In addition to his interest in arms and military affairs, he was a partner in the mercantile establishment of Simon and Henry. They did extensive business with the Indians for which Henry is believed to have supplied the guns. This partnership was dissolved in 1759 when Henry decided to visit England to make some investigations into scientific matters in which he had become interested. He sailed for England with letters of introduction from Dr. Barton, the Rector of St. James Episcopal Church in Lancaster, who came to Lancaster from England.

When Henry arrived in England, he found the country intensely interested in Watt's experiments with the steam engine. Henry's interest in the subject led to his meeting Watt and discussing mutual problems with him. Henry sailed from Plymouth in November, 1761, and arrived in Philadelphia forty-two days later.

in 1776 he became a member of the American Philosophical Society in Philadelphia. his return from England, he was Assistant Burgess of Lancaster from 1765 until 1775. He also served as Assistant Justice of the County Courts in 1770, 1773, and 1777. In 1777 he became Treasurer of Lancaster County, which office he held until his death. His wife filled the office with distinction for the balance of his term and was then appointed for a four-year term.

Henry's familiarity with arms, his previous experience with Braddock and Forbes, and his legal and political experience in Lancaster finally led to his appointment as Superintendent of Arms and accoutrements in the Revolution. Many letters have survived, showed that he was asked to secure arms and accoutrements in the Lancaster area, which was known as "the arsenal of America" in the Revolution. There is a legend that Henry had a barrel mill on Mill Creek, south of Lancaster, where he made arms for the Revolution but there is no evidence of his ownership or occupancy in the records of the Lancaster County Court House.

It has been noted that William Henry was interested in the world of science; in 1776 he became a member of the American Philosophical Society in Philadelphia. He took his seat the same evening with David Rittenhouse and they became lifelong friends.

This short biography of William Henry does not include all the important posts he held throughout his life; but it does focus attention on the fact, in addition to his being a gunsmith, he was a man of outstanding caliber and served his county and country with distinction. He left his home and his family to serve his country at a time when such men were urgently needed. His name can justifiably be placed on a scroll with names like Franklin, Washington, Rittenhouse, and others.

William Henry had three sons, John Joseph I, William II, and Abraham. Abraham became a gunsmith and worked in Lancaster in the late eighteenth and early nineteenth centuries. He was a member of the Lancaster cartel of gunsmiths whose correspondence is recorded in the book *United States Ordnance* by Major James Hicks. He made both rifles and pistols, although only a few have survived that can be identified as his products. Abraham Henry died in Lancaster in 1811.

John Joseph Henry I has gained lasting fame because of his service in the March to Quebec in the Revolution and the story he wrote about this unfortunate mission. The narrative was published in 1812 by his widow after his death in 1811. After the war he returned to Lancaster and entered the law office of Stephen Chambers, whose

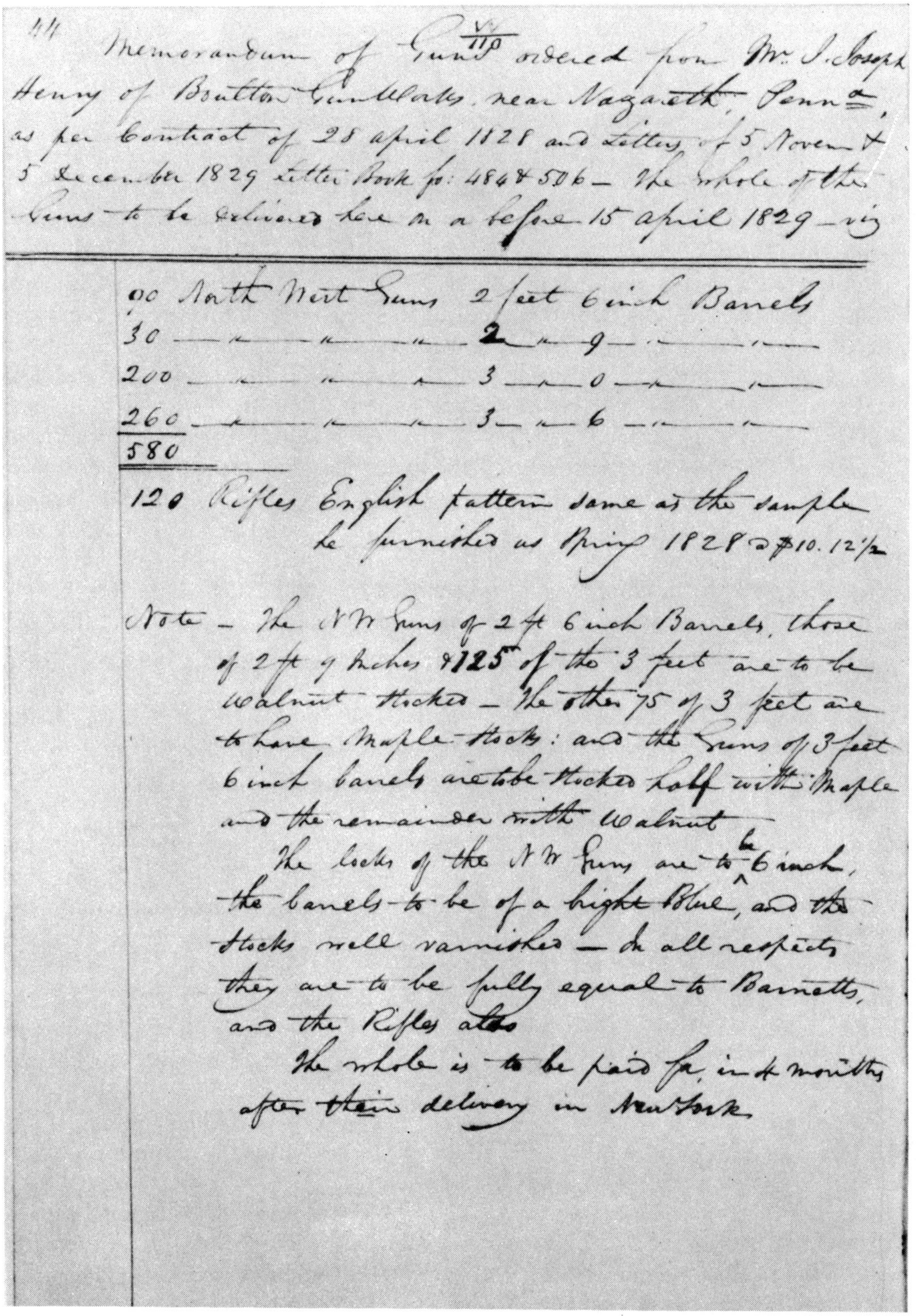
44

Memorandum of Guns 4/110 ordered from Mr. J. Joseph Henry of Boulton Gunworks, near Nazareth, Penna, as per Contract of 28 April 1828 and Letters of 5 Novem & 5 December 1829 Letter Book fo: 484 & 506 — The whole of the Guns to be delivered here on or before 15 April 1829 — viz

90 North West Guns 2 feet 6 inch Barrels
30 — " — " — " — 2 — " 9 — " — "
200 — " — " — " — 3 — " 0 — " — "
260 — " — " — " — 3 — " 6 — " — "
580

120 Rifles English pattern same as the sample he furnished us Spring 1828 @ $10.12½

Note — The N W Guns of 2 ft 6 inch Barrels, those of 2 ft 9 Inches & 125 of the 3 feet are to be Walnut stocked — The other 75 of 3 feet are to have Maple stocks: and the Guns of 3 feet 6 inch barrels are to be stocked half with Maple and the remainder with Walnut

The locks of the N W Guns are to be 6 inch, the barrels to be of a bright Blue, and the stocks well varnished — In all respects they are to be fully equal to Barnetts, and the Rifles also

The whole is to be paid for, in 4 months after their delivery in New York

New York Historical Society

PLATE 210

It is obvious from this memorandum that J. Joseph Henry of Boulton made "North West Guns" for the American Fur Company. He is also known to have made a quantity of Pennsylvania rifles for the same company.

young sister he later married. He was admitted to practice in 1785 and in 1793 was appointed resident Judge of the Second Judicial District of Pennsylvania. Some authorities suggest that he was trained to be a gunsmith in his youth; however, the writer has found no documentary evidence of such training.

William Henry II left Lancaster after the Revolution and opened a shop in the Moravian community of Nazareth in Northampton County. Little is known of his activity in making guns; however, he must have assisted in the planning of the Henry enterprises which came into full production in 1812, the year of his death.

Although virtually nothing is left of the famous Henry factory at Boulton, Pennsylvania, there is evidence there and in the papers of the American Fur Company that it was an extensive and busy place in its day. The three units of which it was composed made it a self-sustaining community, as were most of the "iron plantations" in the eighteenth century. As a matter of fact, the first unit to be built was an iron furnace at Jacobsburg along the old Nazareth-Wind Gap road. The selection of this site was determined by the availability of iron ore and the drop in the Bushkill Creek, which provided water power to operate the furnace bellows. Across the creek from the furnace site, the race for the barrel mill can be easily seen today, although only a crumbling wall of the foundation is evidence that such a building existed there. After barrels were no longer made there but were bought from the various barrel specialists, this mill served the community as a grist mill.

These two adjoining units were really only appendages to the main gun factory, which was located at Boulton, named for Matthew Boulton, an English friend of William Henry I. The deteriorated walls and a few timbers are all that remain to-day; however, this building and its grinding wheels were still standing in 1925 and they are illustrated in *The Kentucky Rifle* by Captain Dillin.

This factory was a complete gun producing unit except for the boring of the barrels, which was done at the mill at Jacobsburg. The mill race ran through the basement of the building, where the water turned the mechanism for drilling and grinding gun barrels. A blacksmith shop was located in the remaining part of the basement, where smith and heat-treatment work were done. The stocks were cut and the guns assembled on the main, or first floor of the factory and the top floor was used for storage purposes. The small frame extention toward the road was used for the storage of finished guns until they were sold locally or shipped to distant merchants in New York or Pittsburgh. In addition to rifles and muskets, the factory produced axes, pistols, and knives.

This business was owned and operated by the sons of William Henry II. In 1821 John Joseph, William III, and Matthew S. Henry formed a partnership which was called William Henry & Co. This name replaced the Boulton Arms Works, which had been used until the new partnership was formed. This combination operated the factory for only about a year, when John Joseph bought complete interest in the factory and moved his inventory from Philadelphia to Boulton. The locks made after 1822 are marked J. J. Henry Boulton. It is not known when John Joseph took his son into the business, but in 1836 James wrote a letter to the American Fur Company office in New York City, telling of his father's death, then James became proprietor of the factory. On June 26, 1837, James wrote to the American Fur

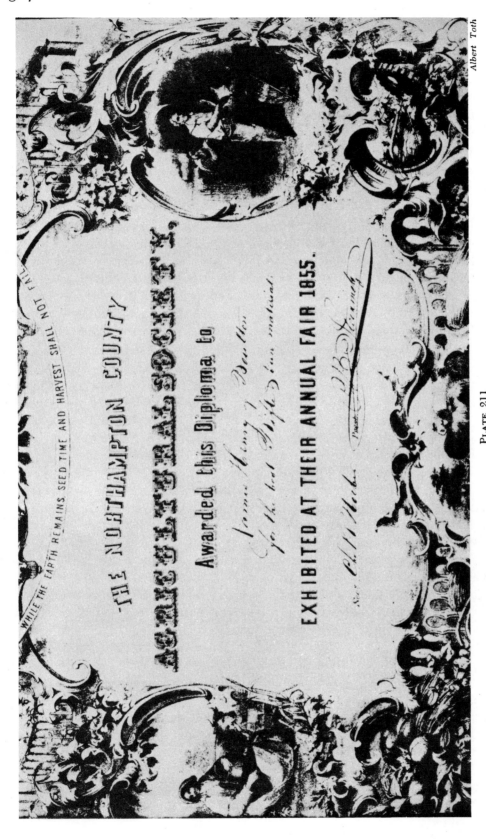

Albert Toth

PLATE 211

Award given to James Henry by the Northampton County Agricultural Society for his exhibit of a rifle and gun material in their annual fair held in 1855.

Company, asking about their need for rifles and explained that, if an order was not imminent, "in common with most manufacturers I am about to discharge my hands for several months."

This lay-off was doubtless to permit the men to harvest their crops or assist farmers who needed help. Harvesting was really a manual operation at that time and many hands were needed to cut the grain and get it into the barns. The Henry correspondence shows that they invariably became busy in the autumn and at times produced as many as two hundred guns in a period of two months.

Later, James Henry took his son, Granville, into the business and the company name was changed to J. Henry & Son. James Henry died in 1895 and the works at Boulton made its last guns about that time.

The third part of the enterprise was located on the side of the Bushkill Creek opposite the factory. Along the hillside a number of residences were built for the men who owned and operated the rifle factory. From their homes they could look down upon the factory, as the old iron masters used to watch their furnaces to see that all activity was supervised and regulated. Although the homes have been renovated to keep pace with the changes of architectural fashion, they continue to stand in groves of trees, suggesting the private living quarters of people of substance.

Beyond the dwellings of the owners, the employees lived in modest houses, of which only a few have survived. The residence of the blacksmith and one or two others can be pointed out. The most interesting area is what is known as "Filetown." When they were not employed at the factory, the people who lived there took lock parts, triggerguards, etc., to their homes and filed and polished them in the old traditions of the craft. There is evidence that similar activity occurred in Birmingham, England, where many locks for Pennsylvania rifles were made.

There is no place called Boulton today. Most of the factory dam has been washed away, the furnace and barrel mill are gone, and only the residences stand on the hill above the creek and the underbrush. The thriving village and the humming gun factory are legends to the natives who live in Belfast or Nazareth, the nearest towns to Boulton and Jacobsburg.

It is well-known by all collectors that guns made by any of the Henry gunsmiths are very scarce. The numerous activities of William Henry I easily explain why he did not make many guns, although there is a musket in the museum of the Lancaster County Historical Society which bears his name on the lock plate. A pair of pistols in the Museum of the Historical Society of Pennsylvania was made by William Henry II, who put his name on the lock plates and "Nazareth" on the top facet of the barrels. A few Pennsylvania rifles are extant that were made by Abraham Henry, although they are not outstanding in design or quality of workmanship. At least one of his pistols has survived. The military products of John Joseph are scarce, but possibly the easiest to acquire of any of the Henry products.

The greatest mystery about their products is concerned with the thousands of rifles that were made at Boulton which seem to have disappeared completely. A letter from John Joseph to the American Fur Company, October 5, 1836, discusses the making of two hundred rifles to be delivered in New York by December 15 of the same year. Such a rate of production suggests that thousands of rifles were made

HENRY'S GUN FACTORY

Here rifles and other fire-arms were made for use in the War of 1812. Built by William Henry, 2nd, about 1800, the famous Henry shotgun was made here as late as 1904. Site about half a mile away.

PENNSYLVANIA HISTORICAL AND MUSEUM COMMISSION

PLATE 212

Pennsylvania Historical and Museum Commission marker telling about the Henry Gun Factory at Boulton.

at the Boulton factory, yet none are known to the author with the name of the company on the top facet of the barrel. It is also interesting to note that despite the fact that many locks are extant marked with the name, J. J. Henry Boulton, their correspondence includes a number of letters directing the American Fur Company to try to obtain locks for them in New York City. From the correspondence we learn that the American Fur Company had a great deal of confidence in the integrity of John Joseph Henry. On one occasion they gave him an order for a great many rifles and asked that he insert the price in the contract form, which he was directed to return to their New York office. It is also interesting to note that some of the contracts called for the use of curly maple for the stocks, although a letter in 1836 pointed out that they had only plain maple for stocks and would not have any curly maple for five or six months.

The records of the Henry factory at Boulton are in the hands of a descendant of the family; they show that, in addition to their contract work with the American Fur Company, they made guns for retail sale at the factory. The identity of some of the buyers is recorded; however, no gun has been found in the vicinity of Nazareth that can be traced to a specific entry in the day books. It is hoped that some of these guns will be brought out of their attic shelter and made available for study, but until that time the collecting fraternity has only the records. These records will be made available in a comprehensive study which is being made in cooperation with the family who owns them.

HENTZ, NICHOLAS
    Main near Cherry, Allegheny, Pennsylvania. 1859-60.

HERSH, JACOB
    Pennsburg, Montgomery County, Pennsylvania. 1861.

HESS, DAVID
    New Tripoli, Lehigh County, Pennsylvania. 1861.

HESS, JONAS M.
    Germansville, Lehigh County, Pennsylvania. 1861.

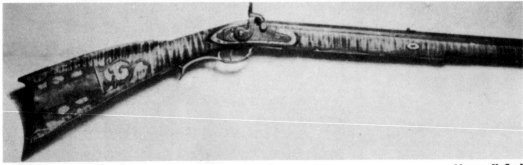

Monroe Hufford

PLATE 213

Rifle with flint lock (now percussion), full stock of curly maple, brass mountings, octagonal barrel with J. Hillegas in block letters on the top facet of the barrel, The piercings in the patch box, the barrel pin escutcheons, and the pleasing contour of the stock are desirable assets of this rifle.

There probably were a number of gunsmiths named Hillegas but the products of J. Hillegas seem to be found most frequently.

HESS, SOLOMON

Overton, Bradford County, Pennsylvania. 1861.

HILLEGAS, JOSEPH.

Joseph Hillegas appeared in the Borough of Pottsville assessment lists in the year 1838, described in the *Transcript of the Triennial Assessment of the Borough of Pottsville for the year 1838.* "Six mills per dollar, George Stichler, Assessor, North Ward. Occupation, gunsmith, owner of one 20 ft. lot on Center Street, one three story brick house, two frame houses on Adams Street, and two horses."

It is known that in 1841 he became a resident of Orwigsburg, then the county seat of Schuykill County, but maintained realty holdings and business in Pottsville.

No will or estate adminstrative record appears in the Register of Wills or Orphan Courts records, therefore it must be presumed that he died intestate or that he moved from the county.

Found in collections are quite a few guns marked J. Hillegas in block letters on the top facet of octagonal barrels. Most of them are of average quality, and he does not seem to have developed a style by which his work can be easily recognized.

HIRTH, AUGUST (Firearms and Machine Shop)

136 & 138 Wood Street, Pittsburgh, Pennsylvania. 1884.

HIRTH, AUGUST OF BROWN & HIRTH

Pittsburgh, Pennsylvania. *J. F. Diffenbacher's Directory of Pittsburgh and Allegheny Cities,* 1885.

HOAK, MATTHIAS

Lancaster, Pennsylvania. Tax lists 1800, 1802, 1803, 1814, 1816.

In 1800, 1802, and 1803, Hoak is listed as a gunsmith, but in 1814 and 1816, he is listed as a barrel ryfler. It must be presumed that he was very apt at that phase of the business and that he felt he could do better if he specialized in it.

HOFF, PETER

York Street, Hanover, York County, Pennsylvania. 1861.

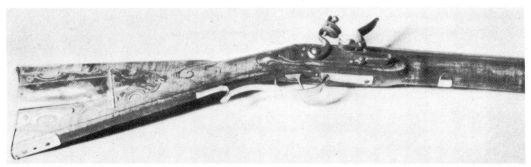

Vincent Nolt

PLATE 214

Rifle with flint lock, full stock of curly maple, brass mountings, octagonal barrel with J. Hoak engraved on the top facet of the barrel. This rifle is carved on the cheek side but its outstanding merit is its beautifully engraved patch box. This pattern was used by a few Lancaster County gunsmiths who made fine rifles.

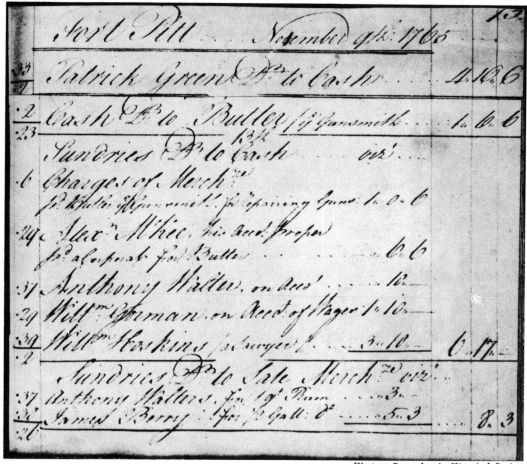

Western Pennsylvania Historical Society

PLATE 215

Photostat of a page from the Day Book of Baynton, Wharton, and Morgan, dated November 9, 1765. The second entry is "Cash DB to Butler/ye gunsmith."

HOFFMAN, JOHN
Lykens Township, Dauphin County, Pennsylvania. Tax list 1828.

HOFFMAN, SILLIAN
Jenner's Cross Roads, Somerset County, Pennsylvania. 1861.

HOKE (HOAK), CONRAD
Strasburg Township, Lancaster County, Pennsylvania. Tax assessment lists 1807, 1809.

HOKE (HOAK), JACOB
Strasburg Township, Lancaster County, Pennsylvania. Tax assessment lists 1800, 1807, 1809.

HOLDRY, HIRAM
Mohn's Store, Berks County, Pennsylvania. 1861.

HOLEMAN, JOHN
Lancaster, Pennsylvania. Tax lists 1814, 1816.

HOLMES, R.
GUNSMITHING. The subscriber, having resumed the above business in Main Street, near J. Boyd's drug store, in the borough of Bridgewater, respectfully informs the public that he is prepared to execute all orders in this line with neatness and dispatch. RIFLES AND FOWLING pieces of the best quality made and kept for sale, at all times—also, repairing done in the best manner. Persons are requested to call and examine his workmanship. Bridgewater, May 30, 1837. *The Western Argus,* Beaver, Pennsylvania. May 31, 1837.

HOLSAPPLE, PHILIP
Center ab High, Pottsville, Pennsylvania. 1860.

HOLTZWORTH, WILLIAM
Lancaster, Pennsylvania. Tax lists 1816, 1820, 1830.

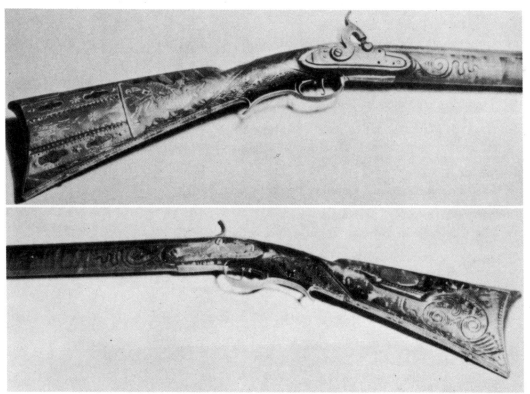

William Reisner, Jr.

PLATE 216

Rifle with flint lock (now percussion), full stock of maple with artificial grain, brass mountings, octagonal barrel with Holtzworth engraved in script letters on the top facet. The finial of the patch box in the shape of a game bird is quite unusual. The piercing in the side plates of the patch box and in the large toe-plate are also unusual features, but occasionally found on other Lancaster rifles.

HOOPER, ROBERT LETTIS, JR. (Musquets)

To be sold by Robert Lettis Hooper, Jr., at his store in Water Street, three doors above Chestnut Street, wholesale or retail.

A Parcel of small, handy musquets, well mounted, and neatly fitted with iron rods, and small bayonets, the locks are large and well made, 3d, 4d, 6d, 8d, 10d, 12d, and 20d nails, pork, common and salt, gammons, a quality of butter in firkins and mackerel by the barrel. *Pennsylvania Journal*, August 18, 1763. No. 1080.

HORN, CONR.

Hazleton, Luzerne County, Pennsylvania. 1861.

HORNER, FREDERICK

Quemahoning Township, Somerset County, Pennsylvania. Tax lists 1805, 1808, 1811.

Jenner Township, Somerset County, Pennsylvania. Tax lists 1815, 1817, 1821, 1834.

HORNER, JACOB

Quemahoning Township, Somerset County, Pennsylvania. Tax lists 1832, 1837, 1849, 1853.

Jenner's Cross Roads, Somerset County, Pennsylvania. 1861.

HORNER, JOHN, JR.

Conemaugh Township, Somerset County, Pennsylvania. Tax lists 1802, 1803, 1806.

HORNER, LEWIS

Jenner's Cross Roads, Somerset County, Pennsylvania. 1861.

HORSTMANN, WILLIAM H. & SONS (Military Store)

51 North Third Street, Philadelphia, Pennsylvania. 1855.

HOWARTER, J.

Lisburn, Cumberland County, Pennsylvania. 1861.

HOWELL, WILLIAM T. (Merchant)

The Commercial Herald, Philadelphia, July 3, 1834:

> GUNS AND PISTOLS. The Subscribers have just received late arrival from Liverpool, a further supply of Guns and Pistols, consisting of
> Double Barrel Flint and Percussion Guns
> Superior double barrel stub or twist do
> A few very superior guns, in mahogany cases, with all the apparatus complete.
> Also, two double barrel Guns. of the manufacture of the celebrated Wesley Richards, of very superior finish.
> Single barrel Flint and Percussion Guns.
> Stub and twist single barrel do
> Long Squirrel Guns, with very small calibers.
> Also, one twisted single barrel gun, sent as a sample, combining the flint and Percussion principle, so that the flint and the percussion lock may be used separately or together.

PISTOLS

Pocket Pistols, with plain and secret triggers.

Belt Pistols, with clasps and secret triggers.

Improved do with patent lock.

Holster Pistols of the usual kind.

For sale at very reduced prices by

WM. T. HOWELL & CO., No. 196 Market Street, 2d door below the Schuylkill Bank.

HUBER, ABRAM

Manchester Township, York County, Pennsylvania. Tax list 1799.

HUMES, JOHN

Near Poplar Lane and North Third Street, Philadelphia, Pennsylvania. *New Trade Directory of Philadelphia,* 1800.

HUMMEL, ADAM

Johnstown Borough, 5th Ward, Pennsylvania. Tax lists 1871, 1873, 1874.

HUMMEL, F.

Market & Water Streets, Lebanon, Pennsylvania. 1860.

HUNSICKER, HENRY

Macungie Township, Lehigh County, Pennsylvania. Tax list 1821. Court House.

HUTCHINSON, R. J.

Lock Haven, Pennsylvania. Tax list 1878.

ICH, CHRISTIAN

Lancaster, Pennsylvania. Tax list 1780.

Although this man is called a smith, and not a gunsmith, in the tax assessment list for 1780, he is probably the man whose name appears on a few muskets made in eighteenth century.

ICKES, JACOB

East St. Clair Township, Bedford County, Pennsylvania. Tax list 1876.

Ickes is known to have made an over-and-under gun with a smooth barrel and the other rifled. His name is on a brass plate which was inlaid on the top facet of a barrel. Later he was known as a wagon maker in his community.

IMHOFF, BENEDICT

Heidelberg Township, Berks County, Pennsylvania. *Pennsylvania Archives,* 3d series, Vol. 18, pages 628, 629.

IRON CITY GUN WORKS

The Iron City Gun Works was founded by William Craig in 1856, who was joined in the same year by another gunsmith, D. J. M'Donald. Their advertisement appeared in the December 5, 1856, issue of the *Pittsburgh Daily Dispatch:*

Wm Craig & D. J. M'Donald. Iron City Gun Works. Wm Craig & Co. Manufacturers of Plain and Fancy Rifles and Shot Guns. No. 118 Third Street, Pittsburgh.

By January 20, 1857, M'Donald seems to have become sole owner of the company and his advertisement appeared in the *Pittsburgh Daily Dispatch* as follows:

> IRON CITY GUN WORKS—D. J. M'Donald, Manufacturer of Plain and Fancy Rifles and Shot Guns, No. 118 Third Street, Pittsburgh.

M'Donald died in 1864; in 1877 H. H. Schutte listed his company as the Iron City Gun Works, which was then located at 330 Liberty Street, Pittsburgh. It is known that he started making guns about 1864 and it is possible that he succeeded M'Donald at the time of his death.

ISRAEL, SAMUEL

Franklin Township, Greene County, Pennsylvania. Tax lists 1809, 1810.

JACOBS, J. H.

Curwensville, Pennsylvania. 1856.

Notice to marksmen—J. H. Jacobs, having located in Curwensville, would hereby inform marksmen and others, that he is prepared to do all kinds of repairing to guns on short notice. Also clocks repaired at his residence. *The Raftsmans Journal*, Clearfield, Pennsylvania. December 10, 1856.

JACOBS, MICHAEL

Warrington Township, York County, Pennsylvania. Census list 1807. Tax list 1813-1814, but not as a gunsmith.

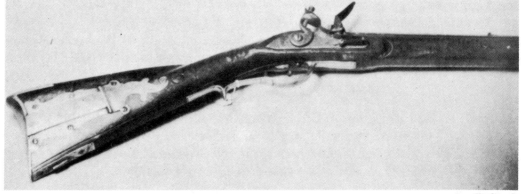

Joe Kindig, Jr.

PLATE 217

Rifle with flint lock, full stock of curly maple, brass mountings, and octagonal barrel marked M. Jacob in script letters on the top facet of the barrel.

The design of the patch box of this rifle suggests that Jacob learned his trade in Lancaster County. His products are rare and little is known about him.

JARECKI, HENRY

Henry Jarecki was born in Posen, Prussia, in 1826 and came to America in 1849. He had served seven years as an apprentice in the trade of brass founding; he established a foundry in Erie the same year he arrived. He also manufactured rifles and stamped on the barrels, "H. Jarecki, Erie, Pa." He is listed in the Pennsylvania

Business Directory of 1861 as a gunsmith. The following advertisement appears in the same publication:

> HENRY JARECKI, State St., bet. 8th and 9th, Erie, Pa. BRASS FOUNDRY and GUN SHOP, Manufacturer and Dealer in Iron Railing, Double and Single Barreled Rifles, Shot Guns, Pistols, Revolvers, Fishing Tackle, Sporting Apparatus, and Fire-gilt Lightning-rod Points, Also Scales, Pumps, Lead pipe, Bells & c. All articles in my line of trade sold at wholesale and retail, at the lowest prices. Repairing in all of these branches neatly executed.

In 1872 he established the Jarecki Manufacturing Company and is not known to have made guns after that year.

JEFFREY, JOHN (Armourer)
Pike Street, Lawrenceville, Pennsylvania. 1839.

JOHNSON, J. H.
Chestnut and North, Lawrenceville, Pennsylvania. 1864. (See Great Western Gun Works.)

JOHNSTON, J. H.
Great Western Gun Works, 621 Smithfield. *J. F. Diffenbacher's Directory of Pittsburgh and Allegheny Cities* for 1886.

JOHNSON, JAMES (Gun Barrel Maker)
Bedford Avenue & Somers, Pittsburgh, Pennsylvania. 1874.

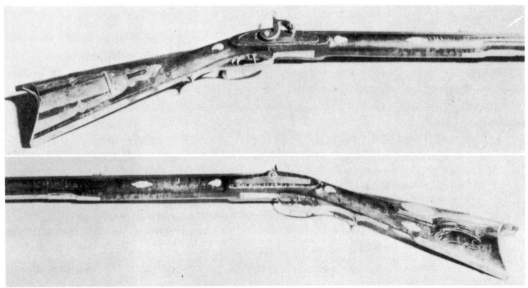

A. Orr Johnston

PLATE 218

Rifle with percussion lock, full stock of curly maple, brass mountings, silver inlays, octagonal barrel 42 inches long marked J. Johnston on the top facet of the barrel in script letters. The form and ornamentation of this gun is typical of the time it was made. The inlays are attractively arranged and reflect the good taste of the maker in decorating his products.

JOHNSON, JOHN

Huntington County, Pennsylvania. Federal Census of 1850.

JOHNSTON, JOHN

Washington Township, Franklin County, Pennsylvania. Tax assessment list 1842.

JOHNSON, JOSEPH

59 Budd Street, Philadelphia, Pennsylvania. 1814.

JOHNSTON, SAMUEL

56 Wayne, Pittsburgh, Pennsylvania. *Fahnstocks Pittsburgh Directory* for 1850.

JOHNSON, WILLIAM

2 Rose Alley, Philadelphia, Pennsylvania. 1847.

JOHNS, ISAAC

Philadelphia, Pennsylvania. Tax list 1780. *Pennsylvania Archives*, 3 series, Vol. 15, page 303.

JONES, ALBERT

Gilmore Township, Greene County, Pennsylvania. 1876.

JORG, JACOB

Berks County, Pennsylvania. *Reading Adler,* January 12, 1818.

Listed as a gunsmith in 1805 in Greenwich Township, Berks County, Pennsylvania tax list. Also listed in 1801, 1802, 1803, but not as a gunsmith.

JOST, CASPAR

Lebanon Township, Dauphin County, Pennsylvania. Tax list 1785.

JOY, ANDREW S.

It is evident from the following newspaper advertisement that A. S. Joy was engaged in gunsmithing in Pittsburgh prior to the date of the advertisement. Since Pittsburgh business directories were published between 1827 and 1839, it is impossible to determine when he opened his gun shop. The following advertisement appeared in the February 2, 1838, issue of the *Pittsburgh Democrat and Workman's Advocate.*

> GUN MANUFACTORY, ST CLAIR STREET, PITTSBURGH, THE subscriber respectfully informs the citizens of Pittsburgh and its vicinity, that he continues the manufacturing, and keeps constantly on hand and for sale, Rifles, Smooth-Bore Shot Guns, Single and Double barreled Rifles, Belt and Pocket Pistols, Powder Flasks and Horns, & c. & C. All kinds of Gun repairing done in the most substantial, and durable manner, on shortest notice. Persons wishing to purchase any of the above articles are requested to call and examine his stock. ANDREW S. JOY.

He also advertised in the same issue for an apprentice from the country about fifteen years of age.

In 1845 his equipment was lost in the great Pittsburgh fire of that year; his losses were estimated to total $150.00. He remained in business, however, and advertised that he would make rifles and smooth-bores on short notice for emigrants

PLATE 219

Rifle with percussion lock, full stock of curly maple, brass mountings, silver inlays, set triggers, octagonal barrel marked A. Joy on the top facet. The fine design and expert engraving of the patch box of this rifle indicate that Joy was a fine craftsman.

to Texas and Oregon. He left Pittsburgh in 1847 but probably continued to make guns in a near-by community. His wife is listed in the Pittsburgh Directory for 1858.

JUDSON, W. H.

W. H. JUDSON, DEALER IN GUNS, RIFLES, PISTOLS, All kinds of Ammunition and Sporting apparatus. Also—Gunsmithing in all its branches done with neatness and dispatch. Sewing machine repairing, Locksmithing, and Bell Hanging promptly attended to. Sign of the NOVELTY IRON WORKS, UNION CITY, PENNSYLVANIA. *Gazeteer & Business Directory of Erie County, Pennsylvania,* 1873-74.

KAMPT, SOLOMON

Hempfield Township, Westmoreland County, Pennsylvania. Tax list 1810, 1811, 1812, 1813, 1814, 1815, 1816, 1817, 1818, 1821, 1823, 1825.

KAPPAL, J.

257 Poplar Street, Philadelphia, Pennsylvania. 1855.

KAUP, LEROY

West Buffalo Township, Union County, Pennsylvania. Federal Census 1850.

KAUPERT, JOHN F.

500 Brook, Philadelphia, Pennsylvania. 1861.

KEARNEY AND GILBERT (Imported)

In Water Street a few doors below Walnut Street. Choice old High Proof'd Barbadoes Rum, x x x Best English whale bone, a large parcel of Musquets with or without bayonets, curious fowling pieces, pistoles, musquetoons or blunderbusses, camp copper kettles and stew pans, several hogsheads of mens strong shoes, English and French sail cloth, x x x some hogsheads of felt hatts, long tavern and short pipes, x x x x guns, 6 and 4 lb. cannon swivel and musquet ball. *Pennsylvania Journal and Weekly Advertiser,* March 8, 1759. No. 848.

KEEFER, ISAIAH

Sylvan, Franklin County, Pennsylvania. 1861.

KEHLER, JOHN

Lancaster Borough, Lancaster County, Pennsylvania. Tax lists 1802, 1803.

KELKER BROS.

17 South Second, Harrisburg, Dauphin County, Pennsylvania. 1861.

KELLER, ELIAS

Yardleyville, Bucks County, Pennsylvania. 1861.

KELLER, JOHN

Carlisle, Pennsylvania. Tax lists 1823, 1832, 1842, 1844.

KELLER, JOHN W.

Louther Street, Carlisle, Cumberland County, Pennsylvania. 1861.

KEPELRING, LEWIS

Berwick Township, Adams County, Pennsylvania. United States Census, 1850.

KERR, MICHAEL

448 North Front Street, Philadelphia, Pennsylvania. *New Trade Directory of Philadelphia,* 1800.

KETTERING, GEORGE

Hempfield Township, Westmoreland County, Pennsylvania. Tax lists 1824, 1825, 1827, 1829, 1830, 1832, 1836.

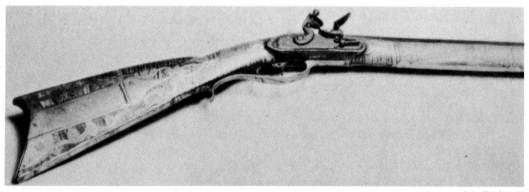

Joe Kindig, Jr.

PLATE 220

Rifle with percussion lock, full stock of curly maple, brass mountings, and octagonal barrel 42 inches long with G. Kettering on the top facet of the barrel.

The design and engraving of the patch box on this rifle focuses attention on the fact that is it one of the finest made in western Pennsylvania. The silver inlays are an attractive feature of the gun and the curl of the maple is also of fine quality.

KEYSER, W. W.

377 North Second Street, Philadelphia, Pennsylvania. 1847, 1855.

KING, CHAMBERS

Washington Township, Armstrong County, Pennsylvania. Tax lists 1863-1867, 1870, 1872.

KING, GEORGE

Sugar Creek Township, Armstrong County, Pennsylvania. Tax lists 1850, 1851, 1857.

Washington Township, Armstrong County, Pennsylvania. Tax lists 1863, 1866.

KING, ISAAC (Whitesmith Business)

The Somerset Whig, Somerset, Pa., January 8, 1818:

WHITE-SMITH BUSINESS, ISAAC KING, Lately from New Jersey, and learned his trade in Philadelphia, RESPECTFULLY Informs the publick in general, that he has commenced the above business, in the borough of Somerset, next door to Mr. John Fleming's and immediately opposite Mr. Jacob Ankeny's inn, in the diamond square, where he will receive and execute all orders in his line of business, with promptitude and on reasonable terms. He has and expects to have on hand, for sale, Guns of all descriptions, Pistols, Swords, Dirks, Carving knives, Powder, Flints, & c. all of the first quality. He hopes from his knowledge of the business and strict attention to merit a share of the patronage of the publick.

January 8.

KING, WILLIAM

Washington Township, Armstrong County, Pennsylvania. Tax lists 1867, 1870, 1872.

KIRLIN, THOMAS

Augusta Township, Northumberland County, Pennsylvania. Tax list 1805.

KISTLER, GEORGE

Maxatawny Township, Berks County, Pennsylvania. 1799.
Berks County, Pennsylvania. Census Report, 1800.

KLEIN, CHRISTIAN

EIGHT DOLLARS REWARD. Ran-away on the 15th instant, from the subscriber living in Lancaster, an indebted servent lad named John McCan.—is about 19 years of age, 5 feet 6 or 7 inches tall, of a dark complexion, lad has a long nose. He speaks both English and German, but English best, and is by trade a gunsmith. He had on when he went away a good hat, a light coloured cassimer coatie, and a nankin waistcoat and breeches.

Whoever apprehends the said Runaway so that his Master may get him again, shall receive the above reward and reasonable charges if brought home, from

Christian Klein, Gunsmith

Lancaster Journal, September 16, 1795.

KLINE, CHRIS

Lancaster, Pennsylvania. 1794.

KLINE, CHRISTIAN

Harrisburg, Pennsylvania. Tax lists 1811, 1817.

KLINE, CONRAD

Conrad Kline is identified as a gunsmith living in Dover, York County, Pennsylvania, in Gibson's *History of York County, Pennsylvania.* He was the last of the Revolutionary soldiers living in Dover Township. At his death his corpse was accompanied to Strayer's Churchyard by the Independent Blues and the Dover Artillerists. The tax records do not confirm any occupation for Conrad Kline.

The 1817-1818 tax assessment lists for Dover do list Andrew Kline as a gunsmith and postmaster. He is also believed to have operated a tavern in the town. His name does not appear on subsequent tax lists as a resident of the area.

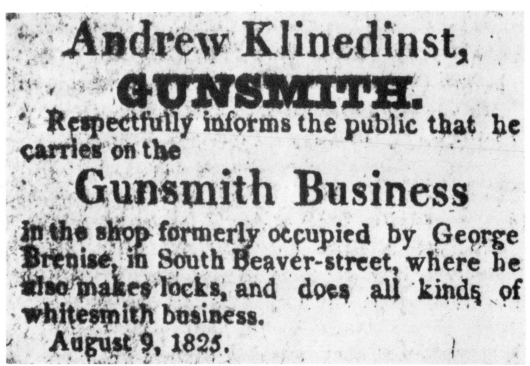

York County Historical Society

PLATE 221

Newspaper advertisement of Andrew Klinedinst which appeared in the *York Gazette,* August 16, 1825.

Joe Kindig, Jr.

PLATE 222

Rifle with flint lock, full stock of curly maple, brass mountings, and octagonal barrel with A. Klinedinst on the top facet of barrel.

KLINE, JACOB

Frankford Township, Cumberland County, Pennsylvania. Tax lists 1828, 1842, 1843, 1844.

KLINE, PHILIP

Halifax, Dauphin County, Pennsylvania. Tax list 1814.

KLINEDINST, ANDREW

York, Pennsylvania. Advertisement in *York Gazette,* August 16, 1825. Deed dated January 3, 1835. Census of United States, 1850.

KNAPPENSBERGER, HENRY

Upper Malford Township, Lehigh County, Pennsylvania. Tax list 1821.

KNAUF, HENRY

Nippenose, Lycoming County, Pennsylvania. 1861.

KNAVE, JACOB

Metal Township, Franklin County, Pennsylvania. Tax list 1807.

KNEPPER, JOSEPH

Summerhill Township, Cambria County, Pennsylvania. Tax lists 1834, 1836, 1840.

KNOUSE, WILLIAM

Marlboro n. West, Philadelphia, Pennsylvania. 1847-1855.

KNOX, ROBERT

Franklin Township, Franklin County, Pennsylvania. Census list 1800.

KNUPP, CHARLES MONROE

Bakersville, Somerset County, Pennsylvania. b. December 9, 1863. d. February, 1939.

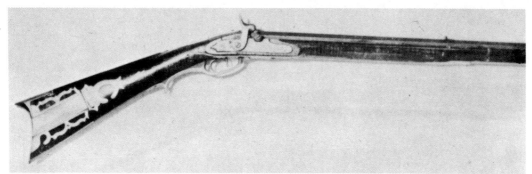

M. T. Stewart

PLATE 223

Rifle with percussion lock, full stock of curly maple, brass mountings, set triggers, octagonal barrel 36 inches long with C. M. Knupp on the top facet of the barrel. Although this rifle was made in the late percussion period, the style of the patch box suggests the late flint-lock period. An identical patch box was used by one of the Dunmeyer gunsmiths on a rifle. The style of lock plate on this gun was used by other gunsmiths in Somerset County.

KOCH, A.
Henrysville, Monroe County, Pennsylvania. 1861.

KOCH, HENRY
Tyrone Township, Cumberland County, Pennsylvania. Tax list 1820.

KOCH, L.
Henrysville, Monroe County, Pennsylvania. 1861.

KOPP, ANDREW
Frankstown Township, Blair County, Pennsylvania. Federal Census, 1850.
Andrew Kopp was sixty-nine years old in 1850 and was probably the father of
George Kopp.

KOPP, GEORGE
Frankstown Township, Blair County, Pennsylvania. Federal Census, 1850.
Frankstown Township, Blair County, Pennsylvania. 1861, 1864, 1869.
George Kopp was thirty-six years old in 1850 and was probably the son of
Andrew. They were neighbors when the census was taken.

KRAFT, JACOB
Lancaster, Pennsylvania. Tax list 1770, 1773, 1780.

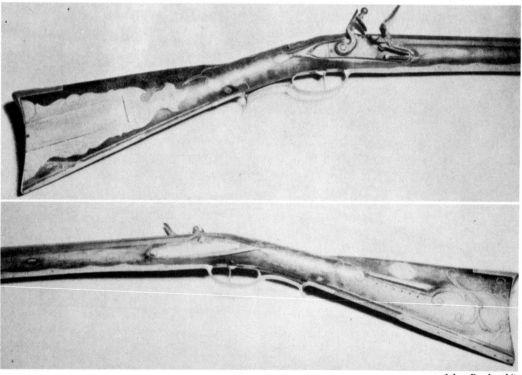

John Fonderwhite

PLATE 224

Rifle with flint lock, full stock of walnut, brass mountings, octagonal barrel with Jacob Kraft engraved in script letters on the top facet of the barrel.

KRAFT, JACOB (Single Freeman)

Heidelberg Township, York County, Pennsylvania. Tax lists 1807, 1808, 1809.

There must have been two Jacob Krafts. The one in Lancaster is known to have been married to Catherine Resor, sister of Peter Resor, and he lived in Lancaster in the 1770's.

The second one, a single man, lived in York County in the early 1800's.

KRIDER, JOHN

NE Second & Walnut Streets, Philadelphia, Pennsylvania. 1847, 1855, 1861.

KRIEGBAUM, GEORGE

Augusta Township, Northumberland County, Pennsylvania. Tax list 1832, 1835.
Shamokin Township, Northumberland County, Pennsylvania. Tax lists 1838, 1840, 1841.

KROTZ, ZIEGMUND

Saw Mill Alley near Spruce, Duquesne, Pennsylvania. 1860-61.

KRYNER, WILLIAM

Montgomery Township, Franklin County, Pennsylvania. Tax list.

KUHNS, PETER

North Whitehall Township, Lehigh County, Pennsylvania. Tax list 1821.

KUNKLE, LEONARD

Harrisburg, Pennsylvania. Tax list 1831.

KUNTZ, JACOB

Germantown Road n. Second Street, Philadelphia, Pennsylvania. 1814.
Cadwallader ab Phoenix, Philadelphia, Pennsylvania. 1847, 1855.

KUNTZ, MICHAEL

Lancaster Borough, Lancaster County, Pennsylvania. Tax lists 1802, 1803.

KUNTZ, PETER

North Whitehall Township, Lehigh County, Pennsylvania. 1860, 1861.

LAIB, CHARLES

Borough Township, Beaver County, Pennsylvania. Tax lists 1849, 1850, 1851.

LAKE, IRA

Shamokin Township, Northumberland County, Pennsylvania. Tax list 1832, 1838.

LALLY, JOHN

German Township, Fayette County, Pennsylvania. Tax list 1811.

LANGEAY, JOHN

The Subscriber takes this method to acquaint his friends and the public in general, that if proper encouragement be given, he will continue to make Cartridges for quick Fire, likewise Balls for the Artillery, and flatters himself, he shall be able to give satisfaction to all who please to favor him with their cutsom, as they may depend on having their orders executed with care and dispatch, by their very humble servant,   John Langeay

N.B. Would be glad to attend any country Battallion who say need his assistance. Enquire of the Printer. *Pennsylvania Journal,* no. 1707. August 23, 1775.

LAMA, MICHAEL

Millheim, Centre County, Pennsylvania. 1861.

LAPKEEHLER, HENRY

Mifflinburg, Union County, Pennsylvania. Federal Census 1850.

LAPPINGTON, WILLIAM

Lawrenceville, Pennsylvania. 1839.

LAUDENSLAGER, HENRY

Fair Oaks, Penn Township, Snyder County, Pennsylvania. Born 1839, died 1912.

LAUFFMAN, P. H. (Hardware Merchant)

28 Wood Street, Pittsburgh, Pennsylvania. 1852.

LAWRENCE, JOHN

Antrim Township, Franklin County, Pennsylvania. Tax list 1786.

LETHER, JACOB

The last name of this gunsmith was spelled a number of different ways, although it is most frequently spelled Leather. Lether was probably the spelling of an indifferent tax assessor and Ledder is the way a German would spell it who had a minimum knowledge of English.

He was one of the gunsmiths who had contracts for muskets, although the writer has never heard of one bearing his name. The following letter tells that he was associated with some famous gunsmiths of Lancaster County in producing such arms:

> To Clement Biddle:
>
> Of the arms manufactured by John Graeff and Abraham Henry at Lancaster, there are stored and ready for delivery seven hundred and forty-two stand. In a short time, they expect to have two hundred more ready for delivery.

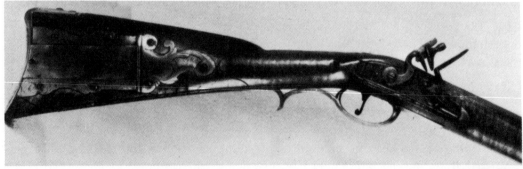

Joe Kindig, Jr.

PLATE 225

Rifle with flint lock, full stock of curly maple, brass mountings, and octagonal barrel marked Jacob Lether on the top facet of the barrel. Rifles by Lether are very rare.

Of these manufactured by Jacob Leather at Yorktown, there are stored and ready for delivery five hundred and nineteen stand.

I have been twice to Strasburg at the manufactory of Fundersmith. I find he has not a single musket ready and only five barrels on hand. He has, I believe, about 200 locks.

Jeremiah Mosher

On February 12, 1800, Governor McKean appointed Peter Gatz of Lancaster in place of Col. Mosher to inspect arms manufactured by Henry and Graeff of Lancaster, Jacob Lather and Conrad Welshans of York, and John Fondersmith of Strasburg.

LEBAN, VALENTINE
Bedford Borough, Bedford County, Pennsylvania. Tax list 1820.

LECHLER, HENRY
Henry Lechler was one of the gunsmiths who was apprenticed in Lancaster, but moved to less competitive territory. In one of his newspaper advertisements he states that he moved from Lancaster to Carlisle to start his business of making guns. His former Lancaster residence is also mentioned in the records of one of his real estate transactions in Cumberland County.

The first evidence of his activity there is in 1798, when he bought six acres, including residence for 150 pounds sterling. His name appears regularly in the tax assessment lists of the borough until 1843.

His earliest guns are of better than average quality and indicate a strong Lancaster influence. A number of guns are known with the daisy finial on the patchbox, a detail which usually indicates some association with the Lancaster area. One is known that shows a York influence in the patch box design. His name was stamped on the barrels of his late guns in block letters.

LECHLER, HENRY JR.
133 North Front Street, Philadelphia, Pennsylvania. 1831, 1840.
15 Arch Street, Philadelphia, Pennsylvania. 1847, 1855.

LEFFEL, DAVID
Shanesville, Berks County, Pennsylvania. 1861.

LEITNER, ADAM (Single Man)
York, Pennsylvania. Tax list 1799.

LEITNER, IGNATIUS
Yorktown, Pennsylvania. Tax list 1783, 1793, 1799. *York Recorder*, May 2, 1800.

Ignatius Leitner—He removed to house next to Jacob Shaffer's store and nearly opposite to Abram Miller Tavern in York Boro—Where he continues to draw deeds, mortgages, Power of attorney, apprentice indenyures, Bulls, Bonds, Notes, States executor and administrators accounts. He will, as usual, clerk at vendues and take inventories and all other instruments of writing done on shortest notice.

N.B. He continues and keeps hands at work in his former branches as making rifles, still cocks, casting rivets, gun mountings, etc., at the lowest prices.

Census list 1800. .

LEITNER, JACOB

Yorktown, Pennsylvania. Tax list 1799.

LEMAN, HENRY E.

In the beginning of this biography of Henry E. Leman, it might be interesting and important to point out that claims have been made on a number of occasions that gunsmiths named Leman worked in Lancaster County in the eighteenth century. Such trade activities might be documented at a later time; however, at the moment the records of the Lancaster County Court House do not support the hypothesis of Leman production before the time of Henry E. Leman. Nor are there any guns known to the writer which can be attributed to a Leman gunsmith of the eighteenth century.

Henry E. Leman was born in Lancaster, Pennsylvania, on March 8, 1812. At the age of sixteen he is reported to have been apprenticed to Melchoir Fordney, one of Lancaster's most outstanding gunsmiths. In 1831 he moved to Philadelphia and worked for the Tryon Company, which was manufacturing guns in a factory

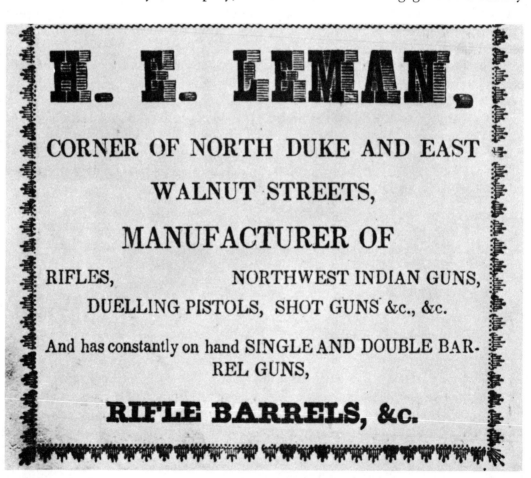

PLATE 226

Advertisement of H. E. Leman in a *Lancaster Business Directory* for 1843. Although there is evidence that Leman was a prolific producer of arms, only a few can be found in collections throughout the country.

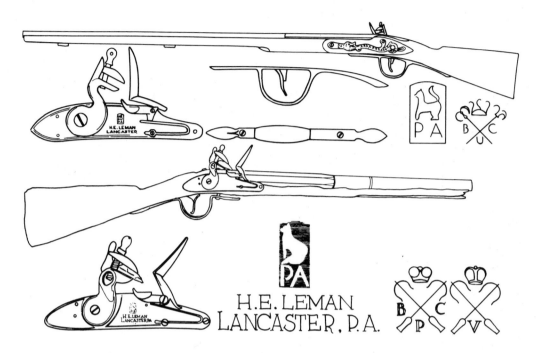

This illustration is from *Guns on the Early Frontiers*
by Carl P. Russel, published by University of California Press, 1957

PLATE 227

The upper sketch is of a trade musket with a flint lock, octagon-to-round barrel 36¼ inches long with a Birmingham proof mark on the left-side facet of the octagon near the breech. The total length of the gun is 51 inches. On the lock plate, in front of the hammer, is a foxlike animal over the letters "PA" and H. E. Leman, Lancaster. The lock-bolt plate is in the shape of a dragon as found on other trade guns. The Birmingham proof mark on the barrel suggests that Leman imported the barrel. He may have also imported the lock and engraved it in his factory in Lancaster. The gun is exhibited at the Kit Carson Museum, Trinidad, Colorado.

The barrel has been sawed off the lower gun which is now owned by Mr. E. A. Hawks of Concord, Massachusetts.

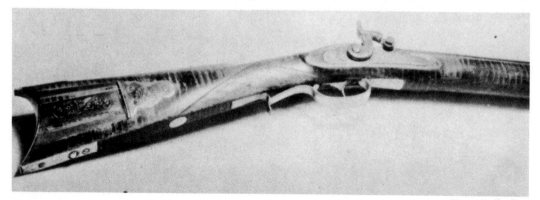

Henry J. Kauffman

PLATE 228

Rifle with percussion lock, full stock of maple with artificial grain, brass mountings, octagonal barrel 40 inches long marked H. Leman, Lancaster, Pa., Warranted. This type of rifle was probably made early in Leman's career. The patch box, trigger guard, and toe-plate are attractively engraved. Much of the artificial grain remains on the specimen.

there. In 1834 he returned to Lancaster and started his business of gun making, which appears to have flourished until 1887.

His first factory was on Mifflin Street, west of Duke. His forge and boring mill were in Upper Leacock Township, along the Conestoga Creek. Its ruined remains can be seen in an area called Oregon, near the highway from Reading to Lancaster. In this mill he welded, drilled, and ground the rifle barrels. The finer hand and machine work was done in the factory on Mifflin Street in the City of Lancaster. There the stocks were also made and the guns finished, ready for sale to a local customer or a distant trader.

A few original records have survived that described Leman's varied business interests.

The papers of the American Fur Company in the Library of the New York Historical Society include some letters written to them by Leman at the beginning of his career. The following letter is dated January 27, 1837:

> Sirs:
>
> I am aware of your formerly receiving Rifles from this place (during my apprenticeship at Rifle Making) and none very lately. I can manufacture Rifles at the following prices,
>
> Single trigger—pan, lock, checkered and engraved $12
> do   do   long tang breech $12
>
> Warranted equal to any manufactured, a sample can be had for inspection.
>
> The small advance since you received Rifles from this place is owing to the advance in Materials and Wages.
>
> H. E. Leman

It is interesting to note that on April 25, 1837 Leman offered them the same rifles at $11.00 each and concluded his letter by saying "please have the goodness to answer this letter."

In 1837 Leman received his first government contract for 500 Indian rifles at $14.00 each. These rifles must obviously have been better, or perhaps had some inlays which his earlier quotation did not include. In 1843 he suggested to Ramsay Crooks, head of the American Fur Company, that his business would be helped and the Indians benefitted if he were permitted to manufacture guns for the Fur Company.

Vincent Nolt

PLATE 229

Rifle with percussion lock marked Leman, Lancaster, Pa., brass mounted with an attractive design engraved on the patch box, brass inlays, octagonal barrel marked H. Leman, Lancaster, Pa. Most Leman rifles with a half stock have round patch boxes and it is possible that this one was changed from a full stock to a half stock, however there is no evidence that a change was made in this gun.

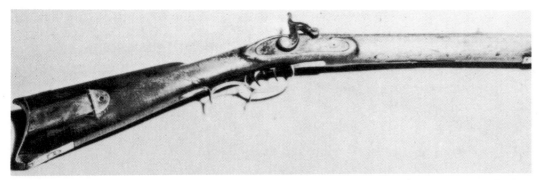

H. J. Kauffman

PLATE 230

Percussion lock rifle, maple stock, plain brass mountings, octagonal barrel 44 inches long, marked H. Leman, Lancaster, Pa., Warranted, on top facet of barrel. This rifle had the usual artificial grain which Leman used, but the style of patch box is rarely found on Leman rifles.

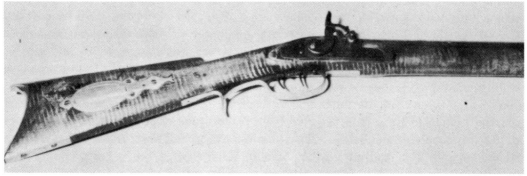

Vincent Nolt

PLATE 231

Rifle with percussion lock marked Leman, Lancaster, Pa. Plain brass mountings, set triggers, plain maple stock with artificial grain, and octagonal barrel marked H. Leman, Lancaster, Pa. It is obvious that Leman used both round and elliptical patch boxes on his rifles.

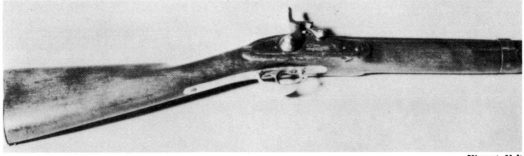

Vincent Nolt

PLATE 232

Musket with percussion lock marked Leman, Lancaster, Pa. Full stock of walnut wood, brass mountings, round barrel 33 inches long, marked Leman, Lancaster, Pa. This gun is identical in size to the "Mississippi" models made by contractors like Tryon and Whitney.

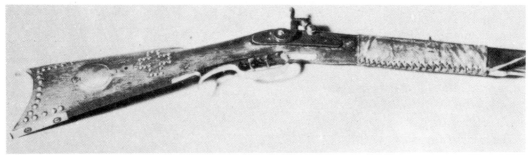

Vincent Nolt

PLATE 233

Rifle with percussion lock, half stock of plain maple, brass mountings, set triggers, and octagonal barrel marked H. Leman, Lancaster, Pa., on the top facet of the barrel.

The brass tacks on the butt and the leather on the forestock are usually considered evidences of Indian ownership of a rifle. The tacks were presumably added by an Indian to decorate the rifle and the laced rawhide to repair a break in the stock.

After 1850 the factory at Oregon was not used and in 1861 his increased business caused him to build a factory at East Walnut and Cherry Streets in Lancaster, where his machines were powered by a steam engine. It is also interesting to note that the 1859-60 Lancaster Business Directory lists a number of men who were known as gunsmiths in the individual listing in the Directory but had only an address for their residence and were not listed under the heading of gunsmiths in the merchantile establishments of the city. These men were probably employed by Leman at this time of expansion in his business and most of them lived in the north end of town near the Leman factory. It is very doubtful if any guns exist that bear their names on the top facet of the barrel. Their names are as follows: Jacob Brock, Lewis Ealer, Benjamin Fox, Andrew Frailey, Samuel Hambright, Levi N. Hart, Christopher Hinkle, Charles Howerter, Henry Howerter, Frederick Konig, John Remly, Adam Ropp, Henry Sheaff, Enoch Stokes, William Troyer, Solomon Weidman, and John Werner. His new factory in which these men worked is standing today, although it is divided into five residences. The men listed as owners of retail gun shops in this Directory are John Drepperd, Junior and Senior, Eicholtz Bros., J. Fordney and H. Gibbs.

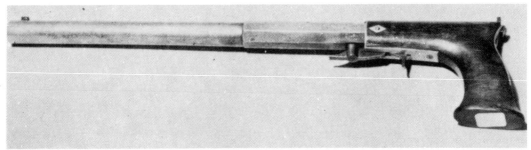

Vincent Nolt

PLATE 234

Pistol with under-hammer percussion lock, stock of plain maple, brass mountings, octagon-and-round barrel marked Leman, Lancaster, on a side facet. This is the only Leman pistol known to the writer.

In 1873 Leman moved to a larger factory at James and Christian Streets, where he continued in business until 1887, when his factory was closed. In 1888 his business is not listed in the Lancaster Business Directory but a Frank B. Leman is listed as a gunsmith at 538 Middle Street, Lancaster, Pennsylvania. The writer is not aware of any relationship between the two men.

In the early years of his business activity Leman is thought to have made most of his own parts, although he certainly made a few guns with Birmingham proof marks on the barrels and possibly English locks. This practise is difficult to

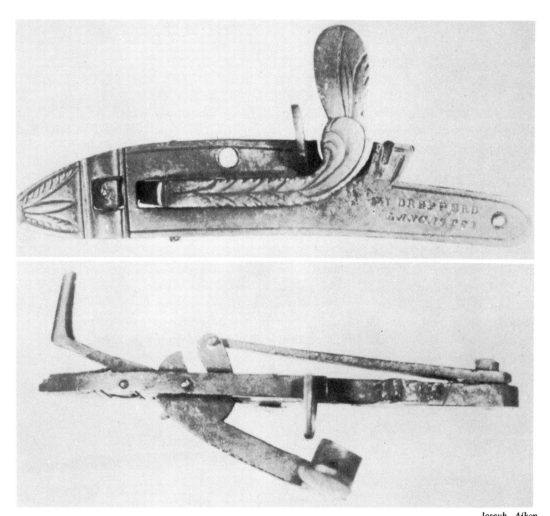

Joseph Aiken

PLATE 235

The invention of the percussion lock doubtless stimulated many craftsmen to improve on the early pattern. The function of this side hammer or "Mule ear" lock was satisfactory but it never was popular with gunners and few of them were made. Some of them were made by men who seem to have been experimenting rather than producing locks in quantity. A side hammer lock in the author's collection has the mainspring on the outside of the lock plate.

Although this lock is the only one known to the writer made by Drepperd of Lancaster, Pennsylvania, it is not surprising that he made one. He was a fine craftsman and it is reasonable that he would try his hand on this strange style. It is also possible that he made it for a customer who specifically asked for such a lock. It is obviously the shape of a standard percussion lock and is beautifully engraved in the style and workmanship of a fine lock maker.

explain in any other way than by the fact that he could import barrels and locks cheaper than he could make them here. His barrels were rifled in his factory and the mountings were cast in a small foundry connected with the business. In 1875 he started buying barrels made by the barrel specialists in Berks County.

Leman made a great variety of guns throughout his career. Perhaps the rarest and most interesting is a type of trade gun with a flintlock which is illustrated in Plate 227. Its barrel is 36 inches long with an octagonal section nine inches long at the breech. On the lock plate a fox-like animal is impressed with the initials "PA." Beneath this mark "H. E. Leman, Lancaster" is engraved. On the left side facet of the barrel a Birmingham proof mark is found and a small replica of the emblem that appears on the lock plate. A typical dragon ornament is used as a lock-bolt plate. The presence of a flintlock on this gun suggests that it was made in the early years of his career.

A long rifle in the author's collection with a full stock and a percussion lock was probably made about the same time as the trade gun, for it has ribbed ramrod pipes identical to those on the trade gun. It has a patch box which reaches to the butt plate and is engraved with an interesting motif. Its barrel is 40 inches long and is octagonal throughout. The stock has a simulated curl, which Leman seems to have used on many of his rifle stocks.

A close examination of Leman's products indicates that in the beginning of his career he was an alert and aggressive business man. He seems to have followed the trends of the times in the style of gun he produced and he certainly made a large variety of guns. It appears that his early sporting rifle with a full-maple stock became a half-stock with the same patch box that he had formerly used. The round and oval patch boxes were later used on the half-stock rifles, of which he apparently made a great many for local trade and shipment to the West.

He also manufactured muskets from the 1840's to the Civil War period. A number are known with 33 inch barrels, which are about the same size and shape of the "Mississippi" models, but Leman's lack the brass patch box. Some of these muskets have iron mountings throughout while some are made of mixed brass and iron parts. He also made the regular models in the early 1860 period, similar to Springfield and other makes.

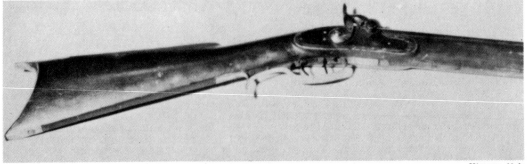

Vincent Nolt

PLATE 236

Rifle with percussion lock marked Conestoga Rifle Company, full stock of maple covered with red paint, brass mountings, octagonal barrel 40 inches long marked Conestoga Rifle Company on the top facet of the barrel.

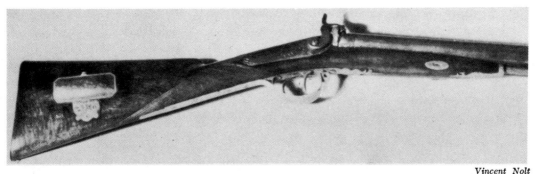

Vincent Nolt

PLATE 237

Double rifle and shotgun with percussion locks, brass mountings, silver inlays and patch-box cover, walnut stock, round barrel marked H. Leman, Lancaster, Pa.

He must have been active in 1885, for the Jos. C. Grubb catalogue for that year included "Half stock Leman rifles with and without a patch box, with extra prices on bores smaller than 150 and barrels over 42 inches long."

The same catalogue includes data on the legendary Conestoga rifles which name Leman is thought to have used for rifles of poorer quality than his standard products. This theory is supported in the catalogue, for his regular rifles are listed in a price range from $10.25 to $11.25, while the Conestoga rifles sold for $7.75 to $9.50, the full stock with a patch box being cheaper than a half stock with a patch box. The Conestoga Rifle from the V. Nolt collection with a coating of red paint is a particularly interesting weapon.

The large number of Leman locks found on guns made by other gunsmiths suggests that he did a considerable business in that line. The appearance of his name on a lock plate can not be regarded as evidence that he made the gun on which such a lock is found.

Leman refused to make breech-loading guns, and it is interesting to speculate how long he could have continued had his business activities not been terminated by his death. By the end of the nineteenth century there was a reduced demand for muzzle-loading guns, and it is doubtful if he could have stayed in business much longer without changing to breech-loading guns.

Henry Leman was the last great gunsmith to have lived in Lancaster; he was spoken of by people who knew him as a man of skill and integrity. The writer has read a number of letters written by him, in which he appears to have transacted his business with courtesy and honesty. If there is a special niche in heaven for gunsmiths, he should be there.

LENNOX, ANDREW
Next door to post office, Pittsburgh, Pennsylvania. 1826.
Fairview (ten miles up Allegheny), Pittsburgh, Pennsylvania. 1837.

LEPLEY, JOSEPH
Southampton Township, Somerset County, Pennsylvania. Tax lists 1863, 1867, 1874.

LIFRED, JOHN (Gun Barrel Maker)
Centre Township, Union County, Pennsylvania. Federal Census 1850.

LILLY, JAMES
German Township, Fayette County, Pennsylvania. Tax lists 1847, 1848.

LILLY, J. PATTERSON
German Township, Fayette County, Pennsylvania. Tax lists 1845, 1846.

LILLY, JOHN
Springhill Township, Fayette County, Pennsylvania. Tax lists 1816, 1817.

LIMERICK, JAMES
Two Coates Court, Philadelphia, Pennsylvania. 1798.

LINS, FRANZ A.
116 Girard Avenue, Philadelphia, Pennsylvania. 1861.

LINS, FREDERICK & FRANZ
563 North Front Street, Philadelphia, Pennsylvania. 1855.

LITTLE, DANIEL (Gun Barrel Maker)
61 Allegheny Street, Pittsburgh, Pennsylvania. 1852.

LITTLE, JAMES
Donegal Township, Washington County, Pennsylvania. Tax lists 1830, 1834.

LITTLE, J. & D.
—. & D. LITTLE, MANUFACTURERS OF RIFLE BARRELS AND TWIST
SHOT GUN BARRELS, CORNER OF ALLEGHENY AND PENN STREETS,
NINTH WARD, PITTSBURGH. *Pittsburgh Business Directory of the Cities of
Pittsburgh and Allegheny,* 1854.

PLATE 238

Advertisement of J. & D. Little in the 1854 edition of the *Pittsburgh Business Directory and Merchant's and Traveler's Guide.*

LITTLE, JAMES (Gun Barrel Maker)
4 Carson Street, Pittsburgh, Pennsylvania. 1850.
63 Allegheny Street, Pittsburgh, Pennsylvania. 1852.

LIVEGOOD, JACOB
Lock Haven, Pennsylvania. Tax lists 1855, 1856.

LLEWELLYN, MATTHEW
Lancaster, Pennsylvania. Contract with the State of Pennsylvania, April 17, 1801.
Pennsylvania Archives, 9 series, Vol. 3, page 1732.

LOCK, JAMES
Wellsboro, Tioga County, Pennsylvania. 1861.

LODGE, JOSEPH
Exchange, Montour County, Pennsylvania. 1861.

LOESCH, JACOB, JR.
Arrived in Salem December 18, 1781. Died in Fayettville, October 8, 1821.

December 28, 1781.

The single Brethren report that Br. Loesch, who recently came from Pennsylvania, will work as a locksmith for the . . . ., and the former grind stone mill can be fitted up for his work shop. It will be well that for the present he does as little work as possible on guns.   March 5, 1782.

Br. Jacob Loesch shall not do anymore gun work at present, as otherwise he will be constantly called on for that work for the public and it will draw too many soldiers to the town.

Moravian Archives, Winston Salem, North Carolina.

LOGAN & KENNEDY (Wholesale Hardware Merchants)
129 Wood Street, Pittsburgh, Pennsylvania. 1841, 1844.

LONG, JOSEPH
Joseph Long was unquestionably one of the outstanding gunsmiths to have worked in central Pennsylvania. He was a Justice of the Peace in Beaver Springs and was regarded as a person of importance in his community. He was born in 1799 and died in 1872.

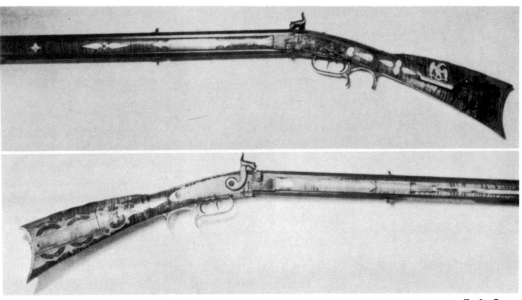

T. J. Cooper

PLATE 239

Double rifle with percussion lock, stock of curly maple, brass mountings, silver inlays, set triggers, octagonal rifled barrels 35 inches long signed Joe Long on the top facet of the barrels.

The workmanship on this gun is of very high caliber. It has a large number of inlays which are distributed from the muzzle to the butt plate. The panels of wood along the barrels are an unusual feature of this rifle with a percussion lock.

Only one flint gun that he made is known, but he was a prolific producer of guns in the percussion era. His octagonal barrels were usually 35 or 36 inches long and were usually marked with the initial J. L. engraved in script letters. A few guns are known to be marked J. Long. The bore of his rifle barrels was usually small. He may have made some fowling pieces, but his distinction is gained from the quality of his rifles.

The openings in the side plates of his patch boxes were half circles, and he used a variety of finials. Many of his guns were highly inlaid with typical motifs of the period; however, he was very partial to a fish pattern. His over-and-under rifle has beautiful side panels of wood along the entire length of the barrels, a feature not usually found on percussion guns.

LONG, RALPH

Beaver Township, Union County, Pennsylvania. Federal Census 1850.

LONGER, JOHN

Milton Borough, Northumberland County, Pennsylvania. Tax lists 1833, 1838.

LOUDENSLAGER, SAMUEL

Mexico, Juniata County, Pennsylvania. 1861.

LOWMASTER, JOHN (Single Man)

York, Pennsylvania. Tax list 1805.

LUTZ, DANIEL Z.

Reinholdsville, Lancaster County, Pennsylvania. 1861.

LUTZ, JESSE

Reinholdsville, Lancaster County, Pennsylvania. 1861.

McCAIN, HUGH

Versaille Township, Allegheny County, Pennsylvania. Federal Census 1800.

McCALLISTER, CALL

Notice to owners. There have been left in the hands of the subscriber a number of guns, pistols, and gun locks, which were repaired by Call McCallister, and the owners of which have neglected to take them away, and to pay for the repairs. NOTICE is therefore hereby given, that unless the owners come forward, on or before the 29th of May next and take them away, they will on that day be sold for the expenses of repairs and costs. John Mercer. April 25, 1820. *The Mercury*, Pittsburgh. April 25, 1820.

McCALY, JAMES

South Huntington Township, Westmoreland County, Pennsylvania. Tax list 1825.

McCAMANT, JAMES

Washington, Pennsylvania. 1797.

James McCamant, Gunsmith, Respectfully informs the public that he has commenced the above business in the Town of Washington, in the house occupied by

William McCamant, where any work in the above line will be done on the shortest notice, and most reasonable terms. *The Western Telegraph and Washington Advertiser,* May 2, 1797.

McCartney, W. G.

ROBBERY.—The shop of the undersigned, corner of Liberty Street and Cherry Alley, was forcibly entered on Monday night last, by some villians, and the following articles, among others, stolen therefrom: One rifle gun, double trigger, with fancy patch box and stock of red color. One rifle gun with single trigger and flintlock. brass bushed and plain box: One English fowling piece, single barreled: Also, two pistols and one smooth pored rifle. Any information which will lead to the recovery of the property, and the conviction of the thieves, will be liberally rewarded. W. G. McCARTNEY, Gunsmith. January 14. *The Daily Commercial Journal,* Pittsburgh. January 22, 1846.

McClanin, David

Wainsburg Town, Franklin Township, Greene County, Pennsylvania. Tax list (undated, but before 1809).

M'Cormick, Robert (Gun Manufacturer)

Wanted immediately. Two good journeymen Clock makers to whom liberal encouragement will be given. Application to be made to Robert M'Cormick & Co. at the gun manufactory, Northern Liberties, Philadelphia. *Aurora,* No. 2618, July 31, 1799.

McCosh, Samuel

NS Liberty, between Hand and Irwin's Alley, Pittsburgh, Pennsylvania. 1826. *Pittsburgh Directory,* 1852. *Pittsburgh Directory,* 1859-60.

McCosh, Samuel

Gastonville, Washington County, Pennsylvania. 1876.

This man was probably the son of the Samuel McCosh who worked in Pittsburgh as early as 1826.

PLATE 240

Advertisement of M'Cosh & Brandt in the 1854 edition of the *Pittsburgh Business Directory and the Merchant's and Traveler's Guide.*

McCLELLAND, ANDREW

German Township, Fayette County, Pennsylvania. Tax lists 1811, 1812, 1813.
Greene Township, Greene County, Pennsylvania. Tax lists 1817, 1822, 1823.
Monongahela Township, Greene County, Pennsylvania. Tax lists 1824, 1825 (deceased).

McCLELLAND, ASA

Franklin Township, Greene County, Pennsylvania. Tax lists 1809, 1810, 1813, 1817, 1821.

McCLELLAND, ENOS

German Township, Fayette County, Pennsylvania. Tax lists 1802, 1803, 1804, 1808, 1810, 1811, 1812.

McCLELLAND, JAMES

German Township, Fayette County, Pennsylvania. Tax lists 1800, 1805, 1808, 1810, 1814, 1815.

McCLELLAND, JAMES AND JOHN

German Township, Fayette County, Pennsylvania. Tax lists 1798, 1799.

McCULLOUGH, W.

Brookville, Pennsylvania.
McCullough is known to have made an over-and-under rifle with a lock marked J. M. Cooper, Warranted, Pittsburgh.

McDONALD, D. J.

118 Third Street, Pittsburgh, Pennsylvania. *Directory of Pittsburgh and Vicinity,* 1859, 1860, 1861.

McFADEN, CHARLES

Connelsville Township, Fayette County, Pennsylvania. Tax list 1833.

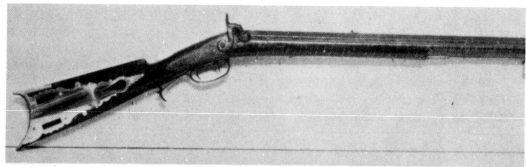

J. T. Herron

PLATE 241

Percussion rifle, curly maple full stock, octagonal barrel 39 inches long, back-action lock, set triggers, plain mountings, marked McKahan and Noble on the top facet of the barrel. The patch box on this rifle is an interesting variation of the common pattern used in western Pennsylvania by a number of gunsmiths. Many craftsmen made two piercings in each side plate while these have only one.

McKahan, John D.
>Washington, Pennsylvania.
>John D. McKahan worked in Washington, Pennsylvania, from 1840 to 1860. He had a varied military record and died of wounds which he received at the battle of Peach Tree Creek, Georgia, on July 25, 1864.

McKahan and Noble
>Washington, Pennsylvania.

McKean, James B.
>Mercer, Mercer County, Pennsylvania. 1861.

Magahan, Abraham
>Huntington County, Pennsylvania. Federal Census of 1850.

Mahla, Philip
>24 Diamond Street, Pittsburgh, Pennsylvania. 1856-57.

Maine, George
>Perry Township, Union County, Pennsylvania. Federal Census 1850.

Makenzie, Duncan
>His Attorney advises all who have left guns to be repaired at the above-mentioned shop to call for and at once pay charges on same. *Pennsylvania Gazette*, No. 162. December 28, 1731-January 4, 1732.

Mallison (Mallisen), Jacob
>Buffalo Township, Allegheny County, Pennsylvania. Census list 1800.

Manger, Michael
>Honesdale, Wayne County, Pennsylvania. 1861.

Mann, George
>Killemoon's Court, Pittsburgh, Pennsylvania. 1826.

Marker, Daniel
>Daniel Marker sold to George Marker on April 26, 1824, a cutter for rifle barrels, two rifle barrels, six rifle gun barrels and fifty gun stocks. It might be presumed that this sale terminated the rifle production of Daniel Marker and also that George Marker was a contemporary of Daniel, but possibly a younger man. Another Marker whose first initial was J. also is known to have made rifles in the Hagerstown, Maryland area.
>The work of George Marker is not known to the writer; however, the J. Marker rifles are of average quality.

Martin, Henry
>George Township, Fayette County, Pennsylvania. Tax lists 1802, 1803, 1804, 1805, 1806.

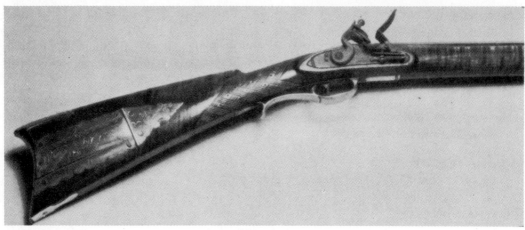

PLATE 242

Rifle with flint lock, full stock of curly maple, brass mountings, octagonal barrel 48 inches long marked M. Martin in script letters on top facet of the barrel. Although Michael Martin was a gunsmith for a number of years, only a few of his products can be found in Pennsylvania collections. The design of the patch box is not a typical Lancaster pattern, but the chequered wrist was used by many gunsmiths in Lancaster County.

MARTIN, MICHAEL

Brecknock Township, Lancaster County, Pennsylvania. Tax lists 1820, 1822, 1826, 1827, 1829, 1836, 1837, 1839.

MARTIN, THOMPSON

WANTED. A Journeyman Gunsmith, of steady habits, will meet with employ, and the highest wages, by applying to Thompson Martin, Elizabeth, Allegheny County, Pennsylvania. None except a first rate workman need apply.

Thompson Martin

The Daily Pittsburgh Gazette, June 10, 1839.

MARTIN, T.

Elizabeth, Allegheny County, Pennsylvania. 1861.

MASON, ALONZO

Monroeton, Bradford County, Pennsylvania. 1861.

MAURER, JOHN (Freeman with Peter Brong)

Lancaster, Pennsylvania. Tax list 1803.

The data from the tax list leads one to think that Maurer was a journeyman gunsmith working for Peter Brong. This hypothesis is further substantiated by the fact that no guns have been found that bear the name of Maurer.

MAYER, GEORGE

22 North Queen Street, Lancaster, Lancaster County, Pennsylvania. 1861.

MEAKIN, GEORGE

Fulmersville, Pike County, Pennsylvania. 1861.

MEALS, JOHN
Butler Township, Adams County, Pennsylvania. United States Census 1850.

MECHLIUS, EDWARD
Halifax, Dauphin County, Pennsylvania. Tax list 1815.

MEDASIA, JOHN NICHOLAS
Union Township, Bedford County, Pennsylvania. Tax list 1876.
Medasia was a fine wood carver and his guns were highly decorated.

MELLEY, HUGH
One Green Street, Philadelphia, Pennsylvania. 1814.

MESSERSMITH, GEORGE
Lancaster, Pennsylvania. Tax list 1802.
George Messersmith was listed as a freeman gunsmith in the tax assessment list only one year and never appears after 1802. He probably never became a journeyman gunsmith, certainly not in Lancaster.

MESSERSMITH, JACOB
Lancaster, Pennsylvania. Tax lists 1800, 1803.

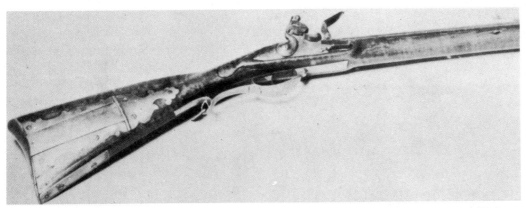

Joe Kindig, Jr.

PLATE 243

Rifle with flint lock, full stock of curly maple, brass mountings, and octagonal barrel 41 inches long marked J. Messersmith on the top facet of the barrel in script letters.

This rifle with its daisy finial on the patch box, simple carving in bas-relief, script signature on the barrel, and flat butt plate, is obviously a product of a gunsmith who worked in Lancaster in the time of the Revolution. It is the only one by this maker known to the writer and the owner.

MESSERSMITH, J.
Messersmith appears as a contributor to the "Hand Account of Continental Rifles" in 1794. His signature on the gun is very similar to the way his name is written on the account.

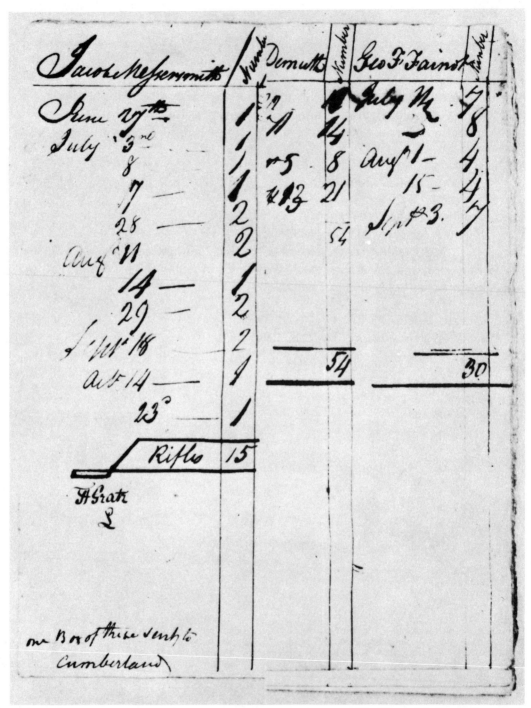

PLATE 244

Jacob Messersmith contributed fifteen rifles to the Hand Account of Continental Rifles made by Pennsylvania gunsmiths in 1794.

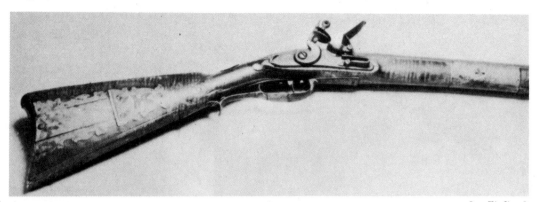

PLATE 245

Rifle with flint lock, full stock of curly maple, brass mountings, and octagonal barrel with J. Metzgar engraved in script letters on the top facet of the barrel.

The designs carved on the cheek side of the butt of this rifle and the outer edges of the patch box strongly suggest that this gun was made by Metzgar while he lived in Lancaster or soon after he moved to Frederick, Maryland. The gun was doubtless made in the last quarter of the eighteenth century.

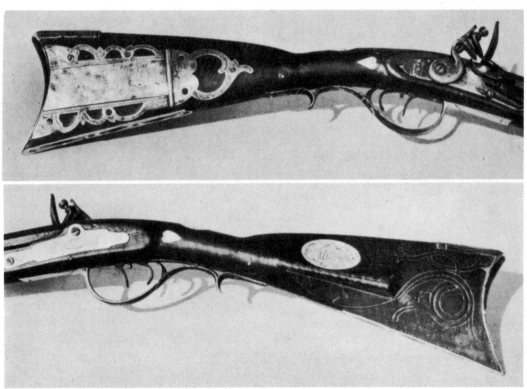

PLATE 246

Rifle with flint lock, full stock of curly maple, set triggers, brass mountings, silver inlays, octagonal barrel 44 inches long with J. Mewhirter engraved in script letters on the top facet of the barrel.

The bow of the trigger guard is unusually large on this rifle and the figure of an Indian engraved on the lid of the patch box is probably unique. It should be noted that there are seven piercings in the patch box and three in the toe plate.

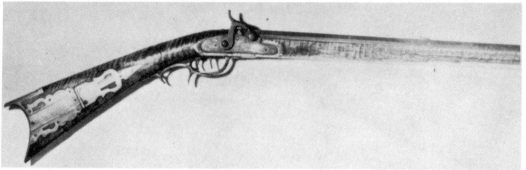

M. T. Stewart

PLATE 247

Rifle with percussion lock, curly maple stock, plain brass mountings, set triggers, and octagonal barrel 38 inches long. J. Mier, Somerset, is engraved in script letters on the top facet of the barrel.

METZGAR, JACOB

Jacob Metzgar probably worked in Lancaster County, Pennsylvania, before he moved to Frederick County, Maryland. The following indenture is recorded in the Court House in Frederick, Maryland.

> This indenture made the fifteenth day of January in the year of our Lord, one thousand seven hundred and eighty-eight, between Jacob Groff of Frederick-town and Jacob Metzgar of the town and county aforesaid, gunsmith, of the other part etc. . . .

Although the Metzgar rifles are very rare, a number are known which are reasonably early and lack the "finesse" of the later makers. One rifle that has survived was probably made in Lancaster and the balance in Frederick.

MEWHIRTER, WILLIAM

Shippensburg Township, Cumberland County, Pennsylvania. Tax lists 1811, 1814, 1828.

MICHLIN, EDWARD

Halifax, Dauphin County, Pennsylvania. Tax list 1817.

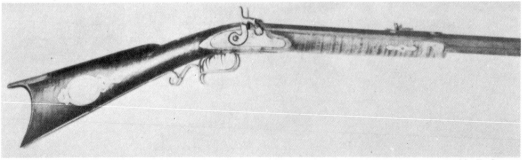

M. T. Stewart

PLATE 248

Rifle with percussion lock, curly maple half stock, brass mountings, set triggers, silver inlays, octagonal barrel 36 inches long with Sam. Meir on top facet of the barrel. The ferrule on the forestock is made of pewter, as many were on half-stocked guns. The trigger guard suggests late nineteenth century production.

While Meir's shop was in Somerset, it was located on Main Street.

MIERS, JACOB

Somerset, Pennsylvania. b. 1793. d. 1873. Tax lists 1822, 1825, 1832, 1837, 1844, 1849, 1850, 1851, 1852, 1853, 1861, 1867.

MIERS, JOHN

Somerset, Pennsylvania. b. 1829. d. June 14, 1909.

MEIR, SAMUEL

Elk Lick Township, Somerset County, Pennsylvania. Tax list 1852, 1859, 1861.
Somerset Borough, Somerset County, Pennsylvania. Tax list 1853.
Salisbury Borough, Somerset County, Pennsylvania. Tax list 1863, 1867, 1872.

MIERS, WILLIAM B.

Somerset, Pennsylvania. b. 1829. d. June 14, 1909.

MILES, JOHN

Gun and Pistol Manufactory, No. 500 North Second Street, ...
Where Merchants, Captains of vessels, and others may be supplied with all sorts of small arms, on the lowest terms and shortest notice.

Also, Organ Guns on a new construction, with three to twelve barrels each, being simple and quick to load, and of utility, surpassing anything of the kind ever made—Specimens of which may be seen as the above manufactory.

John Miles.

Pennsylvania Packet (Claypoole's American Daily Advertiser) no. 5945. April 26, 1798.

MILLER, DAVID

George Township, Fayette County, Pennsylvania. Tax lists 1802, 1803, 1804, 1805, 1806, 1808, 1810.

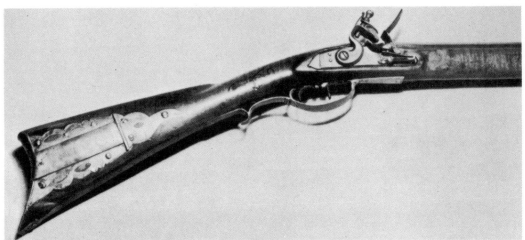

John Fonderwhite

PLATE 249

Rifle with flint lock, full stock of curly maple, brass mountings, octagonal barrel with G. Miller engraved in script letters on the top facet.

The finial of the patch box in the shape of a snake's head is the most outstanding quality of this rifle. Another Lancaster maker named Holtzworth used a patch box that was similar to this one. The products of G. Miller are very rare.

PLATE 250

The business ledger of the Lancaster merchant, William McCord, indicates that John Miller was a gunsmith in the Lancaster area in 1766.

MILLER, GEORGE (Gunsmith With His Father)
Lancaster, Pennsylvania. Tax list 1803.

MILLER, GEORGE
Columbia County, Pennsylvania. Tax list 1821.

MILLER, HENRY (Freeman)
Lancaster, Pennsylvania. Tax list 1840.

MILLER, JOHN
Lancaster, Pennsylvania. Tax list 1771.

MILLER, SAMUEL
Swatara Township, Lebanon County, Pennsylvania. Tax lists 1823, 1829, 1838, 1842, 1844, 1846, 1849.

MILLER, WILLIAM T.
Danville, Montour County, Pennsylvania. 1861.

MILLERON, D.
Smicksburg, Indiana County, Pennsylvania. 1861.

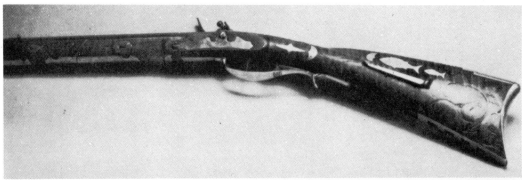

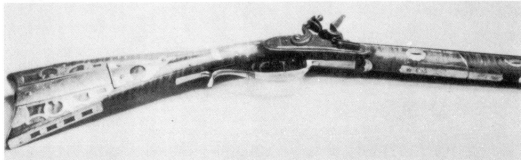

H. L. Murray, Jr.

PLATE 251

Rifle with flint lock, curly maple stock with "take down" feature, brass mountings, silver inlays, octagonal barrel 43 inches long with S. Miller engraved in script letters on top facet of barrel. The piercings in the side plates of the patch box and the toe-plate are attractive features of this rifle. The fish inlays on the cheek side of the rifle are a traditional Christian symbol. They are found on the walls of the catacombs near Rome.

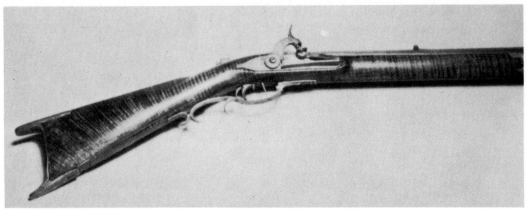

PLATE 252

Rifle with percussion lock, brass mountings, curly maple full stock, octagonal barrel with J. Mills on the top facet. This gun has a stock of fine curly maple and a butt plate that is a late replacement. The location of the main spring on the exterior of the lock plate permitted a small mortise for the lock and provided increased strength where most rifles are usually weak.

MILLS, JOSEPH

Colerain Township, Bedford County, Pennsylvania. Tax list 1821.

Mills made guns of good quality. Some are carved with patterns in relief and some have inlays of silver.

MILLIRON, ANTHONY

Conemaugh Township, Indiana County, Pennsylvania. Tax lists 1805, 1806.

MILLIRON, DAVID

West Mahoning Township, Indiana County, Pennsylvania. Tax lists 1850, 1851.

MILLIRON, JOHN

Hempfield Township, Westmoreland County, Pennsylvania. Tax lists 1802, 1805, 1807, 1808, 1809.

MILNOR, ISAAC

Five Norris Alley, Philadelphia, Pennsylvania. *New Directory of Trade in Philadelphia*, 1800.

MING, WOLERE (Military Articles)

All sorts of Military Articles, such as Cartouche-Boxes, Morocco and other Sword belts, scabbards, Pistol Holders, Rangers Pouches, etc., all made on the best construction by

Wolere Ming

In Market Street 10 doors above the Gaol, where the Military Gentlemen from town or country, may be supplied on the most reasonable terms, and on the shortest notice.

Pennsylvania Gazette, (Philadelphia) Supp. to June 14, 1775, No. 2425.

MITCHELL, JOSEPH

Montgomery, Lycoming County, Pennsylvania. 1861.

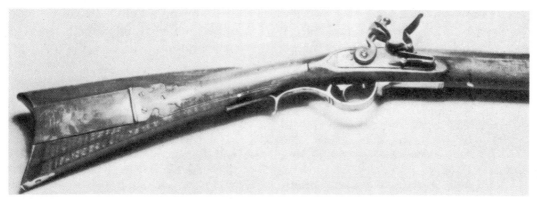

PLATE 253   *Lloyd Nolt*

Rifle with flint lock, full stock of curly maple, brass mountings, octagonal barrel 44 inches long marked John Moll on the top facet of the barrel.

Although this rifle was probably made in the first quarter of the nineteenth century, the design of its two-piece patch box resembles a pattern used at a much earlier time in Northampton County.

MOLL

One of the elusive but productive families of gunsmiths to work in Pennsylvania was the Molls, who lived in Northampton and Lehigh Counties. The data about them has been kindly supplied by Earl S. Heffner, Jr., who wrote a biographical account of the family several years ago. The author has selected only the facts that seem pertinent and important to their gunsmithing activity.

John Moll was doubtless the first significant gunsmith of the group and his name appears for the first time in the tax assessment list for Northampton in 1764. This list includes the names of twenty-eight taxables, an increase of twelve persons over the previous year. On April 28, 1772, John Moll married Lydia Rinker and in the same year he first is recorded as a gunsmith in the *Manuscript History of Northampton County* by Matthew S. Henry. A deed, dated March 17, 1773, tells that John Moll bought a piece of land "containing in bredth on Allen Street (now North Seventh Street in Allentown) sixty feet and depth two hundred and thirty feet in Northampton Town, to hold to him the said John Moll and his assigns forever under the yearly ground rent of Nine Shillings Sterling Money of Great Britian to the Chiefe or Lords of the fee thereof." This property remained a possession of the Moll family for more than a hundred years.

PLATE 254   *Clegg Collection*

Rifle with flint lock (now percussion), full stock of curly maple, brass mountings, octagonal barrel with Peter Moll, Hellertown, engraved on the top facet of the barrel.

It is evident that John Moll was an established gunsmith before the Revolution. On June 8, 1778, Allentown had only three hundred and fifty inhabitants, most of whom took the oath of allegiance. John Moll was among those who took the following oath:

> "I do swear and affirm that I will renounce and refuse all allegiance to George the Third, King of Great Britain, his heirs and successors; and that I will be faithful and bear true allegiance to the Commonwealth of Pennsylvania, as a free and independent state, and that I will not at any time do or cause to be done any matter or thing that will be prejudicial or injurious to the freedom and independence thereof as declared by Congress; and also that I will discover and make known to some Justice of the Peace of said State all treason or traitorous conspiracies which I now know or hereafter shall know to be formed against this or any of the United States of America."

Moll further committed himself to the welfare of his country by becoming a member of the Northampton County Militia; he was never called to duty, however, because his services were utilized in the gun repair shops that were established in Allentown. From October 15, 1777, to December 4, 1777, the factory received the following to repair: 7 pistols, 810 muskets, 847 bayonets, 360 scabbards, 36 rifles, and 25 gun barrels. In the period between October 15, 1777, and June, 1779, the following arms were shipped out from the Allentown shop: 7 pistols, 2 blunderbusses, 2961 muskets, and barrels, 2522 bayonets, 685 scabbards, 83 rifles and 5 carbines.

After the Revolution John Moll apparently prospered; and at his death in 1794, in addition to a stock of tools and the property in Allentown, he left quite a bit of property in South Whitehall and Heidelberg Townships. The intestate inventory of his tools follows:

100 rifle stocks.	1 hand vize.
18 riffle locks.	32 different chisels and gouges.
1 new riffle.	8 moule augers.
1 smooth riffle.	5 different planes.
1 riffle barrel and stock.	13 cut files.
1 new riffle.	3 hammers.
1 smith bellows.	2 pinchers and 1 plyer.
1 anvil.	1 polish steel plyer.
1 anvil.	1 breech pin iron.
1 large smith hammer.	1 brace and Bitts.
7 smith hammers.	2 saws.
3 smith tongs.	2 dressing knives.
2 setts riffle.	1 grindstone.
3 iron augers.	1 scale and weights.
13 riffle augers.	5 tt Old brass.
2 screw plates and pins.	5 tt Sheet brass.
1 bench vize.	4 rifle augers.
1 bench vize.	25 files and rasps.

Also one rifle which was forgot in the inventory.

At the final settlement his estate amounted to three hundred ninety-four pounds, 15 shillings and nine pence. Lydia Moll received one-third of the estate, as prescribed by Pennsylvania law.

John Moll had three sons, John II, born May 13, 1773, John J., who was born in 1776, and Peter Moll, whose birthdate is not known. At the time of his death only John II and Peter were mentioned, although it is believed that John J. was also living at the time. Peter did not become a gunsmith and answered the call to arms in the War of 1812. He survived the war and returned to Allentown where he became wealthy and died many years later.

John Moll II married the daughter of an old and influential resident of the area, named Laurence Newhardt. From this union John III, Jacob, and Peter Moll were born. John was born on November 13, 1796, and Peter was born October 13, 1799. John Moll II carried on his father's business in Allentown; and on April 11, 1820, John Moll II sold the business to his son John Moll III. The document of the sale is recorded in the Lehigh County Courthouse. It is as follows:

> Know all men by these presents that I John Moll of the Borough of Northampton in the County of Lehigh in the state of Pennsylvania, gunsmith, for and in consideration of the sum of one hundred and five dollars lawfull money of the United States to me in hand paid by my son John Moll junior of the same place gunsmith, at and before the ensealing and delivery of these presents, the receipt whereof is hereby acknowledged have bargained, sold and delivered and by these presents do grant bargain sell and deliver unto the said John Moll junior three bench kies, one Grindstone, and boring machine, two screw plates, Cut Bench and two iron bars thereunto belonging twenty-two maple blocks and thirty stocks for riffles fifteen Riffle Augers, one Bellows Sixty-five bushels of Coals, one polishing machine two anvils, Seven hammers one Walnut chest one large copper kettle, two Hives of bees and all the apparatus belonging to sure foundry. To have and to hold all and Singular the Said premises unto the said John Moll, his Executors, Administrators, and Assigns.
>
> Said in the presence of John Horn and Philip Brong.

John Moll III maintained interest in the firm until 1883. In addition to his gun business, he was interested in local politics, and in 1844 was elected to the City Council of Allentown. By 1860 John III had taken his son William H. into the business; they had joint interest in it until John III's death on August 24, 1883. The inventory of his estate listed one-half interest in the business of J. and W. H. Moll, which was valued at eighteen dollars. The property on North Seventh Street was valued at seven thousand five hundred dollars. This property was sold by the executor of the estate.

Peter Moll of Hellertown was the son of John Moll II and the brother of John Moll III. It is thought that Peter started the business in Hellertown about the time that his brother bought their father's business in Allentown. In 1820 Hellertown had thirteen houses, eighteen families, three taverns, two stores, one grist mill, and seventy-three inhabitants. On December 5, 1829, Peter Moll bought a property for one hundred fifteen dollars in Hellertown from Christian Shafer.

Although David Moll is known to have married Elizabeth Weber of Hellertown in 1835, the starting date of the partnership with Peter is not known nor has their relationship been established; although it is thought that David was a cousin or a nephew of Peter. The partnership of Peter and David Moll was dissolved with the death of David on August 31, 1853.

After the death of David, the business became the property of William and Edwin Moll, sons of Peter. Upon the death of William Moll, the business passed to Edwin and David Moll. Nathan Moll was also connected with the business but in what capacity has not been ascertained. The latter owners dealt only in dry goods and groceries.

After the Molls went into the dry goods business and Nathan Moll left for the West, John J. Moll, a grandson of Peter, repaired guns as a sideline until the early 1900's in Hellertown.

Although the products of John Moll I are extremely rare, the writer has seen two rifles that were of fine workmanship. The over-and-under with swivel barrels and a flintlock is one of the few guns of this type that have survived. This gun was obviously made in the Golden Age of gun making in Pennsylvania and its workmanship is in the fine tradition of the craft. A rifle of comparable quality with one barrel was in a Northampton County collection some years ago; however, its location is unknown today.

The rifles of John Moll II are found in many collections but most of them are of average quality. They usually have a two-piece patch box, which may be either engraved or plain. The trigger guards are quite wide and the bottom ramrod pipe often has an unusually wide or long portion overlapping the stock. Many of his guns are made with stocks of plain maple having a reddish finish, which some collectors call a "violin finish."

It is difficult to differentiate between the products of John II and those of John III. A number of Moll rifles are dated. The long guns of P. and D. Moll resemble those of John Moll II and III; However, these men are very famous for their pistols with brass barrels, which are marked "P. and D. Moll, Hellertown," on the top facet of the barrel. The stocks of these pistols frequently have the so-called "violin finish."

MOORE, J. T.
New Freeport, Greene County, Pennsylvania. 1876.

MOORE, HENSZEY, & CO.
427 Market & 416 Commerce, Philadelphia, Pennsylvania. 1861.

MOORE, JAMES
James near Front, Chester, Delaware County, Pennsylvania. 1861.

MOORE, JOHN
Clearfield, Clearfield County, Pennsylvania. 1861.

MORE, WILLIAM (Lived With J. Stodenour)
Colerain Township, Bedford County, Pennsylvania. Tax list 1855.
He is known to have made one double barrel, full-stock gun without a patch box.

MORGAN, JOSEPH

225 North Third Street, Philadelphia, Pennsylvania. *New Trade Directory of Philadelphia,* 1800.

MORGAN, PHILLAMON

Springhill Township, Fayette County, Pennsylvania. Tax list 1818, 1819, 1820, 1822.

MORGAN, GEORGE (Gunsmith)

Philadelphia, August 20, 1776.

Wanted, a Quantity of white Wampum; also a Gunsmith to work by the Year, or as may be agreed on. Apply to the Committee on Congress for Indian Affairs, or to George Morgan, Arch-street. *Pennsylvania Gazette* (Philadelphia) no. 2487, August 21, 1776.

MORRIS, JOHN (Gun-Flint Cutter)

To the Society of Gentlemen, for the Encouragement of Arts, in the different Provinces of North America.

John Morris, Gun-Flint Cutter to His Majesty's Board of Ordnance, in the Kingdom of Ireland, is willing to come and establish that Branch in any of his Majesty's Colonies or Plantations in America, if properly encouraged, for establishing such a useful Branch, whereupon depends the Safety and Protection of his Majesty's Royal Person, His Dominions and Subjects in general. It has always been my Study to propagate such useful Arts, as tend to the Public Good. Therefore, I earnestly entreat your Consideration on this Branch. Likewise the Art of Mines, Minerals, and Mineral Waters, and refining Lead and Copper.

I am, Gentlemen,

A Friend to Liberty and Freedom.

John Morris.

N.B. Please to send your Proposals to me, at William Gun's, Esq.; in Peter Street, Dublin.

Pennsylvania Chronicle, no. 67, April 25, 1768, page 103.

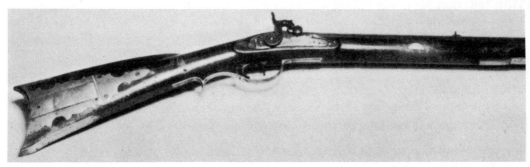

Benson McDowell

PLATE 255

Rifle with flint lock (now percussion), full stock of maple, brass mountings, silver inlays, set triggers, octagonal barrel 44 inches long with A. Morrison engraved in block letters on the top facet of the barrel.

MORRISON, SAMUEL
     Milton Borough, Northumberland County, Pennsylvania. Tax lists 1826, 1829, 1832, 1833, 1838, 1840, 1841, 1843.

MORROW, ABRAHAM
     Abraham Morrow, Gunsmith, Returns his most grateful acknowledgments to those Gentlemen who have heretofore favoured him with their commands—He begs leave to inform the Public, and his Friends in particular, that he has commenced Business again at No. 50, South Third Street, between Chestnut and Walnut streets—Where he intends carrying on the Rifle, Fowling-Piece, Duck-Gun, and Pistol Manufactory in all its Branches. Those Gentlemen who please to honour him with their Commands, will be attended to with Punctuality and Dispatch.
     Philadelphia, July 11.
     N.B. An Apprentice Wanted.
     Pennsylvania Packet (Dunlap's American Daily Advertiser) no. 3887, July 12, 1791.

MORTON, DAVID
     South Huntington Township, Westmoreland County, Pennsylvania. Tax lists 1811-1823.

MOSES, ELIJAH
     George Township, Fayette County, Pennsylvania. Tax lists 1802, 1803.

MOST, HENRY (Gun Stocker)
     146 St. John Street, Philadelphia, Pennsylvania. 1814.

MOYER, DANIEL
     Kimberton, Chester County, Pennsylvania. 1861.

MULL (MOLL), JOHN
     Easton, Northampton County, Pennsylvania. Tax list 1787.

MULL, HENRY
     Lancaster, Pennsylvania. 1740-1751.
     A deed recorded in the Lancaster County Court House, Book C, page 251, dated 1751, tells that Mull was selling a tract of land which he had previously bought from James Hamilton in 1740.

MULL, HENRY, SR.
     Huntington Township, York County, Pennsylvania. Tax list 1783.

MULL, LUDWIG
     Huntington Township, York County, Pennsylvania. Tax list 1797.
     Huntington Township, Adams County, Pennsylvania. Tax list 1799.

MUNSON, H. (Gunsmith and Letter Cutter)
     Corner Second and Liberty, Pittsburgh, Pennsylvania. 1847.

MURROW, ABRAM
     Philadelphia, Pennsylvania. National Census of 1790.

MURPHY, JOSEPH

Washington, Pennsylvania.

Advertisement in *The Washington Examiner*, April 21, 1849.

REMOVAL. The subscriber would most respectfully inform his old friends and the public in general, that he has removed his shop to the East of Main Street on Chestunt, and nearly opposite the Mansion House, where he is prepared to manufacture GUNS of all kinds, from the finest to the plainest finish. All kinds of GUN and PISTOL REPAIRING done with neatness and dispatch.

I will pay the highest price for good curled Maple or Sugar Tree plank, from 1¾" to 2" in thickness, if brought soon.

JOSEPH MURPHY

Wanted—An apprentice to the above business from 15 to 17 years of age; one from the Country will be preferred. April 21, 1849.

MUSSMAN, FRANK

Fifth Extension Tunnel. *Directory of Pittsburgh and Allegheny Cities*, 1866-67.

MYER, PHILIP

130 Fulton Street, Pittsburgh, Pennsylvania. 1850.

MYERS, DANIEL

Washington Borough, Pennsylvania. 1847.

The subscriber respectfully informs his friends and the public in general, that he has secured the services of Mr. John Wehli (formerly Gunsmith in this place) and has just opened a Gun Manufactory on Front Street in the borough of Washington, Lancaster County. He constantly keeps on hand, and makes to order, Guns, Rifles, Pistols, etc.

Repairing done at the shortest notice and in the neatest manner, at the lowest price for cash.

Daniel Myers.

Washington, June 19, 1847.
Columbia Spy, July 17, 1847.

MYERS, GEORGE S.

Apple Grove, York County, Pennsylvania. 1861.

MILITARY STORES, AND PATENT SPUNGE MANUFACTORY.

At No. 14 Chestnut Street, Philadelphia:

There may be had all kinds of Military Stores for the use of Armed Vessels, as cheap as at any other stores in Philadelphia:

Rammers and patent Spunges of all sizes ready covered.

Copper Gun Ladles and Worms for every Bore.

Gunner's Handspikes, plain or shod.

Best salt petre'd Match Rope.

Cannon Priming Horns with Screw Bottoms.

Cannon Priming Wires, Augars and Bitts

Lint-Stocks and portfire stocks ready fitted.

Stolls for Grape Shot, of all sizes.

Cannon Cartridges ready made to every bore.

Gun Aprons.

Cannon and Musket Cartridge Boxes.

Tompions and port Taugles.

Patent covering for Spunges of all sizes.

Musket and cannon Cartridge Paper.

Musket and cannon Powder and Flints.

Magazine, Side, and other Lanthorns.

Boarding Pikes and Cutlasses.

Musket and Pistol Ball and Cartridges with buck shot either empty or filled.

Round, Grape, Cannister, Bar Shot, and Langride, either loose or quilted.

Sky Rockets for Signals, and Fire Arrows.

Hand-cuffs and Leg Shackles.

Port-fire, slow fire and quick match.

Drums, fifes, Powder Cannisters, &c &c.

Signal and other Colours, for shipping of every denomination.

Any Commanders of Vessels, or otherwise, by calling at the above Manufactory, may be furnished with a stated list of the prices of the above military stores, and furnished with any quantity at a few days' notice, as completely as if they themselves were present.

Lead, or Military Stores of any kind, bought at the above Store.

Cannon may be proved for any Merchant, master of vessel, & etc., at a few days' notice, by applying as above.

The proprietors forbear to comment in any way on the utility of the Spunge manufactured by them, as the long and undeniable encouragement it has had from the Board of Admiralty in London, and the generous approbation and encouragement it has met with from the separate Departments of the War and Navy Office in this City, and of armed vessels, induces them to hope for liberal support in their present undertaking.

Federal (Philadelphia) Gazette, no. 3060, August 4, 1798.

NAILER, JAMES

Hempfield Township, Westmoreland County, Pennsylvania. Tax lists 1811, 1812.

NAUMAN, JACOB

Lancaster, Pennsylvania. Tax lists 1800, 1807, 1812, 1813, 1816, 1822.

Nauman is listed as a freeman in the tax assessment lists of 1800, 1807, and 1812, although the assessor wrote married after the 1812 entry. He probably worked most of his life for other gunsmiths, for no guns bearing his name are known in the Lancaster area.

NEEPER, JOHN

Lemoyne Township, Cumberland County, Pennsylvania. Census list 1800.

NEIHARD, PETER

Whitehall Township, Lehigh County, Pennsylvania. Tax list 1786. *Pennsylvania Archives,* 3d series, Vol. 21.

NELSON, ROBERT (Powder Mill)
Antis Township, Huntingdon County, Pennsylvania. 1832.

NETH, JACOB
West Newton, Westmoreland County, Pennsylvania. 1861.

NEVINS, JOHN G.
Buckhorn, Columbia County, Pennsylvania. 1861.

NEWBECKER, PHILIP
Philip Newbecker is listed as a gunsmith in the 1817 tax assessment list for Halifax, Dauphin County. The writer has seen one nice rifle with a 42 to 44 inch barrel. It had little to distinguish it as a product of a Dauphin County gunsmith, but it was nicely balanced and of average workmanship.

NEWCOMER, JOHN
Hempfield Township, Lancaster County, Pennsylvania. Tax list 1788. *Pennsylvania Archives,* 3d series, Vol. 17, page 118.

NEWCOMER, JOHN
Hellam Township, York County, Pennsylvania. Census list 1807.
There probably were two John Newcomers. The senior John Newcomer lived and died in Lancaster County. The John Newcomer who lived in Hellam Township was probably a son.

NEW HART, PETER
North Whitehall Township, Lehigh County, Pennsylvania. Tax list 1821.

NEYHARD, PETER
Whitehall Township, Northampton County, Pennsylvania. Tax lists 1787, 1793.

NICHOLSON, JOHN
To be sold by John Nicholson, Gunsmith, in Front Street near the Drawbridge, a Few Long Duck Guns, Suitable for Shallop Men, etc. *Pennsylvania Journal,* October 17, 1781.

For Sale, at John Nicholson's, Gunsmith, near the Drawbridge, a number of Small Arms for Shipping, such as Muskets, short ditto for tops and close quarters, Blunderbusses with or without swivels, Pistols with ribs or without, Cutlasses, etc., upon the most reasonable terms. *Pennsylvania Journal,* November 24, 1781.

The subscribers work shop in Water Street, was broke open on Tuesday night last, and the following things stolen, viz. one pair new holster pistols, about 10 inches in the barrel, square in the butt, brass mounted with—faced caps; one other pair of round barrel ditto; a drab coloured cloth great coat. *Independent Gazeteer,* September 27, 1783.

Death Notice. Pennsylvania Packet (*Claypoole's American Daily Advertiser*) February 7, 1799.

The friends of the late John Nicholson, and the public in general are informed, that the business will in the future, be carried on by R. B. Nicholson, at the usual place. *Federal (Philadelphia) Gazette*, March 11, 1799.

Notice of his death. *Federal (Philadelphia) Gazette*, no. 3217, February 6, 1799. Adv. of his estate.

NIPES, ABRAM

Longswamp Township, Berks County, Pennsylvania. Census report 1800.

NIPPES, ABRAHAM

130 Dillwyn Street, Philadelphia, Pennsylvania. 1847, 1855.

NIPPES, WILLIAM

254 St. John Street, Philadelphia, Pennsylvania. 1814.

NOBLE, JOHN

Claysville, Washington County, Pennsylvania. 1861.

NOBLE AND LITTLE (Gun Barrel Factory)

Mulberry and Allegheny. *Directory of 1856-57, of Pittsburgh and Allegheny Cities.*

NOLL, JOHN

Washington Township, Franklin County, Pennsylvania. Tax lists 1800-1820.

NOLL, HENRY

Washington Township, Franklin County, Pennsylvania. Tax list 1842.

NORMAN, JOHN

Springfield, Bradford County, Pennsylvania. 1861.

NULL, NATHAN

Seller's Tavern, Bucks County, Pennsylvania. 1861.

OAKS, SAMUEL

A list of letters remaining in the post office Pittsburgh, August 1st, 1793. Samuel Oaks, Gunsmith, Fort Washington, Pennsylvania.

OLDEN, LEIGH

Main below Seventh, Carbondale, Luzerne County, Pennsylvania. 1861.

OLDHAM, THOMAS, JR.

St. Claire Township, Bedford County, Pennsylvania. Tax list 1847.

Oldham is recognized as a maker of fine double barrel guns with full length stocks. He used a unique and nicely proportioned lock on his guns. For a time he was in partnership with Jacob Breigle.

OLENHOUSEN, JACOB

Avenue near Dinwiddie, Pittsburgh, Pennsylvania.

O'NEIL, J. PALMER

66 Fifth Avenue. *J. F. Diffenbacher's Directory of Pittsburgh and Allegheny Cities* for 1885.

OPPELT, EDWIN A.

Clarion Borough, Clarion County, Pennsylvania. Tax lists 1842, 1844, 1845, 1847.

ORTON, JOHN

A New Brick House near to Mulberry Street (commonly called the Arch Street) also a new Cart and Team of Horses, and a Negroe Man, to be Sold by John Orton, Gunsmith, in the Front Street, Philadelphia. *American Weekly Mercury*, no. 308, November 4-11, 1725.

ORWIN, JOHN

Carlisle, Pennsylvania. Tax list 1793-1800.

OVERDORF, JOHN

Brush Valley, Indiana County, Pennsylvania. 1861.

PAINTER, JACOB

Allegheny Township, Somerset County, Pennsylvania. Tax lists 1805, 1806.

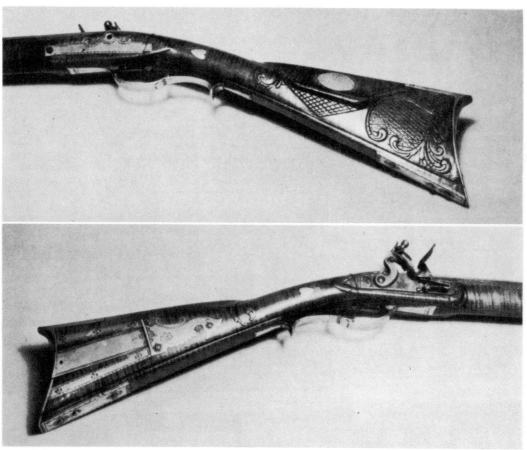

Carl Pippert

PLATE 256

Rifle with flint lock, brass mountings, full stock of curly maple, silver inlays, octagonal barrel marked H. Noll. Henry Noll worked in Franklin County and is thought to have been a son of John Noll. The engraved brass mountings are well done on this rifle and the crosshatching in the carved portions is similar to work done by other gunsmiths in Franklin County.

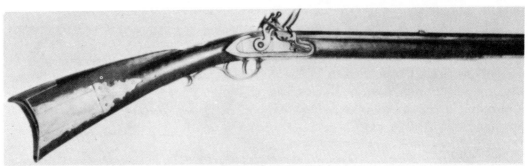

Clegg Collection

PLATE 257

Rifle with flint lock, full stock of curly maple, brass mountings, octagonal barrel with J. Palm on the top facet of the barrel.

PALM, JOHN

Womelsdorf, Berks County, Pennsylvania. United States Census 1850. Business Directory 1860.

PALMER, STEPHEN

Franklin La., Philadelphia, Pennsylvania. 1855.

PLATE 258

Advertisement of Thomas Palmer in a Philadelphia newspaper in 1773. It should be noted that he tells that, "he likewise makes Fowling pieces, of different sizes, such as have been approved of by Gentlemen of this City." It must be presumed from his use of the word "Likewise" that he also made the rifles which are mentioned in the beginning of the advertisement.

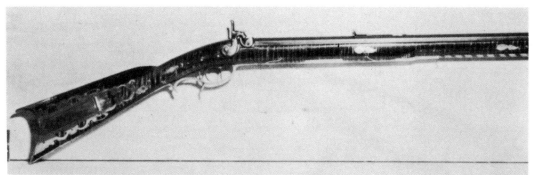

Lloyd D. Norris

PLATE 259

Rifle with percussion lock, full stock of curly maple, brass mountings, silver inlays, set triggers, octagonal barrel 41½ inches long with E. L. Pancoast on the top facet of the barrel.

This rifle is the product of an excellent gunsmith and is in "mint" condition today. The silver inlays make a pleasing contrast with the dark-brown color of the maple stock. Wire inlays are rare in any Pennsylvania rifle, but they are particularly rare in a rifle made in the late period in which this one was made.

PALMER, THEO. (Gunsmith)

Theo. Palmer takes this method to acquaint his Friends and the Public, that he has returned to his former Business, in Market Street, above Fifth Street, in Philadelphia where all sorts of Guns, Pistols, etc., may be had, and repairs done in the most careful manner. He hopes his former customers will favour him with their commands.

N.B. A few Ships Musquets, Pistols, etc., for sale. *Pennsylvania Gazette,* March 27, 1782, No. 2702.

PALMER, THOMAS (Gunsmith)

Adv. for runaway servants, one named Nicholas Linch, brassfounder, One Samuel Bird, upholsterer, one William Sprage, shoemaker. *Pennsylvania Journal,* no. 1700, July 5, 1775.

PANCOAST,

Elizabeth, Allegheny County, Pennsylvania. 1861.

PANNABECKER

It is evident from the census lists, the tax assessment lists, and the deeds in the Lancaster County Court House that Daniel Pannabecker was the first member of the family to be engaged in the business of making guns or gun barrels. Daniel Pannabecker is listed as a gunsmith in the Septennial Census of 1800 and he was living in Cumru Township, Berks County, Pennsylvania. The 1808 and 1809 tax assessment lists in the Lancaster County Court House name him as a resident in Brecknock Township, Lancaster County, but there is no mention of his trade in these lists. Sometime before 1825 he must have started in the business of making gun barrels, for in that year he sold most of his holdings (which include a boring mill and a Tilten (tilt) hammer to three men, probably his sons.

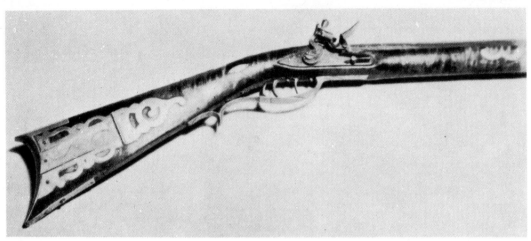

John Fonderwhite

PLATE 260
Rifle with flint lock, full stock of curly maple, brass mountings, silver inlays, octagonal barrel marked Wm. Paul on the top facet.

It is recorded that on September 26, 1825, Daniel Pannabecker sold to Daniel Pannabecker, Jr., five acres of land and half-interest in a boring mill and Tilten hammer, this being part of a larger tract of land which Daniel Pannabecker had previously bought from John and Mary Fry.

Also, on September 26, 1825, Daniel Pannabecker sold to Samuel Pannabecker, gunsmith, seven acres of land and one-half interest in a boring mill and Tilten hammer, this parcel being part of a larger tract which Daniel Pannabecker had previously bought from John and Mary Fry.

Finally on September 26, 1825, Daniel Pannabecker sold to John Pannabecker eight acres of land with its buildings, outbuildings, etc., this part being part of a larger tract of land which Daniel Pannabecker had previously acquired from John and Mary Fry.

It seems obvious that in one day Daniel Pannabecker, Sr., sold most of his possessions to his three sons and that the name and business would be continued by another generation of Pannabeckers.

Later tax assessment lists show that Samuel was a gunsmith in 1834 and in 1839. In the tax list of 1831 John Pannabecker was listed as a "Barlmaker" and in 1834 Jess Pannabecker was listed as a gunsmith. A business directory of 1861 lists Daniel and Jesse as gunsmiths.

Samuel seems to have been the most productive gunsmith of the group and is known to have made some guns with carved stocks of good quality. Most of his guns were made in the flintlock era. A gun is known that is signed J. Pannabecker, which was probably made by Jess, for John is not called a gunsmith.

The Pannabecker name is more famous for its barrels than for its guns. The name is frequently stamped in block letter on one of the side facets or the bottom of the gun barrels. The following advertisement from The (Pittsburgh) *Daily*

Advocate & Advertiser of October 19, 1838, tells of a Pittsburgh merchant who sold Pannabecker barrels:

> TO GUNSMITHS. For Sale, 50 doz. Rifle Barrels, at the reduced price of $30.00 per dozen. Also materials, gun mountings, gun locks and all articles used by gun manufacturers, of all qualities and at lower prices than they can be had at any other establishment in the city. Constantly on hand an assortment of Pannabecker's superior rifle barrels, powder and shot etc. W. H. Brown, Gunsmith, 5th St., one door from Market.

PARK, JOHN
Henderson Township, Huntington County, Pennsylvania. Census list 1821.

PARKS, JOHN
Selinsgrove, Snyder County, Pennsylvania. 1861.

PATTERSON, JACOB
Harrisville, Butler County, Pennsylvania. 1861.

PATTERSON, SAMUEL J.
Rebecca b Bank & Tremont, Allegheny, Pennsylvania. 1858-59.

PAUL, JAMES
Horsham Township, Montgomery County, Pennsylvania. Census report 1800.

PAUL, WILLIAM
Summerhill Township, Cambria County, Pennsylvania. Tax list 1852.

PELOUX, PETER (Armourer)
Gray's R. near Arsenal. 1814.
31 South Street, Philadelphia, Pennsylvania. 1855.

PENNEL, JOSHUA
Southampton Township, Bedford County, Pennsylvania. Tax list 1844.
Guns by Pennel are very rare. He was an average craftsman and used the typical hand-made lock of Bedford County.

PENNYPACKER, WILLIAM
Knauers, Pennsylvania. 1860.

PERKINS, JOSEPH
Philadelphia, Pennsylvania. Tax list 1783. *Pennsylvania Archives*, 3 series, Vol. 16, page 740.

PERKIN AND COUTTY
Perkin and Coutty at the corner of Second and Spruce-streets, Philadelphia, beg leave to acquaint their Friends, and the Public in general that they carry on the Gun and Pistol making in all its branches, where gentlemen may be supplied with Guns and Pistols of the neatest and best quality, on the shortest notice and most reasonable terms.

They also blue and brown Gun Barrels in the neatest manner.
N.B. A small quantity of Ship Musquets to sell.
Pennsylvania Gazette, May 2, 1781, No. 2655-61.

Park Emery

PLATE 261

Rifle with flint lock, full stock of curly maple, brass mountings, set triggers, octagonal barrel marked D. Pollock. The pattern of the patch box on this rifle was used by other gunsmiths in western Pennsylvania in the late flint and early percussion periods.

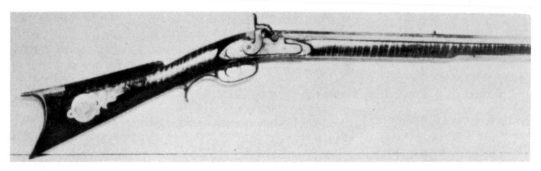

PLATE 262

Rifle with percussion lock, curly maple stock, brass mountings, set triggers, octagonal 38 inch barrel with S. Post on top facet of barrel.

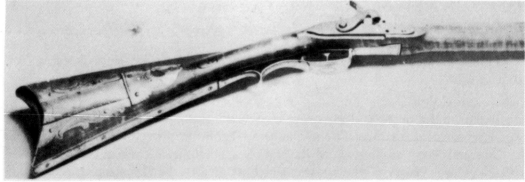

Reaves Goehring

PLATE 263

Rifle with percussion lock (originally flint), octagon-to-round barrel, with H. Albright engraved in script letters on the top facet of the barrel. Stock of curly maple with brass mountings. The horse-head finial on the patch box is a particularly attractive asset of this rifle. The toeplate reaching from the butt plate to the trigger guard is also an uncommon and attractive feature.

J. T. Herron

PLATE 264

This picture of Post with one of the rifles he made was taken a few years before his death. He was one of the last "old timers" to work in western Pennsylvania.

PERREIN, D.

18 Spruce Street, Philadelphia, Pennsylvania. *New Trade Directory for Philadelphia,* 1800.

PETERMAN, ABRAHAM

24 John Street, Philadelphia, Pennsylvania. 1855.

PHARRES, WILLIAM
Brodheadsville, Monroe County, Pennsylvania. 1861.

PHILIPEE, JACOB
Heidelberg Township, Lebanon County, Pennsylvania. Tax list 1842.

PHILLIPPI, DANIEL
Sunbury, Pennsylvania. Tax list 1826.

PICKEL, HENRY
Henry Pickel's name appears in a tax assessment list for York, Pennsylvania, in 1793, although he is listed only as a resident single man without an occupation. He is listed as a gunsmith in the York tax assessment lists for 1795, 1800, and 1804. He is listed as one of the gunsmiths who suffered a loss when the boring mill burned in York in 1800, he is known to have made rifles for the United States Ordnance Department from 1805 to 1808. A description of the rifles and the prices paid for them are reproduced in *United States Ordnance* by Major James E. Hicks.

Only a few of Pickel's products are known to the writer; however, the rifle which is illustrated is one of the fine products of York County gunsmiths known to exist. An additional fowling piece is known, but it has no qualities that distinguish it from other similar guns of the period.

PLANK, WILLIAM
Greenwood Township, Columbia County, Pennsylvania. Tax list 1821.

PLANTS, CHRISTIAN
East Finley, Washington County, Pennsylvania. 1861.

POLLOCK, S. (Gunsmith)
New Castle, Pennsylvania. *Harris' Business Directory of Pittsburgh and Allegheny,* 1841.

POST, S. B.
Washington County, Pennsylvania.
Samuel B. Post was apprenticed to George W. Craft, on Craft Creek, Morris Township, Washington County, Pennsylvania. He was in business at Pleasant Grove, Pennsylvania, and made half-stock guns with parts which he bought in Pittsburgh; however, he rifled the barrels he used. The barrels are marked S. Post in script letters. He died in 1947.

PITTSBURGH FIREARMS CO.
66 Fifth Avenue, Pittsburgh, Pennsylvania. *J. F. Diffenbacher's Directory of Pittsburgh and Allegheny Cities* for 1885.

PRAHL, LEWIS (Armourer and Cutler)
465 North Second Street, Philadelphia, Pennsylvania. 1798.

PRICE, JOHN
Somerset Borough, Somerset County, Pennsylvania. Tax lists 1805, 1806.

PRICE, JOSEPH
 498 North Second Street, Philadelphia, Pennsylvania. *New Trade Directory of Philadelphia,* 1800.

PRINGLE, JOHN
 Cambria Township, Cambria County, Pennsylvania. Tax list 1838.

PROCTOR, WILLIAM
 German Township, Fayette County, Pennsylvania. Tax lists 1815, 1816.
 Menallen Township, Fayette County, Pennsylvania. Tax lists 1816, 1817, 1818, 1819.

QUICK, J. M.
 Laxawaxen, Pike County, Pennsylvania. 1861.

QUINN, KENNEDY
 420 Lynd, Philadelphia, Pennsylvania. 1861.

RAAF, JACOB
 Halifax, Dauphin County, Pennsylvania. Tax list 1820.

RANDALL, JOSEPH C.
 Philadelphia, Pennsylvania. 1861.

RANDOLPH, BENJAMIN
 Holster Pistols, Carbines, and Swords, for the lighthorse, are wanted immediately. Inquire of Benjamin Randolph, in Chestnut street. *Pennsylvania Evening Post (Philadelphia)* no. 347, May 3, 1777.
 (Same as above with who has a quantity of Sheet Iron for sale.) *Pennsylvania Evening Post (Philadelphia)* no. 348, May 6, 1777.

RANEY, STEPHEN
 Barre Township, Huntington County, Pennsylvania. 1809, 1813, 1815.

RAKER, CHARLES
 Bedford County, Pennsylvania. Tax list 1849.

RATE, JACOB
 White Deer, Lycoming County, Pennsylvania. 1861.

RATHFON, GEORGE
 Conestoga Township, Lancaster, Pennsylvania. Tax list 1780.

RATHVON,
 Although only a few Rathvon guns are known in the Lancaster area, the gunsmithing activities of Rathvon are interesting because he apparently was a failure as a gunsmith, and because the reasons for his failure are preserved in an unpublished biography by his son, Simmon Snyder Rathvon. Attention should be focused on the fact that because the man was working in an obscure river town in Lancaster County, most of his business would be in cheap guns or in repairs made quickly while a trader waited. If a man wanted a fine gun, he probably traveled the twelve

to fifteen miles to York or Lancaster, where the finest in the country at that time was immediately available.

The inadequacy of gun trade in the river towns is evident in the fact that John Gonter lived only a short time in Columbia before he moved to Reading, and Jacob Fordney tried the same site for a short time before he moved to Lancaster. It seems obvious that the movements of these two men and the failure of Rathvon that the best place to sell guns in the early nineteenth century was in established communities where a selection was guaranteed to prospective buyers. Rathvon might have survived had he moved, but he lacked the imagination, or horse sense, and he failed.

"My father learned the trade of Gunsmith with a Mr. Gumpf of the city of Lancaster and not a very long period after he was free he took a tour to the wild western country. This might have been about the year 1807 or 1808.
. . .

I do not know how long he remained there but about 1808 or 1809 he located in York, Pennsylvania, where he commenced the business of Gunsmithing, or perhaps worked as a journeyman for someone else.

My father with my mother and my infant sister left York and located at Marietta, Pennsylvania, on the first day of April, 1811 or 1812 where he again commenced the business of Gunsmithing, and was known throughout the neighborhood as the "Gunsmith of Marietta." He had the reputation of being a good artizan in iron and an honest man.

His business, however, was not lucrative, and he did not seem capable of adapting his facilities and his energies to any other calling. As the county improved and the forests were felled before the advances of the sturdy husbandmen and agriculturists; and as public opinion and public morals were undergoing a change, and so also shooting and hunting, prize shooting and gun exercises generally were in a great measure either abandoned or limited to a few. An there also ended my father's business. . . ."

RAUCH, BENJAMIN
     Germansville, Lehigh County, Pennsylvania. 1861.

RAZER (RASURE), JOHN
     German Township, Fayette County, Pennsylvania. Tax lists 1798, 1801, 1803, 1804—"Gone away."

READE, CHARLES
     Springhill Township, Fayette County, Pennsylvania. Tax list 1814.
     Washington Township, Fayette County, Pennsylvania. Tax list 1815.

REDACKER, WILLIAM
     Penn Township, Berks County, Pennsylvania. United States Census 1850.

REDUK, DAVID
     Annville Township, Dauphin County, Pennsylvania. Tax list 1800.

REED, CHARLES
     Washington Township, Fayette County, Pennsylvania. Tax lists 1816, 1819.

REED, SAMUEL
　　302 Apple (Kensington), Philadelphia, Pennsylvania. 1855.

REEDY, LEONARD
　　The name of Leonard Reedy is doubtless one of the most important ones to be added in recent years to the list of gun makers in Pennsylvania. The addition has been made through the combined efforts of several researchers who worked on the problem in their spare time for a number of years. Unfortunately, only the location where he worked in his later life is known and nothing is known about where he was born or learned his trade. Although Reedy worked in a frontier town, he certainly was not born nor had he learned his trade there.

　　The search for data about Reedy started when a very perceptive gun collector from Lancaster, Pennsylvania, spotted in the Fort Ticonderoga collection of arms a signed gun similar to a fine unsigned gun which he had in his collection. The designs of the patch box and the bas-relief carvings were very similar, so there was good reason to conclude that the two guns were made by the same craftsman. Although the signature was very difficult to see, close examination revealed the name, L. Ready. The published biographical data on gun makers included no such name, so the search was temporarily halted.

　　The physical characteristics of the guns suggested that they were made in Berks County, Pennsylvania, where the "Roman nose" type of butt design was used by

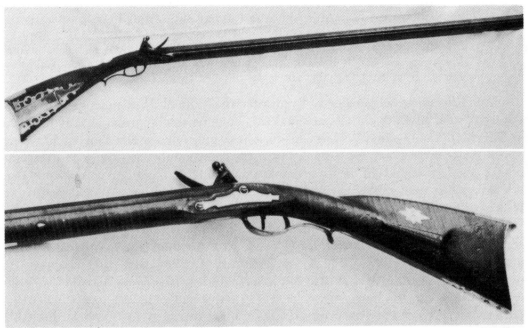

Lee Boyer

PLATE 265

　　Rifle with flint lock, full stock of curly maple, brass mountings, silver star on the cheek side of the butt, and an octagonal barrel 44 inches long with L. Reedy engraved in script letters on the top facet of the barrel.
　　A number of Reedy's rifle stocks are carved in bas-relief but on this one he used the incised technique. Although this rifle lacks some of the details of his fine products, its form and workmanship is evidence that Reedy was a fine craftsman. His products are very scarce and only a few are signed.

many gunsmiths. There were also two rivets in the patch box catch, which is a feature also used by Berks County gunsmiths. The Berks County hypothesis was partially substantiated by the discovery in the *Pennsylvania Archives* that a Leonard Reedy had served in the War of 1812 in the First Brigade, Pennsylvania Militia, under Lt. Col. Adam Richers, and that Reedy was registered as a resident of Schuylkill County, Pennsylvania. Schuylkill County was formed in 1811 from Berks and Northampton counties, so it was very likely that Reedy originally lived in Berks County. This discovery focused the research on the records of Schuylkill County, but nothing was found there concerning Leonard Reedy.

Finally, an over-and-under gun was found with the name. L. Reedy, and Kratztown engraved on the top facets of the barrels. The original theory of Berks County residence was revived because it was thought that Kratztown might be a distortion of the name, Kutztown. A thorough search of the records and graveyards in the Kutztown area was unproductive of information about any Reedy residents in the area.

Several years later, while the writer was researching the tax records of Dauphin County, it was discovered that Leonard Reedy, gunsmith, was a tax-payer in Lykens Township, Dauphin County, Pennsylvania. Further research revealed that Reedy lived in the small town of Gratz, where he had bought a property in 1825. *A History of the Counties of Dauphin and Lebanon in the Commonwealth of Pennsylvania* by Willam Eagle describes the town as follows:

> Gratz was laid out by Simon Gratz. (Of Philadelphia) It is situated on the road leading from Millersburg to Reading. . . . This town, located on the Old Reading Road, was the center and the field of the old-time Militia Musters, at which thousands used to assemble to witness the evolutions of the battalions. The ridge on which the borough stands was in old times called "Wild Cat Ridge" from its being the abode in pioneer times of wild cats.

It is not known where Reedy lived after the War of 1812 until he purchased a tract of land in Dauphin County in 1825, but one might presume that he lived in Schuylkill County and perhaps made a few guns there. His moving to Gratz can be easily understood, for a small town was being established there and its location on the frontier would create a demand for guns. It has been pointed out that it was a militia center, this in addition to its being located on the main road from Millersburg to Reading, might also produce a market for his skills.

He lived in a log house near the center of the town and his shop was on the same property. It is thought that the house is still standing, but its original identity has been obscured by the addition of a clapboard siding and other changes. He owned other tracts of land in the community and it is obvious that his superior craftsmanship was the background for a successful career in the new small town. He was a Justice of the Peace from 1834 until his death in 1835 and he probably held other positions of importance in the town of which no records have survived.

Upon his death he was buried in the Lutheran and Reformed Cemetery in Gratz. His gravestone is cut with the following information: "In Memory of Leonard Reedy, who departed this life April 10, 1835. Aged 62 years, 7 months, 10 days." His wife died on July 15, 1867.

Reedy's distinction as a gunsmith is based on his production of some fine guns, which are distributed in collections throughout the country. A description of them might be prefaced by mentioning the fact that he also left an account book, the only one in existence to chronicle the business affairs of a Pennsylvania gunsmith.

This account book missed destruction by a narrow margin, for it was discovered in the possession of an aged and indifferent owner. Soon after its discovery the owner died, and because of an earlier knowledge of it, one of Leonard Reedy's direct descendants became its owner. This book is an invaluable document, as it records his gunsmithing activity for about twenty years. The names of the buyer and the prices of many of his guns are preserved in the book, as well as the records of many repair jobs, such as fixing a trigger, or mending a stock. There is also a record of selling a "dubble barrel" gun which may be the one that has the inscription, L. Reedy, Kratztown, on the barrels. It is interesting to note that he recorded the birth dates and names of his children in the ledger. These entries and most of the early business entries he wrote in German, but his later business transactions were entered in English.

Like most gunsmiths, Reedy made guns of different quality, although he seems to have perpetuated the early quality of workmanship to a late date in his pioneer town. His best guns are comparable to the best that were made anywhere. They were not extravagantly carved, but his use of scrolls and crosshatching is interesting and effective. He used three designs for his patch box covers, two with solid side plates, and one with openwork which was late and typical of the period. His patch boxes were engraved with considerable skill, as were his eight-pointed stars on the cheek side of the stocks. The panels for his locks and side plates indicate that he was trained in the early traditions of the craft, which he seemed to follow in most of his guns. One of his products is known to have incised carving and a number are plain guns with slender long fore stocks and other attractive features. He used the so-called "hand-made" locks on some guns and bought the common English type for others. The name on the top facet of his barrels is usually engraved in thin lines which are difficult to read, except the "over-and-under," which is done in deep bold lines. There is no obvious explanation for his spelling his name "Ready" instead of 'Reedy" on a few of his guns, although there obviously was a transition in his writing from German to English, which could account for such an irregularity. This change might also account for his using "Kratztown" when the word should have been "Gratz" or "Gratztown."

REEDY, B. E.

Reedy was 44 years old and listed as a gunsmith in the enrollment of men liable for military service in the Civil War. It is noted in the record that he had a crippled hand and wrist. He lived in the town of Donaldson in Fraley Township, Schuylkill County, Pennsylvania, in 1862. He was probably the son of Leonard Reedy of Gratz.

REEDY, E.

Lykens Township, Dauphin County, Pennsylvania.
E. Reedy was a son of Leonard and lived about three miles from his ancestral

town, Gratz. A map, dated 1862, of Lykens Township shows the E. Reedy residence with a blacksmith shop adjoining it.

A plain match gun is known with E. Reedy engraved in script letters on the top facet of the barrel.

REIFFSNYDER, JOHN
Reading, Pennsylvania. *Pennsylvania Archives,* 3d series, Vol. 18, page 532.

REINFRIED, LEO
1325 Frankford Avenue, Philadelphia, Pennsylvania. 1861.

REITENBACH, WILLIAM (Single Freeman)
Lancaster, Pennsylvania. Tax list 1840.

REITER, LEONARD (LENHARDT)
Heidelberg Township, Berks County, Pennsylvania. Tax list 1800.

RESOR, (see ROESSER)

RHODES, FRED
Entered a "Rifle, double barreled" in the second annual Allegheny Fair. *Pittsburgh Mercury,* November 25, 1823.

RICHARD, HARMON (Single Freeman)
Somerset Township, Somerset County, Pennsylvania. Tax list 1852.

RICHE, HENRY
Poplar Lane ab St. John, Philadelphia, Pennsylvania. 1814.

RILEY, EDWARD
28 South Third Street, Philadelphia, Pennsylvania. 1814.

RINEER, MICHAEL
Conestoga Township, Lancaster County, Pennsylvania.

RINGLE, MATHIAS
Blairsville, Indiana County, Pennsylvania. Tax lists 1835, 1842, 1868, 1872.

RIPPY, HUGH
Notice is hereby given to those persons having guns repaired by the subscriber, and now in his possession, to come and redeem them within three weeks from this date, otherwise they will be sold for the expense of repairing and all persons indebted to the subscriber are desired to make payment. Produce will be received till the first of June next. HUGH RIPPY, May 8. *The Pittsburgh Gazette,* May 23, 1789.

ROBERTSON, WILLIAM
SE Second & Cock, Philadelphia, Pennsylvania. 1855.

ROBINS, WILLIAM E.
Elk Run, Tioga County, Pennsylvania. 1861.

RODES, JOHN
Schaefferstown, Lebanon County, Pennsylvania. 1861.

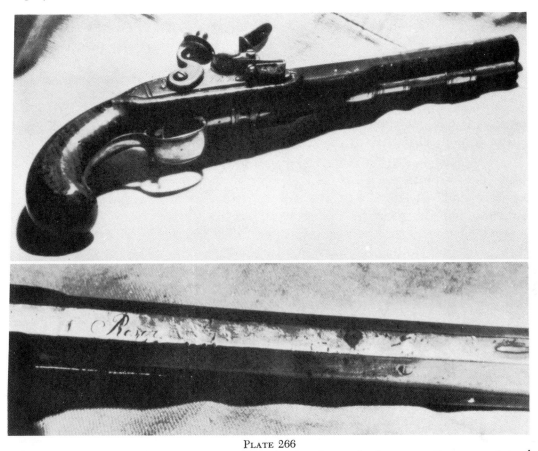

PLATE 266

Pistol with flint lock marked J. Resor, full stock of curly maple, brass mountings, an octagonal brass barrel 43 inches long marked J. Resor on the top facet. This pistol was probably made by Resor in Pennsylvania before he moved to Cincinnati.

ROESSER, MATHIAS

The Roessers, despite the fact that only a few guns can be identified as their products, must be regarded as one of the most important families in the history of gunsmithing in Pennsylvania. They are significant because Mathias Roesser was one of the earliest gunsmiths to have worked in Lancaster and because three generations of Roessers worked between 1740 and 1845, carrying on their gunsmithing activities in a number of communities. Mathias worked in Lancaster, Pennsylvania; Peter, his son, worked in Lancaster and Hagerstown. Their name is most frequently spelled Resor; however, the following spellings can be found in tax assessment lists and other documents: Reeser, Roesor, Razor, Reasor, Rosser.

The progenitor of the family is known to have been Matthias Roeser (ship list spelling), who arrived in America from Rotterdam on September 1, 1736. Another passenger on the same boat, Jonathan Hager, a gunsmith, gave his name to the city of Hagerstown, Maryland. The association of these two men might account for the fact that Peter, Mathias' son, moved to Hagerstown when he left Lancaster in the mid-1780's.

Mathias Roesser has always been regarded as an important gunsmith in Lancaster; there is a legend that the famous William Henry was apprenticed to him. Jordan's "Life of William Henry" states this as a fact, although unfortunately, there is no documentary proof of this relationship.

There is proof that Mathias came to Lancaster in 1740, for at that time he bought a tract of land on King Street from James Hamilton, a property which was sold at his death in 1771. This act establishes him as one of the earliest gunsmiths in the county; possibly he was really the first one.

It is probable that he worked as a gunsmith at that time. He was 28 years old when he came to America and most Europeans served their apprenticeship from the age of 14 to 21. It should also be noted that only four years elapsed from the time he landed until he bought the property in Lancaster, which might indicate that he was working and saving money here rather than serving as an apprentice at his trade. This evidence also points to the fact that he was one of the gunsmiths who worked in Pennsylvania but was apprenticed abroad. Others could doubtless qualify for this category, but evidence concerning their early lives and the probability of their being trained in Europe is lacking.

Attention should also be focused on the fact that at his death in 1771, he left one of the most complete inventories of gunsmith tools that has been found to date. In it are listed most of the tools of a gunsmith who made a complete gun. It included a barrel anvil, a rifling bench, a boring bench, and crucibles for casting brass, along with more common tools, such as grindstones, hammers, hatchets, saws drills, compasses, etc. It is obvious from the tools that he owned that he did not buy barrels and gun furniture from the local hardware store of Philip Schaefer, or John Miller.

There is no record of his son, Peter's birth, but there is a record in the Lancaster County Court House that Mathias' oldest son, Jacob, refused the family homestead and Peter bought the interest of his brothers and sisters in it. Peter later

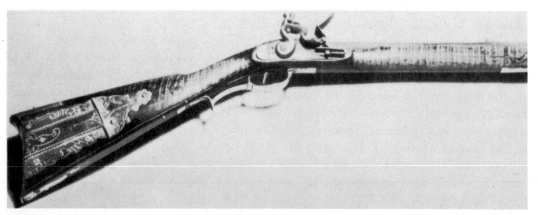

H. J. Kauffman

PLATE 267

Flintlock rifle, (lock not original) curly maple stock, octagonal barrel 46 inches long, brass mountings, marked P. Resor in script letters on the top facet of the barrel. Although this rifle was probably made by Resor after he left Lancaster, the daisy finial on the patch box suggests his earlier training in Lancaster. The screw in the tail end of the trigger guard was also used by other gunsmiths in Lancaster. The engraved designs are done in a very bold manner. Only a few Resor products are known to be in local collections.

sold it to Jacob Kraft, gunsmith, who was married to Peter's sister, Catherine. The tax list of 1773 indicates that Peter Roesor was living with Jacob Kraft; he was probably living in his old homestead, then owned by Kraft.

There is a record that Peter Resor married Catherine Welshans, daughter of Joseph Welshans, a York, Pennsylvania gunsmith, in the First Reformed Church of York on April 16, 1775. It is possible that Welshans was apprenticed to a Lancaster gunsmith, perhaps Matthias Roesser, and that the family friendship culminated in the marriage of these two young people.

Tax assessment lists of 1773 and 1780, and the record of six baptisms of Resor children in the First Reformed Church of Lancaster between 1776 and 1784, indicate that Peter was a gunsmith in Lancaster throughout the period of the American Revolution. Peter saw barrel mills being build and grist mills changed to barrel mills. He saw blacksmiths being taught to be gunsmiths and it is possible that men and machines worked around the clock. These men must have produced a large number of guns, but unfortunately few signed, or unsigned ones, have survived to hold a place of importance in the gun collections of the mid-twentieth century.

Tax assessment records show that Peter's associates were Christopher Breidenhardt, Jacob Dickert, Peter Gonter, John Graeff, Jacob Kraft and John Miller. By 1780 Frederick Fainot and Jacob Messersmith had joined the group, and by 1785 Stophel Gumpf and Christian Klein were included.

The conclusion of the war is thought to have caused a surplus of gunsmiths in Lancaster, so several moved to more attractive markets. About 1785 Peter and his wife Catherine moved to Hagerstown, Maryland, and the records of the Zion Reformed Church in that community indicate that their children, Johan and Elizabetha, were baptised there on Feb. 22, 1789 and October 17, 1793. The 1810 Census of Franklin County, Pennsylvania, shows that the Resors had moved to Mercersburg at that time and that the family consisted of one adult male and two adult females. It is obvious that Peter's son, Jacob, was grown by this time and living at some other place in Pennsylvania; records indicate that he moved to Cincinnati in 1811. Jacob might have spent a few years at gunsmithing in Pennsylvania on his own before he moved to Ohio.

Jacob Resor was born in Lancaster, Pennsylvania in 1784 and married Margaret Wolf, probably in Mercersburg, who was born in Little York, Pennsylvania in 1788. After moving to Cincinnati, he immediately started a gunsmith business on the west side of Main Street between Front and Columbia (now 2nd St.), and later added a tin and coppersmithing business. An advertisement in the *Liberty Hall and Cincinnati Gazette*, July 22, 1816 indicates that he made guns as usual but was also concerned with old copper, brass and pewter. In 1819 he started the Phoenix Iron Foundry, which later developed into the Monitor Stove and Range Company, one of the largest foundries of its type in the country at that time.

A number of books about the history and industries of Cincinnati mention the importance of the Resor enterprises, but little is known about his gunsmithing activities. The writer owns a fine Pennsylvania pistol that is signed "J. Resor" on the lock and on the top facet of the octagonal brass barrel. There is no proof that it was made in Pennsylvania, but it is distinctly different from his Cincinnati products. These have a silver plate on the top of the barrel, engraved with his name and "Cincinnati."

Lacking any proof that Jacob's father, Peter, moved to Cincinnati, we presumed that he had died in Franklin County. After a thorough perusal of Franklin County records failed to produce any such evidence, the search was abandoned. Later, when spelling of the name was discovered, it was definitely determined that Peter Reasor died in Lancaster County, Pennsylvania.

The writer has examined only a few long guns with the name P. Resor engraved on the top facet of the barrel; the style of the guns indicates a strong Lancaster influence. Two had typical daisy finials on the patch boxes and were engraved with deep bold cuts. It is doubtful if Peter ever developed a style that was different from that which he learned in Lancaster. Although it is possible that other Resor products exist, they are very scarce and usually of a better than average quality.

ROHR, JOHN FREDRICK (Joh. Friederich Rohr)
Philadelphia, Pennsylvania.

John Frederick Rohr, awl, saw and armour maker, living near the Red Lion in 2d St. in Philadelphia, expects (D.V.?) to go to England at the next good opportunity, and from there across Holland to Germany. He will go to Hamburg, Berlin, Leipsiz, Zwickau, &c.

All those who are indebted to him by bonds, notes, book-debts, or in any other way, are earnestly admonished to pay honestly.
Staatsbote, no. 561. October 2, 1772.

ROSS, SAMUEL W. (Gunsmith)
12—Fifth, Pittsburgh, Pennsylvania. *Fahnstock's Pittsburgh Directory*, 1850.

ROSS, WILLIAM
Luzerne Township, Fayette County, Pennsylvania. Tax list 1796.

ROSSEL, JOB
Connellsville Township, Fayette County, Pennsylvania. Tax list 1849.

ROTH, CHARLES
Main & Union, Wilkes-Barre, Luzerne County, Pennsylvania.

ROTH, GEORGE
Heidelberg Township, Lebanon County, Pennsylvania. Tax list 1826, 1842.

RUGH, DANIEL
Blairsville, Pennsylvania. 1836, 1837. Listed as a whitesmith in 1842.

SACKETT, J. T.
J. T. SACKETT, Manufacturer of and Dealer in Rifles, Shot Guns &c. Also Horse shoer and Blacksmith. This business was established many years ago. It embraces the manufacture and sale of Muzzle Loading Rifles, Shot Guns, and Re-

PLATE 268

Rifle and shot gun with percussion lock, walnut stock, round barrels, one rifled and the other smooth, marked J. Sackett, Saegertown, Pa. The pattern of the brass mountings on this gun indicates that it was made late in the nineteenth century.

volvers. In connection with this he carries a line of Breech Loading Rifles and Shot Guns, both double and single barreled, also ammunition, &c. He also manufactures a very superior Violin, which has attained much celebrity for its excellence. These have been used by some of the best violinists of Boston, that center of American Musical culture, where they elicited the warmest commendation, and were preferred to others of celebrated make and more costly price. Added to the above is the blacksmith department, which it is only necessary to say, is complete in all its details. Horse Shoeing is one of the specialties, as is also repairing in all its various branches of the business. The facilities are good and the situation favorable to the convenience of patrons, while the trade transacted is largely distributed throughout the surrounding neighborhood. Mr. J. T. Sackett, proprietor, is a native of Crawford County, and has been for many years, filling a much desired niche in the business of the town. (Saegertown)

From a *History of Crawford County:*

SAILOR, HENRY
Harrisburg, Pennsylvania. Tax list 1792.

SANKEY, WILLIAM
Union Township, Mifflin County, Pennsylvania. Federal Census 1850.

SAUP, ANDREW
Bedford Borough, Bedford County, Pennsylvania. Tax list 1841.

SAYLOR, JACOB
Bedford Borough, Bedford County, Pennsylvania. Tax list 1776.
Thought to have been a gunsmith at that time.

SCHALK, GEORGE
Union Street, Pottsville, Schuylkill County, Pennsylvania. 1861.

SCHOENER, HENRY
North Fourth & Walnut, Reading, Pennsylvania. 1860.

SCHRECKENGOST, LINCOLN

Lincoln Schreckengost was the son of William. He was born January 28, 1865, and died June 15, 1949. There is a family tradition that William taught his son Lincoln the trade of gunsmithing, although he is not listed by that trade in tax lists because his major occupation was operating a general store in Putneyville.

SCHRECKENGOST, PETER

Kittanning, Armstrong County, Pennsylvania. Tax lists 1870, 1871.

SCHRECKENGOST, WILLIAM

Putneyville, Armstrong County, Pennsylvania. Tax lists 1857, 1862, 1867, 1881.

SCHREIDT, JOHN

Patentee of town lot in Reading in 1758. *History of Berks County in Pennsylvania*, Morton Montgomery, 1886.

SCHREINER, GEORGE

Pittsburgh, Pennsylvania.
Master armourer, U. S. Arsenal (Allegheny Arsenal) 1841.

SCHROYER, GEORGE

Heidelberg Township, York County, Pennsylvania. Tax list 1793.
Antrim Township, Franklin County, Pennsylvania. Tax list 1805.
Hookstown Road, W. P. *Baltimore Business Directory*, 1810-1815.

SCHROYER, GEORGE, JR.

Heidelberg Township, York County, Pennsylvania. Tax list 1793.

SCHULER

The Schuler brothers, Joseph, John, and Samuel, were of German descent and were possibly the sons of John Schuler, a gunsmith living near Quakertown in 1811. Joseph was the youngest and the first to live in Liverpool, Pennsylvania. His guns are quite rare, for other interests, such as being Sheriff of Perry County from 1838 to 1841, and serving in the Legislature of Pennsylvania from 1871 to 1875, occupied much of his time. He was born on June 22, 1811, and died on March 6, 1879.

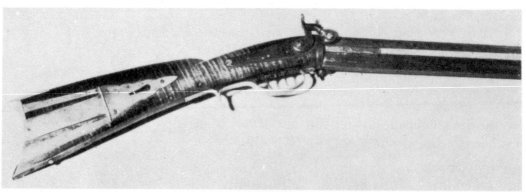

Collection Hemil Kline

PLATE 269

Percussion double rifle with one lock, octagonal barrels 34 inches long, both rifled and swivel at the breech, John Schuler, Liverpool, Pa. in block letters on top facet of each barrel.

Photo by Ray Smith

PLATE 270

The Schuler gun shop in Liverpool, Pennsylvania, has been used as a residence in recent years.

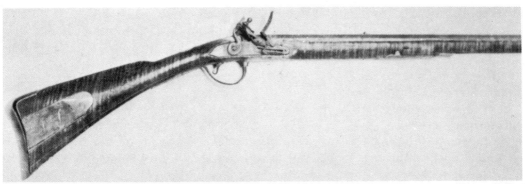

Monroe Hufford

PLATE 271

Rifle with flintlock, full stock of curly maple, brass mountings, and octagonal barrel. The side hinge of the patch box of this rifle is not found on many rifles; however, G. Weiker (one of the maker's neighbors) used it on most of his rifles and H. Gibbs of Lancaster made at least one rifle with a similar arrangement on the lid. The J. S. engraved on the lid of the patch probably are the initials of Jacobus Scout.

John and Samuel Schuler moved to Millerstown, Perry County, Pennsylvania, before finally settling in Liverpool. The three brothers worked together in Samuel's old store-room, which is standing today, although it has been converted into a residence. John was born on January 22, 1804 and died on March 19, 1879; Samuel was born on December 19, 1799 and his death occurred on August 17, 1875.

The success of these men can be attributed to the quality of their products. They made a conventional long, single-barrel rifle which was known for its accuracy by those within a fifty mile radius of Liverpool, and it was frequently inlaid with small pieces of silver in a variety of patterns. The brass-work on their rifles was expertly done and their patch box patterns resembled those used in Lancaster, Pennsylvania, by the Gumpfs and the Gibbs. They also made a number of over-and-under rifles, and John is known to have specialized in making heavy rifles for target shooting.

Their location near the mountains, the Pennsylvania Canal, and the Susque-hanna River, was also an asset to their business. In the middle of the nineteenth century there was big game in the mountains and a great deal of river traffic, both creating a demand for the products of the brothers who worked in Liverpool.

SCHUTTE, HENRY H.
     Pittsburgh, Pennsylvania. 1864-1877.

SCHWEITZER, ABRAHAM
     The fact that Abraham Sweitzer was a contributor to the Hand Account of Rifles in Lancaster, Pennsylvania, in 1794, and that he was married to the daughter of Jacob Fordney of Lancaster, strongly suggests that he started his trade in the Lancaster area. His name appears in the tax assessment lists of Franklin County in the 1820's; he died there in 1832.

The details of his Lancaster guns are not evident in the guns he made in Franklin County. His carving and engraving are the work of a skilled craftsman.

A gunsmith named J. Sweitzer is known to have worked in the early nineteenth century in Franklin County, Pennsylvania, and the style of his products suggests that he was a son of Abraham Sweitzer. Another gunsmith, who signed his guns "A. Switzer," is known to have worked at Bellefonte, Centre County, Pennsylvania, in 1861.

SCOUT, J.
     Although no guns are known today that were made and signed by Jacobus Scout there is a long tradition that the guns with side opening patch boxes and J. S. engraved on them were made by him. In the Museum of the Bucks County Historical Society there is a gun that is attributed to him which he is thought to have given to his friend, John Fritch. This gun was handed down through the Longstreth family, Daniel Longstreth being a mutual friend of Fritch and Scout.

Jacobus Scout seems to be a person who has caused quite a bit of confusion. In Davis' *History of Bucks County*, 3 vols., volume 1, page 192 we find the state-ment "Scout's Christian name was James, or Jacobus." Earlier in that same para-graph we find the statement: "Cobe Scout, mentioned in connection with Fitch, his friend, and intimate companion, was an eccentric character in Warminster, made his home part of the time with Charles Garrison, who lived on the road from Davisville to the Montgomery county line in the first house on the west side. Fitch taught Scout the art of silversmithing to which he added gunmaking."

In the proceedings of the *Historical Society*, Vol. 1, pages 89-90 in a paper written by Rev. D. K. Turner in 1883, we find: "He (John Fitch) came to Penn-sylvania in 1777, when he was 34 years of age, and resided in the lower part of Warminster, where he established himself in his calling in a wheelwright-shop, belonging to Jacobus Scout, or "Cobe" Scout as he was familiarly styled." Later in the same article it speaks of Fitch presenting his petition a second time to the

Legislature "supported by certificates from Rev. Irvin, Abraham Lukens, Seneca Lukens, Daniel Longstreth, James Scout and John Folwell, of Bucks County . . ."

In Davis' *Life of John Davis,* page 183, in speaking of Cobe Scout he says "His silver spoons were held in high estimation by housewives of three-quarters of a century ago, and his long rifles were equally celebrated."

In MacReynold's *Place Names in Bucks County,* page 183 we find that when John Fitch fled Trenton, N. J., at the outbreak of the Revolution "He sought security later in a less frequented place and passed on to Charles Garrison's and Cobe Scout's, and taught Cobe the art of silversmithing and possibly gunmaking."

We do not find him listed in the tax records as a gunsmith. The following is the tax record of Warminster Township:

> 1785—James Scout
> 1786—James Scout—"place of abode" Abraham Sutfins
> 1788—James Scout—at his own house
> 1789—James Scout—silversmith
> 1793—James Scout—35 acres, 1 horse 1 cow
> 1791—James Scout
> 1794—James Scout—37 acres, 1 horse 1 cow
> 1796—James Scout—stone house and weaver's shop 35 acres 1 horse 1 cow
> 1797—James Scout—single freeman—36 acres 1 horse 2 cows
> 1798—James Scout—stone house and log stabling 36 acres 1 horse 2 cows
> 1799—James Scout—stone house and log stabling 36 acres 1 horse 2 cows
> 1800—James Scout—stone house and log shop and stabling 36 acres 1 horse
>   2 cows
> 1801—James Scout—stone house and log shop etc. 36 acres 1 horse 2 cows
> 1802—James Scout—stone house 36 acres 1 horse 2 cows
> 1803—James Scout—36 acres 1 horse 1 cow
> 1804—James Scout—36 acres 1 horse 1 cow
> 1805—James Scout—36 acres 1 horse 2 cows
> "Cobe" Scout died in 1829 at the age of ninety.

SEDWICK, GEORGE

Rimersburg Borough, Clarion County, Pennsylvania. Tax lists 1859, 1861.

SEEBROOKS, WILLIAM

Martic Township, Lancaster County, Pennsylvania. Tax list 1807.

SELL

The 1793 tax assessment list for Germany Township, York County, Pennsylvania, lists three tax payers by the name of Jacob Sell. One had a sawmill, another was a merchant, and the third a gunsmith. The date of this reference suggests that Jacob Sell, Senior, was working there at that time. He was born about 1750 and died about 1825.

The rifles made by Jacob Sell, Senior, fall within the Golden Age of gunmaking in Pennsylvania and are among the finest that were made. Some have sliding wooden covers for their patch boxes and show other evidences of late eighteenth century styles. It has been previously mentioned that covers of this type were used from 1750 to the very end of the Golden Age; however, the later rifles with these covers conform in most respects to the period in which they were made.

His four-piece brass patch boxes are superb in their design and workmanship. He used a variety of patterns, although the one in which a man's head is used as a finial is doubtless one of his most attractive patterns. It has three piercings in each side plate and the finial. The C scrolls are attractively arranged and the engraved patterns conform to the general form of the side plates and finial.

His design, carved in bas-relief on the cheek side of the stock, is based on a capital C in a horizontal position with extravagant serifs at the ends of the letter. Under the cheek rest are two panels with cross-hatchings, and at the front of the cheek rest a small capital C is carved. His carving might be described as primitive in style, as contrasted with the refined style of his son, Jacob Sell.

The junior Jacob Sell was also a fine craftsman, although his work is more repetitive and less varied than that of his father. His rifles are executed in a refined style and superior quality of craftsmanship. He probably started working about 1800, when the York-Adams County group were at their best.

It seems reasonable to conclude that Jacob, Junior, and Fredrick Sell were sons of Jacob, Senior; however, the senior status is given to the older Jacob only because he is known to have lived and worked in an earlier period than Jacob, Junior, and Fredrick.

Fredrick is first recorded as a gunsmith in the 1807 census record for York, Pennsylvania. He is called a freeman, which suggests that he was starting his trade at that time. Although he finally settled in Littlestown, Pennsylvania, the occurrence of his designs in the work of other gunsmiths, such as J. Ernst, suggests that he traveled around the countryside as a journeyman before he married and settled permanently in Littlestown.

Although he did not sign all of his rifles, Fredrick Sell had a unique style so that most of his products can be easily recognized by one who is familiar with his work. Some of the features of his rifles were used by other contemporary craftsmen. His patch boxes had four to nine piercings and were exquisitely engraved. He used a number of patch box finials; his finest one, however, is the head of a bird, plucking feather from its wing. An extravagant array of C scrolls and cross-hatching can be found on many of his patch boxes.

His carved patterns on the cheek side of the stock suggest that he was influenced by the master carver of York County, George Eyster. His inter-related C scrolls and flower motifs are expertly executed and attractively arranged on the flat portions of the stock.

He is known to have used a few brass lock plates in his flintlocks and signed them with his initials. Some rifles have as many as ten to twelve inlays, which are cleverly arranged on the various parts of the stock.

SENSENY, JEREMIAH
    Chambersburg, Franklin County, Pennsylvania. 1861.

SETTLE, JOHN
    Cashtown, Adams County, Pennsylvania. 1861.

SHAFFER, HENRY (Freeman)
    Lancaster, Pennsylvania. Tax lists 1797, 1798.

SHALLENBERGER, DANIEL

Bullskin Township, Fayette County, Pennsylvania. Tax lists 1822, 1829.

SHALNON, HUGH

Fifth near Germantown, shop near Shippen, Philadelphia, Pennsylvania. 1814.

SHANNON, WILLIAM

Seven Cutler, 21 Passyunk near Fifth, Philadelphia, Pennsylvania. 1814.

SHARPS, C. & Co.

336 Frankford Road, Philadelphia, Pennsylvania. 1855.
30th below Bridge, Philadelphia, Pennsylvania. 1861.

SHEAFF, HENRY

Lancaster, Pennsylvania. Tax list 1834.

SHEETZ, HENRY AND PHILIP

We, the subscribers, gunsmiths of Mecklenburg in the County of Berkley, do certify that we can make and deliver, at our shop in this Town, to Mr. Thomas Rutherford, or any other person legally appointed by the Honble the Committee of Safety to Secure and Pay for them, twenty-four good and well fixt Rifle guns per month, at the rate of Four Pounds and Ten Shillings Virginia Currency each, or in lieu thereof twenty-four good and well fixt muskets with sufficient bayonets at the rate of Four Pounds......Like Currency each.

Certified under our hands this 28th Day of May, 1776.

> Thomas Worley
> Philip Sheetz
> Henry Sheetz

SHELL, DANIEL

Lower Paxton Township, Dauphin County, Pennsylvania. Tax list 1825.

SHELL, JOHN

West Hanover Township, Dauphin County, Pennsylvania. Tax list 1837.

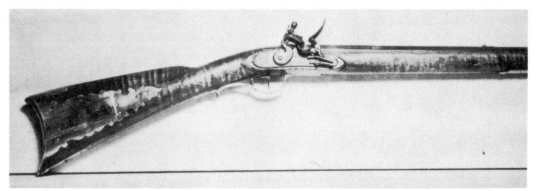

Robert McMurtrie

PLATE 272

Rifle with flint lock, full stock of curly maple, octagonal barrel with John Shell engraved on the top facet of the barrel. The form of this gun is particularly graceful and the design of the patch box also suggests that John Shell was a sensitive artist as well as a good craftsman.

Herman Dean

PLATE 273

Rifle with flint lock, full stock of curly maple, brass mountings, octagonal barrel with M. Shell engraved on the top facet of the barrel.

This rifle by Martin Shell is a fine example of the work done in Dauphin County, Pennsylvania in the eighteenth century. The design of the patch box was used, with some variations, by a number of makers, but this one compares favorably with the best examples. The cheek side of the butt is extravagantly carved. The contour of the stock and the fine curl of the wood are also important features of this fine rifle.

SHELL, MARTIN

Paxton Township, Dauphin County, Pennsylvania. Tax list 1788.

SHELL, J.

Linglestown, Dauphin County, Pennsylvania. 1861.

SHEIBNER, JOHN

Mechanicsburg, Cumberland County, Pennsylvania. 1861.

SHELLENGER, DANIEL

Connellsville Township, Fayette County, Pennsylvania. Tax lists 1830, 1832, 1833, 1834.

SHENNEFELT, NICHOLAS

The following information about Nicholas Shennefelt is copied from the *History of Clarion County*, 1887, by A. J. Davis:

> Nicholas Shennefelt was born in Centre County Feb. 4, 1799. He married Keziah Greenland in Trough Creek Valley, Huntington County, on March 30, 1823. Their early home was in McConnellstown, Huntington County, where he was a gunsmith. Their first son was born there in 1825. In 1835 he moved to Redbank Township, Armstrong County. When Clarion County was created in 1840 this area became a part of Porter Township in the new county. His shop here was located at Leatherwood near Brinkerton. In 1850 he moved to Clarion Borough where he remained until his death on October 13, 1871.

SHENER, JOHN

Reading, Pennsylvania. Census report 1800.

SHENER, WILLIAM

Reading, Pennsylvania. Census report 1800.

SHERRY, JOHN

Beaver Township, Clarion County, Pennsylvania. Tax list 1850.

SHERRY, JOHN, JR.

Beaver Township, Clarion County, Pennsylvania. Tax lists 1848, 1851, 1853.

SHERRY, MICHAEL

Beaver Township, Clarion County, Pennsylvania. Tax lists 1844, 1851. Business Directory, 1861.

SHERRY, PETER

Derry Township, Westmoreland County, Pennsylvania. Tax list 1810.

SHERRY, X.

Knox, Clarion County, Pennsylvania. 1877.

SHILLITO

The Shillito family is believed to have migrated from the northern part of Ireland and settled in Franklin County, Pennsylvania, about 1740. Samuel Shillito, the first in a line of gunsmiths, was born in Chambersburg in 1793. For a time he lived at Fort Loudon, Franklin County, where S. M. Shillito, his first son, was born November 8, 1824.

The son worked with his father from the time of his apprenticeship until the father's death in 1852, when he took over the business and continued it until the destruction of Chambersburg in 1864. S. M. Shillito, Jr., served for some time as Burgess of Chambersburg and for six years was a clerk in the Chambersburg Postoffice. He also served for fifteen years as a member of the Board of Education.

It is recorded in the *History of the Burning of Chambersburg* that the S. M. Shillito property, a two-story brick building on the north side of Market Street, was burned with a loss of $1500.00. Although a few Shillito rifles have survived, an evaluation of them leads only to several dubious conclusions. Their rifles are typical of those made in Franklin County at that time, a number being lavishly inlaid with pieces of silver. Most of them seem to have been made in the percussion era. It is difficult to determine which of the two men made the guns which the writer has examined; however, it is more probable that they are the products of the son, rather than of the father.

SHOEMAKER, JACOB
New Bethlehem, Pennsylvania. Tax lists 1858-1868.

SHOFF, JACOB
Cavernon Township, Berks County, Pennsylvania. Census report 1800.

SHONFELT, NICODEMUS
Name entered as a gunsmith with line drawn through. Probably indicating that he moved or died.
Union Township, Huntington County, Pennsylvania. 1820.

SHOUGH, JACOB
Back Noble near Third, Philadelphia, Pennsylvania. 1814.

SHOUGH, JOSEPH
German Township, Fayette County, Pennsylvania. Tax lists 1809, 1810, 1814, 1816. 1815 G. Smith & Farrier.

SHOUP, GEORGE
Jackson Township, Cambria County, Pennsylvania. Tax list 1832.

SHOWALTER, JOHN (Freeman)
Lancaster, Pennsylvania. Tax list 1840.

SHOWALTER, JOHN
Mill Street, Brookville, Jefferson County, Pennsylvania. 1861.

SHRIVER, JOHN
John Shriver, gunsmith, of Hanover, Pennsylvania, sold a parcel of land to Rev. Christopher Gobrecht in Heidelberg Township, York County, Pennsylvania, on December 17, 1793. In 1799 a John Shriver was listed as a gunsmith in the tax assessment list of Mt. Pleasant Township, Adams County, Pennsylvania.

Although both of these references may have referred to the same man, the existing rifles signed with the name, J. Shriver, suggest that two markers by that name worked in Pennsylvania. One is thought to have worked in the period of the Revolution and the other in the early nineteenth century. There is, of course, a strong possibility that a father and son relationship existed between the two men but this has not been proved by documentary evidence.

There is little similarity in the products of the two men. The rifle illustrated in Plate 19 is one of top quality in the style of the York-Adams County group of craftsmen. The piercings in the patch box, the engraving on the patch box and inlays, and the patterns carved in bas-relief all suggest production in York County.

SHROYER, GEORGE

In the Pennsylvania Archives, 3rd series, Vol. 18 the name of George Shroyer appears as a gunsmith living in Berks County in 1768. It is not known when he moved, but in 1775 he bought a parcel of land in Hanover, York County, Pennsylvania, presumably to build a residence and gun shop there. The terms of his purchase contract were that he had to build a house at least eighteen feet square with a chimney of brick or stone within two years after the date of the purchase transaction. He is known to have been living in Hanover, in 1813, for he is listed as a gunsmith in the tax assessment list for that year, although his name was then spelled Shreyer.

The fact that Shroyer was listed as a gunsmith as early as 1768 focuses attention on the fact that he made rifles in the transition era in Pennsylvania. His early guns have thick butts and heavy stocks throughout. The carved patterns in. the bas-relief technique are simple, yet expertly executed. His engraving is of good quality and the designs of his patch boxes vary. Some of his guns have a steel insert in the butt plate, a procedure which was used by other gunsmiths in the Hanover area to minimize the abrasive action of the ground on the butt plate, while the rifle was being loaded.

There were two gunsmiths by the name of George Shroyer, the one presumably the son of the other. The second one appears to have worked in a later period; his guns, however, are comparable in quality to those made by the elder George Shroyer.

SHULTZ, HENRY

Richland, Lebanon County, Pennsylvania. 1861.

SHUNK, ISAAC

Lancaster, Pennsylvania.

SIBLE (SIPLE), JACOB

Lancaster, Pennsylvania. Tax list 1770.

The tax list record tells that Jacob Sible lived with widow Sible. It is likely that he was a gunsmith and was living with his mother. It is possible that the Christian Seibel, listed in the Lancaster tax assessment list for 1802 as a freeman gunsmith, was a son of Jacob.

SIDES, HENRY

Bedford Township, Bedford County, Pennsylvania. Tax list 1796.

SIEGFRIED, DANIEL (Rifle Barrel Maker)

Wernersville, Pennsylvania. 1860. Census of 1850.

SIEGFRIED, JOHN (Gun Barrel Maker)

Lower Heidelberg Township, Berks County, Pennsylvania. Census of 1850.

SILKNITTER, SOLOMON

Huntington County, Pennsylvania. Federal Census of 1850.

SILVIES, JACOB
Hempfield Township, Westmoreland County, Pennsylvania. Tax lists 1827, 1829, 1830.

SINCLAIR, JOHN
Lancaster Borough, Lancaster County, Pennsylvania. Tax list 1802, 1803, 1820.

SINER, JOHN T.
Lawrence below Franklin, Philadelphia, Pennsylvania. 1847, 1855.

SINK, WILLIAM
Conemaugh Township, Cambria County, Pennsylvania. Tax list 1830.

SIPES, CHARLES
Buffalo Township, Allegheny County, Pennsylvania. Census list 1800.

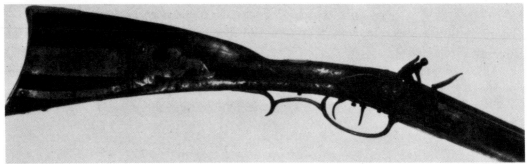

Joe Kindig, Jr.

PLATE 274

Rifle with flintlock, full stock of curly maple, brass mountings, and octagonal barrel with C. Siple on the top facet of the barrel.

SIPLE, CHRISTIAN
Lancaster, Pennsylvania. Tax list 1802.
Middletown, Pennsylvania. Tax list 1808.
The Lancaster tax assessment list for 1802 lists a Christian Seibel as a freeman gunsmith with Jacob Heaffer. Siple was obviously starting his trade at that time and was working for, or living with, Jacob Heaffer. Possibly he was doing both.

SKILLEN, CHARLES
Conaquanessing Township, Allegheny County, Pennsylvania. Census list 1800.

SLAYSMAN, CHARLES
Indiana Borough, Indiana County, Pennsylvania. Tax lists 1850, 1859, 1860.
East Church Street, Indiana, Pennsylvania. 1876-77.

SLAYSMAN, GEORGE
Lewistown, Mifflin County, Pennsylvania. Census list 1821.
Woodbury Township, Huntington County, Pennsylvania. Tax lists 1825, 1830, 1833.

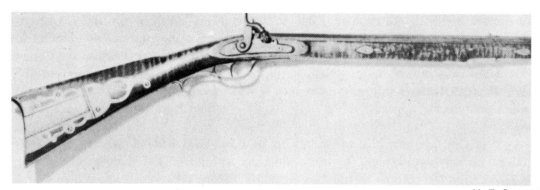

PLATE 275

M. T. Stewart

Rifle with flintlock now (percussion), full stock of curly maple, brass mountings, octagonal barrel 40 inches long with G. Slaysman on the top facet of the barrel. The shape of the butt plate suggests that this rifle was made by Slaysman in the early part of his career. The similarity of the patch box to a style used in Franklin County might be explained by the fact that Huntington County adjoins Franklin County.

SLAYSMAN, GEORGE

Punxsutawney, Jefferson County, Pennsylvania. 1861.

SLONAKER, GEORGE

Union Township, Bedford County, Pennsylvania. Tax list 1849, Bedford Court House.

Slonaker's guns were a bit heavier than the typical Bedford County product. He used handmade and commercial locks on his guns, many of which have very attractive patch-boxes.

SMALL, JACOB

Moon Township, Allegheny County, Pennsylvania. Tax list 1800.

SMALL, JOHN

George Township, Fayette County, Pennsylvania. Tax lists 1802, 1803, 1806.

SMITH, A. B.

Although Abia Smith was a member of an important Smith family in Pennsylvania, his major contribution to this publication is his indenture which is in the

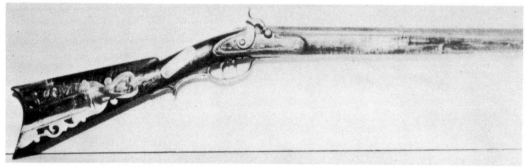

PLATE 276

J. T. Herron

Rifle with percussion lock, brass mountings, full stock of curly maple, octagonal barrel 45 inches long with A. B. Smith on the top facet of the barrel. The fine engraving on the patch box and the forty-five inch barrel are unusual features of this rifle.

possession of his daughter, Mrs. Ellen Watt, who has kindly permitted it to be reproduced (in the data about the apprenticeship of a gunsmith) for all who are interested in such matters. A few indentures of gunsmiths are known to exist but this is the only one of a Pennsylvania rifle maker that was available for reproduction. It is particularly interesting because it was executed in the nineteenth century when the terms of apprenticeship were greatly changed from those of the eighteenth century.

It is also interesting to note that on July 28, 1863 Abia Smith was granted a patent for an improvement in breech-loading ordnance. The following paragraph is taken from the records of the United States Patent Office:

> The object of my invention is to reduce breech-loading ordnance to the utmost simplicity, lightness, and facility of manipulation, together with all necessary strength and security, and wholly without leakage of gases at the discharge.

The rifle illustrated here indicates that he was a rifle maker and the indenture indicates that he had been apprenticed to Joel Ferree of Findley Township, Allegheny County, Pennsylvania, in 1836. His affection for his master is indicated by the fact that he named one of his sons Joel Ferree Smith. Abia Butler Smith was born September 11, 1818 and died March 29, 1900.

SMITH, GAMALIEL
Huntington County, Pennsylvania. Federal Census of 1850.

SMITH, HENRY
Hempfield Township, Westmoreland County, Pennsylvania. Tax lists 1832, 1836, 1851, 1855.

SMITH, JACOB
Murrysville, Westmoreland County, Pennsylvania. 1861.

SMITH, LORENS
Penn Avenue, Scranton, Luzerne County, Pennsylvania. 1861.

SMITH, MARTIN
Lancaster Borough, Lancaster County, Pennsylvania. Tax list 1816.

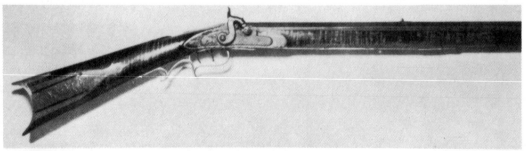

T. J. Cooper

PLATE 277

Rifle with percussion lock, full stock of curly maple, octagonal barrel 37 inches long with S. Smith on the top facet of the barrel. This rifle was probably made after the Civil War in Huntingdon County where a number of gunsmiths made rifles with heavy barrels and light stocks.

SMITH, PETER

Ennisville, Huntington County, Pennsylvania. 1861.

SMITH, SAMUEL

Redstone Township, Fayette County, Pennsylvania. Tax lists 1823, 1831.

SNEEVELY, JACOB

Harrisburg, Pennsylvania. Tax list 1817.

SNYDER, JACOB

Liberty Township, Bedford County, Pennsylvania. Tax list 1846.
Retailer of Merchandise and Gunsmith. Tax list 1849, Bedford Court House.
Snyder's guns are average quality. His log shop is standing in Liberty Township.

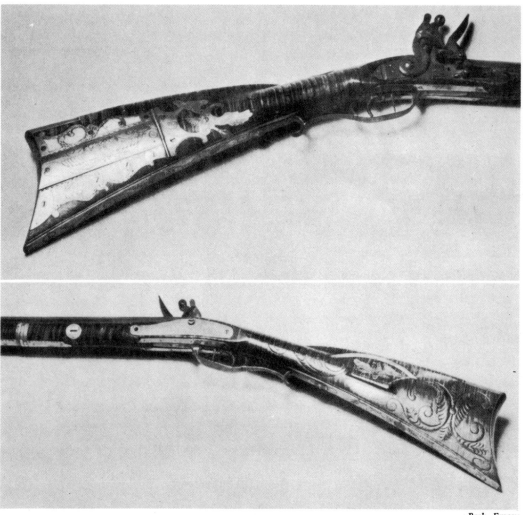

Park Emery

PLATE 278

Rifle with flintlock, full stock of curly maple, brass mountings, octagonal barrel with brass plate on which is engraved George Spangel, Liverpool, Pa.

The patch box on this rifle is an extravagant display of design and workmanship. The eagle finial is beautifully executed and engraved. The ivory inlays in the piercings of the side plates are probably unique. The toe-plate is unusually long and cleverly engraved.

SNYDER, TOBIAS
Hollidaysburg, Pennsylvania. Tax lists 1848, 1849.
Hopewell Township, Bedford County, Pennsylvania. Tax list 1857.
Tobias was a brother of Jacob Snyder. His guns are rare and average quality.

SNYDER, WILLIAM
Flatwood, Fayette County, Pennsylvania. 1861.

SOLOMON, THEODORE
Washington (West Philadelphia), Philadelphia, Pennsylvania. 1847, 1855.
Market n 31st., Philadelphia, Pennsylvania. 1861.

SPANG AND WALLACE
Sporting Store, 94 North Third, 1847, 1855.

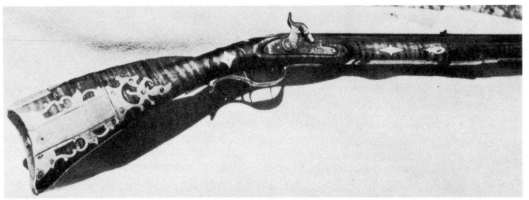

Nixon Collection

PLATE 279

Although this rifle was not signed by its maker, the design of the patch-box finial resembles the
one on the rifle which is signed Geo. Spangel, Liverpool, Pa.

SPANGLER, SAMUEL
Stony Creek Township, Somerset County, Pennsylvania. Tax lists 1823, 1829,
1832, 1834.

SPEIGHT, ADAM
Beaver Township, Union County, Pennsylvania. Federal Census 1850.

SPECHT, ELIAS
Beavertown, Snyder County, Pennsylvania. 1820-1890. Federal Census 1850.

SPRINGER, ISAAC
Potter, Beaver County, Pennsylvania. 1861.

SROYER, LEWIS
George Township, Fayette County, Pennsylvania. Tax list 1806.

STACK, JOHN (Gun Barrel Smith)
Annville Township, Dauphin County, Pennsylvania. Tax list 1807.

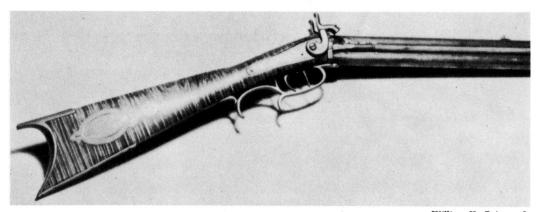

PLATE 280

William H. Reisner, Jr.

Double rifle with two percussion locks, brass mountings, set triggers, curly maple stock, round barrels 36 inches long with Stapleton on top of barrels. The wood of this gun has very superior curl in it. The trigger guard suggests late production.

STAHL, WILLIAM
>   307 Ridge Avenue, Philadelphia, Pennsylvania. 1855.

STAKE, JOHN
>   Hempfield Township, Westmoreland County, Pennsylvania. Tax lists 1817, 1818, 1819, 1820, 1821, 1822, 1823, 1825, 1826, 1830.
>   The tax assessor changed the spelling of this name in 1823 from Stake to Steck.

STALL, CHRISTIAN
>   Harrisburg, Pennsylvania. Tax list 1817.

STAPLETON, JAMES
>   Todd, Huntington County, Pennsylvania. 1861.

STARE, JOHN
>   Harrisburg, Pennsylvania. Tax list 1792.

STEEVER, ADAM
>   Union Township, Huntington County, Pennsylvania. 1824, 1828, 1833.

STEWART, GEORGE
>   Lewistown, Pennsylvania. Federal Census 1850.

STOUDENOUR, JACOB
>   Colerain Township, Bedford County, Pennsylvania. Tax list 1825. Business Directory, 1861.
>   Stoudenour made guns in the flint and percussion era. He was a very prolific maker and some of his guns are highly decorated.

STRICKEL, SAMUEL
>   Heidelberg Township, York County, Pennsylvania.

STROHWEG, ANDREW
>   Water Street, Butler County, Pennsylvania. 1861.

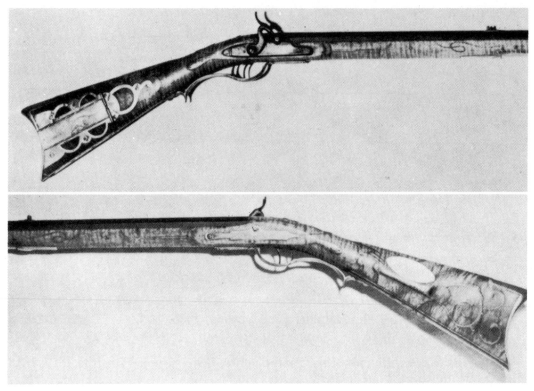

F. A. Farber

PLATE 281

Rifle with percussion lock, full stock of curly maple, brass mountings, and octagonal barrel, attributed to Jacob Stodenour who lived in Colerain Township, Bedford County, Pennsylvania. The round end on the tail of the lock plate is found on a few other guns made in Bedford County but is not as common as the lock plate with a tail. Stodenour was one of the early makers in Bedford County and the radius of the stock plate on this rifle indicates that it was made at an earlier date than most Bedford rifles were made.

STUEBYEN, C.
    Saxonburg, Butler County, Pennsylvania. 1861.

STUNKARD, R.
    New Grenada, Pennsylvania.

SUBERS, JAMES
    158 M. Road, Philadelphia, Pennsylvania. 1855.

SUTTON & DUNSETH
    SUTTON & DUNSETH, GUNSMITHS, request all persons indebted to them to make payment on or before the 1st of March, otherwise their accounts will be put in the proper officers' hands for recovery. Pittsburgh, January 29, 1799.
    N.B. Those who have left old guns to repair are requested to call for them soon, or they will be sold for repairs.
    The Pittsburgh Gazette, February 2, 1799.

SUTTON, GEORGE
    Pittsburgh, Pennsylvania. Federal Census 1800.

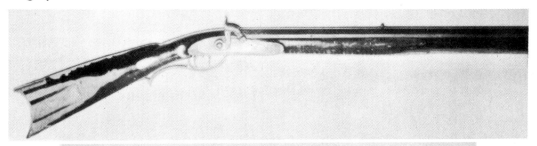

Aprile the 18 /07
New Grenada Fulton Co
Mr Noah. McFleagle Sir i Resieved
yours inquiring Whather i Cou Sende the
Gun Bye Express i can send hit but
hit Will have to gailing Round to git
to you if you Wonte hit Expressed give me
the Adress to Ship to a bout the Money
i think hit Wod cum safe By mail in
a leter i have sente a heape of money in leters
& Never loste Enny yet i dount let the Poste
Master know Enny thing a bout sending
hit Dont git hit Registerd a tell i cante
tell you Jeste When i will have yougun don
i hante got a barrel the Rite Nute but i have
alot on the Way now tha Will soon cante hit
Wonte be long till i will have hit maid for
you   yours truly

Robert F. Stunkard

T. J. Cooper

PLATE 282

Rifle with percussion lock, full stock of curly maple, silver inlays, set triggers, octagonal barrel 37
inches long and 1⅛ inches wide at the muzzle, with R. F. Stunkard on the top facet of the barrel.
   Although Stunkard's rifle is a typical product of the time and place he worked, the letter which
he wrote to a prospective customer must be regarded as "rare."

SWEIGART, ADAM
    Halifax, Dauphin County, Pennsylvania. Tax list 1815, 1817.

SWEIGER, WILLIAM
    Elliotsburg, Perry County, Pennsylvania. 1861.

SWEIGERT, WILLIAM
    Sanille Township, Perry County, Pennsylvania. Federal Census of 1850.

SWITZER, A.
    Bellefonte, Centre County, Pennsylvania. 1861.

SYLVIS, JACOB
    Salem Cross Roads, Westmoreland County, Pennsylvania. 1861.

SYPHERS, JOHN
    Waynesburg, Greene County, Pennsylvania. 1876.

TETLEY, JOHN OF BOWN & TETLEY
    h 37 Fayette Street, Pittsburgh, Pennsylvania. 1852.

THOMAS, WILLIAM
    202 St. John Street, Philadelphia, Pennsylvania. 1814.

THOMPSON, GEORGE W.
    Thompson, George W.—Gunsmithing of all kinds done neatly and promptly.
Dealer in guns, pistols, powder and shot. East Walnut Street, Washington. *Caldwell's*
Atlas of Washington County, Pennsylvania, 1876.

TOPPER, HENRY
    Napier Township, Bedford County, Pennsylvania. Tax list 1835.

TRAYER, JOHN
    George Township, Fayette County, Pennsylvania. Tax lists 1802, 1803.

TREPPERT, JOHN
    Lancaster, Pennsylvania. Tax lists 1834, 1840. (See Drepperd biography)

TRISSLER, JOHN
    Lancaster, Pennsylvania. Tax lists 1816, 1820.

TROUT, JOHN
    Williamsport, Lycoming County, Pennsylvania. 1861.

TROUTMAN, BENJAMIN
    Southampton Township, Somerset County, Pennsylvania. Tax lists 1810, 1811,
1817.

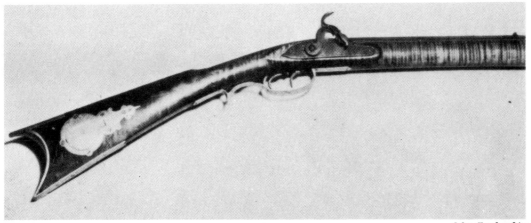

John Fonderwhite

PLATE 283

Rifle with percussion lock, full stock of curly maple, brass mountings, octagonal barrel marked D. B. Troutman. Although this gun is of average quality, Troutman is known to have made at least one very fine gun.

TROUTMAN, DANIEL B.

Londonderry Township, Bedford County, Pennsylvania. Tax list 1858.

Wellersburg, Somerset County, Pennsylvania. Tax list 1867.

Troutman's residence is very near the Bedford and Somerset County line, which accounts for his appearance on both tax lists. His guns were of average quality. He used both handmade and imported locks.

TROUTMAN, THOMAS

St. John Street, Philadelphia, Pennsylvania. *New Trade Directory of Philadelphia,* 1800.

TRUITT BROS. & CO.

529 Market Street, Philadelphia, Pennsylvania. 1861.

TRUMP, HENRY

Bullskin Township, Fayette County, Pennsylvania. Tax lists 1807, 1808.

TRYON

The Tryon history starts with the apprenticing of a young man named George Tryon to a Philadelphia gunsmith by the name of Getz. In 1811 the young protégé joined his master in the business; and, at the age of twenty, bought out his master's interest and established the George W. Tryon Company at 165 N. Second Street, Philadelphia.

George Tryon enlisted in the service of his country in the War of 1812 but was returned to civil life to operate his business, which was making a vital contribution to the war effort. No sizeable gains were made in the business until 1829, when a large property was bought at 134 N. Second Street, in Philadelphia. The front portion of the first floor was used as a sales room and forges for gunwork were set up in the rear portion. The family lived on the second floor.

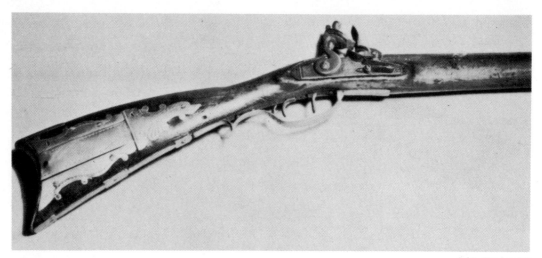

John Fonderwhite

PLATE 284
Rifle with flintlock, full stock of maple, set triggers, octagonal barrel marked Tryon, Phila. A number of Tryon's military products have survived but their sporting rifles are very rare.

In 1836 Edw. K. Tryon, son of George W., was admitted as a partner in the business and they became importers as well as manufacturers. Among the new items of the expanded business was fishing tackle from England.

Their workshops were busy making Pennsylvania rifles. They were one of the few Philadelphia gunsmiths to make this famous arm, a number of which have survived until today. Although the workmanship is good, their design is not typical of the country product. They used a number of patch box patterns, one of which closely resembles the pattern usually associated with the rifles of Derr and Mauger in Berks County. In addition to making guns, their shops were busy in the 1830's converting flint guns to percussion ignition. In 1841 they made a number of the famous "Mississippi" muskets for the Republic of Texas.

Although they continued to make guns, their business slowly changed to the wholesale selling of sporting goods, which is its major interest today.

TUCKER, JONATHAN (Armourer)
Gray's Road n Arsenal, Philadelphia, Pennsylvania. 1814.

TYLER, JOHN (Armourer)
The Captains of the Association in the city of Philadelphia are desired to deliver all the arms belonging to the state in the hands of their respective companies, to Mr. John Tyler, armourer in Eighth Street, between Market and Chestnut Streets, who is authorized to receive them.

George Henry
Lieutenant of the city of Philadelphia.
Pennsylvania Evening Post, no. 352, May 15, 1777.

UMHOLTZ, JACOB
Lykens Township, Dauphin County, Pennsylvania. Tax list 1825.

UNANGST, ISAAC
West Beaver Township, Union County, Pennsylvania. Federal Census 1850.

VANDERGRIFT, JEREMIAH
115 Green Street, Philadelphia, Pennsylvania. 1814.

VANDERSLICE, JACOB
Rose & William (Kensington), Philadelphia, Pennsylvania. 1847, 1855.

VANSCRIVER, BENJAMIN
67 Virgin Alley, Pittsburgh, Pennsylvania. 1859-60.

VARMER, JOHN
St. Clair Township, Allegheny County, Pennsylvania. Tax list 1800.

VOSBURG, ORVIN
Port Alleghany, McKean County, Pennsylvania. 1861.

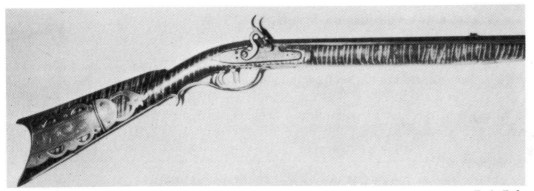

F. A. Farber

PLATE 285

Rifle with percussion lock, full stock of curly maple, brass mountings, set triggers, and octagonal barrel. The initials on this rifle are attributed to Benjamin Franklin Vore, who lived in New Paris Borough, Bedford County, Pennsylvania.

VORE, BENJAMIN FRANKLIN
New Paris, Bedford County, Pennsylvania. Tax list 1889.
Vore's guns were slightly different from the traditional Bedford County pattern. They were usually very long and slender. He used the typical hand-made lock of the area.

VORE, BENJAMIN
Elk Lick Township, Somerset County, Pennsylvania. Tax lists 1836, 1838, 1839.

WALKER, JAMES
George Township, Fayette County, Pennsylvania. Tax list 1803.

WALKER, JOHN
Lancaster Borough, Lancaster County, Pennsylvania. Tax list 1802, 1803.

WALKER, JOSEPH

George Township, Fayette County, Pennsylvania. Tax lists 1799, 1800, 1802, 1803.

WALKER, JOSEPH

Shippensburg, Pennsylvania. Tax list 1842-1843.

WALKER, SAMUEL

Hublersburg, Centre County, Pennsylvania. 1861.

WALLACE, DAVID

Sardis, Westmoreland County, Pennsylvania. 1861.

WALLACE, JOHN

Freeport, Armstrong County, Pennsylvania. Tax lists 1858, 1864, 1868.

WALTER, JOHN

Shartleysville, Berks County, Pennsylvania. 1861.

WARD, JOHN

St. John Street, Philadelphia, Pennsylvania. 1798.

WARD, MILLER & CO.

GUN-BARRELMAKERS, YORK COUNTY, NEWBERRY T. P., PENNSYL-VANIA. Persons wishing to purchase the above article can obtain them by addressing a few lines to the subscribers. The gun-barrels are of the best quality, and warranted to be made of the best hammered iron. *The Democrat & Workingmen's Advocate,* Pittsburgh, January 19, 1838.

WASHBURN, IRA

South Gibson, Susquehanna County, Pennsylvania. 1861.

WATERS, JOHN

Carlisle, Pennsylvania. Tax lists 1779, 1782.

WATT, CHRISTOPHER

176 St. John Street, Philadelphia, Pennsylvania. 1814.

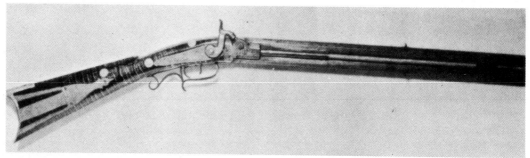

T. J. Cooper

PLATE 286

Double rifle with percussion lock, stock of curly maple, brass mountings, set triggers, octagonal barrels 32 inches long with John Watt on the top facet of a barrel. The silver inlays on this gun are half dimes.

WATTS, JOHN

John Watts, the son of James and Elizabeth McBride Watts, was born November 2, 1813. He died July 4, 1885, and is buried at Mattawana, Mifflin County, near McVeytown, Pennsylvania.

On January 15, 1839 he married Elizabeth Berryman and sometime before the Civil War, this couple bought a large farm in Lack Township, Juniata County, Pennsylvania. His land adjoined the Willow Run district, which has always been noted as excellent country for hunting and fishing. Watts operated his gunshop on this farm property for many years and presumably made many of his guns there. The farm has been abandoned and is now grown over with timber, but old-time residents of the area continue to call it the "Watts place."

After closing his shop on his farm property, he rented a spring-house loft from Squire John Patterson at Peru Mills, Pennsylvania. It is not known exactly when Watts stopped producing guns in this spring house, but the structure was still standing in 1950.

Watts is thought to have been a prolific maker. Sam Woodside, an ardent gun collector on the contemporary scene, tells that most families living in Lack and Tuscarora Townships owned one of his guns while he lived in that area. Most of his rifles had maple stocks, which were artificially striped as were many guns late in the nineteenth century. Watts used a center punch to mark "J. W." on the top facet of his barrels between the breech and the rear sight.

Watts had one son, James, who learned the trade of gunsmithing from his father, and a son-in-law named David Wagner, who also learned the trade and set up in business for himself in Sherman's Valley, Perry County, Pennsylvania.

WEBER, MATTHIAS

1512 North 2d Street, Philadelphia, Pennsylvania. 1855.

WEEKS, D.

D. WEEKS, PRACTICAL GUNSMITH, 139 State Street, Erie, Pennsylvania. Dealer in rifles, breech and muzzle-loading shot guns, gun materials, etc. Also Sealer of Weights and Measures for Erie County. *Gazeteer & Business Directory of Erie County, Pennsylvania*, for 1873-74.

WEHLI, JOHN

(See Daniel Myers)

WEIKER, GEORGE

Only a quick examination of a gun made by George Weiker is needed to convince the observer that he is looking at an unusual product of a Pennsylvania gunsmith. Other makers used a patch box lid that was hinged at the side instead of the end; a few signed their names on patch box lids, some have similar trigger guards, ramrod pipes, and incised carving; but no gunsmith is known to have used these details in the manner that Weiker used them.

The unique arrangement of these qualities has always focused attention on, and caused curiosity about, the area in which this man worked. This interest was aroused because it was assumed that if his residence were established, that

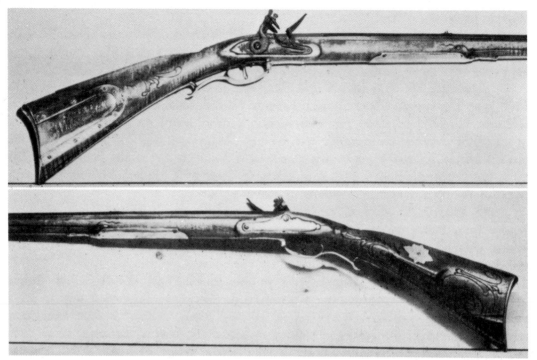

Henry J. Kauffman

PLATE 287

Flintlock rifle, maple full stock, brass mounted, silver inlay on the cheek side, octagonal barrel 48 inches long.

Although this rifle has an unusually long barrel its most unusual feature is the signature of the maker (G. Weiker) on the lid of the patch box. On a few of his products he is known to have included the price on the lid of the patch box which was usually $15. Weiker was an expert in the technique of incised carving. His rifles are rare and usually command a high price because of his novel method of advertising.

information would lead to a knowledge of where other men worked whose guns resembled Weiker's in some ways. The more standard details of his guns, such as the pattern of the lower ramrod pipes, the shape of his trigger guards, and the contour of the stock, suggested residence in the Allentown, Pennsylvania, area. Research for this book confirmed this suggestion when it was learned that G. Weiker lived in Richland Township, Bucks County, Pennsylvania. This discovery was particularly rewarding when it was also established that Jacobus Scout, who is thought to have signed initials J. S. on side-hinged patch boxes, was also a resident of Bucks County for many years.

The biographical information about Weiker is very limited. The first fact to be established was that his first name was George. Only G. appears with his last name on patch boxes; and though it always had been assumed that his first name was George, only the recent discoveries about him proved beyond any doubt that this was actually his name.

His father, whose name also was George, had been a blacksmith in the area for quite a few years before the name George, Junior, appears on the tax assessment lists. The occupation of George, Junior, was not secured from the tax assessment lists but from a transfer of real estate which must have occurred when George,

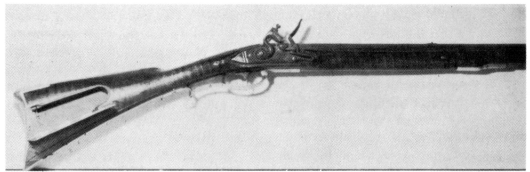

Christian E. McMurtrie

PLATE 288

The side hinge movement of the patch box lid was a favorite variation which a number of gunsmiths used, however, most of the rifles made by G. Weiker have this feature.

Senior, seemed to be retiring from business. Before the transfer the father was called a blacksmith in the tax assessment lists, and after the transfer he was called a gentleman, the usual implication being that then he had no occupation.

The document which finally called Weiker a gunsmith starts as follows: "This indenture, made the thirtieth day of July in the year of our Lord one thousand eight hundred, between George Weiker of Richland Township county of Bucks and the State of Pennsylvania, gunsmith, of the one part, etc. . . . ." After this transaction Weiker seems to have disappeared, and nothing is known of his subsequent residence. His name appeared in the tax lists for only a few years without any indication of his occupation. He was presumably a young man who worked as a gunsmith in that area for only a short time. It is hoped that additional research will uncover the later activities of this very interesting craftsman.

WEINBERGER, JOHN L.
Johnstown, Cambria County, Pennsylvania. 1861.

WEIR, JAMES (Brushes)
Pennsylvania.
Wires and brushes for Firelocks, after the best and most approved construction of the most experienced officers, Made and Sold by James Weir at the corner of Church Alley, in Second Street, at the low rate of five shillings per dozen. Black Ball of the best quality may be had at said shop, with a reasonable allowance were purchased by the quantity. Orders from the country will be faithfully and punctually executed. *Pennsylvania Evening Post*, no. 149, January 4, 1776.

WEISS, WILLIAM
Lancaster Borough, Lancaster County, Pennsylvania. Tax lists 1802, 1803, 1819, 1820, 1821.

WELSHANTZ
Although very few products of the Welshantz family are known today, they were unquestionably one of the important families connected with the trade in York, Pennsylvania. Two rifles that have "A. W." on the top facet of the barrel are known: the age of the guns and their style suggest to Joe Kindig, Jr., that

they were made by Abraham Welshantz. A man with that name is known to have lived in York in the late eighteenth century. Although he has not been documented as a gunsmith, the use of the two initials, the age of the rifle, and its general style strongly suggest that possibility.

Any early tax assessment list of York contains the name of Joseph Welshantz; he is not listed as a gunsmith, however, until the tax list of 1779. In this list he is joined by another Welshantz, named Jacob, who is also a gunsmith. Joseph was taxed in 1783 for one "boring mill" and it is entirely possible that most of the Welshantz family were connected with the mill rather than with the production of guns. As owners of a boring mill they might be called gunsmiths on a tax list, despite the fact that they actually did not produce guns. It is also possible that Jacob was connected with the gunsmithing production of George Eyster, for they both attended the same church and lived in the same area. A number of fine rifles made by Eyster are known.

In 1783 Joseph, Sr., Joseph, Jr., and Conrad Welshantz were listed as gunsmiths in York, Pennsylvania. In the 1811 tax assessment list of Harrisburg, Jacob is listed as a gunsmith; a George Welshantz is known to have been a gunsmith in the borough of Milton, Pennsylvania in 1826 and 1832.

A number of guns are known which bear the Welshantz name and one very fine one, which was made by Conrad.

WENZEL, HERMAN
    82 Van Braam. *Directory of Pittsburgh & Allegheny Cities* for 1872-73.

WENZEL, HIRAM
    327 North Avenue, Allegheny, Pennsylvania. 1878-79.

WENZELL, J. H.
    Smithfield. *Directory of Pittsburgh & Allegheny Cities* for 1870-71.

WERNER, C. L.
    122 Ohio Street, Allegheny, Pennsylvania. 1874.

WETZEL, DANIEL
    Hereford, Pennsylvania. 1860.

WETZEL, HENRY (Gun Barrel Maker)
    Middle Creek Township, Union County, Pennsylvania. Federal Census 1850.

WETZEL, JOHN
    Sheimersville, Lehigh County, Pennsylvania.

WHITE, JOHN
    John White was probably the son of the famous gunsmith, Peter White. Both of them worked in Union township, Fayette County—Peter from 1820 to 1834 and John from 1835 to 1840. John moved to Pittsburgh around 1840 and opened a shop on Ferry St. He moved quite frequently and is listed at a different address in each of the Pittsburgh directories from 1844 to 1858.

On Sept. 4, 1848, he inserted the following advertisement in the *Pittsburgh Daily Dispatch*: "A GOOD WORKMAN at the Gun Smith business wanted immediately, having a large contract of No. 1 Patent Mincinger's Guns to fulfill for Arkansas Territory. Apply to JNO. WHITE, Gun Smith, on Fifth Street, Pittsburgh, Pa."

Mincinger, was David Mincsinger of Beaver, Pa., who had invented a breechloading percussion gun in 1848. He was granted Patent Number 6, 139 on Feb. 27, 1849, but it appears he was in production before that time. His invention is better known today for its cartridge, or removable chamber, than for the gun which fired it. The latter had a hinged trap door, something like the Snider, and took a tapered steel cartridge having a regular percussion nipple mounted on one side. This projected through a hole in the trap door and was fired by the hammer. The patent drawing resembles a regular percussion rifle, having a scroll trigger guard and normal percussion lock. Production must have been very small for they are almost unknown to the collector today.

In 1859 White moved to the town of Rochester in Beaver County. This is close to Mincsinger's home town of Beaver and it is possible they were still working on the latter's patent. He left Rochester in 1861 and from then until 1864 his whereabouts are unknown. In the latter year he again returned to Pittsburgh, where he is listed in the directories as a gunsmith until 1867.

WHITE, JOHN R.
Reading, Berks County, Pennsylvania. 1861.

WHITE, LEVI
Isabella Street, Allegheny, Pennsylvania. 1850.

WHITMORE & WOLF (Wholesale and Retail Hardware Merchants)
Liberty & St. Clair, Pittsburgh, Pennsylvania. 1841, 1844.

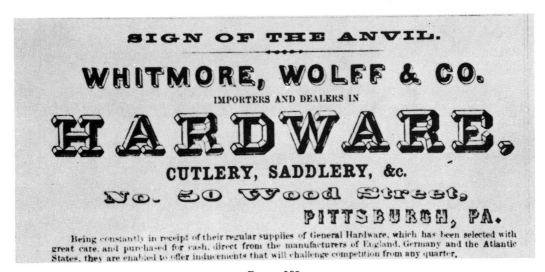

PLATE 289
Advertisement of Whitmore, Wolf & Co. in the 1854 edition of the *Pittsburgh Business Directory and Merchant's and Traveler's Guide.*

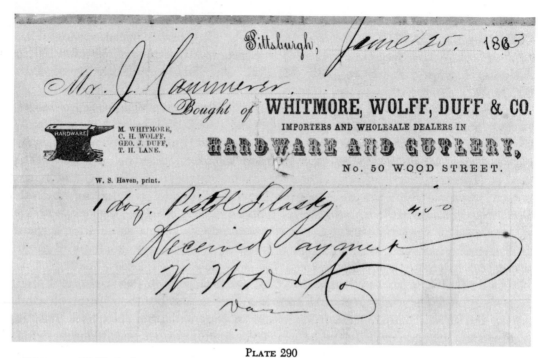

PLATE 290

Whitmore, Wolff, Duff & Co.

WHITMORE, WOLFF, DUFF & Co., (Importers and Retail Dealers in Hardware)
No. 50 Wood Street, Pittsburgh, Pennsylvania. 1871-72.

WICKHAM & Co.
No. 94, Market Street, three doors above Third Street, have just received from
the manufacturers in England, an assortment of Hardware, Military and Sportsmen's
Articles, all selected by M. T. Wickham, among which are extensive assortment of
Lancashire and Sheffield files, consisting of 230 kinds.
Steel of the following descriptions, viz.-Cast, Hunstmans, Shear, German, Blister,
Crowley, Sword, Coach, and Small Spring, &c &c. 15 kinds, assorted from one-quarter
inch to the largest size.
A great variety of Fowling pieces, Pistols, Locks, and component parts of each,
with every article necessary to equip either the Fowler or Angler. *The Independent
Balance* (Philadelphia), March 4, 1818.

WICKHAM, WILLIAM W. (Chief Armourer)
United States Arsenal, Philadelphia, Pennsylvania. 1814.

WIGLE, JACOB
South Huntington Township, Westmoreland County, Pennsylvania. Tax lists
1812, 1813.
Rostraver Township, Westmoreland County, Pennsylvania. Tax lists 1814, 1816.
Franklin Township, Fayette County, Pennsylvania. Tax lists 1819, 1820, 1821,
1822.

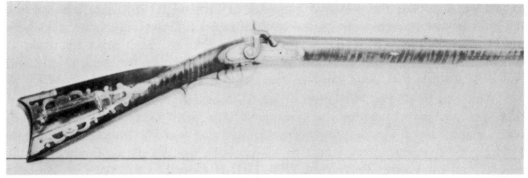

J. T. Herron

PLATE 291

Rifle with percussion lock, full stock of curly maple, brass mountings, set triggers, octagonal barrel 40 inches long with A. Williams on the top facet of the barrel. The brass plate on the wrist of the gun is one example of the poor repair techniques used by later craftsmen and owners of rifles.

WILLIAMS, ABE

Craft Creek, near Prosperity, Washington County, Pennsylvania.
Morris Township. Tax lists 1839-1845.

Williams made both flint and percussion guns. His name was often engraved on a brass plate which was inlaid on the top facet of his barrels. He worked from 1830-1860.

WILLIAMS, LEVI

Greene Township, Greene County, Pennsylvania. Tax lists 1820, 1822.
Monongahela Township, Greene County, Pennsylvania. Tax lists 1824, 1825, 1826, 1827.

WILLIAMS, LEWIS

Greene Township, Greene County, Pennsylvania. Tax lists 1820, 1822, 1823.
Monongahela Township, Greene County, Pennsylvania. Tax lists 1824, 1826, 1829, 1833.

WINEBERGER, LEONARD

South End Bedford, Johnstown, Pennsylvania. 1876-77.

WINGERHOLTER, MARTIN

274 Penn Street, Pittsburgh, Pennsylvania. 1860-61.

WINNER, JAMES

104 Walnut Street, Philadelphia, Pennsylvania. 1814.

WINTABLE, ABRAHAM

Back 437 North Third Street, Philadelphia, Pennsylvania. 1814.

WISE, NATHANIEL

Union Township, Mifflin County, Pennsylvania. Federal Census 1850.

WOLF, HENRY

Although not one of the well-known gunsmiths of Pennsylvania, Henry Wolf was, nevertheless, an important member of the fraternity in his day. For over twenty years he was the principal gunsmith in Pittsburgh, at a time when it was the most important settlement on the western frontier. Unfortunately no rifles bearing his name are known today and it is possible that he didn't mark his work. Of course, frontier conditions were not conductive to long life for guns of any sort, and it is possible that none survived the hazardous conditions of the time.

Wolf was located in Pittsburgh at least as early as 1787, for his name appears that year on the petition for the creation of Allegheny County. At that time he was a man of less than thirty-three years of age and possibly associated with John DeHuff, whose name appears next to his on both the Allegheny County Petition of 1787 and the Census Records of 1790. DeHuff moved to the town of Washington in 1793 and worked there as a gunsmith until 1803.

The picture that we can draw today of Henry Wolf is that of a brave man and a good mechanic, but it is also true that he must have been pretty hard to get along with. Aside from being embroiled in several lawsuits, no less than three of his apprentices ran away at various times. The first of these was Hugh Cook Glass, who left in the spring of 1795, taking with him "a continental rifle." Although Glass was twenty years old and presumably near the end of his apprenticeship, it is obvious that Wolf didn't particularly care to have him back, for he offered a reward of only six pence "without reasonable charges." The next to run away was eighteen-year-old Joshua Bennet, who left in February of 1808. Wolf was more eager for his return, since he offered a reward of "six dollars and reasonable charges or three dollars for securing him in jail so that his master may get him again," this despite the fact that Bennet was advertised as being fond of company and drink. The third runaway was fourteen-year-old James Mahaffy, who left in May, 1808, and for whom a reward of two dollars was advertised.

Of Wolf's bravery there can be little doubt, for he was most probably the "Henry Woolfe" who stole into Fort Pitt one rainy night in the summer of 1794 and rescued Major Kirkpatrick from the Whiskey Rebels. This act not only endangered his life but could have ruined his business, since nearly the entire county was in violent agreement with the rebels. Wolf was at that time a second lieutenant in the Second Regiment of Allegheny County Militia and they, too, were on the side of the rebels. In fact, the only persons supporting law and order were the land owners and artisans of Pittsburgh, who were afraid the rebels would burn the town.

In connection with his gunsmithing activities Henry carried a stock of gunpowder for the use of his patrons. An advertisement in the *Pittsburgh Gazette* on March 18, 1797, stated: "JACOB FERREE'S BEST RIFLE POWDER to be sold by HENRY WOLF, Gunsmith in Pittsburgh." A similar advertisement appeared in the *Gazette* in the fall of 1806 but this one was for "Powder of a superior quality made by Jonathan Egley." Wolf's workmanship was probably a good calibre, for in 1801 we find that the County Commissioners asked him to make a screw for the county seal. He did it and charged them $14.00, the price of a good rifle at that time.

In March of 1808 Wolf advertised that he would pay generous wages to a journeyman gunsmith who understood stocking and that he would also take one or two apprentices to that business. He advertised again in June of the same year and that is the last he is heard of. He is not listed in the Census of Allegheny County for 1810 and there is no record of his death; so it is possible that he moved, perhaps to Ohio, as so many others were doing at that time.

WOLF, OTTO
147 Third Street, *Woodward & Rowlands' Pittsburgh Directory* for 1852.

WOLFGANG, MICHAEL
Hegins, Schuylkill County, Pennsylvania. 1861.

WOODCOCK, AMOS (Powder Mill)
Woodberry Township, Huntington County, Pennsylvania. 1832.

WOODS, ABSOLOM
German Township, Fayette County, Pennsylvania. Tax lists 1816, 1818.

WORKMAN, JOHN
Lower Mahanoy Township, Northumberland County, Pennsylvania. Tax list 1838.

WORELY, HENRY
Mohn's Store, Berks County, Pennsylvania. 1861.

WORLEY, CALEB
Greenwood Township, Cumberland County, Pennsylvania. Census list 1800.

WORLEY, DAVID
Donegal Township, Washington County, Pennsylvania. Tax lists 1823, 1841.

WORLEY, THOMAS (See Sheetz)

WURFFLEIN, ANDREW
122 North 2d. Street, Philadelphia, Pennsylvania. 1855.

WURFFLEIN, JOHN
98 South Third Street, Philadelphia, Pennsylvania. 1855, 1861.

WYSONG, SAMUEL
Union Township, Bedford County, Pennsylvania. Tax list 1877.
Wysong is known to have made one gun with a 48-inch barrel.

YEAGER, JACOB
Huntington County, Pennsylvania. Federal Census of 1850.

YITWELLER, ANTHONY
Blair County, Pennsylvania. Federal Census 1850.

YOHN, PHILIP
Providence Township, Montgomery County, Pennsylvania. Census list 1800.

YOST, JOHN (Single Man)
York, Pennsylvania. Tax list 1805.

Vincent Nolt

PLATE 292

Rifle with percussion lock, curly maple, full stock, brass mountings, set triggers, octagonal barrel 41 inches long with J. Young on the top facet of the barrel. The style of the patch box and the curve on the butt plate suggest mid-nineteenth century production.

YOUNG

Boalsburg, Centre County, Pennsylvania. 1861.

YOUNG, JOHN

Easton, Pennsylvania. Tax list 1787.

YOUNG, PETER

37 North Second Street, Philadelphia, Pennsylvania. *New Trade Directory of Philadelphia*, 1800.

YOUNG, WILLIAM & BROS.

131 Northampton Street, Easton, Northampton County, Pennsylvania. 1861.

YOUS, JOSHUA

Greencastle, Franklin County, Pennsylvania. 1861.

ZAHM, MATTHIAS

Lancaster Borough, Lancaster County, Pennsylvania. Tax list 1816.

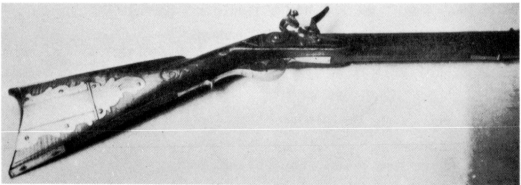

Joe Kindig, Jr.

PLATE 293

Rifle with flint lock, full stock of curly maple, brass mountings, and octagonal barrel marked F. Zorger on the top facet of the barrel.

This is one of the fine guns made in York, Pennsylvania in the late eighteenth century. The carving is skillfully executed, the patch box is an interesting design, and the entire rifle is evidence of Zorger's superior craftsmanship.

ZAHRINGER, EUGENE

Corner O'Hara and Mulberry Alley, Pittsburgh, Pennsylvania. 1860-61.

ZEHRINGER, EGAN (Pistol Maker)

Corner O'Harra & Mulberry Alley, Pittsburgh, Pennsylvania. 1860-61.

ZINK, ALBERT

Zink was 25 years old when he was listed in the "Enrollment of Citizens within the borough of Port Carbon, Schuylkill County, liable to Military Service, by Order of the President of United States, August 9, 1862."

ZOLLINGER, GEORGE

Harrisburg, Pennsylvania. Tax list 1811.

Carlisle, Pennsylvania. Tax lists 1823, 1842.

ZORGER

Fredrick Zorger is known to have been a "Resident Gunsmith" in York, Pennsylvania, at the time of the Revolution and he is similarly listed in the tax assessment lists for York in 1800 and in 1804. Rifles have been found in the York area inscribed with the names, G. Zorger and C. Zorger, although the relationship, if any, of these gunsmiths to Fredrick is not known.

The rifles of Fredrick are of high quality and typical of the York pattern. The finial of his patch boxes usually has the drooping feather pattern with two piercings. His carving and engraving are of excellent quality and he is regarded as one of York's outstanding gunsmiths of the eighteenth and early nineteenth centuries. Two of his pistols have survived and are illustrated in this survey under the heading of pistols.

At least one rifle made by G. Zorger is known, which is also of excellent quality. C. Zorger appears to have been of a later generation; he made some rifles with heavy barrels. They have attractive patch boxes and are carved in the incised technique.

Glossary

BACK ACTION LOCK. A side lock used on late percussion guns. The mainspring is behind the hammer and is attached to the rear of the tumbler with a link.

BACK SIGHT. The sight nearest the breech end of the barrel.

BAYONET. A dagger, first fitted into the bore of a gun, but later attached by a ring to the exterior of the barrel at the muzzle.

BLUNDERBUS. A muzzle-loading gun with a large flare at the muzzle.

BORE. Refers to the diameter of the hole in the barrel.

BREECH. The end of the barrel holding the charge before it is discharged.

BREECH (PATENT). A casting of iron or steel incorporating the breech plug, the breech tang, and the nipple into one piece.

BREECH PLUG. A metal plug screwed into the breech end of a muzzle-loading gun.

BREECH TANG. A projection of the breech plug which overlaps the stock of the gun, through which a bolt or screw is turned to attach the barrel to the stock.

BRIDLE. A band of metal attaching the pan to the frizzen in a flintlock, or a metal plate which covers the tumbler and the sear in a flint or a percussion lock.

BUTT. The part of a long gun which is rested against the body when the gun is discharged.

BUTT CAP. A metal cap over the back end of the stock, usually associated with pistols.

BUTT MASK. A butt cap in the form of a face in metal.

BUTT PLATE. A plate of metal covering the butt end of a long gun.

CARBINE. A light short arm, often used by the cavalry.

COCK. An old term used for the hammer of a flintlock.

COMB. The top edge of the butt end of the gun. Many guns of the eighteenth century had large combs.

DOG LOCK. A form of safety catch used on the exterior of early flintlock plates.

DOUBLE GUN. A gun with two barrels.

ESCUTCHEON. A plate of metal to protect wood from abrasion or other injury, such as barrel pin escutchens.

FERRULE. The metal cap on the forestock of a gun.

FINIAL. The terminating point of various gun parts such as patch boxes, lock-bolt plates, etc.

FLASH GUARD. The rising back portion of the pan on a flintlock, which presumably offered some protection from the flash of the powder.

FORESIGHT. The sight on the muzzle end of the barrel.

FORESTOCK. The portion of the stock near the muzzle end of the barrel.

FRIZZEN. The pan cover which the flint strikes to discharge the gun.

FRIZZEN SPRING. A small spring which activates the frizzen.

FURNITURE. The metal mounts of a gun.

HAND GUN. Formerly applied to all guns held by hand, but now only to pistols and revolvers.

HOLSTER. A case, usually made of leather, to carry a hand gun, attached to a saddle or belt.

INCISE. To cut or engrave, usually, below the surface of wood or metal.

INLAY. A small piece of metal or wire inletted into the stock for decorative purposes.

LANDS. The raised portions in a rifled barrel.

LOCK. The mechanical device to discharge a firearm.

LOCK-BOLT PLATE. A strip of metal on the side of a gun opposite the lock to protect the stock from the abrasive action of the lock bolts. The attractive early form slowly deteriorated into a simple washer for locks with only one screw.

LOCK PLATE. A heavy plate of iron or brass to which the various lock parts are attached.

MAIN SPRING. The main spring in most gunlocks is mounted inside the lock plate and exerts pressure on the tumbler when the gun is cocked. When the trigger is pulled, the pressure of the main spring thrusts the hammer forward with a sharp action and discharges the gun.

MATCHLOCK. The earliest form of gunlock mechanism. A lighted match, or cord, was brought in contact with the powder in the pan by pressing the trigger. It was the simplest form of mechanical ignition and was followed by the wheel lock, which was the most intricate mechanism ever used to discharge a gun.

MUSKET. A portable firearm with a large smooth bore. Usually regarded as an arm designed for military use.

MUZZLE. The end of the barrel farthest from the gunner, when held in position for shooting.

PAN. A shallow trough on the top of a flintlock, adjacent to the barrel, in which the priming powder is placed.

PAN COVER. An obsolete term for the frizzen.

PATCH BOX. A compartment in the butt end of a rifle to carry patches and the grease which was applied to them to facilitate loading.

PINS. Small round or flat pieces of metal, used to hold the barrel to the stock.

PISTOL. A small firearm, usually held and fired with one hand.

PISTOL, (HORSE). A pistol with a long barrel, carried in a holster attached to the saddle.

POWDER FLASK. A flat flask of metal to carry gunpowder.

POWDER HORN. A tapering round horn used to carry gunpowder. The large horns contained powder for shooting and the small ones were used for priming powder.

PRICKER. A short length of wire with a loop handle used to remove fouled powder from the touchhole of the barrel.

PROOF MARKS. Marks on the breech end of the barrels, indicating that they had been tested prior to their being used in the gun. Many European barrels have such marks but they are rarely found on Pennsylvania rifles.

RAMROD. Rod for ramming the charge from the mouth of the barrel to the breech. Ramrods for Pennsylvania rifles were usually made of hickory wood and had a spiral stripe. Ramrods with this original stripe are very rare.

RAMROD PIPES. A short tube of metal under the forestock to carry the ramrod when not in use. The bottom one is sometimes called the "tailpipe."

RELIEF (BAS). A design which is not three dimensional is described, done in relief; and when low or flat, the technique is called bas-relief.

RIFLE. A gun with a barrel having a number of groves cut on its bore to reduce friction and impart a rotary motion to the bullet. A few rifle barrels have straight grooves instead of spiralling ones.

SEAR. The part of a gunlock which engages the tumbler and keeps the gun at full or half-cock.

SEAR SPRING. A spring shaped like a V, which bears against the sear and prevents action in the lock until the trigger is pulled.

SET TRIGGER. Although a few single set triggers are known, most of them are comprised of two triggers. In these there is a delicate spring assembly, which gives the sear a sharp impact when the set trigger is released. The relayed action through the two triggers permits a more sensitive release than if only one trigger is used.

SIDE HAMMER. A type of hammer used on percussion locks, which operates in a horizontal plane rather than vertically. They are sometimes called "mule ear hammers."

SIDE PLATES. The two plates on either side of the patch box lid.

SNAPHAUNCE. An early form of flintlock first used in Europe in the late sixteenth century, although most examples were made in the seventeenth century. It was very popular in Spain.

STEEL. A strip of hardened metal fastened to the frizzen to produce a spark. If the frizzen were hardened, it was called the "steel."

STOCK. The part of a Pennsylvania rifle which is made of wood, usually of curly maple.

TOE-PLATE. A metal band on the bottom edge of the stock adjoining the butt plate.

TOUCHHOLE. The hole in a barrel through which the spark passes to ignite the main charge.

TRIGGER GUARD. A bowed piece of metal mounted on the bottom edge of the stock to protect the trigger from accidental tipping.

TRIGGER PLATE. A small piece of metal mounted on the bottom edge of the stock. It has a tapped hole into which the breech tang screw is turned and a slit through which the trigger moves. The trigger is usually not connected to it, its major function being to confine the movement of the trigger.

TUMBLER. The lock part to which the hammer is attached. The portion inside the lock has notches cut into it to engage the sear at half and full cock.

WHEEL LOCK. A complicated lock mechanism which replaced the earlier matchlock. In it the cock (hammer) held a piece of pyrites, which contacted a rotary mechanism and produced a spark. Its large and intricate mechanism was replaced by the snaphaunce and flintlock in the seventeenth century.

Bibliography

Primary Sources in Pennsylvania

United States Census of 1850

Adams County	Berks County	Mifflin County
Beaver County	Blair County	Union County
Bedford County	Huntington County	

Deeds, Wills, and Intestate Inventories,

Adams County	Franklin County	York County
Berks County	Fayette County	Frederick County, Maryland
Bucks County	Lebanon County	
Dauphin County	Lehigh County	

Tax Assessment Lists,

Adams County	Cumberland County	Lehigh County
Armstrong County	Dauphin County	Montgomery County
Beaver County	Fayette County	Northampton County
Bedford County	Franklin County	Northumberland County
Berks County	Greene County	Schuylkill County
Bucks County	Indiana County	Venango County
Butler County	Jefferson County	Washington County
Cambria County	Lancaster County	Westmoreland County
Clarion County	Lebanon County	York County

Fort Pitt Day Book of Baynton, Wharton, and Morgan

Secondary Sources

An Essay on Shooting, Printed for T. Cadell in the Strand, London, 1787

BECK, HERBERT, *Henry E. Leman, Riflemaker,* Lancaster County Historical Society, Bulletin, Vol. XL

DUNKLEBERGER, GEORGE F., *The Story of Snyder County,* The Snyder County Historical Society, 1948

Deane's Manual of the History and Science of Fire-Arms, Longmans, Brown, Greene, Lingmans, & Roberts, Publishers, London, 1858

EAGLE, WILLIAM H. and others, Editors, *Pennsylvania Archives,* Harrisburg, 1890

FREEMANTLE, T. F., *The Book of the Rifle,* Longmans, Green and Co., New York and Bombay, 1901

GEORGE, J. N., *English Guns and Rifles,* The Stackpole Co., Harrisburg, Pennsylvania, 1947

GLENDENNING, JAN, *British Pistols and Guns 1640-1840,* Cassel and Company, London, 1951

GREENER, WILLIAM, *Gunnery in 1858,* Smith Elder & Co., London, 1858

HICKS, JAMES E., *United States Ordnance,* 1940

371

HOWITT, WILLIAM, *The Rural and Domestic Life of Germany*, Carey, Hartt, Philadelphia, 1843

JORDAN, FRANCIS, *The Life of William Henry*, 1910

MULHEARN AND PUGH, *A Traveler's Guide to Historic Western Pennsylvania*, University of Pittsburgh Press, 1954

MANN, JAMES G., *European Arms and Armour, Wallace Collection Catalogues*, Part III (Gallery XI) Printed for the Trustees by William Clowes and Sons, Ltd., London, 1945

MONTGOMERY, MORTON L., *History of Berks County*, Everts, Peck, and Richards, Philadelphia, 1886

New York Historical Society Quarterly, Volume xxxvi, April, 1952

PETERSON, HAROLD L., *Arms and Armour in Colonial America*, The Stackpole Company, Harrisburg, 1956

RUPP, DANIEL L., *The History and Topography of Dauphin, Cumberland, Franklin, Bedford, Adams, and Perry Counties*, Gilbert Hills, Lancaster, 1845

RUPP, DANIEL L., *History of Lancaster County*, Gilbert Hills, Lancaster, 1844

RUPP, DANIEL L., *History of Northampton, Lehigh, Monroe, Carbon, and Schuylkill Counties*, Hickock and Cantine, Harrisburg, 1845

RUSSEL, CARL, *Guns on the Frontier*, University of California Press, 1957

STELLE AND HARRISON, *The Gunsmith's Manual*, Excelsior Publishing Company, New York, Reprinted by Thomas G. Samworth, Plantersville, South Carolina

URE, ANDREW, *A Dictionary of Arts, Manufactures and Mines*, D. Appleton and Company, New York, 1856

Index

Initial letters of proper names only are capitalized;
plates and their numbers appear in bold-face type.